JUNG and TAROT

JUNG and TAROT
An Archetypal Journey

Sallie Nichols

with an introduction by
Laurens van der Post

SAMUEL WEISER, INC.
York Beach, Maine

First published in 1980 by
Samuel Weiser, Inc.
P.O. Box 612
York Beach, Maine 03910

Reprinted 1982

ISBN 0-87728-480-6 (hardcover)
ISBN 0-87728-515-2 (paperback)
Library of Congress Catalog Card No.: 80-53118

Cover design by Barbara Factor

Typeset in 10 pt. Souvenir by
Friedland Company
New York, N.Y.

Layout by Alden Cole

Printed in the U.S.A. by
Noble Offset Printers, Inc.
New York, N.Y. 10003

To

Culver Nichols

My thanks to the following friends who helped launch this Tarot Trip, and without whose advice and encouragement our ship would never have made home port: Janet Dallett, Rhoda Head, Ferne Jensen, James Kirsch, Rita Knipe, Claire Oksner, Win Sternlicht, William Walcott, and Lore Zeller.

Acknowledgements

For permission to use copyright material, the author gratefully makes the following acknowledgements:

Chatto and Windus Ltd. for permission to quote from Alan McGlashan's *The Savage and Beautiful Country*.

Wesleyan University Press for permission to quote from Joseph L. Henderson's *Thresholds of Initiation*.

Spring Publications, Box 1, University of Dallas, Irving, Texas for permission to quote from Marie-Louise von Franz's *An Introduction to the Psychology of Fairy Tales;* Marie-Louise von Franz and James Hillman's *Lectures on Jung's Typology;* Aniela Jaffé's "The Influence of Alchemy on the Work of C.G. Jung" from *Spring, 1967;* Emma Jung's *Anima and Animus;* Alma Paulsen's "The Spirit Mercury as Related to the Individuation Process" from *Spring, 1966;* Marie-Louise von Franz's *The Problem of the Puer Aeternus;* C.G. Jung's "Interpretation of Visions" from *Spring, 1962;* Kristine Mann's "The Shadow of Death" from *Spring, 1962;* Amy I. Allenby's "Angels as Archetype and Symbol" from *Spring, 1963.*

Princeton University Press for permission to reprint excerpts from *The Collected Works of C.J. Jung.* Bollingen Series XX, Vol. 7: *Two Essays on Analytical Psychology,* trans. R.F.C. Hull, copyright 1953, 1966; Vol. 9, I: *The Archetypes and the Collective Unconscious,* trans. R.F.C. Hull, copyright 1959, 1969; Vol. 10: *Civilization in Transition,* trans. R.F.C. Hull, copyright 1964, 1970; vol. 11: *Psychology and Religion: West and East,* trans. R.F.C. Hull, copyright 1953, 1968: Vol. 13: *Alchemical Studies,* trans. R.F.C. Hull, copyright 1967: Vol. 14: *Mysterium Coniunctionis,* trans. R.F.C. Hull, copyright 1965, 1970: Vol. 15: *The Practice of Psychotherapy,* trans. R.F.C. Hull, copyright 1954, 1966: Vol. 17: *The Development of Personality,* trans. R.F.C. Hull, copyright 1954: Vol. 18: *The Symbolic Life,* trans. R.F.C. Hull, copyright 1950, 1953, 1955, 1958, 1959, 1963, 1968, 1969, 1970, 1976: Vol. 19: *General Bibliography of C.G. Jung's Writings,* compiled by Lisa Ress with collaborators, copyright 1979; C.G. Jung, *Psychological Reflections: A New Anthology of His Writings,* ed. Jolande Jacobi and R.F.C. Hull, Bollingen Series XXXI, copyright 1953, 1970; From Joseph Campbell's *The Mythic Image,* Bollingen Series C, copyright 1974. From Erich Neumann's *The Great Mother,* trans. Ralph Manheim, Bollingen Series XLVII, copyright 1955.

Macmillan Publishing Co. for permission to quote from W.B. Yeats' *Mythologies,* copyright 1959; from *Collected Poems,* copyright 1961.

C.G. Jung Foundation for permission to quote from Aniela Jaffé's *The Myth of Meaning,* English translation by the C.G. Jung Foundation; from Edward F. Edinger's *Ego and Archetype,* copyright 1972; from Edgar Herzog's *Psyche and Death,* published by G.P. Putnam's Sons, New York, for the C.G. Jung Foundation for Analytical Psychology; from Marie-Louise von Franz's *C.G. Jung, His Myth in Our Time,* copyright 1975.

William Morris Agency for permission to quote from Paul Huson's *The Devil's Picture Book,* copyright 1971.

Random House, Inc. for permission to quote from W.H. Auden's *The Age of Anxiety,* copyright 1947.

The University of Chicago Press for permission to quote from Mircea Eliade's *The Forge and the Crucible,* copyright 1978 by the author.

The Viking Press Inc. for permission to quote from *The Portable Blake* (William Blake), copyright 1946.

Prentice-Hall, Inc. for permission to quote from John Weir Perry's *The Far Side of Madness.*

Oxford University Press for permission to quote from *The Poems of Gerard Manley Hopkins* (eds. W.H. Gardner and N.H. MacKenzie).

Harcourt Brace Jovanovich, Inc. for permission to quote from T.S. Eliot's *Collected Poems 1909-1962,* copyright 1963, 1964 by the author.

W.W. Norton & Company for permission to quote from *The Divine Comedy*, trans. John Ciardi, 1977 edition; from Rainer Maria Rilke's *Duino Elegies,* trans. J.B. Leishman and Stephen Spender, copyright 1939.
Routledge & Kegan Paul Ltd. for permission to quote from C.G. Jung's *The Tavistock Lectures* (now C.W. Vol. 18, Princeton University Press).
Cambridge University Press for permission to quote from Erwin' Schrödinger's *My View of the World,* copyright 1964.
Doubleday & Company for permission to quote from "Symbolism in the Visual Arts" by Aniela Jaffé in *Man and his Symbols* by C.G. Jung, copyright 1964, Aldus Books London.
Tarot of Marseilles printed by J.M. Simon/Grimaud, France.
Tarot cards from the IJJ Swiss Tarot Deck (copyright 1974), the Rider-Waite Tarot Deck (copyright 1971) and the Visconti-Sforza Tarocchi (copyright 1975) reprinted by permission of U.S. Games Systems, Inc., New York and AGMuller, Switzerland;
The Aquarian Tarot painted by David Palladini, printed by Morgan Press, Dobbs Ferry, N.Y., reprinted by permission;
The Tate Gallery, Private Collection, London, for permission to reprint William Blake's *Satan Exulting Over Eve*;
Illustration on p. 321 reprinted by permission of The Philosophical Research Society, Inc.;
Musee de Cluny, France, for permission to reprint Auguste Rodin's *The Hand of God*;
Princeton University Press for permission to reprint from C.W. 12, *Psychology and Alchemy*, Figures 36, 60, 91, 213, 226.

All efforts have been made to contact copyright holders of material quoted in this book. However, if we have unwittingly infringed copyright in any way, we offer our sincere apologies and will be glad of the opportunity to make appropriate acknowledgement in future editions.

Contents

List of Illustrations

Introduction

One of the main sources of misunderstanding of the nature and magnitude of Jung's contribution to the life of our time, is due to the assumption as common, alas, among his followers as among others, that his overriding interest was in what he came to call "the collective unconscious" in man. It is true he was the first to discover and explore the collective unconscious and to give it a truly contemporary relevance and meaning. But, ultimately it was not the mystery of this universal unknown in the mind of man but a far greater mystery that obsessed his spirit and compelled all his seeking, and that was the mystery of consciousness, and its relationship with the great unconscious.

It is not surprising, therefore, that he was the first to establish the existence of the greatest and most meaningful of all paradoxes: the unconscious and the conscious exist in a profound state of interdependence of each other and the well-being of one is impossible without the well-being of the other. If ever the connection between these two great states of being is diminished or impaired, man becomes sick and deprived of meaning; if the flow between one and the other is interrupted for long, the human spirit and life on earth are re-plunged in chaos and old night. Consciousness for him is therefore not, as it is for instance for the logical positivists of our day, merely an intellectual and rational state of mind and spirit. It is not something which depends solely on man's capacity for articulation, as some schools of modern philosophy maintain to the point of claiming that that which cannot be articulated verbally and rationally is meaningless and not worthy of expression. On the contrary, he proved empirically that consciousness is not just a rational process and that modern man precisely is sick and deprived of meaning because, for centuries now since the Renaissance, he has increasingly pursued a slanted development on the assumption that consciousness and the powers of reason are one and the same thing. And let anyone who thinks this is an exaggeration just consider Descartes' "I think, therefore, I am!" and he ought immediately to identify the European hubris which brought about the French Revolution, fathered a monstrous off-spring in Soviet Russia and is spawning subversion of the creative spirit of man in what were once citadels of living meaning like churches, temples, universities and schools all over the world.

Jung produced evidence from his work among the so-called "insane" and the hundreds of "neurotic" people who came to him for an answer to their problems, that most forms of insanity and mental disorientation were caused by a narrowing of consciousness and that the narrower and more rationally focussed the consciousness of man, the greater the danger of antagonizing the universal forces of the collective unconscious to such a point that they would rise up, as it were, in rebellion and overwhelm the last vestiges of a painfully acquired consciousness in man. No, the answer for him was clear: that it was only by continually working at an increase of consciousness that man found his greatest meaning and realization of his highest values. He established, to put it back into its native paradox, that consciousness is the abiding and deepest dream of the unconscious and that as far back as one could trace the history of the spirit of man to where it vanishes over the last horizon of myth and legend, it has incessantly strived to achieve ever greater and greater consciousness; a consciousness which Jung preferred to call "awareness." This "awareness," for him and for me, included all sorts of non-rational forms of perception and knowing, all the more precious because they are the bridges between the inexhaustible wealth of, as yet, unrealized meaning in the collective unconscious, always ready to carry reinforcements for expanding and strengthening the consciousness of man engaged in an unending campaign against the exactions of life in the here and now.

This, perhaps, is one of his most important contributions to a new and more significant understanding of the nature of consciousness: it could only be renewed and enlarged as life demanded it to be renewed and enlarged, by maintaining its non-rational lines of communication with the collective unconscious. For this reason he rated very highly all non-rational ways along which man in the past has tried to explore the mystery of life and stimulate man's conscious knowledge of the expanding universe around him into new areas of being and knowing. This is the explanation of his interest, for instance, in astrology and this, too, is the explanation of the significance of Tarot.

He recognized at once, as he did in so many other games and primordial attempts at divination of the unseen and the future, that Tarot had its origin and anticipation in profound patterns of the collective unconscious with access to potentials of increased awareness uniquely at the disposal of these patterns. It was another of those non-rational bridges across the apparent divide between unconscious and consciousness to carry night and day what should be the growing stream of traffic between darkness and light.

Sallie Nichols, in her profound investigation of Tarot, and her illuminated exegesis of its pattern as an authentic attempt at enlargement of the possibilities of human perceptions has in some such form as I have of necessity described in so over-simplified a fashion, performed an immense service for analytical psychology. Her book enriches and helps us to understand the awesome responsibilities laid upon us by consciousness. Moreover she has done something in her book which people who profess to recognize the great work done by Jung, so often fail to do. Jung, as a profoundly intuitive person, was compelled by his demonic vision, not to stay long with any particular aspect of his vision. It needed all that he had of reason and the method of the devout scientist that he was, to give him the will to stay long enough with a particular stage of his work to establish its validity empirically. But once that was done he had, as it were, to strike his intellectual tent and send the caravan of his mind on its way to the next stage of his unending journey. His spirit, inevitably in an age so imperilled as ours (an intuitive soul exhorted him), was a spirit desperately in a hurry. As a result almost everything he accomplished needs enlargement. And Sallie Nichols, in this book, has done Jungian psychology and all those who try to serve it, an immense service by the way in which she has enlarged the story and our understanding of the role of an important non-rational source of consciousness. On top of it all, she has done so not in an arid academic fashion, but as an act of knowing derived from her own experience of Tarot and its strangely translucent lights. As a result her book not only lives but quickens life in whomever it touches.

Laurens van der Post

The Tarot Trumps

LE MAT
THE FOOL

LA PAPESSE
THE HIGH PRIESTESS

III

L'IMPÉRATRICE
THE EMPRESS

L'EMPEREUR
THE EMPEROR

V

LE PAPE
THE POPE

VI

L'AMOUREUX
THE LOVER

VII

LE CHARIOT
THE CHARIOT

VIII

LA JUSTICE
JUSTICE

VIIII

L'HERMITE
THE HERMIT

LA ROUE DE FORTUNE
THE WHEEL OF FORTUNE

LA FORCE
FORCE

XII

LE PENDU
THE HANGED MAN

XV

LE DIABLE
THE DEVIL

XVII

L'ÉTOILE
THE STAR

LE MONDE
THE WORLD

1. Introduction to the Tarot

The Tarot is a mysterious deck of cards of unknown origin. At least six centuries old, this deck is the direct ancestor of our modern playing cards. Down through the generations, the figures depicted on these cards have enjoyed many incarnations. It is a testimony to the vitality and wisdom of the ancient Tarot that, although it had spawned such an active child as the playing cards we use today, the parent deck itself did not retire. In Central Europe, these quaint Tarot cards have remained in constant use for gaming and fortunetelling. Now, in America, the Tarot has suddenly surfaced into public consciousness. Like the puzzling figures which pop up unexpectedly in our dreams, these Tarot characters seem to cry out for our attention.

Dramatic eruptions of this kind usually mean that neglected aspects of ourselves seek recognition. No doubt, like our dream figures, the Tarot personalities have intruded themselves into our complacency in order to bring us messages of great import; but modern man, steeped as he is in a verbal culture, finds the nonverbal picture language of the Tarot difficult to decipher. In the following chapters we shall explore ways to approach these mysterious figures and catch sparks of understanding.

A journey through the Tarot cards is primarily a journey into our own depths. Whatever we encounter along the way is *au fond* an aspect of our own deepest, and highest, self. For the Tarot cards, originating as they did at a time when the mysterious and irrational had more reality than they do today, bring us an effective bridge to the ancestral wisdom of our innermost selves. And new wisdom is the great need of our time – wisdom to solve our own personal problems and wisdom to find creative answers to the universal questions which confront us all.

Like our modern cards, the Tarot deck has four suits with ten "pip" or numbered cards in each. The four Tarot suits, are called wands, cups, swords, and coins. These have evolved into our present suits of clubs, hearts, spades, and diamonds. In the Tarot deck, each suit has four "court" cards: King, Queen, Jack, and Knight. The latter, a dashing young cavalier mounted on a spirited horse, has mysteriously disappeared from today's playing cards. The handsome Knight pictured here (fig. 1) is taken from an Austrian transition deck – meaning a design which falls historically somewhere between the original Tarot cards and our modern deck. As we see, the vitality of this Knight was such that he persisted in the deck after his suit had already changed from coins to diamonds.

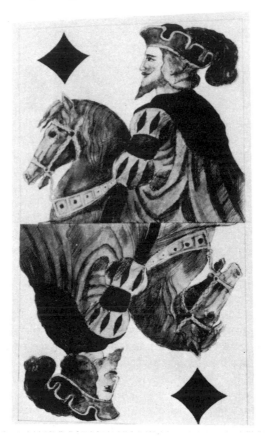

Fig. 1 Knight of Diamonds

That this symbol of single-minded purpose, courtliness, and courage should have disappeared from today's playing cards may indicate a lack of these qualities in our present-day psychology. The Knight is important because we shall need his courage and questing spirit if our journey is to be a successful one.

Equally significant, and certainly as mysterious, is the amputation from our modern deck of the Tarot Trumps, which are the cards that will be the landmarks for our journey. These Trumps – sometimes called Atouts – comprise a set of twenty-two picture cards which do not belong to any of the four suits. Each of these cards bears an intriguing name (THE MAGICIAN, THE EMPRESS, THE LOVER, JUSTICE, THE HANGED MAN, THE MOON, and so forth), and the cards are numbered. Arranged in sequence, the Trumps seem to tell a picture story. It will be the focus of this book to examine the twenty-two Trumps in sequence and to puzzle out the story they tell.

Like the alchemical *Mutus Liber* (which incidentally appeared later), the Trumps can be viewed as a silent picture text representing the typical experiences encountered along the age-old path to self-realization. How and why such subject matter found its way into the Tarot, which was and still is essentially a deck of playing cards, is a mystery that has puzzled generations of scholars. Only one vestige of the Trumps remains in our modern playing cards: the Joker. This odd fellow who leads such an elusive life in every pack of cards is a direct descendant of a Tarot Trump called THE FOOL, with whom we shall soon become acquainted.

Theories about the origin of this Fool and his twenty-one companion Trumps are various and fanciful. Some imagine that these cards represent the secret stages of initiation in an esoteric Egyptian cult; others maintain, and this with more historical probability, that the Trumps are of Western European origin. Several reputatable scholars, among whom A. E. Waite and Heinrich Zimmer, suggest that the Trumps were concocted by the Albigenses, a gnostic sect which flourished in Provence in the twelfth century. It is felt that they were probably smuggled into the Tarot as a veiled communication of ideas at variance with the established Church. One contemporary writer, Paul Huson, views the Tarot's origin as a mnemonic device used chiefly in necromancy and witchcraft. Another contemporary writer, Gertrude Moakley, pioneered the ingenious theory that the Trumps are of exoteric origin, being simply adaptations of illustrations from a book of Petrarch's sonnets to Laura. This book was called *I Trionfi*, a title which translates both as "The Triumphs" and "The Trumps."

In Petrarch's sonnets a series of allegorical characters each fought and triumphed over the preceding one. This theme, a popular one in Renaissance Italy, was the subject of many paintings of the period. It was also dramatized in pageants in which these allegorical figures, elaborately costumed, paraded around the castle courtyards in decorative chariots accompanied by knights on horseback in full regalia. Such parades, called carousels, are the origin of our modern merry-go-round. On today's carousels, while children play at being brave knights riding handsome steeds, their grandparents can enjoy a more sedate ride in a golden chariot.

Fig. 2   The Chariot (Sforza Tarot)

Figure 2 shows Tarot number seven, THE CHARIOT, as pictured in a fifteenth century commemorative deck designed and executed by the artist, Bonifacio Bembo, for the Sforza family of Milan. These elegant cards, some of which can be seen in the Pierpont Morgan Library in New York, are painted and illuminated in brilliant colors on a diapered background of gold over red with touches of silver. It is good to recall that such triumphal cars as the one pictured here are still an important feature of Italian festivals, and that the delightful rocking-horse spirit of its horses remains forever on parade in our modern carousels.

Actually, very little is known about the history of the Tarot cards or about the origin and evolution of the suit designations and the symbolism of the twenty-two Trumps. But the many imaginative hypotheses as to the cards' inception, and the numerous visions and revisions inspired by their pictorial symbology attest to their universal appeal and demonstrate their power to activate the human imagination. For the purposes of our study, it matters little whether the Tarot Trumps sprang from the Albigenses' love of God or Petrarch's passion for Laura. The essence of their importance for us is that a very real and transforming human emotion must have brought them to birth. It seems apparent that these old cards were conceived deep in the guts of human experience, at the most profound level of the human psyche. It is to this level in ourselves that they will speak.

Since it is the aim of this book to use the Tarot as a means of getting in touch with this level of the psyche, we have chosen as the basis for discussion the Marseilles Tarot, one of the oldest designs available today. Playing cards being perishable, the "original" Tarot no longer exists, and the few remnants of old decks still preserved in museums do not correspond exactly with any pack currently in print. Thus no present-day Tarot can be called in any sense authentic. But the Marseilles version, in general, preserves the feeling tone and style of some of the earliest designs.

There are other reasons for choosing the Marseilles deck. First, its design transcends the personal. There is no evidence, for example, that it was created by one individual as are most of our contemporary Tarot decks. And second (again unlike most contemporary Tarot packs), the Marseilles deck comes to us unaccompanied by an explanatory text. Instead it offers us simply a picture story, a song without words, which can haunt us like some old refrain, evoking buried memories.

This is not the case with contemporary Tarot decks, most of which were devised by a known individual or group, and many of which are accompanied by books in which the authors set forth in words the abstruse ideas which they have presumably presented in the picture cards. This is the case, for example, with the cards and texts created by A. E. Waite, Aleister Crowley, "Zain," and Paul Foster Case.

Although the text which accompanies the Tarot in such cases is usually introduced as an elucidation of the symbols portrayed on the cards, the net effect is more that of an illustrated book. In other words, it is as if the Tarot cards were devised as illustrations for certain verbal concepts rather than that the cards erupted spontaneously first and the text was inspired by them. As a result, the personalities and objects pictured in these cards seem more allegorical in character than symbolic; the pictures appear to illustrate verbalized concepts rather than suggesting feelings and insights wholly beyond the reach of words.

The difference between a Tarot deck accompanied by a text and the Marseilles deck which stands alone is a subtle one; but it is important in terms of our approach to the Tarot. To our way of thinking, it is the difference between reading an illustrated book and walking into an art gallery. Both are valuable experiences, but they are quite different in their effect. The illustrated book stimulates intellect and empathy, connecting us with the insights and feelings of others. The art gallery stimulates imagination, forcing us to dip down into our own creativity and experience for amplification and understanding.

Another difficulty with some Tarot decks is that a number of these have affixed to the Trumps extraneous symbols borrowed from other systems, implying that there is an exact correlation between the Trumps and other theological or philosophical theories. For example, in some decks each of the Trumps is marked with one of the twenty-two letters of the Hebrew alphabet in an attempt to connect each Trump symbolically with one of the twenty-two paths of the Cabalistic Sephiroth. But there exists no uniform agreement as to which Hebrew letters belongs to which Tarot. Commentators have also affixed alchemical, astrological, Rosicrucian, and other symbols to the Tarot. Here also confusion reigns, as one can see by contrasting the ideas of Case, "Zain," Papus, and Hall in this regard.

Since all symbolic material derives from a level of human experience which is common to all mankind, it is, of course, true that valid connections can be made between some of the Tarot symbols and those of other systems. But this deep layer of the psyche, which C. G. Jung termed the unconscious, is, by definition, *not* conscious. Its images do not derive from our ordered intellect, but, rather, in spite of it. They do not present themselves in a logical manner.

Each philosophical system is merely an attempt on the part of the intellect to create a logical order out of the seeming chaos of imagery arising from the unconscious. Intellectual categories are a way of systematizing our experience of this nonverbal world. Each is a kind of grid system superimposed, if you like, over the raw experience of our most profound human nature. Each such system is useful, and in that sense, each one is "true" – but each is unique. Viewed one by one, these various patterns offer us convenient pigeonholes for organizing psychic experiences. But to superimpose these many grids, one atop the other, would be to distort their symmetry and destroy their usefulness.

Lest through such confusion we lose our way in the Trumps, we make no attempt in this book to correlate the Tarot symbolism with that of other disciplines. For the most part we shall confine our discussion to the Trumps as they appear in the Marseilles deck, picturing other versions of the cards only when these seem to offer insights that enrich their meaning. We shall try, as Jung did with symbolic material, to amplify by analogy, leaving the symbol's ultimate meaning, as always, free and open-ended.

In defining the scope of a symbol, Jung often stressed the difference between a symbol and a sign. A *sign,* he said, denotes a specific object or idea which can be translated into words (e.g., a striped pole means barber shop; an X means railroad crossing). A *symbol* stands for something which can be presented in no other way and whose meaning transcends all specifics and includes many seeming opposites (e.g., the Sphinx, the Cross, etc.).

The pictures on the Tarot Trumps tell a symbolic story. Like our dreams, they come to us from a level beyond the reach of consciousness and far removed from our intellectual understanding. It seems appropriate, therefore, to behave toward these Tarot characters pretty much as we would if they had appeared to us in a series of dreams picturing a distant unknown land inhabited by strange creatures. With such dreams, purely personal associations are of limited value. We can best connect with their meaning through analogy with myths, fairy tales, drama, paintings, events in history, or any other material with similar motifs which universally evoke clusters of feelings, intuitions, thoughts, or sensations.

Since the symbols pictured in the Tarot are ubiquitous and ageless, the usefulness of these amplifications will not be confined to this book. The Tarot figures, in various guises, are ever present in our lives. By night they appear in our sleep, to our mystification and wonder. By day they inspire us to creative action or play tricks with our logical plans. We hope that the material presented here will help us to connect with our dreams – not only with those which come to us at night, but with the hopes and dreams of our daylight hours as well.

Fig. 3 Map of the Journey

Note: A full color Map of the Journey appears at the back of the book.

2. Map of the Journey

Before setting out on a journey, it is a good idea to have a map. Figure 3 is such a map. It shows the territory we shall be covering in this book. Pictured here are the twenty-two Trumps as they appear in the Marseilles Tarot which, as already indicated, is based on some of the earliest surviving designs. The way the cards are arranged in this map offers us a preview of the kinds of experiences we may expect to encounter along the way.

The best way to get at the individual meaning of these cards for oneself is to approach them directly, as one would the paintings in an art gallery. Like paintings, these Trumps are so-called projection holders, meaning simply that they are hooks to catch the imagination. Speaking psychologically, *projection* is an unconscious, autonomous process whereby we first see in the persons, objects, and happenings in our environment those tendencies, characteristics, potentials, and shortcomings that really belong to us. We people the exterior world with the witches and princesses, devils and heroes of the drama buried in our own depths.

Projecting our inner world onto the outer one is not a thing we do on purpose. It is simply the way the psyche functions. In fact projection happens so continuously and so unconsciously that we are usually totally unaware it is taking place. Nevertheless these projections are useful tools toward gaining self-knowledge. By viewing the images that we cast onto outer reality as mirror reflections of inner reality, we come to know ourselves.

In our journey through the Tarot Trumps, we shall be using the cards as projection holders. The Trumps are ideal for this purpose because they represent symbolically those instinctual forces operating autonomously in the depths of the human psyche which Jung has called *the archetypes*. These archetypes function in the psyche in much the same way as the instincts function in the body. Just as a healthy newborn babe arrives with a built-in tendency to suckle or to startle at a loud noise, so his psyche also shows certain hereditary tendencies whose effects can be similarly observed. We cannot of course see these archetypal forces, as indeed we cannot see instincts; but we experience them in our dreams, visions, and waking thoughts where they appear as images.

Although the specific form these images take may vary from culture to culture and from person to person, nevertheless their essential character is universal. People of all ages and cultures have dreamed, storied, and sung about the archetypal Mother, Father, Lover, Hero, Magician, Fool, Devil, Savior, and Old Wise Man. Since the Tarot Trumps picture all of these archetypal images, let us look briefly at some of them as they appear on our map. By doing so, we can begin to familiarize ourselves with the cards and demonstrate how powerfully these symbols act in all of us.

In our map, the Trumps from number one through number twenty-one are set out in sequence to form three horizontal rows of seven cards each. THE FOOL, whose designation is zero, has no fixed position. He strides along at the top, looking down on the other cards. Since he has no pigeonhole, The Fool is free to spy on the other characters and can also burst unexpectedly into our personal lives with the result that, despite all conscious intentions, we end up playing the fool ourselves.

This archetypal Wanderer, with his bundle and his staff, is very much in evidence in our culture today. But, being a product of our mechanized world, he prefers to ride rather than walk. We can see his present-day counterpart, with beard and bedroll, standing by the roadside, extending a hopeful smile and a thumb in our direction. And if this character represents an unconscious aspect of ourselves, we are bound to react emotionally to him in one way or another. Some may instantly feel moved to stop and give the hitchhiker a lift, recalling how they, too, in their younger days once en-joyed a period of carefree wandering before settling down into a more stable pattern of living. Others, who never played the fool in their youth, may reach out to this wanderer instinctively because he represents an unlived aspect of themselves to which they feel unconsciously drawn.

It can happen, though, that another person might have a negative reac-tion to this young fellow – a reaction so instantaneous and violent that he suddenly finds himself literally trembling with rage. In this case the driver may jam his foot down on the accelerator, clench his teeth, and literally flee the sight of this innocent bystander, muttering imprecations about his "slovenly ways." He may wish he could get his hands on this "young fool," chop off his hair, give him a good bath and shave, and then set him down in a forty-hour week "where he belongs." "Such irresponsibility makes me sick," he mutters. As a matter of fact his hostility is so overpowering that he may actually begin to feel sick. When he arrives home, he may find himself drained of energy and unaccountably weary. But next day, when (and if) the obsessive chattering in his head has somewhat abated, a small space may open up within which a question can find whispering room: "Why shouldn't this young hitchhiker wander about if he likes? What harm is he doing?" But the "harm" to the observer is already done. The mere sight of this fellow has opened up a can of worms. And these come wriggling and tumbling out as a dozen questions, each demanding an answer: What would it be like to live like that fellow – to smash one's alarm clock – to throw away one's possessions – to spend this entire spring and summer just roving under the wide blue sky – and so forth.

There being no way to stuff these worms back into the can, our driver may find himself immobilized at home trying to answer these questions and dreaming impossible dreams. Perhaps, with luck, he may find ways to make some of his dreams come true. Strange things can happen when one confronts an archetype.

Reactions to the Fool will of course be as many and varied as the personalities and life experiences of those who confront him. But the point is that being touched by an archetype will always evoke an emotional reaction of some kind. By exploring these unconscious reactions, we can uncover the archetype that is manipulating us and free ourselves, to some extent, from its compulsion. As a result, next time one meets this archetypal figure in outer reality, his response need not be so irrational and automatic as the one described above.

In the instance just cited, the emotional turmoil that seeing "the fool" touched off and the self-examination that ensued may not have eventuated in any dramatic change in the life style of the person in question. But, after seriously considering other possibilities, he may well conclude that the life of a vagabond is not for him. He may find that, all things considered, he prefers the stability and convenience of a home, and that he likes a car and other possessions enough to sweat it out at the office in order to buy them. But, through examining other possibilities, he will have come to choose his life style more consciously; and having made friends with his hidden impulse to play the fool, he may find ways to express this need within the context of his present life.

In any case, the next time he passes a happy wanderer on the road, he will feel more empathy for him. Having now chosen his own life he may be more willing to let others choose theirs. And having come to terms with the renegade in inner reality, he will no longer feel so hostile and defensive when such a figure presents itself in outer reality. But, most important of all, he will have experienced the power of an archetype. The next time he speeds along in his car he will realize that he does not sit alone in the driver's seat. He will know that mysterious forces are at work within him which can guide his destiny and absorb his energy in unforeseen ways. And he will be on the alert for these. The Fool is a compelling archetype and, as we have seen, one very much in evidence today. But all the figures of the Tarot have their own kind of power, and being ageless, they are all still active in ourselves and our society. By way of illustration let us now look at the seven Trumps pictured in the top row of our map.

The first of these is called THE MAGICIAN. It pictures a magician about to perform some tricks. He calls them tricks, and that is exactly what they are. He is getting ready to trick us. His seeming magic will be done with mirrors, specially constructed cards, top hats with false bottoms, and sleight of hand. We know this is the case, and our intellect is a-chatter with epithets like "charlatan" and labels like "rubbish." But to our dismay we observe that the rest of our body is already moving in the direction of this magician, and our hand is now surreptitiously reaching into our pocket to extract a coin for admittance to this magic show. It is stealing our money to subject us to swindle.

And later, as we sit in the audience waiting for the show to begin, we notice that our heart is beating faster than normal and that we are holding our breath. Although our mind knows that what we shall see will at best be a demonstration of skill and manual dexterity, the rest of us behaves as if something truly miraculous were about to happen. We behave this way because, in the deepest levels of our being, we still inhabit a world of true mystery and wonder – a world that operates outside the limits of space and time and beyond the reach of logic and causality. We are attracted to this outer magician so compulsively and irrationally because within each of us there exists an archetypal Magician even more attractive and compelling than the one before us, one who stands ready to demonstrate for us the miraculous reality of our inner world whenever we feel ready to turn our attention in his direction.

No wonder our intellect skids to a stop and digs its heels in at the mere idea of magic. If our mind admits to this kind of reality, it risks losing the empire which its reason has built brick by brick throughout the centuries. And yet the compulsion of the Magician is so strong in our culture today that many bridges between his world and ours, over which reason can begin to walk with some assurance, are at last being built. Various para-psychological phenomena are being examined under scientifically controlled conditions. Transcendental Meditation is attracting thousands of followers by offering objective proof of the salutary effects of meditation on blood pressure and anxiety states. Through the use of biofeedback machines and other devices, various other forms of meditation are being explored, and convincing research is in progress on the effects of meditation on cancer. In our century, it seems, the worlds of magic and reality are becoming one. Perhaps by studying THE MAGICIAN we can bring about a new unity within ourselves.

The second card in the top row of our map is LA PAPESSE, or Lady Pope, sometimes called THE HIGH PRIESTESS. She may be seen as symbolizing the archetype of the Virgin, a familiar one in the myths and sacred writings of many cultures. The virgin birth is a motif frequently observed in the beliefs of so many peoples, separated in both time and geography, that its origin can only be explained as an archetypal pattern inherent in the human psyche.

The Virgin archetype celebrates a humble receptivity to the Holy Spirit and a dedication to its embodiment in a new reality as the Divine Child, or Savior. In our culture, the biblical account of the Virgin Mary dramatizes this archetype. LA PAPESSE is a somewhat crude representation of the Virgin of the Annunciation as she is depicted in Catholic art. There she is often pictured seated, with the Book of the Prophets spread open before her, as in the Tarot.

The Virgin archetype has caught the imagination of artists and sculptors for centuries, and for every woman the fact of pregnancy marks her as one singled out to be the carrier of a new spirit. But today she has become active in a different way. For it is the Virgin, it seems, who has inspired what is most truly feminine and courageous in the women's liberation movement. Just as the Virgin Mary was chosen for a destiny uniquely her own for which there was "no room at the inn," so woman today is called to fulfill herself in ways to which our collective society still closes its doors. As the Virgin was forced by her vocation to forego the comfortable anonymity and security of traditional family life, carrying her burden alone, and bringing her new spirit to birth only in the most humble of circumstances, so women today, for whom the new annunciation has sounded clearly, must sacrifice their security and endure loneliness and humiliation (often in circumstances more trying than the routine of housewifery and motherhood) in order to bring into reality the new spirit that stirs within them. In this endeavor the Virgin might well be accorded a special niche for veneration, because she still shines forth today as a unique symbol of the pervasive force of the feminine principle. Although dedicated to the service of the spirit, the Virgin has never lost touch with her own femininity. It seems significant that Mary, one of the most powerful figures in our Judeo-Christian heritage, should have remained in our culture a paradigm of the utterly feminine woman.

The next two cards in our Tarot sequence, THE EMPRESS and THE EMPEROR, symbolize the Mother and Father archetypes on the grand scale. Little need be said here about the powers of these two figures, for we have all experienced them in relation to our personal mothers and fathers or other human beings who stood for us as their surrogates. As children we probably all saw our parents enthroned as the "good," "nourishing," "protective" mother, and the "omniscient," "courageous," "powerful" father. When, being human, they failed to enact these roles according to our script, we often then experienced mother as the archetypal Black Witch or Bad Stepmother and father as Red Devil and Cruel Tyrant. It took many years of outlandish projecting before we could finally see our parents as human beings who, like ourselves, possessed many potentials for both weal and woe.

Even as adults, if our parents are living we may still discover some areas in which we revert to the habit patterns of youth and play "child" to their parenthood in a variety of ways. When this happens, we may feel moved to go to our parents and "have it out" with them, if possible. But from the Jungian point of view, the proposed confrontation with the parents, even if possible, is not necessarily the first step toward clarification of our problem. For here too (as in the case of the driver and the hitch-hiker) the archetypes are at work. Quite apart from the personalities and actions of our parents (however limited and unconscious these may be), we would be having similar problems with whoever stood in their shoes as long as we had not come to terms with the Mother and Father archetypes within ourselves. Chances are that both we and our parents are puppets in an archetypal drama, manipulated by giant figures operating above and behind our conscious awareness.

As long as this is the case, however much good will, determination, confession, or whatever takes place in a confrontation between the puppets themselves, the result can only be further entanglement in the strings. Obviously the first thing to do is to turn around and face the puppeteers so that we can see what they are up to and, if possible, untie or loosen some of those strings. In later chapters we shall confront the Empress and the Emperor and suggest some techniques for freeing ourselves from the hidden wiles of these master manipulators. The discovery of this archetypal layer of the unconscious and the presentation of techniques for confronting it is one of Jung's great contributions to psychology. For without the concept of the archetypes, we would forever be caught in a never ending circular dance with persons in outer reality. Without techniques for separating the personal from the impersonal, we would endlessly project on our parents, or others in our environment, archetypal behavior patterns which no human being can possibly embody.

Tarot Trump number five is THE POPE. In Church dogma the pope is God's representative on earth. As such he is infallible. He represents an archetypal authority figure whose power surpasses that of father and emperor. In Jungian terms he represents the archetypal Old Wise Man. Obviously, to project such superhuman wisdom and infallibility on any human being – even the pope himself – might be questionable.

The archetype of the Old Wise Man, dramatized in the biblical Hebrew prophets and Christian saints, is still a powerful one today. He appears in our society frequently as a beturbaned guru or an elderly bearded wanderer in white robe and sandals. Sometimes he has undergone training in some spiritual discipline, Eastern or Western, and sometimes he appears without portfolio. If we receive such a new acquaintance on sight with overwhelming adulation or turn our backs on him in instant rejection, we can be sure that the archetype is at work. But coming to know such a person as a human being can help us to see that spiritual illumination is, after all, a personal rather than an institutional matter.

The Tarot, being itself both old and wise, has pictured the archetypal Old Wise Man in two ways. THE POPE of card five shows him in his more institutional form, and THE HERMIT of card nine pictures him as a mendicant friar. When we come to study these two cards, we shall have a chance to contact these figures as forces within ourselves. Coming to know these archetypes will help us to determine to what extent the qualities they symbolize are embodied in ourselves and in persons of our acquaintance.

The card that follows THE POPE is called THE LOVER. Here a young man stands transfixed between two women, each of whom seems to claim his attention, if not his very soul. Surely the eternal triangle is an archetypal situation vivid in our own personal experience. The plot pictured in THE LOVER needs no elaboration here for it is the basis of about ninety percent of the literature and drama extant in the world today. Anyone who wishes to refresh his memory on that score need only turn on his television more or less at random.

In the sky above and behind the Lover, a winged god with a bow and arrow is about to inflict a fatal wound that may resolve the young man's conflict. The little god, Eros, is of course an archetypal figure, and so is the young man. He personifies a youthful ego. The ego is technically defined as the center of consciousness. It is the one in us who thinks and speaks of itself as "I." In THE LOVER, this young ego, having to some extent freed himself from the compulsive influence of the parental archetypes, is now able to stand alone. But he is still not his own man, for, as we see, he remains caught between two women. He is unable to move. The principle action in this picture is taking place in the unconscious realm of the archetypes hidden from his present awareness.

Perhaps the poisoned arrow from heaven will fire him up and set him in motion. If so, we shall observe with interest what happens next because, from now on in our Tarot series, this young ego will be the chief protagonist of the Tarot drama. In this sense we shall often refer to him as the hero, for it is his journey along the path of self-realization that we shall be following.

In card seven, called THE CHARIOT, we see that the hero has found a vehicle to carry him on his journey, and it is piloted by a young king. When a young king appears on the scene in dreams and myths, he usually symbolizes the emergence of a new guiding principle. In the fourth card, THE EMPEROR appears as the authority figure. He is an older man, seated, and drawn so large that he fills the entire canvas. In THE CHARIOT the new ruler is in motion and drawn to human scale, meaning that he is more active and approachable than an emperor; and, more important, he is not alone. He is seen to function as part of a totality with which the hero begins to feel a connection.

But the king pictured here is as young and inexperienced as the hero himself. If our protagonist has crowned his ego king and placed it in command of his destiny, his journey forward will not be smooth.

With THE CHARIOT we come to the last card in the top row of our map. This row we are calling the Realm of the Gods because it pictures many of the major characters enthroned in the heavenly constellation of archetypes. Now the hero's chariot carries him down into the second row of cards, which we will call the Realm of Earthly Reality and Ego Consciousness because here the young man sets forth to seek his fortune and establish his identity in the outer world. Freeing himself increasingly from containment within the archetypal "family" pictured in the top row, he sets out to find his vocation, establish a family of his own, and assume his place in the social order.

Having discussed "the gods" of the top row, we shall now run through the cards in the next two rows much more rapidly in order to get an overall view of the general plot that follows. The first card in the second row is JUSTICE. The hero must now evaluate moral problems for himself. He will need her help to weigh and balance difficult questions. Next comes THE HERMIT, who is carrying a lantern. If the hero no longer finds the illumination he seeks within an established religion, this friar can help him to find a more individual light.

The card following THE HERMIT is THE WHEEL OF FORTUNE, symbolizing an inexorable force in life which seems to operate beyond our control and with which we must all come to terms. The next card, called STRENGTH or FORTITUDE, pictures a lady taming a lion. She will help the hero to confront his animal nature. Perhaps his initial confrontation will not be wholly successful, for in the following card, THE HANGED MAN, we see the young man hanging upside down by one foot. He appears to be unharmed but he is, for the moment at least, completely helpless. In the next card he faces DEATH, an archetypal figure before whose scythe we all stand helpless. But in the final card of this second row, TEMPERANCE, a helpful figure appears. She is an angel, and she is engaged in pouring liquid from one vase into another. At this point the hero's energies and hopes begin to flow again and in a new direction. Heretofore he has been engaged in freeing himself from the compulsion of the archetypes as they affect him personally in the world of human beings and events, and in establishing an ego status in the outer world. Now he is ready to turn his energies more consciously toward the inner world. Whereas before he sought ego development, his attention now turns toward a wider psychic center which Jung has termed the *self*.

If we define the ego as the center of consciousness, then we might define the self as the all-encompassing center of the entire psyche, including both conscious and unconscious. This center transcends the puny "I" of ego awareness. It is not that the hero's ego will no longer exist; it is simply that he will no longer experience this ego as the central force which motivates his actions. From now on his personal ego will be increasingly dedicated to service beyond itself. He will become aware that his ego is merely a small planet revolving around a giant central sun – the self.

All along his journey the hero will have had flashes of this kind of insight; but as we follow his fortunes through the archtypes of the bottom row we shall see his awareness widen and his illumination increase. For this reason we will call the bottom row on our map the Realm of Heavenly Illumination and Self-Realization.

The first card in this bottom row is THE DEVIL. He represents Satan, that infamous fallen star. Whenever this fellow drops into our garden he brings with him, willy-nilly, a flash of light, as we shall see when we come to study him later on. The next four cards in sequence are called THE TOWER OF DESTRUCTION, THE STAR, THE MOON, THE SUN. They picture various stages of illumination in an ascending order. The card that follows these four is called JUDGEMENT. Here an angel with a trumpet bursts into the hero's awareness in a glorious blaze of light to wake the sleeping dead. On the earth below, a young man rises from the grave as two older figures stand by in attitudes of prayer and wonder at this miraculous rebirth.

With the final card of the Tarot series called THE WORLD, the self, now fully realized, is bodied forth as a graceful dancer. Here all the many opposing forces with which the hero has been struggling are united in one world. In this last Tarot figure, sense and nonsense, science and magic, father and mother, spirit and flesh, all flow together in a harmonious dance of pure being. In the four corners of this card, four symbolic figures stand witness to this ultimate miracle.

Now we have completed our quick preview of the twenty-two Trumps as set forth on our map. As we follow the hero's fortunes through these cards, we shall be observing their interconnections on the horizontal axis – how each experience encountered along the way evokes the one that follows it. When we come to study the cards in the bottom row, we shall also be making connections on the vertical axis between these Trumps and those directly above them on the map.

Let us illustrate what we mean. As the cards are arranged in our map, they can be seen not only as three horizontal rows of seven cards each but also as seven vertical rows of three cards each. As we shall discover, the three cards in each vertical row are connected with one another in a significant way. For example: the first vertical row presents THE MAGICIAN at the top, THE DEVIL at the bottom, and JUSTICE sitting as mediator between the two. Many connections can be made between these three cards, but one of the more obvious might be that the seemingly benign MAGICIAN of card one and the magical DEVIL of card fifteen must both be taken into consideration in our lives. For if we don't "give the devil his due" he'll take it anyway; if we ignore him, he will operate from behind in a destructive way. So the cards of this first vertical row may be saying that as long as we use both pans of JUSTICE's scales, there will be less chance of either magician playing tricks behind our backs.

As we shall see later on, the cards in the second horizontal row, the Realm of Earthly Reality and Ego Consciousness, often act as mediators between the Realm of the Gods above and the Realm of Illumination and Self-Realization below. In fact, all the Trumps in the second row, like its first card JUSTICE, are specifically concerned with equilibrium. For example: STRENGTH is engaged in establishing an equilibrium between herself and a lion, and TEMPERANCE is absorbed in creating a balanced interaction between the two urns that she holds. In more subtle ways, all the other cards in this row can be seen to symbolize some kind of harmonious balance between opposing forces. For this reason it might be useful to subtitle the second horizontal row the Realm of Equilibrium.

From what has already been said, it is easy to understand why Jung chose to call this kind of self-realization *individuation*. By confronting the archetypes and freeing oneself somewhat from their compulsion, one becomes increasingly able to respond to life in an individual way. As we have seen, the behavior of those with little awareness of the archetypes is predetermined by unseen forces. It is almost as rigidly programmed as the instinctual behavior of the birds and bees who always react to certain stimuli in a preordained way, so that mating, nest building, migration, and so forth, are carried on in identical patterns throughout the generations. But when a human being has achieved some degree of self-awareness, he is able to make choices that are different from those of the flock and to express himself in ways that are uniquely his own. Having contact with his own true self he will no longer be prey to the chatter of other selves, inner and outer. What "they" are doing and saying will have less influence upon his life. He will be able to examine current social customs and ideas and adopt them or not as he chooses. He will be free to act in ways that fulfill his deepest needs and express his truest self.

It is important to note here that as a person gains the independence to be a nonconformist, he also gains the self-assurance to be a conformist. As Jung has often stressed, an *individuated* person is not the same as someone who is *individualistic*. He is not driven to conform to custom, but he is equally not driven to defy it. He does not try to set himself apart from his peers by affecting peculiar dress or by exhibiting outlandish behavior. On the contrary, because he so truly experiences himself as a unique expression of the godhead, he is under no compulsion to prove it.

Whenever we meet such a person, he is usually indistinguishable at first glance from others in the group. His overt behavior and dress may be in no way remarkable. He may be actively engaged in conversation, or he may be relatively quiet; but almost instantly some indefinable quality in his way of being may attract us to him. It is as if everything about him—his clothes, his gestures, his way of sitting or standing—belongs to him. Nothing about him is superimposed. Everything he says or does appears to arise from his deepest center, so that even his most ordinary remark shines forth with new meaning. If he is silent, his silence, too, seems to belong. It is a comfortable silence both for him and for us. Often such a person in silence will seem more present and active than those who are participating in more overt ways. Because he is in contact with his deepest self, our deep self responds, so that sitting in silence with this kind of human being can open up new vistas of awareness. Being at home with himself, he is instantly at home with us—and we with him. We feel as if we have known him forever. The communication between us is so open and easy that we understand him; and yet, he puzzles us. On the one hand, he is the most unusual person we have ever met, and on the other, he is just like us. He is a paradox.

The self is indeed the most paradoxical and elusive of all the forces operating in the deep unconscious. It is the self which will propel the hero forward from the parental womb to seek his destiny in the outer world; and it is the self which will bring him home at last to the realization of his own uniqueness. As we follow the hero along his journey, we will share vicariously in his experiences as they are pictured in the Trumps.

There are many techniques for putting ourselves in touch with the cards. Each person will find his own way into the pictures, but we offer here a few suggestions that others have found useful. For example; some like to keep a Tarot scrapbook. They find that the Trumps jump to life when relevant material is collected about them. Once attention is paid to them, the Tarot characters have a way of popping up in unexpected ways. It often happens, for instance, that related news items, photographs, prints, and references to the Tarot begin to appear quite magically and with amazing frequency.

Also, studying a specific card seems to unlock hidden stores of creative imagination so that sudden insights and ideas can burst forth into consciousness—seemingly from nowhere. These wispy creatures of the imagination are as ephemeral as butterflies. If we don't catch them instantly, they may disappear forever. But when such bursts of creativity occur, often we don't have time to sit down and give them our full attention. It is helpful to have some fixed place ready to capture and hold them

safe for future reference: a place where we can jot down the bare plot of a
story, draw a quick sketch for a future painting, or set down the opening
lines of what may become a poem. If we have some aptitude in the arts,
we may want to develop these ideas later. If not, we may wish to refer to
them again in connection with our personal Tarot trip. In either case, a
scrapbook or loose-leaf notebook with several pages devoted to each
Trump offers convenient storage for this material and a ready-made filing
system for easy access.

All of us react differently to different cards. Some cards attract us;
some repel us. Some cards remind us of people we know or have known
in the past. Some are like figures in dreams or in fantasies. Others bring us
entire dramatic episodes. Perhaps the important point here is that when
we really focus on a Tarot card and then follow as the card itself leads, we
become open to new and exciting experiences.

The Trumps are best studied in sequence. Their numerical order
creates a pattern both throughout the deck and within ourselves. And to
follow that pattern, our imagination will provide the passport. There are
many ways to stimulate the imagination. Included here are a few ideas that
others have found useful.

Approach each card directly before reading the chapter about it. This
offers you a chance to react freely and naively to whatever is pictured
there. It is a good idea to study the card for a few minutes, and then jot
down "off the top of your head" any reactions, ideas, memories, and
associations (or even four-letter words) that come to mind. Remember,
these notes are for your eyes alone, so let fly with the pen. Don't censor
anything, however farfetched it seems, for it may connect you with important insights later on.

Since, as with human personalities, first impressions are often more
significant than they appear at the time, jot down *everything* verbatim.
Please don't attempt to analyze, evaluate, or label whatever you have written. Just file it away for future consideration. Later, when you have come
to know this Tarot Trump, it will be interesting to compare your first impressions of it with your later reactions. Whatever turns up, just muse on it
as you go about your daily affairs. Hold these happenings in your heart as
you might do with a poem—but keep your reason at arm's length. The
Tarot people are creatures of the imagination. The spotlight of intellect will
send them scurrying underground.

Since the Tarot characters cannot tell us verbally about themselves,
we must use every sensory means to feel into their essence. One surprisingly effective way to do this is to color the cards. The Marseilles deck is not
available in an uncolored version, but one can easily create an uncolored
set of Trumps by making Xerox reproductions of those in the regular deck.
Invariably, students who have made and colored their own cards in this
way find that doing so adds a new dimension to their understanding.

Whatever you do (or don't) in relation to the cards, remember that all suggestions presented here are offered simply *pour le sport.* They are chiefly useful as devices to warm up our imagination and lure the Tarot characters out into our world where we can get a better look at them.

It is axiomatic that symbols and the feelings or intuitions that they inspire do not come labeled "right" or "wrong." As will be repeatedly demonstrated in this study, it is characteristic of symbolic material to embrace many opposites and to include seeming paradoxes. Living as we do most of the time in an Either/Or world of fixed opposites, it may be some comfort to know that in the world of feelings, intuitions, sensations, and spontaneous ideas that we are about to enter, we can pretty much discard the Either/Or yardstick we generally use to make practical choices in everyday life. We are about to step into the land of imagination, that magic world whose key words are Both/And. In reacting to a given Tarot Trump, we can't be "right" if we try – and by same token we can't be "wrong." So let us react to the Tarot in any way we like with a light heart and a free hand. Allow room for everything; expect nothing. Let your imagination play. Enjoy – enjoy.

These, then, are some of the ways to explore the meaning of the cards. From time to time we shall add other do-it-yourself suggestions for any who are interested. In the following chapters we shall amplify the meaning of each Trump by presenting themes from myth, literature, drama, and the pictorial arts which seem to enrich its message. These are not offered as conclusions but rather as springboards for the imagination. The final dimension of this study, the dimension of depth, is one which only the reader himself can fully explore; only he can relate these findings to his individual life.

Each must discover his own way into the nonverbal world of the Tarot. Although we shall follow certain signposts along the way, the cards themselves, as we have seen, are not signs; they are symbols. No precise definitions can be given to them. They are pictorial expressions which point beyond themselves to forces no human being ever completely understands. Today, man is at least beginning to realize that the more he remains unconscious of archetypal forces, the more power they have to rule his life.

So let us contemplate the symbols. Let us watch them move, connecting us with the deepest roots of our history and with the seeds of our undiscovered selves.

THE FOOL

Fig. 4   Le Mat (Marseilles Deck)

3. The Fool in Tarot and in Us

> If a man would persist in his
> folly, he would become wise.
> — WILLIAM BLAKE

THE FOOL is a wanderer, energetic, ubiquitous, and immortal. He is the most powerful of all the Tarot Trumps. Since he has no fixed number he is free to travel at will, often upsetting the established order with his pranks. As we have seen, his vigor has propelled him across the centuries where he survives in our modern playing cards as the Joker. Here he still enjoys confounding the Establishment. In poker he goes wild, capturing the king and all his court. In other card games he pops up unexpectedly, deliberately creating what we choose to call a misdeal.

Sometimes when we have lost a card we ask the Joker to pinch-hit, a function that well suits his motley hue and love of mimicry. But most of the time he serves no overt purpose. Perhaps we keep him in the deck as a sort of mascot in much the same way that the court maintained its jester. In Greece it was believed that keeping a fool about the premises warded off the evil eye. Retaining the Joker in our deck may serve a similar function, since playing cards are reportedly "the devil's pictures."

The Joker connects two worlds – the everyday, contemporary world where most of us live most of the time and the nonverbal land of imagination inhabited by Tarot characters, which we visit occasionally. Like Puck, King Oberon's jester, our Joker moves freely between these worlds; and like Puck, he sometimes mixes them up a bit. Despite his tricky ways, it seems important to keep the Joker in our modern deck so that he can connect the modern "games people play" with the archetypal world of the ancestors. No doubt he observes and reports on our doings to Someone Up There.

To act as the king's spy was, in fact, an important function of the court jester. Being a privileged character, the fool could easily mingle with any group nosing out gossip and assessing the political temper. There is an old

Italian saying, still current, "To be like the Fool in *Tarocchi*," (Tarot) which means to be welcome everywhere.

The Shakespearean fool could act as the king's alter ego in other important ways too, notably in *King Lear* where he seems to symbolize a kingly wisdom not attained by Lear himself until the end of the play. According to James Kirsch,[1] Lear's fool personifies the central core of the psyche, the guiding force which Jung has called the self. In the Tarot series, as we shall see, the Fool sometimes play a similar role. And like his Shakespearean counterpart, this Jester is restless – all over the stage – popping up now here now there and then disappearing before we can catch him. He likes to be where the action is, and if there isn't any, he creates some.

Portraits of court jesters frequently picture them with dogs. Like the king's dog, the fool was thought of as belonging to the king, and both accompanied their master everywhere. One can imagine that the relationship between these two court "animals" must have been an intimate one, more so even than that of master and beast, for they were, in a sense, siblings.

In many Tarot decks, the Fool is shown with a small dog which is nipping at him as if to communicate something. In the Marseilles Tarot (Fig. 4) we are left to imagine the nature of the dog's message. In the Waite version of the Tarot (Fig. 6) the animal appears to be warning his companion of impending danger. In any case, the Fool is in such close contact with his instinctual side that he does not need to look where he is going in the literal sense; his animal nature guides his steps. In some Tarot cards the Fool is pictured as blindfolded, further emphasizing his ability to act by insight rather than eyesight, using intuitive wisdom instead of conventional logic.

Like the foolhardy third brother in fairy tales who rushes in where angels fear to tread, and by doing so wins the hand of the princess and her kingdom, the Fool's spontaneous approach to life combines wisdom, madness, and folly. When he mixes these ingredients in the right proportions the results are miraculous, but when the mixture curdles, everything can end up in a sticky mess. At these times the Fool can look pretty foolish which (being a fool) he has the good sense not to mind. He is often pictured like Bottom, wearing asses' ears because he knows that to admit ignorance is the highest knowledge – the necessary condition of all learning.

Our inner Fool urges us on to life, where the thinking mind might be overcautious. What seems like a precipice from afar may prove to be only a small gulley when approached with the Fool's gusto. His energy sweeps everything before him, carrying others along like leaves in a fresh wind.* Without the Fool's energy all of us would be mere pasteboard.

*The energizing aspect of The Fool is nicely depicted in Manley Hall's *An Encyclopedia Outline of Masonic, Qabalistic and Rosicrucian Symbolic Philosophy*, The Philosophical Research Society, 1968, Plate CXXIX. There The Fool, "life-sized," strides across the page bearing affixed to his costume the rest of the Tarot Trumps, shown as small cards.

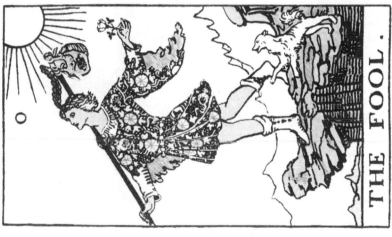

Fig. 7 Aquarian Deck

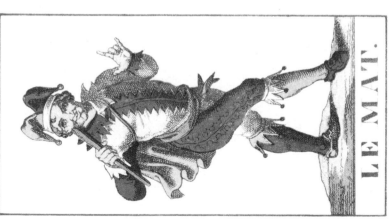

Fig. 6 Waite Deck

Fig. 5 Swiss Deck

In his book *The Greater Trumps,*[2] Charles Williams explores a similar idea. Here the Fool is the central character of the Tarot Trumps. To see him dance is to plumb the mystery of all creation, for his essence is all-inclusive and his paradoxes many. He strides forward yet he looks backward, thus connecting the wisdom of the future with the innocence of childhood. His energy is unconscious and undirected, yet it seems to have a purpose of its own. He moves outside space and time. The winds of prophecy and poesy inhabit his spirit. Although he wanders with no fixed abode, he endures intact throughout the ages. His multicolored costume spins a rainbow wheel offering us glimpses of eternity. As patterns in a kaleidoscope appear and disappear, so the Fool pops in and out of our world, erupting into the Tarot Trumps from time to time as we shall see.

His many-sided nature is expressed by his bauble, a replica of his own head in cap and bells, with which he is often pictured in earnest conversation. This idea is embellished in many subtle ways. In some decks, a serious Fool holds up a mirror whose image grins or sticks out its tongue. In one fifteenth century Austrian deck, a female joker holds a mirror up to – us! The mirror image here, a glum-looking masculine figure, is inscribed "Female joker looking at her grinning idiot's face in the mirror."[3]

Many of the ambiguities of the archetypal Fool are illustrated in a French deck of unknown origin which was given to me about thirty years ago, and which I have seen pictured nowhere else (Fig. 8). In this card the Fool is depicted as an old beggar man, white bearded, and blindfolded. In his right hand he holds a bauble (his alter ego) in such a way that it precedes and guides his faltering steps. Perhaps it shakes its bells to warn the Fool of the crocodile lying in wait below. The little dog barking at his master's heels also sounds an alert of impending danger. As further indication that this old mendicant is in tune with his instinctual side, he carries a violin under his left arm. Its music will accompany him when he sings for his supper at the next village and will help to keep his soul in harmony and peace along the lonely road.

In marked contrast to Waite's young Fool, whom we saw about to set forth on his adventures, this old wanderer is approaching the end of his long journey home. He is not blind, but he wears a blindfold, indicating a voluntary willingness to forego the stimuli of outer scenes and events so that he can contemplate life with the inward eye. He has also outgrown the need for human companionship. He now devotes himself to dialogue with his intuitive self, as personified by his bauble, and to the wordless companionship of his little dog. The age-old tradition of the archetypal sad, wise Fool, kept alive in drama and art through the centuries, is dramatized today in the Chaplinesque clown and the sad jesters whose world gaze meets ours from the canvasses of Picasso, Rouault, and Buffet. The sad Fool is close kin to the archetypal Old Wise Man, a character whom we shall see personified as the Hermit of Tarot number nine.

Le Fou

Fig. 8 The Fool (Old French Tarot)

The Jester's place in the Trump sequence is appropriately quixotic. In some decks, as number zero he leads the pack. In others he is assigned the number twenty-two and as such brings up the rear of the Trump parade. In our view, the question of whether the Fool is first or last is irrelevant; he is neither, and both. For, being a creature of perpetual motion, he dances through the cards each day, connecting the end with the beginning — endlessly.

As might be expected, the details of the Fool's costumes combine many pairs of opposites within their design. His cap, although originally conceived as a satire on the monk's cowl, nevertheless betrays a serious connection with the spirit. Its bell, echoing the most solemn moment in the mass, calls man back to the childlike faith of fools, ringing out St. Paul's exhortation: "Let us be fools for Christ's sake."

The Jester's talisman, a coxcomb with bells, similarly combines a serious truth with lighthearted trappings. The cock foretells the dawn of a new awareness, a reawakening to ancient truths. This miracle, it appears, will be enacted not in the starry heavens above, but once again in the filth and hubbub of the barnyard. In place of iridescent doves and angels with golden trumpets, the Fool offers us the crowing of a cock, that bright and fertile bird with connections in Gethsemane. In the light of these comments, it seems doubly appropriate that the Albigenses, the probable originators of the Trumps, should have chosen to disguise themselves as fools. Feeling betrayed by the corruption of the Church, they too proclaimed a new spirit; and they must have enjoyed fooling the authorities by smuggling their revolutionary ideas into a deck of playing cards.

Symbol par excellence for the union of many kinds of opposites is, of course, the Fool's motley. Its variegated colors and haphazard design might seem to bespeak a discordant spirit; yet within this apparent chaos, a pattern is discernible. Thus the Fool presents himself as one bridge between the chaotic world of the unconscious and the ordered world of consciousness. In this way he is related to the Trickster archetype, as will be discussed later.

The word "fool" is derived from the Latin *follis*, meaning, "a pair of bellows, a windbag." One Austrian Tarot shows the Fool in monk's cowl and bells, playing on a bagpipe.[4] Today, circus clowns sometimes carry a set of bellows or beat one another over the head with empty bladders, thus maintaining a connection with the windy folly of their origins. Bellows furnish the oxygen needed for combustion in much the same way as the Fool furnishes the spirit, or impetus for action. He "fires us up." The Tarot Fool occasionally wears a feather in his cap, further emphasizing his connection with the heavenly spirit. But the Jester can also be a windbag, full of hot air, as the name "buffoon" (from the Latin *bufo*, meaning "toad" and the Italian *buffare*, "to puff") suggests.

Always within the Fool *les extrêmes se touchent*. William Willeford calls our attention to the fact that the jester has traditionally been connected with the phallus, both in the sense of lewdness and of fertility.[5] The phallus was worn by the Fool's Greek and Roman counterparts and by the Renaissance *Arlecchino*. A more contemporary example of this theme is illustrated by Punch – the title figure of the British humor magazine – who has a colossal phallus. The European court jester often carried a bladder shaped like a phallus. His bauble with its two pendant bells is obviously a fertility symbol, his "tool." At the same time this toy is also the Fool's sceptre, connecting him directly with the king as an alter ego.

Sometimes the Fool, depicted more outspokenly as the king's counterpart, is shown wearing a crown. A crown is symbolically a golden halo, open at the top to receive illumination from above. Thus, both king and fool are seen to be divinely inspired. As the king ruled by divine right, so

his counterpart had a right equally divine to criticize him and to offer
challenging suggestions.

Pictured here (fig. 9) is a modern king and his jester. Shockingly
similar in physiognomy, these two personages wear identical crowns of a
most peculiar kind. These head coverings are square and black and solid at
the top so that they have the effect of miniature roofs, protecting the
wearers both from the illumination of heaven and from its tears. Many find
such crowns worthless today, and those who wear them have been called
"squares." Such head coverings seem to make their wearers all look and
behave alike. As this illustration shows, it is sometimes hard to tell which is
the king and which the fool. It was the function of the king's jester to re-

Fig. 9   King and Jester

mind him of his follies, of the mortality of all men, and to help him to guard against the sin of hubris or overweening pride. A jester who is almost identical with the king cannot properly serve these functions; nor can he ward off the "evil eye." And, as the "Watergate tragedy" of the early 1970s demonstrated, a court composed entirely of yes-men is doomed.

Because the Fool encompasses the opposite poles of energy, it is impossible to pin him down. The minute we think we have caught his essence, he slyly turns into his opposite and crows derisively from behind our backs. Yet it is his very ambivalence and ambiguity that makes him so creative. Speaking of this aspect of the Fool, Charles Williams has said: "(It) is called the Fool, because mankind finds it folly till it is known. It is sovereign or it is nothing, and if it is nothing then man was born dead."[6] The Fool encompasses all possibilities.

It seems significant that today the young in heart ot all ages often wear a medley of colors and affect rags and patches, baubles and bells. Many also become wanderers, traveling about with their worldly goods slung carelessly over their shoulders. Alan McGlashan,[7] in his book *The Savage and Beautiful Country*, sees these phenomena as unconscious attempts to reach back into the creative soil of Eden to reactivate the boundless power of the first creation. Many contemporary young people drop out of recognized institutions of higher learning to search for wisdom more profoundly rooted in the soil of their essential being. Perhaps the psychedelic colors of the 60's and 70's presaged the dawn of new consciousness for all mankind.

The Fool's French name, Le Fou, cognate with the word "fire," echoes his connection with light and energy. As the Jester himself might put it, "I *am* light and I *travel* light." (They do love to pun.) A symbol of Promethean fire, the archetypal Fool personifies the transforming power which created civilization – and which can also destroy it. His potential for creation and destruction, for order and anarchy, is reflected in the way he is presented in the old Marseilles Tarot. He is pictured walking his own way, free of all encumbrances of society, without even a path to guide him; yet he wears the conventional dress of the court jester, indicating that he holds an accepted place within the ruling order. At court he plays a unique role as the king's companion, confidant, and privileged critic. Like the Navajo trickster Coyote, the fool is accorded a special role in the social order. His presence serves the ruling powers as a constant reminder that the urge to anarchy exists in human nature and that it must be taken into account.

The maintenance of jesters at court and in the households of titled families began in ancient times and continued until the seventeenth century. This practice dramatizes the idea that we must make room for the renegade factor in ourselves and admit him to our inner court, which means psychologically we must *admit to him*. It is usually a good idea to place our Fool out front where we can keep an eye on him. Excluded from consciousness he can play jokes on us which, although "practical," are difficult to appreciate. Accepted in our inner council, the Fool can offer us fresh ideas and new energy. If we are to have the benefit of his creative vitality, we must put up with his unconventional behavior. Without the Fool's blunt observations and wise epigrams, our inner landscape might become a sterile wasteland. Thus the belief that "to keep a fool at court wards off the evil eye" is no antiquated superstition; it represents a psychological truth of enduring value.

Another technique used in earlier times to insure society against unexpected uprisings of latent destructive urges was to set aside certain periods of universal permissiveness, such as the celebrated Feast of Fools, when all conventions were temporarily suspended. On these occasions the natural order of things was turned upside down. The most sacred rituals were parodied in obscene fashion; dignitaries of Church and State were ridiculed, and all underdogs were allowed to give vent to year-long repressions of hostility, lust, and rebellion.

Today the spirit of such saturnalia survives in a watered-down form in carnivals such as Mardi Gras and Fastnacht, and to a lesser extent in Hallowe'en, New Year's Eve, April Fool's Day, circuses, parades, rodeos, rock festivals, and other events where a holiday spirit prevails. The recent eruption in our culture of black magic and increased interest in the activities of witches and warlocks indicates that we need to include the irrational in more acceptable ways.

There are many less dramatic possibilities for admitting the Fool into our lives. One of these is to admit freely to our own foolishness. Whenever we are able to do this in a conflict situation, the results are disarming. Meeting with no resistance, antagonism falls on its face, and one's adversary is left making a fist at thin air. More significant, the energy we ourselves formerly spent defending our own stupidity is now freed for more creative use. Whenever one protagonist can open his heart to admit the Fool, it usually happens that hostility is dissipated in laughter, and all parties to the conflict end up shaking their heads with Puck over the foolishness of mortal man. All in all, the Fool is a good character to consult whenever we find that our best-laid plans have gone askew, leaving us hopelessly adrift. At these times, if we listen we can hear him say with a shrug, "He who has no fixed goal can never lose his way."

As mentioned earlier, there are many versions of the Tarot. Several examples of the Tarot Fool are presented here because each of these dramatizes an important side of his complex personality. The first of these, an old Swiss card (Fig. 5) shows him as *puer aeternus*, a youth of immortal vigor – several centuries old. His wand suggests Papageno's magic flute, which could set his enemies dancing, thus dispelling their wrath. Surely a fine way to avoid disharmony and war if we can but catch the tune.

The flute also suggests that infamous trickster, the Pied Piper. (There is in fact a German deck that pictures the joker specifically as the Pied Piper followed by a pack of enchanted rats.) In a similar way, the enchanting Swiss Piper can lure us away from conventional ways of thinking and back to the children's land of fantasy and imagination. But we must beware of his magic; if we should forget to pay the piper, this Tarot Trickster could hold us prisoners in the instinctual world, dancing like rats to his tune, helpless until we have paid him his due. It behooves us to keep a good relationship with our Fool. Then, like him, we can journey freely back and forth between the worlds of airy fantasy and earthly reality.

A good example of such a working arrangement between the adult world and that of the eternal child is symbolized in the story of Peter Pan. This famous boy, like the Pied Piper, lured children away from the Establishment. Although he did not wear a fool's coxcomb and bells, Peter could fly and he liked to crow like a cock. Like the archetypal Fool, he embraced the opposites, for he had a dark shadow which he wisely kept sewn to him so that it could not get lost or forgotten.

When Peter Pan abducted Mrs. Darling's children to the Never-Never Land she was desolate, so Peter made a deal with the Establishment: Wendy could live at home most of the time on condition that she drop by the Never-Never Land once in a while to help with the spring house-cleaning. Perhaps if we welcome the Fool into our world, he will teach us to fly and will offer us similar safe-conduct trips to his world, provided of course that we help him tidy it up a bit. Obviously he needs our ordered intellect in his Never-Never Land as much as we need his vitality and creativity in our Ever-Ever Land.

The Fool's trickster aspect is indeed a tricky one. As Joseph Henderson observes, the Trickster is thoroughly amoral. He submits to no discipline and is guided wholly by his experimental attitude toward life; yet it is out of the Trickster figure that the Hero-Savior ultimately evolves. A necessary concommitant to this transformation is that the youthful Trickster must endure punishment for his hubris. Hence, to quote Henderson, "the Trickster impulse provides the strongest resistance to initiation and is one of the hardest problems education has to solve because it seems a kind of divinely sanctioned lawlessness that promises to become heroic."[8] It is perhaps in long overdue recognition of the heroic potential of youth that society today tolerates unconventional dress, behavior, and even lawlessness in young people. That many older people, too, are adopting youthful dress and habits may indicate an unconscious attempt to contact in themselves an unfulfilled heroic potential.

Sometimes this unconscious attempt to contact the unfulfilled heroic potential within can erupt in strange and even violent ways. One notorious example in recent years is the attempt by a young woman called Squeaky Fromm to assassinate President Ford. Not content to play the Jester's archetypal role as an impudent balance wheel for established rules and customs, Squeaky set out to eliminate the Establishment altogether. "It didn't go off," she reported. But this misguided young Fool did achieve immortality of sorts when a photograph of her appeared, complete with red fool's cap, on the cover of *Newsweek* magazine for September 15, 1975 (Fig. 10).

Fig. 10   Squeaky Fromme as The Fool

In our journey toward individuation, the archetypal Fool often demonstrates both the resistance and the initiative inherent in his nature by influencing our lives in less drastic and more creative ways. His impulsive curiosity urges us on to impossible dreams while at the same time his playful nature tries to lure us back to the laissez-faire childhood days. Without him we would never undertake the task of self-knowledge; but with him we are always tempted to dawdle by the wayside. Since he is part of ourselves cut off from ego-consciousness, he can play tricks on our thinking mind; embarrassing slips of the tongue and convenient lapses of memory are the least of these. Sometimes his jokes, even more practical, lure us into situations where the ego would never dare.*

It seems evident that the Fool, as Trickster-Hero, can play good or bad tricks depending on one's point of view. To quote Marie Louise von Franz, such a figure "half a devil and half a saviour . . . is either destroyed, reformed, or transformed at the end of the story."⁹ In the following chapters we shall attend the Tarot Fool and/or hero throughout the twenty-one stages along the way of his transformation. Surely many miracles must take place before the mad conglomeration of energies symbolized by the prancing Jester of card zero can emerge in card twenty-one as The World, a serene dancer moving to the harmonies of the spheres.

In the Swiss deck, The Fool is called Le Mat, meaning literally "the dull one." Oftentimes, court fools were actually mentally retarded. Although dull in matters of intellect, they were felt to have a special relationship to the spirit. Calling such a fool "an archetypal religious figure," von Franz connects him with the *inferior function,* Jung's term for an undeveloped aspect of the psyche. In her *Lectures on Jung's Typology,* she equates the Fool with "a part of the personality, or even of humanity which remained behind and therefore still has the original wholeness of nature."¹⁰

Affectionately referred to as God's folk, or *les amis de Dieu,* such fools were cared for and cherished by society. This custom survives in a vestigial form today among country people whose "village idiot" is supported and protected by the whole town. But in more so-called civilized communities, these aberrations from the norm are no longer tolerated so that such people are shut away in institutions.

If The Fool went by his Italian name, Il Matto (The Mad One), he would surely be put away by our society, for insanity is a condition of the human spirit much feared today. Here too the conventional Establishment has become increasingly intolerant of behavior that deviates from whatever it has chosen to call normal. No doubt the alarming increase in the use of drugs is attibutable in part to the increased rigidity of the previous genera-

---

*For example, my inner Fool led me into Jungian analysis one day over twenty years ago "just for one hour – to see what it was like!" I am still there, in a sense, for the journey never ends.

tion. Apparently only drugs could put consciousness sufficiently to sleep so that the artificial barriers between the two worlds could be broken down. Now many who have used drugs to blast their way out of a too-rigid cultural prison find themselves stranded on the other side, unable to find shelter of any kind in the chaotic winds of psychosis. Mental illness is increasing at an alarming rate. Ironically, but not surprisingly, the thing we feared most has come upon us.

Paradoxically, the way to true sanity often leads through childishness and madness. In certain primitive ceremonies, doctor and patient "act mad" in order to turn the prevailing evil order into its opposite. In *King Lear*, the central figure, helpless as a child, must wander on the heath, exposed to raging tempests within and without, before he can arrive at a new and kingly clarity of soul. It is characteristic of Shakespeare's insight that Edgar, disguised as a fool, leads Lear to sanity. The Fool can play the devil, luring us to madness; but he can also help us find our way to salvation.

Commenting on the Savior aspect of both child and madman, McGlashan has this to say:

> Man must return to his origins, personal and racial, and learn again the truths of the imagination. And in this task his strange instructors are the child, who has but half entered the rational world of time and space, and the madman, who has half escaped from it. For just these two are in some measure released from the remorseless pressure of daily events, the ceaseless impact of the external senses, which burden the rest of mankind. They travel light, this curious pair, and go on far and solitary journeys, sometimes bringing back a gleaming branch from the Gold Forest through which they have wandered.[11]

The Fool as potential Savior is charmingly depicted in a Tarot designed in the first decade of this century under the direction of A.E. Waite. This delightful young page with his beflowered garments and his rose seems almost androgynous, combining masculine and feminine qualities in a happy blend. In many primitive cultures the gods and the first humans were believed to be bisexual, thus symbolizing the primordial state of wholeness which existed before the separation of the opposites – heaven and earth, male and female.

This Fool's costume connects him, then, both with the primal power of the Creator and with the innocence of the newly created. Despite the precipice yawning before him, Waite's young Fool prances along without a care. His head is wrapped in cloudy dreams of a perfect world free of all mishap, and his heart yearns for romance and adventure. He looks as naive as Parsifal. Like Parsifal, the Great Fool, he has no notion what question to ask of life or even that one is required; but he has a little dog who can smell out danger and help him to avoid it.

As with Parsifal, the Fool's connection with his instinctual side has the potential to save not only himself but all mankind as well. In this connection, Joseph Campbell has often made the point that it was precisely Parsifal's complete reliance on his native intuition that prompted him to disregard conventional good manners and the advice of his elders, so that in the end he asked the one simple question needed to redeem the Waste Land. Perhaps Waite's dreamy Fool will save himself – and us. Like Prince Mishkin in Dostoevsky's *The Idiot,* Waite's Fool personifies the redemptive power of simplicity plus faith. And like all fools, he has been touched by the hand of God.

God touched the fool in many ways. In bygone times bodily deformities were looked upon as a special mark of the Lord; so dwarfs, hunchbacks, and the clubfooted were often chosen to be fools at court or in royal houses. Sometimes, ambitious parents even created such deformities by binding or other means, so that their offspring might aspire to the coveted position of fool. Regardless of whether these maimed ones were touched by the miraculous hand of God or by the underhanded tricks of man, they often proved to be human beings of unusual depth and wisdom. Excluded by their physical handicaps from the activities and interests of the average man, through their loneliness and suffering these people were forced to discover resources within themselves. The irony of the sad clown, a frequent theme in the arts, has been immortalized on canvas by Picasso and Rouault and on the stage, notably in *Rigoletto* and *Pagliacci,* though perhaps nowhere so eloquently in terms of human dignity and the ability of the spirit to transcend suffering as in Velasquez' *Don Sebastian de Morro.*

The Fool, be he court jester, trickster, or circus clown, is always touched with the sadness and loneliness of any figure who stands outside the cosy anonymity enjoyed by the average man. One Tarot figure that catches this solemn note is, significantly, a newly hatched Fool from a contemporary deck called the Aquarian Tarot (Fig. 7). Unlike the Fools of many other decks, who are pictured moving toward the right (traditionally the direction of consciousness), this wanderer is turned toward the left (the sinister, unconscious side). All other Fools are stepping out into the extraverted world of action, symbolizing the evolution of consciousness through external experience. The Aquarian Fool, unlike most youths of past generations, has turned away from this kind of reality to pause thoughtfully on the brink of another world. Perhaps like many young people of this age, he is setting out to explore the inner world of dreams and visions.

By far the most solemn of all the Fools, this fellow is the only one who seems to be looking where he is going. He appears to be directing his gaze at some distant goal. Although he is pictured as a young man, there is nothing of the devil-may-care gaiety or bounce of youth about him. It is as if he is setting out quite consciously on the path of self-realization with a dedication and purpose usually achieved only in the second half of life. One might feel that he is retreating from life before he has lived it. Perhaps he feels that our world and its values offer him no opportunity for self-fulfillment. Ideally, he will return from his inward journey inspired to create a new and challenging world more worthy of his effort.

The Aquarian Fool mirrors the seriousness and the sadness of young people today who have the fate to be born into a world which is foreign in every way to the world which their parents have known. As Margaret Mead has often pointed out, anyone born since World War II is stepping into a scientific and cultural climate unknown and forever unknowable by their parents. The problem is not merely the ordinary generation gap, but a cultural abyss so enormous that it is almost as if young people today had all landed on a new planet, both physically and psychologically.

No doubt this is the very abyss that Waite's young page did not see coming. What a contrast between that turn-of-the-century Fool and the contemporary Aquarian Fool! When one looks at this new voyager he feels confident that this young man, too, has the capacity to become the Hero-Saviour who slays the dragon and leads us all to a new kingdom. But first it seems that we all, young and old, must get our heads out of the clouds and face the abyss of reality together. We may even have to fall into the abyss to find common ground on which to build a new world.

In the Marseilles Tarot, The Fool is numbered zero, a fact worthy of our attention, for the number under which a card was "born" sheds light on its character and destiny. Like the stars, numbers shine with an eternal reality that transcends language and geography. They have been called "the bones of the universe" because they are archetypes symbolizing the interrelationship of all things mortal and immortal. Words express man's ideas; numbers express God's realities.

The concept of zero, unknown in the ancient world, did not appear in Europe until the twelfth century. The discovery of this apparent "nothing" enlarged man's thinking in important ways. Practically, it created the decimal system, and philosophically it concretized the astounding paradox that "nothing" is really something, and that this nothing occupies space and contains power. It seems appropriate that zero should have been assigned to The Fool. In the old Italian game of *Tarocchi*, The Fool, true to form, had no value of itself, but augmented that of any card with which it was combined. Like the empty, worthless zero, The Fool's magic can turn one into one million.

The power of zero is inherent in its circular form. To experience the essential qualities of this form, it is helpful to contrast the feel of a circle with that of a square. Suppose that you wanted to draw a perfect circle. First you would set one foot of your compass down at a spot which is to become the center of your circle. Now you are ready to draw the circle's circumference. But until you have pinpointed its center, you cannot begin to draw a circle. There is no chicken-or-egg about it; the center comes first, is in fact central to the whole concept of "circle," a fact not true of any other geometric figure.

A circle with a dot at its center is the universal sign for the sun, source of all warmth, light, and power. This hieroglyph also stands for the World Egg from whose fertile center all creation arose and continues to arise. The Fool, whose motley has been called the ever moving garment of the motionless center, like his number zero, expresses nothing and contains everything.

Try drawing a freehand circle in the air. This motion is so natural and easy that having started, it is almost impossible to stop. One can feel how the circle has come to symbolize natural wholeness, perpetual motion, and infinity. Not so, of course, with the square. To draw even the most primitive rectangle requires four separate motions, and to draw a perfect square demands precise measurements. It is not a thing to be done with one twist of the wrist. The perfect square is found nowhere in nature; it is definitely man's creation.

Man is intimately connected with circular motion every second of his life through the pattern of his breathing and the coursing of his bloodstream. Our life's journey, too, is a circular one as we move from the unconscious intuition of childhhood through knowledge and back to the intuitive perception, which is the wisdom of old age. A circle has unique properties; it is indivisible and indestructible, hence it is immortal. Not so the square. Try this experiment. Cut out a circle from paper or cardboard, cut it into halves and then ask someone what the two pieces are. Chances are the person will say "two semicircles" or "a circle cut in two." Then present a square cut into halves either diagonally or vertically, again asking what these are. This time your subject will probably reply "two triangles" or "two oblongs," as the case may be. In either event the original square has been lost, whereas the circle maintained its identity throughout. The zero, too, is similarly indestructible, for it cannot be changed by addition, subtraction, multiplication, or division.

The circle reflects the shape of the eternal planets and of the great dome of the sky, connecting these with our earthly globe and reminding us that we, too, float in heavenly space. Standing in a circular room whose outer wall is constructed entirely of glass, one could embrace the universe. But we choose instead to live in square boxes whose windows hold up preselected views for our inspection, screened to exclude nature. We like to portion out the world according to the pattern of man rather than to expose ourselves to the free flow of all nature which is the habitation of the patternless Fool.

From what has been said so far, it is easy to see how the Fool's emblem has become the symbol for the unmanifest deity, for the primal chaos or void from which the cosmos and all its creatures arose. It has been connected with the Cabalistic *En Soph,* or Limitless Light, the active principle of existence prior to its manifestation in matter – the nothing from which all things proceed. As such it is also the alchemical *prima materia,* or ground of being, "the stuff we all start with."

The circle also symbolizes the Garden of Eden, paradise, that blissful state of unconsciousness and innocence that mankind experienced before falling into the stony realities of consciousness. It represents the happy womb in which we all were contained as children "once upon a time," before knowledge of the forbidden opposites slithered into our garden. Many paintings show the Garden of Eden as a circle, notably Paolo's *Expulsion,* in the center of which is a beautiful round green world surrounded by a rainbow. It is the Fool's world – and his colors – the habitation from which he visits us occasionally, trailing clouds of everlasting glory.

In the sky above Eden, Paolo shows us the Lord pointing a stern finger at Adam and Eve whom he has cast out of the garden to journey homeless and wandering forevermore. We can identify with those two. How we all long to go home again – to crawl back snugly into the womb of time! The nostalgia we feel for our childhood and the place of our birth reflects this great longing to be contained once more in the Perfect Round.

In many paintings, a circle in the heavens represents a holy place, a sacred *temenos,* wherein heavenly powers miraculously appear – where the divine "breaks through" into human awareness. In our Tarot this device is used in several cards, as will be discussed in later chapters. In this connection it is of interest that the word "cipher" connects with the Hebrew *Sephiroth*, the ten points on the Cabalistic Tree of Life where God's power is made manifest.

In his *God Creating the Universe,* William Blake has used this device effectively to portray what he has called "the secret habitation of the ever invisible Deity" (Fig. 11). Here a bearded Deity, very visible indeed, reaches out a long arm from the holy circle where, compass in hand, he is about to create our microcosmic world in the image and likeness of the Perfect One above. Since the Deity cannot create our world without first fixing its center, Blake's painting reassures us that our world also has a central core of order and meaning hidden within its depths, if we can but find our way to it.

There are a thousand ways in which our world reflects the Great Round above. Many ages and cultures have created temples and churches in circular form, of which Stonehenge, Hagia Sophia, and the Temple of Delphi are prominent examples. The etymology of the word "circle" again connects with much that has already been said. The words "church" and "kirk" are related to circle, and the Greek word *kirkos* (hawk) was the pic-

Fig. 11   God Creating the Universe
(*Ancient of Days* by William Blake. Reproduced from the original in the Henry E. Huntington Library and Art Gallery.

ture name for the priesthood. So we can see that as a voyager of the spirit, The Fool comes honestly by his zero and earns that feather in his cap as well.

A magic circle was thought to keep out the evil spirits and to concentrate energies within its borders. King Arthur's Round Table had such a mysterious significance, and it is sometimes pictured with the Holy Grail appearing miraculously at its center as the knights seated around it marvel. Any round table, clock, or zodiac also illustrates another characteristic of the Fool's magic circle; it gathers persons or ideas together *within* a relationship rather than setting them apart from one another in a hierarchy of importance. A circle has no head or foot, and any person or thing on its circumference is equidistant from its central point. That is why diplomats usually sit at a round table to thrash out international problems.

Certain discs of great contemporary interest (and very much connected with the Fool) are flying saucers, those little circles that zero in on our world from worlds presumably above and beyond our comprehension. The fact that a new and strange "heavenly circle" is seen, or believed to be seen, so frequently today might mean, as Jung has suggested (in "Flying Saucers: A Modern Myth"),[12] that a new image of wholeness is about to burst into consciousness. But these flying saucers suffer the fate of all new insights; they are dismissed as "foolish" and labeled "nothing," as is the Jester himself. *Nothing is a perfect symbol for the state of undivided wholeness before the creation of things.* The world of everyday experience, described by the Hindus as "The Ten Thousand Things," is truly an illusion created by man. Both psychologically and physically we create the world we see. Everything in it comes from nothing at our birth and will return to nothing at our death. This nothing is outside time and space. It is pure nature, the essence behind the veil.

"We make vessels of clay," observed Lao-tzu, "but their true nature is in the emptiness within." To contact this natural emptiness again, to replenish our spirit from its inexhaustible well of silence, this is the object of most meditation exercises. We cannot find a new creative word until we have plumbed the primal silence that existed before the first Word of Creation.

The idea of the circle as both the beginning and the end of the journey is symbolically expressed by the Uroboros, or Tail Eater, that mythical snake who creates, feeds on, and transforms himself by swallowing his tail. His circular form stands for the original state of unconscious nature, the primeval womb before the creation of the opposites and for the state of wholeness, the union of the opposites, desired at the end of the journey.

According to St. Bonaventure, "God is an intelligible sphere whose centre is everywhere and whose circumference is nowhere."[13] To pin the Fool down, even within the wide world of the circle, is impossible. Perhaps we might say he represents a redemptive factor within ourselves that urges us on towards individuation. He is that part of us which, innocently yet somehow quite knowingly, finds itself embarked upon the quest for self-knowledge. Through him, we fall into seemingly foolish experiences which we later recognize as crucial to the pattern of our lives.

Jung defined the ego as "the center of consciousness." The self is the term he used to denote the center of the entire psyche, a center of expanded awareness and stability. As the Tarot Fool in his circular dance will show us, the self is not a thing we create nor is it some kind of golden carrot held by life always in front of our nose. The self is there in the beginning. The ego is, if you like, *made* – but the self is *given*. It exists at our birth – and before our birth and after our death. It is with us always, waiting for us to come home and yet urging us on, for there is no turning back. Our voyage, like the Fool's, is a circular one. To quote Jung:

> The ego stands to the self as the moved to the mover, or as object to subject. . . . The self, like the unconscious, is an a priori existent out of which the ego evolves. It is, so to speak, an unconscious prefiguration of the ego. It is not I who create myself, rather I happen to myself.[14]

The Fool's iridescence cannot be caught and impaled on words. But the above quotation seems to capture at least some of his dancing colors. Let us say that the Tarot Fool is the self as an unconscious prefiguration of the ego. It seems to me that even the Fool might find this sufficiently ambiguous! If he is laughing, it is to remind us that humor is an important ingredient in all our relationships and a necessary commodity for any journey.

William Butler Yeats understood this. He went about collecting amusing stories from the country folk of Ireland. In one of these, called "The Queen and the Fool," we learn that our Tarot Fool is still alive today in Ireland and up to his usual tricks. Those who have seen him say that he wears a little pointed beard and likes to pop up unexpectedly in odd places.

> I have heard one Hearne, a witch doctor, who is on the border of Clare and Galway, say that 'in every household' of Faery 'there is a Queen and a fool,' and that if you are 'touched' by either you never recover, though you may from the touch of any other Faery. He said of the fool that he was 'maybe the wisest of all,' and spoke of him as dressed like one of 'the mummers that used to be going about the country.' . . . The wife of the old miller said, 'It is said they (the Faery) are mostly good

neighbors, but the stroke of the fool is what there is no cure for; anyone that gets that is gone."[5]

From the stroke of The Fool one never recovers. And who would want to!

Fig. 12   Le Bateleur (Marseilles Deck)

4. The Magician: Creator and Trickster

Out of other things thou wilt never make the One,
until thou hast first become One thyself.

Dorn

The Fool, we said, expresses the spirit of play, footloose and fancy-free with boundless energy, wandering restlessly about the universe with no specific goal. Heedless of what's to come, he even looks back over his shoulder. The Magician (Fig. 12) has come to rest, at least temporarily. His energy is directed to the objects before him which he has singled out for special attention. They are set on the table of reality which will confine his activity within its boundaries so that his energy does not spill over and run away. He evidently has a plan. He is about to do something – to perform for us.

If the Fool is that impulse deep in the unconscious that sets us on the quest, then the Magician might symbolize a factor in us that directs this energy and can help to humanize it. His magic wand connects him with his ancestor, Hermes, the god of revelations. Like the alchemical Mercurius, who possessed magical powers, the Magician can initiate the process of self-realization which Jung called individuation, and he can guide our journey into the underworld of our deepest selves. Man has always recognized a power transcending the ego, which he sought to propitiate through magical rites.

The Fool and the Magician are both at home in the transcendental world. The Fool dances about in it like an unconscious child; the Magician journeys through it as a seasoned traveler. Each is related to the Trickster archetype, but in different ways. The differences between the Fool and the Magician in this respect parallel those between a practical joke and a magical performance. The Fool plays tricks *on* us; The Magician arranges demonstrations *for* us. The Fool perpetrates his surprises behind our backs; the Magician can perform his magic before our eyes if we will attend his performances. The Jester fools us and makes us laugh; the Magician mystifies us and makes us wonder.

The Fool is a loner, his method is secretive. He pops up suddenly crowing "April Fool" and is gone again. The Magician will include us in his plans. He welcomes our attendance at his magic show, sometimes even inviting us on stage as his accomplice. Some degree of cooperation on our part is necessary for the success of his magic. But with the Fool our complete unconsciousness is the sine qua non for success.

The Fool is a happy-go-lucky amateur; the Magician is a serious professional. As the Fool's magic is wholly spontaneous, he is often as surprised as we at its result. If it fails, he is unconcerned, bounding along to the next adventure with a shrug. With the Magician it is quite otherwise, for he is a dedicated artist. When one of his creations fails, he is concerned and tries to understand why. The Fool's designation being zero, the wide world is his oyster. He is interested in everything and cannot be bothered with anything. Like the Eternal Boy of every age, he spins fanciful dreams, leaving their execution for someone else to accomplish. The Magician, being Tarot Trump number one, has a very different psychology. He is interested in discovering the one creative principle behind diversity. He wants to manipulate nature, to harness its energies. The most primitive magic rites were connected with fertility. They were ceremonies to propitiate the gods in order to insure plentiful crops and fertile women. The Fool has no such plan. He merely wants to enjoy nature.

The Marseilles Magician holds his wand in one hand and in the other a golden coin. The hand is central to all magic. It is symbolic of man's power to tame and shape nature consciously, to put its energies to creative use. Quicker than the eye, the Magician's hand creates illusion more rapidly than our thinking mind can follow it. His hand is also quicker in the sense of "more alive" than man's plodding intellect. The human hand seems to have an intelligence of its own; it has been called "the fleeting moment of creation that never stops."

The Magician's gift for miracle and for deception is manifold. By directing our attention away from the golden coin, he can ensnare and befuddle us with his sleight of hand. Like human consciousness itself, an aspect of which he symbolizes, the Magician can create maya, the magic illusion of "the ten thousand things." For, by making the objects on his table disappear, he can dramatize the simple truth that every object, every thing, is but an *appearance* of reality. It is we who create the world which appears to exist. By transforming one object or element into another, the Magician reveals another truth; namely that underneath the "ten thousand things," all manifestations are one; all elements are one and all energies are one. Air is fire, is earth, is rabbits, is pigeons, is water, is wine, is ONE! All are whole and all are holy. The Magician helps us to understand that the physical universe is not the result of The Original Life Power acting *on matter*, rather it is the result of the Life Power acting *upon itself*. *Out of itself* the One Power builds all shapes and forms, all force, and myriad of structures.

Originally, only the gods or their earthly representatives, the priests, were felt to have this magic power. One such figure was Hermes Trismegistus, a mythical figure variously associated with the Egyptian god Thoth and the Greek god Hermes. It was he who left us this succinct summary of the topic now under discussion: "All things are from this One, by the meditation of The One, and all things have their birth from this One Thing." As already indicated, this expresses a truth on both the macrocosmic and the microcosmic planes of existence.

Magic is sometimes called the science of hidden relationships. Be it miracle or trick, one underlying essence of this art is revelation. The Magician has power to reveal the fundamental reality, the *isness* that underlies all. He represents a wonder-working aspect of ourselves which can divine the hidden wellsprings of life and open them up for creative use. This kind of revelation is beautifully symbolized in the story of Moses who, divining hidden waters, smote the rock with his miraculous staff until its springs gushed forth to slake the thirst of his people. "Blessed are they that hunger and thirst. . . ." In the service of a vital, human need, miracles can occur. One might say that miracles can *only* happen in response to a need transcending the ego.

In the picture *Moses Striking Water from the Rock* (Fig. 13), the importance of this transcending necessity is illustrated in a most dramatic way. Here the thirsty people are more prominently featured than Moses himself. They are shown crowded together at the waters, each absorbed in drinking his fill. No one seems concerned with the miracle worker, least of all Moses himself, who is busy wielding his staff, intent on the job at hand. He is not centrally located in the scene nor is he set apart from the others. Instead he appears as one of the group, joined with his people both pictorially and emotionally by the advent of the miraculous waters. The flow of these waters and the circular rhythm of the design seem to emphasize the idea that we are witnessing one event involving two poles of equal importance: on the left, the people's need and hope; on the right, Moses' awareness and dedication. Without both factors, no miracle could take place. Were the thirsty people eliminated from this illustration, the magus would inevitably become its central figure and his magic, if operable at all, merely a prideful trick, an ego trip in the service of nothing beyond personal vanity.

According to Jung, all magic, miracles, and parapsychological happenings have one ingredient in common: an attitude of hopeful expectancy on the part of the participants. Jung found this hopeful attitude to be

Fig. 13   Moses Striking Water from the Rock

a major ingredient in the success of the Rhine experiments at Duke University in which participants "divine" the symbol imprinted on a card which they cannot see. Commenting on this phenomenon, Jung says:

> The test person either *doubts* the possibility of knowing something one cannot know, or *hopes* that it will be possible and that the miracle will happen. At all events the test person being confronted with a seemingly impossible task finds himself in the archetypal situation which so often occurs in myths and fairy tales, where a divine intervention, i.e., a miracle, offers the only solution.[1]

In describing these events, Jung has also used the terms "archetype of the miracle" and "archetype of the magic effect."

It is understandable that the Magician who lives in the depths, at the psychoid level of the unconscious where there exist no divisions of time, space, body and soul, matter and spirit (and where the four elements themselves have not been separated out of the great void), should have the power to put us in touch with the great Oneness of perfection, health, and harmony. But since this great void is also the Whole from which all will be born, it contains, of necessity, all opposites. Small wonder then that the Magician's character is a maze of contradictions. As Wise Man he can lead us to the manger or perform The Miracle of Camelot. As Trickster, he can be found at the village fair and is not above deliberately befuddling gullible customers, sometimes even making their money disappear. It is some consolation to know that, being a descendent of the wily Mercury, the Magician comes by his duplicity honestly. Like Mercury, messenger of the gods, he connects inner and outer, above and below, partaking of both.

Some modern Tarot decks (notably the Waite version) present Trump number one as the priestly "good" Magician, eliminating entirely his more questionable aspects. We shall return to this later but, for the moment, be it noted that the Marseilles version alone offers us the full enchantment of the Magician's multiple facets. At first glance, his motley costume (Fig. 12) reminds us of the Fool, an appropriate connection since both characters partake of the Trickster archetype. As with the Fool, the Magician's variegated colors suggest the incorporation of many disparate elements, but here the opposing colors are more consciously arranged vis-à-vis one another. In comparison with the more haphazard design of the Fool's costume, the Magician's alternating patches of color seem deliberately placed to suggest both opposition and interaction, contrast and coordination. Each foot, leg, hip, breast, and shoulder seems clothed with an almost studied disregard for the color selected by its opposite member. Their colors fairly vibrate with alternate repulsion and attraction so that they seem to emit sparks of electric energy.

The theme of creative antithesis is further emphasized in the Magician's hat brim which suggests a figure eight lying on its side. This pattern, called the "lemniscate," is the mathematical sign for infinity. As pictured here, the almost hypnotic sweep of the brim's red outline connotes the movement of the opposites, each endlessly changing into the other, as in the Chinese symbol Tai Chi, which shows the ceaseless interaction of yang and yin, the positive and negative forces inherent in all nature. If you concentrate on the Magician's hat brim by candlelight in the dark of the moon, he will make it move for you. Seen thus, it becomes the perpetual motion of creation.

The two ellipses of this lemniscate, joined by a large hump or bridge in the middle, can also be seen as a pair of giant spectacles. If you put on these magic eyeglasses you may catch a glimpse into new dimensions of reality. These glasses are not rose-colored. What we shall see in this new dimension is a natural phenomenon. It is not pie-in-the-sky nor the manifestation of some vague "other world." The experiences which the Magician offers us are as indigenous to our nature and as rooted in our terrestrial environment as are the plants that we see growing at his feet.

It is significant in this connection to recall that the Fool's costume had no touch of green. As we noted, he was not planted in our reality. His was the free-flowing energy of the wholly unmanifest. Here the Magician organizes this energy for creation, preparatory to its embodiment in reality. The Fool's cap was yellow, the color of fiery sun power. At its tip was affixed one tiny red ball, or perhaps it is a bell, worn jauntily like a token drop of blood. With the Magician this red blood comes alive, coursing and flowing through the lemniscate hat-brim. He "gives his blood" to the situation, he is committed to the task before him. The golden yellow, now centered and shaped into a large ball, becomes the crown of the Magician's hat. That this magic sun power belongs to the Magician's person as well is suggested by the fact that his curls are tipped with gold. His hair resembles Medusa's snaky locks, again recalling this Trickster's dual nature.

The Magician's wand, like an orchestra conductor's, is an instrument for concentrating and directing energy. Energy needs direction. Only with man's conscious cooperation can it be shaped to human use. The maestro at his podium uses his baton to coordinate and modulate the energies of his players, creating from otherwise chaotic sound a harmonious, rhythmic pattern. So does this Tarot maestro seem about to orchestrate the energies of the objects before him. He holds his wand in his left hand, indicating that his power is not a result of intellect and training but is rather a natural, unconscious gift. Often magicians use the forefinger itself as a wand to direct attention and to concentrate energy. One of the most beautiful pictorial representations of this is Michelangelo's well-known *Creation* on the ceiling of the Sistine Chapel. In this painting the index finger of the Supreme Magus, phallus-like, imparts the creative life-force to the hand of Adam. One can feel the loving flow of this inseminating energy as it passes from the hand of God to that of Adam, and through him to all God's creatures.

We have spoken of the Magician's ambiguous nature; how, on the one hand, he can put us in touch with the Great Round of unity and how, on the other hand, he can help us to separate out its elements for examination. That one being can perform such diverse and seemingly antithetical functions seems magical; but that he can perform these dual functions at one and the same time seems a miracle of unbelievable proportions. This, however, he can do.

In an illustration by Goltzius from Ovid's *Metamorphoses* (Fig. 14), we see the Grand Magus himself actually performing this miracle. The picture is called *The Separation of the Elements*, yet it is apparent that the wholeness of the Great Round is in nowise destroyed by this activity. On the contrary, it is as if its true essence now stands, for the first time, fully revealed. Our inner Magician performs this same kind of magic by helping

Fig. 14   The Separation of the Elements
(Goltzius, Hendrick. From a set of illustrations for Ovid's Meta-
morphoses Engraving. The Metropolitan Museum of Art, New
York. Gift of Mrs. A.S. Sullivan, 1919.)

us to examine and discriminate the elements of our inner worlds in such a
way as to reveal, rather than destroy, its essential unity.

Since his task is one initiated and exemplified by the Creator, it
behooves us to have another look at Goltzius' dramatization of it so that we
can understand what is happening here. In this picture, God – or "kindlier
nature" as Ovid calls him – appears to be wholly absorbed in his dance of
revelation. Apparently this separation of the elements is a difficult operation even for the Creator. It evidently requires perfect concentration.
Sometimes it seems a sticky, tricky business, a bit like pulling taffy. Other
times it appears to be more like a dance with veils, involving superhuman
dexterity and perfect timing. The problem may be how to tear away the
veils that hide the central reality without becoming entangled and
smothered in these outer trappings. What passionate intensity it requires,
this dervish dance whereby a new unity is revealed and a new world
brought into being!

On the microscopic level, the ego alone cannot effect this magic.
Only our inner Magician can master the intricate choreography of revelation. Only he can demonstrate the correspondence between the central
core and its outer wrappings; only he can reveal that they are both made of
the same stuff.

In a different way, the magic of the alchemists demonstrated a correspondence between inner and outer. They saw in the elements and transformations taking place in their chemical retorts the elements and transformations within their own psychic nature. Their avowed aim was purely external and chemical: by applying heat to certain mixtures, they hoped (they said) to uncover the creative seed or essence underlying all matter and thereby to transform the baser metals into gold. They spoke of this as "liberating the spirit concealed or imprisoned in matter."

In their writings however, the alchemists repeatedly hinted that the gold they really sought was not outer gold, but rather that transcendent, inner gold at the center of the psyche that Jung calls the self. In *Psychology and Alchemy* Jung gives a detailed account of the various stages of this Great Work, as the alchemists called their experiments. Jung demonstrates how the various alchemical stages referred to in their writings (liquification, distillation, separation, coagulation, etc.) correspond in many ways to the various stages through which the human psyche evolves, matures, and moves toward individuation. Jung describes how, by working with the elements "out there," the alchemists achieved an intuitive connection with similar kinds of transformations within their inner nature. He shows how, through this outer work, they connected with, intuitively understood, and thereby influenced, the inner work as well. In other words, the alchemists, whether or not they understood consciously what they were doing, were actually using their chemical experiments as "projection holders" in somewhat the same way that we are using the Tarot cards. The contents of the alchemists' retorts were air, earth, fire, water, salt, lead, mercury, and other such things, whose interactions they studied and so came somewhat to understand their own inner chemistry. Our materials are the twenty-two Trumps, whose interaction we are studying in a similar way and for similar reasons.

Central to the alchemists' work was a figure called Mercurius, whose paradoxes were limitless. The alchemists referred to him as both "the world-creating spirit" and "the spirit concealed or imprisoned in matter." They called him "the transforming substance" and, at the same time, "the spirit indwelling in all living creatures." In short, Mercurius was both the transformer and the element that needed to be liberated and transformed.

Our mercurial spirit (whom we might label the inner Magician) also shares these ambiguities. He is the "world-creating spirit" – yet he is "concealed and imprisoned" in the matter of our dark unconsciousness. If he is to function as "the transforming substance," we must find ways to liberate him from captivity and bring him out into the light of conscious awareness.

According to the alchemists, man himself stood in this dual role as world creator and imprisoned one – as redeemer and the one in need of redemption. For they felt that salvation and redemption were not bestowed from on high; these they believed were achieved only through the Great Work to which they dedicated their lives: the liberation of the spirit contained within themselves and within all nature.

We too need to find ways to free our imprisoned spirit so that he can function as "the transforming substance" with power to change our inner world and affect the outer one. We shall need his help to find our way around in the darkness of inner nature and to at last unveil the self, the central sun of our being now eclipsed in darkness, so that it can shine forth in a new way. To the extent that we succeed in doing this, we as individuals are changed and human nature itself is transformed.

Speaking psychologically, it is through the interaction between human consciousness and the primitive, unconscious archetypes, that what is unconscious moves toward the light, and the quality of human consciousness itself slowly evolves toward expanded awareness. More and more we are coming to understand that the human psyche, like the human body, is not static; that both of these, as well as we ourselves, are (like all natural phenomena) processes in evolution. We no longer tend to picture the Creation as a fixed moment when the Creator "did" this or "said" that for all time. Rather, we view creation as a continuous ongoing event – an eternal dialogue as it were between the one which is our small Magician and the One which is God, the Grand Magus.

Artists throughout the ages have tried to picture the Creation for us. We have already discussed several of these pictorial representations. But none of them so effectively catches the essence of the Creation as a process in which both Creator and Created are involved as does Rodin's sculpture entitled *The Hand of God* (Fig. 15). In this marvelous study, we see Adam and Eve embracing, cradled and sheltered in the supporting hand of the Almighty. Here the human figures actually appear to be evolving from the stuff of the Creator's hand, so that human and superhuman together form one supreme Whole. In this picture, the miracle of creation is not presented as a *fait accompli,* an act performed soley by the Grand Magus. Instead, Creator and Created alike are involved together in the act of becoming. They are co-creators in a process which transcends both.

The Magician of the Marseilles deck, with his electric coloring and his lemniscate hat, symbolizes such a process. The feeling of "becomingness" is also reflected in the symbolism of the Magician's number, which is one. The number one is symbolic of the yang, or masculine power. It is light, bright, active, penetrating, and is associated with heaven and spirit. Yet, for all its seeming forthrightness, this number has hidden ambiguities, for its very concept implies *another.* The idea of one can only be experienced in relation to at least one other. The number one is said to represent man's consciousness because, like man, it stands erect connecting heaven and earth. But consciousness also implies a duality – observer and observed. It is as if, hidden in the rib of our Magician, there is already contained the feminine principle, whose number is two. As the white yang "fish" of the

Fig. 15 The Hand of God (Auguste Rodin)

Tai Chi symbol carries the dark eye of its counterpart, so embedded in the pure spirit of the Magician is a dark spot of feminine ambivalence.

The Marseilles deck alone catches these subtle nuances. In the Waite version, for example, only the positive yang aspects of the Magician are shown (Fig. 16). No motley Trickster at the crossroads, this magus appears against a backdrop of pure, golden light among lilies and roses. He wears priestly robes and a solemn expression. In his right hand he holds aloft a wand indicating that his powers are under conscious control and are dedicated to the heavenly spirit above. With his left hand he points earthward, dramatizing the Hermetic maxim "As above so below." It is worth noting that, although this Magician's wand has two poles, both of them are white. Thus the masculine spirit is doubly emphasized whereas the dark feminine yin is excluded altogether. "White above and white below" suggests a static, sterile universe ruled by rigid perfectionism.

Fig. 16 Waite Deck

The setting in this card seems contrived: in place of the informal, natural background of the French card, Waite has planted his Magician in a cultivated bower of symbolic lilies and roses. Waite eliminates most of the ambiguities of the Marseilles version and, with these, much of its vitality. The flamboyant hat, with its roller coaster brim and its golden crown, has disappeared entirely, leaving instead a small black lemniscate that hovers ghostlike above the Magician's head, offering us little to nourish the imagination. The Magician's snaky, gold-tipped curls have been replaced by the severe no-nonsense coiffure of the priestly Establishment. The table of the magus has also been tidied up – questionable articles such as dice, balls, and other oddments of unknown origin and dubious purpose have been swept, so to speak, under the table. In their place we now find only the four objects representing the four Tarot suits, these all neatly arranged and ready for use.

All in all, the kind of magic pictured in the twentieth-century English card is very different from that in the old French one. These differences reflect two mutually exclusive attitudes about the way of individuation and about the Magician's role in the process. For example, Waite's Magician seems to experience the transcendent power as located "up above." His rigid body stance and gestures indicate that he will bring illumination to earth by an act of will according to established ritual. Only the vertical axis is stressed; his gestures do not include the horizontal, which is the dimension of human relationship.

In contrast, the French Magician's pose and the wide sweep of his hat include the horizontal dimension as well. He appears to operate less by will and more by imaginative play. His casual setting allows room for the unexpected. And above all, his posture is not tense and rigid, for this lively fellow is not concerned with future perfection. He is caught in the creative moment of the ever present *now*. The impromptu atmosphere of the Marseilles card reminds one that the miracles of Jesus were also performed quite casually by the wayside and that his wisest parables were spontaneous responses to the living moment.

The Magician's French name, Le Bateleur, means "the juggler." One can imagine him tossing all the objects on his table into the air in a continuous rhythmic design, not unlike that of his lemniscate hat. In a painting by Marc Chagall entitled *The Juggler*, the central figure is pictured manipulating time itself, symbolized by an enormous watch which he flaunts almost like a banner. The ability to transcend the restrictions of ordinary time has always seemed to be magic of an especially godlike kind. The Magician demonstrates this magic in several ways. First, as seer he brings into present reality ideas and potentials that ordinarily lie hidden from us "in the future." This ability to divine is indeed Divine, for through it we touch the timeless world of the immortals.

Another way in which the Magician juggles time is through his ability to speed up natural processes in apparent defiance of the laws of time. As a smith speeds up the transformation of metals by applying intense heat, so can the Magician effect transformations of consciousness by applying the heat of emotional involvement. In ancient times smiths were thought of as magicians. Their powers were considered divine as is evidenced by the fact that one of their numbers was the Olympian god Hephaestus.

As Juggler, the Magician creates magic patterns in space-time. All artists are magicians, for they juggle the forms of everyday life into transcendental patterns. They strip away all unessential details, baring the basic structure underlying all appearance so that through each of a dozen different paintings of a dozen individual trees, the essence of treeness shines forth.

Sculpture is also a kind of magic revelation. Artists in this medium often say that they do not create their figures. Instead they simply chisel away all superfluous material so that the image already implicit in the basic stone can stand free. This idea is beautifully dramatized in Michelangelo's famous statue, fittingly called the *The Captive*. It depicts a slave struggling to free himself from a block of marble in which he is still partially imprisoned. In the same way, writers strive to liberate their ideas from the mass of entangling verbiage that tends to obscure them. The problem is not so much to find words as to weed out the excess, so that the image can stand clear. All of us have no doubt experienced the truth of that old adage: "If one had more time, one could write fewer words."

As we have seen, the alchemists, too, dedicated their lives to freeing the spirit imprisoned in matter. Significantly, although they were looked upon by their contemporaries as magicians, they spoke of themselves as artists. Analytical psychologists are also artists and, in the sense in which we have been using the term, magicians. For out of the *massa confusa* of our daily lives, our conflicting urges, and confused images, they help us to find the underlying pattern: the unique one in ourselves which touches the universal One of all mankind.

The word "magic" is cognate with imagination, a necessary ingredient for all creativity in the arts, and in the sciences as well. Who would have imagined that we could fly to the moon? Yet somebody did, and that's how we got there. We achieved this magic because lots of "somebodies" had this image and concentrated their energies upon it. Just imagine what could happen if every living human being "imaged" peace and directed his energies toward its realization. We magicians could indeed work miracles.

But the magic of human consciousness is a two-edged sword. We can use it to shape a brave new world or crack open a Pandora's box of hidden devils to destroy our world and all life on this planet. The temptation to misuse power is a hidden aspect of any archetypal figure; but since the powers of the Magician are so primitive and subtle, this temptation is his special *bête noire*. It is perhaps in recognition of this fact that the Magician's "black beast" is specifically pictured in card fifteen, where we shall meet him as the Magician's shadow, the Devil.

In Jungian terms, the shadow is a figure appearing in dreams, fantasies, and outer reality that embodies qualities in ourselves which we prefer not to think of as belonging to us, because to admit to these would tarnish our image of ourselves. So we project these seemingly negative qualities onto someone else. Such a person seems always to haunt our dreams, disturbing the atmosphere by saying or doing inappropriate or even downright devilish things. In outer reality, a person onto whom our shadow is projected usually acts as a constant irritant or "grater." Almost everything he says or does rubs us the wrong way. Even his most casual remark can get under our skin, where it festers for days, weeks, or even months. It won't let us alone, so that we find ourselves constantly involved emotionally with this unwelcome personality. Often this involvement is external as well as internal with the result that, as if by black magic, this obnoxious person, whom we "never want to see again," keeps popping up persistently and irrationally in our daily lives.

Like Robert Louis Stevenson's famous shadow, he is ever present in our garden, where he "goes in and out with us" in such a distressing way that we too cry out: "What can be the use of him?" That he should have any use at all is more than we can see. But if he, and we, are persistent, we discover that this unwelcome character is useful – even necessary – to our well-being in many ways.

For one thing, he holds in thrall through the magic of projection not only negative characteristics that belong to us but many positive potentials as well. And, as we soon discover, if we are to claim these good qualities as our own, we shall have to accept the negative ones as well. Getting to know and accept our shadow as an aspect of ourselves is an important first step toward self-knowledge and wholeness. Without our shadow we would remain but two-dimensional beings, paper thin, with no substance.

Enlarging our aperture of awareness to admit the shadow as a member of our inner family is difficult; but in some ways it is easier than it sounds. Because, as we come to know this dark character, we discover that much of his murkiness was chiefly caused because he inhabited the darkness of our own unconsciousness. As we gradually allow him to step forth into the light, we begin to find that even his most annoying qualities seem less dark and their weight less difficult to bear. Ideally, when (and if) our sun ever reaches its full zenith, we may have incorporated into ourselves so many of these shadowy aspects that, like the child in Stevenson's garden, we can almost say of our shadow, "there is none of him at all." But in the meantime (which decoded means *a lifetime*) the shadow will be in evidence somewhere, because as energies formerly devoted to resisting the shadow gradually become available for more creative use, we find the courage and strength to look deeper and deeper into our own darkness to discover still more shadowy figures.

Since shadow figures can appear in many guises, wrestling with them is a forever battle. No sooner do we recognize and accept one aspect mirrored in a person of our acquaintance than up he pops again in another form. Now it is no longer that old friend next door but a new neighbor across the street who sets our teeth on edge. And once again we find ourselves bewitched, fascinated, and obsessed. But this time we are wary. Before allowing ourselves to be lured into sterile rounds of circular thinking, fuming, and emoting, we might remember to confront our inner Magician and persuade him to stop playing his devilish tricks. If we approach him firmly but courteously, he may even help us to retrieve that part of ourselves that has somehow moved across the street.

Fortunately we shall never have to accept the Devil as our personal shadow, nor do we find ourselves projecting his full weight upon our neighbor. Whereas our neighbor may well embody the *personal shadow*, the Devil represents for us what Jung has called the *collective shadow*, meaning a shadow figure so enormous and all-encompassing that it can only be borne collectively by all mankind. Neither the suprahuman creativity of the Magician nor the infrahuman destructiveness of the Devil belongs to us personally. Both of these characters are archetypal figures representing instinctual tendencies whose full powers are above and beyond our grasp. But, nonetheless, each of us does possess some of the magic of consciousness and, to the extent that we have this kind of power, we stand prey to the devilish temptation to misuse it. To resist this temptation requires a high degree of discipline and self-knowledge.

Shakespeare understood this problem. In *The Tempest*, he dramatizes both the problem and its solution with true poetic insight. Here Prospero, a duke deprived of his kingdom by the machinations of former friends, retires to a desert island where he studies the magic arts and plots vengeance on those who have betrayed him. Through his magic, he liberates the spirit Ariel, imprisoned long ago in a tree trunk by a wicked witch. But Prospero, in turn, subjects Ariel to slavery, forcing this good spirit to serve his own black ends, which involve conjuring up a fatal storm to bring shipwreck and death to those who have betrayed him. Later, through the good influence of Ariel, Prospero voluntarily abandons his vengeful plot, makes friends with his enemies, and frees Ariel and others whom he has held slaves to his black magic. In the denouement he renounces forever this kind of magic, leaves the island where he has reigned supreme, and returns to the mainland of collective humanity where he vows to live his life and use his creative gifts in a more human and conscious way.

Prospero, isolated in his magic world, is an excellent example of the archetypal Magician. No one of us is such a Magician. We cannot call forth storms at will nor, literally speaking, free airy spirits imprisoned in matter and force them to cooperate. But, through the miraculous magic of modern science our Prospero has split the atom, letting loose spirits more powerful than any storm. We have already seen this energy hideously misused, and we are aware that forces potentially even more horrendous are available to be let loose upon the world.

No one of us is individually responsible for the magic of science nor for the horrors of its misuse. But all of us collectively must bear this burden. Unless we can free our good spirit from its present bondage to our materialism, greed, and vengeance, we will surely be destroyed by our own black magic. At the eleventh hour, we must somehow help our Prospero to find his way back to the mainland of common humanity.

Most of us feel helpless in this situation. And probably there is very little the average person can do directly to effect a change at the top. We are indeed small drops in a very large bucket. But there is, luckily, a direct connection between the clarity of each of these little drops and the quality of the collective waters as a whole. Whenever, in our personal lives, we renounce the comfortable magic of one small black projection, or whenever we abandon the vicious temptation to vengeance, the world consciousness is clarified and the dark shadow that hovers over our planet is lightened. Whenever, like Peter Pan, we take time to retrieve our own small shadow and stitch it securely to our puny self, we will have done more than we may imagine possible to mend the world's woes.

The reason for this – and the point is a crucial one – is that the correspondence between inner and outer can no longer be considered merely an analogy: It has now become a proven, scientific fact. This connection between spirit and matter intuited by the alchemists, mystics, and poets of many cultures, and expressed in a vague and metaphorical way, has now been found by scientists to be much more actual and direct than was heretofore imagined possible. The alchemical idea that our inner Magician was a "world-creating spirit" has been demonstrated in various ways to be far more than mere poetic truth.

Probably the most familiar proof that we do indeed create the objective world is offered by the scientific experiments conducted with light. In these it was conclusively proven that, under two different sets of carefully controlled experimental conditions (each equally valid), the nature of light was observed to be, on the one hand, "waves," and on the other, "corpuscles." And despite all subsequent efforts to do so, these two diametrically opposite scientific facts refuse to be reconciled. The "real" light will not stand up and make itself known to us. The ultimate essence of nature remains concealed. Nor will Nature ever reveal herself, scientists say.

The fault, they explain, is not with our man-made instruments for observing outer reality, but with our human selves – with the limitations of our sensory apparatus. No instrument devised, however refined and exact, can ever offer us an unobstructed view of the world "out there." We are forever, it seems, doomed to experience the nature of light as both "waves" and "corpuscles," both of which are admittedly created not "out there" but "in here," within our psychophysical selves. It is we ourselves who "create" the world. Nature remains, and will ever remain, a mystery.

It now seems evident that the reality of the psyche is the one reality – the only reality. Long ago, a Zen monk put it this way: "This floating world is but a phantasm. It is momentary smoke." Sir Arthur Eddington, the astrophysicist, after devoting his life to the investigation of so-called outer reality, summed up his findings in approximately these words: "Something out there – we don't know what – is doing something we don't know what."

So we are stuck with one world, which we sometimes experience as "outer" and sometimes as "inner." That the correspondence between these two aspects of the one reality should now be revealed as scientifically and mathematically exact seems less surprising than formerly. But the duality of our intellect is so ingrained that these revelations still seem magical. For example: the fact that physicists can postulate and accurately describe a potential new element which later does, in fact, manifest itself in outer nature. Or that mathematicians (quite independent of astronomical observations) have succeeded in working out the laws of planetary orbit with such exactitude that their formulae were subsequently found to tally precisely with the way these planets behave in nature.

In *The Myth of Meaning*, Aniela Jaffé comments on the miraculous way these independent mathematical calculations tally so exactly with scientific fact. "This seems most astonishing," she says, "and can be satisfactorily explained only by postulating an 'independent objective order' that 'imprints' both man and nature, or human thinking and the cosmos."[2] It is as if, at the psychoid level, the archetypal patterns of the inner world correspond exactly with those of outer reality.

Most of us can cite astounding instances where an inner pattern suddenly corresponded with an outer one in a miraculous way, where no causal connection could be found between the two events. In these situations, an inner image suddenly materializes in outer reality, just as if we had conjured it forth. For example, we find ourselves haunted by the persistent memory of a childhood friend whom we have not heard from in twenty years. Then suddenly, out of the blue, we receive a wholly unexpected letter, telephone call, or visit from this friend.

Synchronicity is the term Jung used to denote this kind of coincidence between internal states and external events. Jaffé further clarifies Jung's meaning, elucidating it as follows:

> By "synchronistic phenomena" Jung meant the meaningful co-
> incidence of a psychic and a physical event which cannot be
> causally connected with one another and are separated in space

or time (for instance, a dream that comes true and the event it predicts). Such coincidences arise from the fact that space, time, and causality, which for our consciousness are discrete determinants of events, become relativized or are abolished in the unconscious, as has been statistically demonstrated by the ESP experiments of J. B. Rhine. Consciousness breaks down into processes that which is still a unity in the unconscious, thereby dissolving or obscuring the original interrelationship of events in the "one world."

Synchronistic phenomena are like an irruption of that transcendent unitary world into the world of consciousness. Always they are unpredictable and irregular, because not based on causality, and they arouse astonishment or fear because they make nonsense of our habitual categories of thought. The paradoxical unity of being which they reveal was identified by Jung with Dorn's *unus mundus*.[3]

It is our inner Magician, of course, who is responsible for these miraculous eruptions of the unitary world into our everyday world of space and time, cause and effect. In order to observe how this works, let us say that we are sitting down (as you probably are) reading this book. Under "normal" circumstances, we should expect to proceed through the Trump series, page by page, studying the cards in numerical sequence as outlined. By viewing them thus sequentially in space-time, we expect to see how each card evolves from the preceding one: how the first card, in a sense, *causes* the second one and so on. According to the linear thinking to which we have become accustomed, we should expect to see card twenty-one, The World, only at the end of this book. "In the course of time," as the saying goes, we shall have "traveled through" the Trump series, arriving ultimately at the final card which pictures the unitary world, the alchemical *unus mundus*, which exists beyond space and time.

But suppose, now, that just as we think this thought, our book should unaccountably fall to the floor face up and open at the very page that pictures The World. Probably we should all agree that this correspondence between inner thought and outer happening was a miraculous coincidence, transcending logical categories of space and time and cause and effect. By offering us this unexpected glimpse of the transcendent world, our inner Magician would have temporarily derailed our mechanistic train of thought and offered us a numinous experience of the enduring One beyond all man-made categories.

As our Trickster shuffles the order of our cards, we can hear him say with a smile, "You see – everything was *here* all the time. It's only because your aperture of awareness is such a narrow slit that you experience events sequentially, one by one. Come! Have another look at the world with the great, round eyes of my magic spectacles!"

Whenever a synchronistic event intrudes itself into our complacent, ordered world, it shakes us to the bone and makes us look at the world with great round eyes in search of its possible meaning.

In his pioneer work in this field, Jung originally defined synchronicity as *meaningful coincidence*. But later on, the more objective concept of *acausal orderedness* came to replace this idea of *pre-existent meaning*. The archetype in the collective unconscious is seen as the ordering factor; the meaning is a quality man must create for himself.

Jaffé goes on to elucidate this as follows:

> Experience has shown that synchronistic phenomena are most likely to occur in the vicinity of archetypal happenings like death, deadly danger, catastrophes, crises, upheavals, etc. One could also say that in the unexpected parallelism of psychic and physical happenings, which characterizes these phenomena, the paradoxical, psychoid archetype has "ordered" itself: it appears here as a psychic image, there as a physical, material, external fact. Since we know that the conscious process consists in a perception of opposites which throw each other into relief, a synchronistic phenomenon could be understood as an unusual way of becoming conscious of an archetype.[4]

When I first began working with the Tarot cards, synchronicities in connection with the Trumps began to happen with increasing frequency. One of the most startling of these, appropriately enough, concerned the Magician. Ultimately this event caused me to look at the world – and at myself – with new eyes. But at first I did not connect with the idea expressed by Jaffé that such a phenomenon "could be understood as an unusual way of becoming conscious of an archetype." It took several years for me to find keys to its hidden meaning.

The incident concerns a print of Rodin's *Hand of God* (Fig. 15). I had borrowed a copy of this print for study and wanted very much to have one of my own. It seemed to me that the hand, as represented here, made wondrously real the androgynous qualities of the Creator. It expressed the masculine strength and support of the father combined with the womblike shelter and tenderness of the mother. I like the way these two poles of creation, the yang and the yin, were shown as part of the Primal One, and were echoed again in the embrace of Adam and Eve. Being a woman, I especially cherished the fact that Eve was directly connected with the Creator via her own personal contact rather than via Adam as his rib or chattel. I was moved by the way the hand of the Almighty and the two human figures seemed involved together in a process. With these emotions very much in my heart, I began searching everywhere for a print of this Rodin sculpture, but I could not find one. Then one day, while waiting for a friend in her living room I casually pulled out a magazine from among many on the bottom shelf of a table. The magazine fell open to a photograph of Rodin's *Hand of God*.

I was astounded, of course, and quickly turned to the front cover to see which current periodical I had thus blindly selected. To my profound amazement I discovered that the magazine I held was one long out of print; this issue itself was over a dozen years old! It was titled *Wisdom*, January, 1957. That the magus should choose *Wisdom* as his vehicle seemed most appropriate. Equally so was the magic way in which he juggled time so that this periodical should be there waiting for me after all these years. I felt that something beyond pure chance was operating here. I did not feel that my desire for this picture had *caused* it to appear, but I did feel that this synchronistic event must hold a special message for me.

No doubt synchronistic events occur much more frequently than we realize, and doubtless all would prove worthy of remark if we could but learn to be more aware. Luckily for me, the miraculous appearance of the Rodin print could not escape notice nor could it be buried in the trivia of the days and weeks that followed. I felt that the *Hand of God* had offered me a precious insight but I found myself at a loss to decode its message.

It took me over a year of *sturm und drang,* of trial and error, before I could connect with the personal meaning of this experience. But, as is usually the case with these miraculous happenings, the effort to tune in on their special meaning proved rewarding. Since synchronistic happenings are one of the ways our inner Magician can best communicate with us, it is important to learn to decode his hidden language.

How does one go about decoding a synchronistic happening in order to determine its meaning? Each of us must find his own way to do this. I share here some personal experiences, hoping that some of the techniques which have evolved through them will be useful to others. These events taught me much about the uses (and abuses) of magic.

When I first started writing about the Tarot cards, several incidents occurred such as the one just described where a needed picture or bit of information was "magically" supplied. At first I was so excited about the externals of each event and so bewitched by its miraculous occurrence that I entirely missed its deeper implications. I felt that such happenings merely indicated that I was meant to have the picture or information involved. I felt that life must be saying yes to my desire to write this book. These were not unreasonable conclusions, but the trouble was that they kept the more personal emotional implications of such happenings at arm's length. As a result I became fascinated by the external magic of these events rather than moved to connect emotionally with their possible meaning. As these synchronicities started to occur with increasing frequency, I began to get more and more bewitched by them. Soon I developed quite an inflated notion about my own magic qualities. I began to imagine that I must have unusually attractive (in every sense of the word) powers. Certain clichés appropriate to this state of mind rattled about in my skull: "I must live right," "I'm in Tao," etc. I hadn't exactly got the notion that the Almighty was my copilot, but I was getting to feel rather precious and special.

Fortunately, before I had taken off into the stratosphere entirely, I came across the following timely warning by Jung:

> Miracles appeal only to the understanding of those who cannot perceive the meaning. They are mere substitutes for the not understood reality of the spirit. This is not to say that the living presence of the spirit is not occasionally accompanied by marvelous physical happenings. I only wish to emphasize that these happenings can neither replace nor bring about an understanding of the spirit, which is the one essential thing.[5]

I began to realize how the enormous fascination with parapsychological happenings, so prevalent in our culture, could indeed become "a mere substitute for the not understood reality of the spirit," and I saw that I, too, had allowed myself to become so enthralled by their magic that I had neglected to use these synchronicities as a bridge to self-understanding. It seemed more practical, then, to curb my tendency to flap my wings and crow about my "marvelous synchronicities" and turn this energy toward exploring the possible meaning of these events for me.

Granted (I thought) that I was perhaps "meant" to have pictures and other information about the Tarot, why (I began to wonder) did some of these things fall into my hands magically, while the rest had to be sought out in the usual ways? I came to the conclusion that the items which simply appeared in response to my wish must fulfill a deeper and more personal desire than the overt need for the picture itself. Applying this insight specifically to the miraculous appearance of Rodin's *Hand of God*, I began to ask these kinds of questions: "What lack (or unrecognized potential) in my life does this picture represent? Where do I long for the hand of God to touch my daily life?" Naturally, the answers to these questions are so personal as to be almost incommunicable.

Although this incident took place several years ago, I write of it here in the present tense, for layers of its hidden meaning continue to unfold. I am discovering that, as I become less befuddled by the "magic" of these synchronicities, I grow more free to connect with the insights they have to offer. In other words, as with the figure of *Moses Striking Water*, when "peoples' thirst" is in the picture the Magician cannot be central. *Together* they create the miraculous event which transcends both but which at the same time keeps one's feet on the good earth of human reality.

According to Jung, when synchronicities occur it means that an archetypal power has been activated. Since the Tarot Trumps symbolize such powers it is understandable that they should stimulate happenings of this kind. If you are keeping a Tarot notebook, it might be useful to record any such experiences which do take place. Here are a few suggested ways for tapping the hidden meaning of these miraculous events. You will no doubt discover many others.

One way to begin is by asking the kinds of questions suggested above: *What in me needed this happening? What lack (or potential) in me does this represent?* You might want to jot down whatever answers come to mind. Try to catch in words the flavor of persons or objects involved in the synchronicity. Let your pen wander where it will: doggerel, free verse, or freer nonsense. Try doodling or casually drawing any shapes or figures that pop up on your inner screen. Artistic achievement, be it understood, is not the point to this endeavor. If you "have no talent" so much the better, for you'll not be tempted toward perfectionism and can enjoy playing with your feelings in a carefree way.

Sometimes a synchronistic happening does not lend itself to any of the above approaches. In this case, one can occasionally get at its message *retrospectively* by simply observing what, if anything, actually happened *after* the synchronistic event. Once more, a personal experience will serve to illustrate. This took place many years ago in Zurich, where I had gone for personal analysis and study. My Magician was in one of his most tricky moods that day, for he had somehow contrived to lock me *inside* my apartment just at the moment I was to set forth for an appointment with my analyst. When, the following week I related the odd coincidence to my therapist, I anticipated in reply some profound discourse on the meaning of synchronicity. Instead the doctor burst into loud laughter. When he could speak again, he asked a significant question: "What did you do with your time *instead?*" Examining in detail what I had done with this hour "instead" proved so rewarding that, twenty years later, I still regard this small happening as one of the most meaningful events of my life for it dramatized in an unforgettable way how I reacted to frustration. Instead of accepting the inevitable and using the lost hour creatively, I squandered it on futile attempts to outwit fate. When all tricks to break out of my prison by external means had failed, I escaped psychologically by getting quite tipsy.

Since the Magician is an artist rather than a dictator, he asks that we interject a word of caution. In following up on any suggestions presented here, do keep a light touch and a playful mood. Coming to terms with the meaning of synchronistic events is not intended as a work project. Rather, the atmosphere suggested is one of exploration. All questions and techniques set forth in this book are intended to be poetic and suggestive, not didactic and directive. To approach a miraculous event as a job or as homework can only serve to bury the very emotional content we seek. We might better ponder the meaning of synchronistic events as we go about our daily routine. The most world-shaking "Aha's" usually occur when we are showering or washing the dishes.

Synchronicities are natural phenomena. There is no evidence that they are devised by fate in order to teach mankind moral lessons. Like the fruits and flowers, they are products of nature. They grow spontaneously in our garden, awaiting discovery. They present themselves for our nourishment and delight.

Many synchronistic happenings involve inner images that miraculously materialize in the external world. All images tend to materialize in this way; it is their nature to seek expression in outer reality. Like Michelangelo's *Captive*, visions yearn to be born, struggling against our lethargy and indifference to free themselves from the unconscious. Knowing this, we sometimes use images quite consciously – counting sheep for instance to induce sleep, or visualizing a placid scene or a mandala to calm ourselves when we feel confused. Increasing numbers of people set aside a time each day when they try to implant favorable images in the unconscious by self-hypnosis or other techniques. But such procedures are of limited value. The unconscious is, by definition, unconscious. One cannot manipulate its activities by will power. A more useful technique might be simply to *observe* one's inner thoughts, feelings, and images – to allow whatever pictures appear spontaneously to flow across one's inner screen. The shock of observing what we are "really like" underneath will already effect a change. The inner Magician can help us to become aware of the visions of power, vengeance, cupidity, or whatever, which actually exist within us; so that we can confront these aspects with a more conscious standpoint. The Magician can also help us to discover and bring our creative imaginings into reality. In this way conscious and unconscious will become related in a meaningful way.

An old alchemical maxim reads: "What the soul imagines happens only in the mind, but what God imagines happens in reality." When the Unitary World erupts into our consciousness, perhaps we do catch a glimpse of the world as God imaged it.

How, then, are we to view our Tarot Magician in Jungian terms? Is he the ego consciousness that creates illusion or the self-awareness that dispels it? Is he man's will or is he Divine Intention? The answer is that he is both. For it is through consciousness that we become entangled in the world of things and categories, and it is through consciousness that we extricate ourselves from its confusions. The Magician creates the maze and he guides us through it. In this sense man can be viewed both as the redeemer and as the one to be redeemed. With The Fool, ego and self were closely allied, for it is out of the self that the ego evolves. If the Fool symbolizes "the self as an unconscious prefiguration of the ego," then the Magician might be seen as the embodiment of a more conscious connecting link between the ego and the self.

Calling him "that uninvited guest," Alan McGlashan equates the Magician with the central character of our dreams, the Dreamer, who is both the experiencing subject and the observed object of the dreams, a "ghostly guide" into realms of the unconscious. Of this Dreamer, McGlashan says:

> Like the mysterious Juggler of the Tarot Pack, the Dreamer is continually doing the apparently impossible, capsizing our solemn ultimates of birth and death, manipulating space and time with a breath-taking impudence, riding roughshod across all our most treasured and assured convictions.[6]

We know that dreams do come true. In innumerable ways we "dream up" the world we live in, our personalities, and our goals – all in accordance with our inner images. Some images occur in daydreams when we are awake, when the motor of our conscious mind is idling. These are easy to catch. But the archetypal images that appear in dreams when our conscious mind is completely turned off come from the deeper levels of the psyche and are harder to recall. Here again the Magician can help by teaching us the trick of stepping into his dream world.

The first step, of course, is to remember our dreams. For those who "don't dream" it is helpful to replace this negative thought with an attitude of hopeful expectation. Many nondreamers find that keeping a pencil and paper at one's bedside usually establishes a connection between daytime consciousness and the world of dreams. The paper may remain blank for several days – or longer – but if you lie quietly upon awaking, with eyes shut, ultimately a wisp from last night's dream will float across your inner screen. Maybe at first you will catch only one phrase or a vague picture. Nevertheless, write this down. Often this in itself will bring up other images or even a complete drama. It is very important to write everything down immediately, for dreams are easily forgotten.

Since these dream images do play such a large role in shaping our lives, it behooves us to get acquainted with them. That is what this book is all about. The twenty-two Trumps picture archetypal personalities and situations. By coming to know these Tarot figures we learn to recognize them when they appear in our dreams. Paying attention to our dreams – even if we never do anything further with them – will have an effect on our lives. As we behave toward the unconscious, so will it behave toward us. Dream characters, like our friends and relatives, need to be taken seriously. They like to feel that we are interested in them and their doings – that we are involved with them.

The Magician helps to involve us in the world of dreams. Whereas the Fool wanders in and out of our world occasionally, the Magician takes a stand vis à vis us. The Fool may bring us seemingly impossible dreams, but the Magician will get them up on the table for consideration. It is he who helps us to make our dreams come true.

All of us share in the Magician's magic power. Ours is the potential for illumination and enterprises as yet undreamed of. Ours is also a destructive power of gigantic proportions. We can blow up our planet; we can bury it and ourselves under the weight of a billion plastic gadgets; or, we can cherish and protect our natural environment and humanity. The choice is ours. Perhaps to the extent that our inner Magician makes us aware of our dreams, our nightmares need never come true.

Fig. 17   La Papesse (Marseilles Deck)

5. The Popess: High Priestess of Tarot

> The world will change less in accordance
> with man's determinations than with
> woman's divinations.
>
> —*Claude Bragdon*

Tarot Trump number two pictures a lady pope of ancient and mysterious origin (Fig. 17). Historically there never was a female pope, but for several centuries a woman called "Pope Joan" enjoyed a lively existence in the public imagination. Disguised as a priest, this legendary personage ultimately rose through the orders to become pope. No one suspected that "Pope John" was a woman until the fact was revealed one day in an embarrassing manner. In the midst of a solemn papal procession, "Pope John" suddenly gave birth to a baby!

This tale has no foundation in outer fact, but like all myths it involves an inner truth so obvious that it is often ignored. The chief creative activity that distinguishes Joan from John—the relevant and revealing factor—is childbirth. This genius for making babies is woman's secret power and her public weakness.

Although the real Pope John might rule vast spiritual and temporal kingdoms, he could not have performed this everyday miracle. Man may propagate and celebrate the Divine Spirit but it is through woman alone that the spirit is made flesh. It is she who catches the divine spark in her womb, protects and nourishes it, and ultimately brings it forth into reality. She is the vessel of transformation.

From the masculine viewpoint of law and order, Joan's creative act might appear as an unfortunate accident that interrupts the civilized procession. What a shock it might be to be faced with the bloody mess of reality—the squalling babe and all those diapers—in the midst of pomp and circumstance. How inconsiderate of untidy Nature to interrupt so rudely the celebration of pure spirit! But even as man says this, he must acknowledge the tremendous importance of woman's power. "Pure spirit" is pure nonsense. Unless winged inspiration is caught, brought to earth and grounded in reality, it scatters itself aimlessly and to no purpose. Without birthing there could be no procession. Unless the spirit is truly made flesh its papal celebration could have no meaning.

So, here before us in card two sits Woman. Although she is called the Popess, she is not literally the pope's wife. Since, in sequence, she follows the Magician, who is a priestly wise man, or magus, we may think of her as a High Priestess, which is what she is actually called in some of the modern decks. The Magician represents the primary yang, or masculine creative principle. The Popess can be seen to symbolize the primary yin, or feminine aspect of the godhead. She embodies the qualities of Isis, Ishtar, and Astarte, all goddesses who reigned over the rituals of women's mysteries. In her spiritualized aspects she appears as the Virgin Mary and as Sophia, Divine Wisdom. Her number two is a number sacred to all female deities.

The Popess is a substantial, rather heavy female figure, seated—possibly enthroned. She wears the ceremonial robes and tiara of the Church, thus representing a spiritual power beyond her individual person. In her hand she holds an open book, no doubt a holy book, symbolic of the Divine Word. Perhaps she is musing on what she has just read. Perhaps she holds the book open so that we too may see the Word . . . . see how it was written "in the beginning." In paintings of the Annunciation, the Virgin Mary is often similarly pictured with an open book; she holds the book of the Prophets, which foretells her destiny as carrier of the Divine Child. Here in the Tarot it would seem that the book has a similar meaning, indicating that it is through the Popess that the spirit will be *real*-ized, brought down into reality. Traditionally, woman does not make the law, she is the instrument of its enactment; she does not control her destiny, it will evolve as it was written. This woman takes no action to seek out her fate, for the essence of the feminine is receptivity. She does not choose; she is chosen. It will happen to her as it was foretold "in the beginning."

The yellow yoke across the Popess's breast might indicate that she accepts her fate, that she will bear her burden with oxlike patience and serve the spirit with humility. It emphasizes the horizontal axis of the cross, the dimension of earthly reality. It connects right and left, conscious and unconscious, binding them together in a practical way. Similarly, her right and left hands unite to hold the book of prophecy; she accepts the Word with all her being. This feeling of commitment is echoed in the white wimple, not unlike that worn today by certain orders of nuns and by women making their first communion. Worn generally in medieval times, the wimple is today retained as a sign of special dedication to the Holy Spirit. It hides the woman's hair, her "crowning glory," symbol of sexual attraction and seductive power. But the Popess is bedecked with a jeweled tiara which calls attention to a glory more precious than mortal hair. Its beehive shape connotes everlasting fertility, instinctive organization, and life-giving nourishment. Its three tiers show that this power manifests itself in all the worlds: in heaven, on earth, and under the water.

The three-tiered headdress also connects its wearer with the three-faced witch Hecate, a dark pre-Olympian figure with whom the Popess must share dominion in the three worlds. Our Tarot lady symbolizes a refinement and spiritualization of instinctual nature seemingly eons removed from the vengeful Hecate; yet the Popess by no means sits complacent on her throne. Her beehive headdress serves as a constant reminder that the instincts, when thwarted, can attack with vicious stings, for they guard their honey jealously. Behind the Popess is hung a large veil or curtain supported by two pillars glimpsed briefly below the veil on her right and again beneath her left elbow. She is obviously seated at the entrance to something – perhaps a temple or inner sanctum whose mysteries she guards.

One can appreciate the mysterious qualities of the Popess by contrasting her with the Magician. He is pictured standing outdoors in an open field. Everything about him – the lemniscate shape of his hat, the wand poised high in one hand, the little ball held so delicately between the finger and thumb of his other hand, together with the implements and tools of his trade on the table before him – all suggest action. He is about to do something. Even his gold-tipped hair, falling freely from under his hat, seems alive. His stance with feet outspread is that of a maestro at his podium, about to conduct a performance. Like the conductor, the Magician is not fixed permanently at this spot. When this performance is finished, he will move on to other fields. Nor is he bound by the limitations of terrestrial time. The extravagant curves of his lemniscate hat connect him with infinity – indicating that its wearer has access to magic dimensions of impersonal awareness transcending the mundane realities of time and space.

But not so the Popess. She is almost rooted in place, passively seated, immobile. One feels that she has been sitting there always and will continue to do so until the end of time. Whereas the Magician's hat and wand suggest action and experiment, her tiara and book indicate containment and tradition. In contrast to the Magician's freedom in space, her pillars mark the limitations of hard reality.

The Magician's power is fire: hot, bright, flashing sun power. The Popess's power is water: cool, dark, fluid, moon power. He controls by quick force, knowledge, and idea. She rules by slow persistence, love, and feminine patience.

The pillars reiterate the duality expressed in the Popess's number two. Her essence is paradox. She encompasses all, embracing both good and evil – even life and death. She who is the mother of life must also preside over death, since all that lives in the flesh must one day die in the flesh. Only the unconfined light of pure spirit is immortal.

The Magician's magic, like his sex, is out in front. The Popess's magic is veiled and hidden, like her hair. Is it concealed by the curtains behind her? Does she keep it "under her hat"? Or is it buried within the waters of her womb? Wherever it is concealed, woman's secret, like nature's, will always remain hidden from penetration of masculine consciousness. On the base of a statue of Isis in Saïs, the following words are inscribed: "I am everything that was, that is, that ever will be. Nor has any mortal man ever been able to discover what lies under my veil." Hers is the realm of deep inner experience; hers is not the world of external knowledge.

One feels that the Magician's power is somewhat under his conscious control, that he can "call the shots." This is not the case with the Popess: The nature of her magic is hidden even from her. It happens in part "behind her back," as it is pictured. She is the custodian of birth and of rebirth but she does not control them.

In primitive cultures, woman was seen as the sole source of life. This was because sexual intercourse was not understood to be connected with pregnancy. Man was felt to have no role in the process of conceiving. He was even experienced as an intruder, a force destructive to creation, as is exemplified mythologically in the tale of the rape of Persephone. Since man's role in the life process was not understood, each woman who became pregnant must have felt herself to be mysteriously and unaccountably chosen by the gods. As with Mary, the news of her fate must have seemed to descend inexplicably like an annunciation from heaven. Childbirth was a holy mystery, and it was woman's mystery. The first known sacred precincts were those set aside for childbirth. Later on, temples were erected on these sites. Thus the feminine principle embodied in Isis, Ishtar, Astarte, and later in Mary, came to be connected not only with birth into the body but also with rebirth into a new dimension of awareness transcending the flesh.

Today, despite the pill, sex education, and women's liberation, childbirth still remains, thank God, a holy mystery. Planned parenthood is spoken of glibly, but the truth is that each pregnancy occurs (or not) by the grace of God. Every prospective mother, however willing, must still be chosen by fate to assume this role. The miraculous happening itself is still a mystery, and still woman's mystery. It happens to her. With a man, the act of propagation happens outside himself, both physically and psychologically. A man may sire a dozen children without ever becoming aware that he has done so. But with a woman, conception and the child itself happens within her body – at the very center of her being. From the moment that she has conceived, whether she knows it or not a woman is quite literally *with child*. Whatever her intellectual attitude may be, deep in the unconscious of every woman pregnancy is still experienced as a fateful annunciation. For her, every birth is a recreation of the Divine Child.

It seems significant that today women are beginning to re-establish a conscious connection with the *experience* of childbirth. Through natural childbirth and other drugless techniques, women are able to remain conscious at the moment of giving birth so they can connect emotionally and spiritually with the experience and participate consciously in this supreme act of creation. More significant still is the fact that husbands, far from being excluded from the "sacred precincts," are invited to participate in the ritual of childbirth and to share the experience as cocreators. At last, feminine creativity and the feminine principle (too long denied in our culture) are coming into their own.

Women's Liberation is sometimes narrowly viewed as a movement to free women from the drudgery of housework and from the prejudices of men in all areas of life. But what is actually involved is the liberation of both men and women from slavish subservience to the masculine principle, a ruler whose long-established autonomy has now become tyranny for both men and women. At its deepest level this movement is not a war between sexes, but rather a painful struggle on the part of both sexes to liberate The Popess from the dungeons of unconsciousness and to elevate her to her rightful place as coruler with her masculine counterpart. The present psychological and social revolution can be seen as an enactment in human terms of the Assumption of the Virgin Mary which was pronounced dogma by the Catholic Church in recent years. Theologically, the Virgin now has a secure place in Heaven on the right hand of God. But, after centuries of spiritual genuflexion to the father principle (so long dominant in our Judeo-Christian culture), it is difficult for women as well as for men to accord equal billing to the female principle.

One of our problems may be that the concept "equal but different" is a difficult one for our competitive society in which every person, place, or thing is instantly computerized, evaluated and labeled. It would appear that in our effort to experience the sexes as equals we sometimes tend to obliterate their differences. Understandably the present transitional phase is one of confusion for everyone; but it seems particularly so for those of us brought up in an era when sexual differences, however much distorted by the culture, were nonetheless clearly defined. Not so today. Simple housewives stride past us in the supermarkets got up like something out of the Hell's Angels; football heroes, once chary of apron strings, now pose for the press wearing the entire apron – and curls! More confusing still is the uniform dress and conduct of the so-called unisex, wherein everybody wears long hair and blue jeans and everybody totes his/her own bedroll and suitcase; and there is scarcely a clue as to which person is which sex.

Maybe we don't deserve to know who is which or need to (assuming of course that the individuals themselves have a good grasp of the facts of life). But we can echo Ogden Nash's bemused admiration of the turtle, in which sex is similarly concealed: "I think it clever of the turtle / in such a fix to be so fertile." It can only be hoped that a new "equal but different" role for both men and women is about to be born. One of the ways we can assist in its delivery might be through a fuller, more conscious experience of the long-neglected feminine principle and an understanding of how it operates in all of us, both men and women.

As a first step, let us clarify our terminology. The terms masculine and feminine, as Jung uses them, are not intended to correlate with the physiological dichotomy man-woman. For this reason concepts such as yang-yin or Logos-Eros are helpful because they make it clear that what we are concerned with here are two life principles, both of which operate in all men, all women, and all of nature. Yet, to retain some sexual overtone in our language seems important too. Sex is a paradigm in human experience for the realization of the opposites and their ultimate transcendence. Through the otherness of sexual relationship we come to experience the dynamic power of the opposites in our guts, and through the ecstasy of their reconciliation we glimpse intimations of a wholeness transcending mortal flesh.

Thus the terms masculine-feminine are used here to denote positive and negative poles of energy whose dynamic interaction propagates, motivates and illuminates our lives. For example, just as a man's body has secondary female characteristics, so his psyche—his moods and behavior—is affected by his so-called feminine side whose personification Jung has called the *anima*. When a man is unconscious of his anima, he can be fully swayed and destructively influenced by her. When he becomes aware of her and her needs, she can inspire him and lead him to his own totality. In Jungian terms, the Popess would represent for the man a very high development of the anima. It is she who would symbolize the archetypal figure which relates him to the collective unconscious. For a woman, the Popess could be a highly differentiated form of Eros; she would symbolize womanliness, a spiritually developed self.

The many facets of spiritual femininity cannot be caught in words nor even in pictures; but I have selected some illustrations that may amplify and enrich the meaning of this card. Perhaps by considering these pictures we can connect with the "moon magic" in ourselves. For all of us, men and women alike, have available within us the powers of both the Magician and the Popess. Without these two poles interacting in us there could be no life—no creativity.

One of the illustrations (Fig. 18) shows an alabaster statue of an ancient moon goddess, symbol of fertility and reproduction, probably Astarte. She represents a much more primitive form of the feminine principle than the one we have been examining; but underneath the robes of civilization, the blood of Astarte runs in The Popess's veins – and in ours. These female deities were moon goddesses because the phases of the moon were believed to control all birth, growth, and decay. Even to-

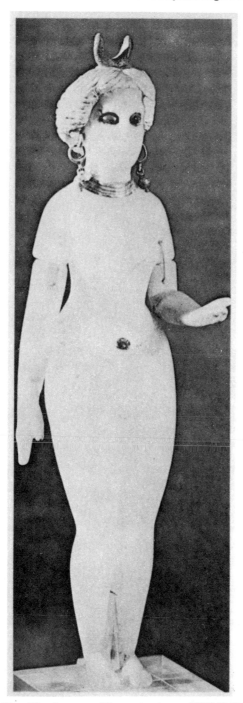

Fig. 18   Astarte   (Mesopotamian c. 2000 B.C.)

day many so-called "civilized" farmers consult the almanac before planting their crops.

Moon power is very subtle but very strong. It controls the mighty tides, hence the tears of Isis were said to govern the waters of the Nile. In contrast to the sun which is constant, predictable, and bright, the moon is inconsistant, veiled, and dark. Woman's nature is moody, changeable as the moon, which can bring life-giving nurture, drought, or destructive floods, depending on the whim of the Great Goddess.

Both sexes are subject to the whims of the goddess, but women through their kinship with her are usually more aware of her influence and prepared to deal with it. The rhythm of the menstrual cycle, with its accompanying changes of mood, helps a woman to expect the unexpected and to recognize and accept the irrational as part of life. Woman's temperament, like that of the goddess, is more related to rhythms of nature than to systems of logic.

A man's situation is different. Both physiologically and psychologically he is usually less attuned to the ebb and flow of his moods than is woman. As a result, the goddess can take him by surprise. Sometimes she appears to usurp his entire personality so that a man in this state seems almost to speak with her voice, in a womanish, irrational, and even hysterical way. One can imagine that the Moon Goddess pictured in Figure 18 might be vindicative and ruthless when crossed. Just look at those eyes! Notice also the "third eye," located not in her forehead but in her belly, at the navel, center of all.

The element with which she connects is water. In most creation myths, water is depicted as the original receptive, productive, and form-building power. From the depths of the ocean, out of the cradle endlessly rocking, rose all creation—all forms of life. Out of the deep unconscious rose consciousness itself. For, as the individual embryo is contained and nourished in the amniotic fluid, so each individual identity is contained and nourished in the deep unconscious of every newborn babe. Thus it is from the unconscious that consciousness is born.

Symbolically woman is indeed water: *mare, mer, mère,* and *Mary.* Her connection with water is emphasized in the twentieth-century English version of the Popess pictured here (Fig. 19). This card is from the Waite Tarot and is called The High Priestess. Here the lady's garments flow into and become water. This stream, woman-like, will follow the line of least resistance, adapting itself to the contours of the earth, moving ever downward to collect in pools and lakes which mirror the sky. The feminine nature is reflective. Through immersing himself in the depths of woman, man comes to know himself. By looking into the images in the deep unconscious, we come to know ourselves.

Fig. 19 Waite Deck

Duplication, duplicity, and also memory belong to the feminine side. In his book *The Two Hands of God,*[1] Alan Watts reminds us that when Isis reassembled the dismembered body of Osiris she literally re-membered him. Remembering is not a mere mechanical act, such as pulling a photograph out of a file. It is basically a restorative and creative act. For when we remember someone we recreate his image. To the bits and pieces of scattered fact about the person or situation in question, we add an important piece of ourselves; an emotional content out of our own experience. Thus, by remembering someone, we create a new entity. We bring the forgotten one back to a new wholeness, and we reinstate him in the collective world.

The creative act of memory is the special province of the feminine principle. It is always colored by emotion. In fact, as Watts reminds us, our word "memory" is derived from the Old English *mournan*, meaning "to mourn." Thus mourning indeed "becomes Electra." This ability to connect in a creative way with their emotions also belongs to men who are in contact with their feminine side. It is the particular gift of the poets to help us to "weep for Adonais."

Our Western culture tends to emphasize the light, pure aspect of womanhood, so that it is difficult to find examples in European art that portray spiritual woman as *rooted in the body*. A case in point is the Popess as depicted in the Waite deck. This turn-of-the-century English deck was designed under the direction of the scholarly A. E. Waite and executed by Pamela Smith, who created stage sets for Yeats's plays. In it the lady pope suffers significant changes. This priestess is pictured as a beautiful young woman sitting proud and straight. The waters at her feet support a crescent moon. Although she is enthroned between the Pillars of Solomon against a backdrop of ancient fertility symbols, with a scroll marked "Tora" in her lap and wearing Hathor's own crown, the lady herself looks British to the bone. Despite the complex symbology of her setting – or perhaps because of it – she seems to me a passionless figurehead, remote from her surroundings and disconnected from her body. What a far cry this chaste, post-Victorian maiden from the horned Astarte – she of the glowing belly and the fiery eyes!

Waite's twentieth-century priestess is perfect and beautiful and to the manner born – but something is missing. In contrast to the Popess, with her comfortable body and her wise old eyes, this young woman seems to be untouched and pure – too good to be true. In a similar way the Virgin Mary is sometimes so romanticized and idealized that she appears to be bodiless and ethereal. Today, with the Doctrine of the Assumption, the Virgin's body has become acceptable to Heaven – and to us. Perhaps the time is also ripe for the word "virgin" to be reinstated in its original force and meaning.

Nowadays we speak of a virgin as one who is sexually pure. But originally the word "virgin" had nothing whatever to do with physical chastity. "Virgin" meant simply "an unmarried woman." As Esther Harding points out,[2] since she belonged to no man, a virgin belonged to herself in a special way. Thus she was free to give herself to God; she was psychically open to the Holy Spirit. Virgin in this sense was the Delphic Oracle. No disembodied spirit she, floating about in pallid gauze and ectoplasm. The Pythian goddess sat strong and solid in her flesh; for in order to receive the impact of the Holy Spirit, the vessel needs to be strong. What it means to be "chosen by God" is movingly dramatized in Par Lagerkvists's novel *The Sybil*. This book, which won the Nobel Prize for Literature in the fifties, is worth rereading as amplification for certain aspects of the Popess.

As the powers of the Popess are essentially nonverbal, you may find (as I have) that a good way to enrich your feeling for this archetypal aspect of yourself is to search out pictures that personify her many qualities. Another useful technique for coming to know this mysterious figure is to approach her directly. If the atmosphere (and the stars) are right, you may come away with new insights.

In explanation of this method, I include here an illuminating conversation which I had with the Popess recently on the subject of her position as number two in the Tarot sequence. I had been wondering if being second made her feel second-rate. Whatever her feelings, I observed that she wasn't trying harder. There she sat as she had done for centuries, immobile and serene, knowing whatever she knew and apparently secure in that wisdom. What was her secret? As I approached the Popess's throne with this question in mind, she stiffened imperceptibly and part of her fled for cover (as is the way with introverts). When all her inner hatches were secured, the lady acknowledged my presence and granted me an audience with one gracious inclination of her head.

Madam Popess, many women today feel that you should be Tarot number one. Do you agree with them?

"Mercy no!" she replied. "You see, for centuries now number one has belonged to the Magician. It suits him perfectly, don't you think? The number one is slim and mobile like his wand, ideal for his kind of magic. But it wouldn't do at all for carrying a baby, or cooking a pot of soup, or brewing up a plot. No, for my magic that funny fat number two is just right. I'm very happy with it."

After this, the lady fell silent, allowing herself to sink down into the ancient well of memory. As she did so, years fell away and her face began to glow with the freshness of Eden's garden. "You know," she said with a little shrug and a girlish laugh reminiscent of Eve, "for an even number, two is a little odd, don't you think? I mean, two is fat and substantial like a pot, yet it's also kind of curly and elusive, like a snake . . . ."

At this point, the speaker closed her eyes and drifted away again with a little smile remembering. . . . At length she aroused herself with an effort, resuming the poise and demeanor of the Popess. "Pay no mind to those Freudians, child," she said. "They don't understand snakes at all. There are lots of things they don't understand about our wicked, wily, wonderful number two! Yes, I'm quite contented with woman's place," she concluded softly, humming a little tune in her throat.

But wouldn't you rather be first?

There followed another long pause. "I gather you read from left to right," she said finally, her eyes fixed on a point about a foot above my head and several centuries deep.

But, Madam, whichever way one reads, in counting, the number one always comes first!

"That's right, my dear," she said placidly, "and the number two comes second. Mathematics was hard for me, too, at first, but you'll soon get the hang of it."

But surely it's better to be first?

"Ah, me!" she sighed. "What a chore you moderns do make for yourselves with all that evaluating. No wonder you invented computing machines to do some of it for you."

So you're against evaluating? You must think, then, that whether one is first or second amounts to the same thing.

"Oh, no. Not at all the same. Different. Quite different. That's the whole point, don't you see? Not better or worse – just different. Each place has its flavor – like spices – or perfumes. I like to think of us as flowers – the Magician as a goldenrod and me as a rose."

Yes, I see. But there are a couple of things that still bother me. They say that Eve was an afterthought of the Creator – Adam's rib, you know. Is this true?

"Nonsense! Adam's rib was completed before he was, if it comes to that. Adam just didn't get around to noticing her until later, that's all.

"I have a picture here somewhere that tells the whole story. It shows exactly what happened in Eden at the Creation, and what is still happening today. You do know," she said, looking at me intently while she searched in the folds of her robe for the picture, "you do know," she repeated, "that in many ways you children are still caught in Eden. Your creation isn't finished yet – that's a job that you (like all God's children everywhere) must finish for yourselves. . . .Ah, here's that picture!" she cried, producing this stunning illustration by William Blake (Fig. 20).

"Now it's plain to see that Eve isn't anybody's *rib!* She's a goddess, rather, and like all such immortals, she emerges full-grown – a miraculous birth. Behind her, rises her glorious snake. *Aren't they both beautiful!* But Adam is asleep; he doesn't know she exists. Today he's beginning to wake up to her reality, but he still doesn't know much about her. Actually, Eve herself isn't yet quite convinced of her reality. If you'll look at her face, you'll see that she's still caught in a dream, poised, like Shakespeare's Miranda, on the threshold of a Brave New World.

"Blake titled his picture, *The Female From His Darkness Rose*. Many people nowadays say that it was *in spite of* Adam's darkness, not *from* it, that Eve managed to get herself born. They emphasize that word "spite," too, as they recount how Eve (poor thing) has struggled all these years against her man's unconsciousness, suffering the many black looks (and black eyes) he has given her along the way! But that isn't the way Blake painted it, or said it. And it isn't the way I feel about it either. Blake says it was *from* Adam's darkness – almost you might say *because* of it, that Eve came into being. (I do wish she could find it in her heart to offer him a little more gratitude – and a little less spite!)

Fig. 20 "The Female from His Darkness Rose"
(*The Temptation of Eve* by William Blake. Crown Copyright,
Victoria and Albert Museum, England, Reprinted by permission.)

"Just imagine: theirs was a Jehovah-world of strict commandments and prohibitions, and Lord Adam was its heir apparent. It was only in the shadow of his sleeping darkness that a safe womb could be found for her conception, and a secret space for her growth. Adam (bless him) saved his darkness for her, and nourished her with his dreams. He dreamed of her constantly, you know – and longed for her. So it was really because of his dreams of her and his need that she found a way to come true. Don't you see?

"Naturally the Eve of his dreams didn't correspond to the Eve of reality. But, at first, neither of them knew that. And since she had risen from his dreams, she simply embodied them, having found as yet no essence of her own. Today, as she discovers who she is, he will uncover new dreams to dream. One day he'll dream true. You'll see.

"Oh, his first dreams were inadequate, there's no denying. First dreams often are. But they are the seeds of all reality, my dear. Remember that."

For a few moments, the Popess and I sat silent, musing together over the sleeping Adam. Then she said suddenly: "Never mind what they may say when they're awake, child. They nourish us with their dreams and they long for our true reality. *Don't ever forget that!*" After a pause while I remembered not to forget, the Lady turned to me and said gently, "I believe you had one more question?"

Well, this one has to do with the sun and moon. There's a rumor that the moon is a second-rate light, simply a reflector of the sun's mighty glory – that she has no essence or divinity of her own. How do you feel about that?

"Dear me," said The Popess shaking her head. "Whoever starts such rumors – not a woman you may be sure! Luckily, I have something here which will set your heart at rest." With this the lady produced from her voluminous cloak a picture. "You see," she continued, "here is a very fine portrait by Raphael – *The Almighty Creating the Two Great Lights.* You can see with your own eyes how He personally made both the sun and the moon at the same time, one with each of His two hands. (Fig. 21)

"No," she continued, "the whole question of first or second is really irrelevant. Two is the number of all life; one alone can do nothing. Even the Lord, you know, needed the two before he could begin the task of creation. There is another famous portrait of Him that demonstrates this quite clearly – Blake's *God Creating the Universe* (Fig. 11) It shows the bearded

Fig. 21 God Creating the Two Great Lights
(Raphael. Fresco painting from The Vatican. Reprinted by permission.)

Creator with a compass in His hand, reaching a long arm down from the Great Round of Heaven. He is in the act of drawing the microscopic circle in the image and likeness of the macrocosmic one. In order to do this He – even He – needed to use both legs of the compass: the one to fix and stabilize the center of His circle and the other to describe its circumference. Yes, even the Almighty would have been powerless with one alone. To make a whole, one needs the two . . . one needs the two."

Fig. 22   L'Impératrice (Marseilles Deck)

6. The Empress: Madonna, Great Mother, Queen of Heaven and Earth

Generation is the mystery by which the spirit unites
itself to matter, by which the Divine becomes human.

Papus

At first glance, the Empress (Fig. 22) looks enough like the Popess to be
her sister. Whenever sisters appear in myths, dreams, and fairy tales, they
often represent two different aspects of the same family or essence—in this
case the feminine principle. If we were to go by their names alone, we
might jump to the conclusion that the Popess represents spiritual femininity, whereas the Empress rules over the mundane kingdom. But this is not
the case, for the Empress's golden sceptre displays the orb of earthly reality
surmounted by the cross of spirit. This ability to connect heaven and earth,
spirit and flesh, is in fact one of the Empress's chief attributes, as further
evidenced by the way her throne suggests a pair of golden wings. In some
versions of the Tarot she is even pictured as a winged goddess. The golden
eagle emblazoned on her shield is further evidence of her connection with
the spirit. The eagle soars to tremendous heights; his habitat is as inaccessible as Mt. Olympus. In the myth of Eros and Psyche, it was, significantly,
an eagle who helped Psyche to catch the waters of life and contain them in
a vessel.

In the preceding card the atmosphere is static, rooted, with the emphasis on protection and containment. In this card the eagle suggests motion on the vertical axis, bespeaking liberation and transformation. It is as if
the Popess shows us spirit caught in the womb of matter, whereas in the
Empress we see spirit born anew out of the flesh, thus creating a new entity
which partakes of both. The Empress's connection with the spirit is further

indicated by the way she embraces the golden eagle, almost as if he were alive, for this royal bird obviously represents a living force with which she feels emotionally connected. The fact that a similar bird also appears on the shield of the Emperor (Trump four) indicates that this golden eagle is the family coat of arms or talisman. As such, its image would exert a very subtle, powerful influence over this royal couple and their empire.

Perhaps because the female eagle is larger than the male, this bird is often a feminine symbol. This is the case in alchemy where the eagle is interchangeable with the phoenix, a bird that symbolizes the spiritualization of instinct. Certainly the Empress's eagle appears, appropriately, to be ascending. In the reign of the Popess (the Virgin) the spirit descended into matter. With the Empress (the Mother) the spirit is freed from matter and rises heavenwards as the Son, the Redeemer.

In this context the Empress's golden bird, which connects heaven and earth, holds a special meaning for us today because (as Jung has often pointed out) Christianity in our era has lost its body, its earth, its emotion. We must, as he says, return to the body in order to recreate the spirit—in order to give it a new reality in human experience.

One of the most eloquent pictorial representations of the spirit contained or created in the body is the *Vierge Ouvrante*, a fifteenth-century statuette made of painted wood (Figs. 23 and 24). As Erich Neumann describes her:

> Seen from the outside, the "Vierge Ouvrante" is the familiar and unassuming mother with child. But when opened she reveals the heretical secret within her. God the Father and God the Son, usually represented as heavenly lords who in an act of pure grace raise up the humble earth-bound mother to abide with them, prove to be contained in her; prove to be "contents" of her all-sheltering body.[1]

That the Albigenses also knew this "heretical secret" seems evident by the sheltering embrace within which the Empress enfolds the golden eagle and by the way she holds her sceptre in the left (unconscious) hand, thus showing that her connection with the Holy Spirit is instinctual – that it comes from within rather than descending from above. Also, her sceptre is not held upright but rests casually aslant – a further indication that the Empress rules intuitively rather than according to man-made laws. Her dominion is flexible, almost quixotic at times, because her heart has reasons inaccessible to the mind. But although she allows her sceptre to fall away from her, she clasps the eagle to her. Obviously the power of love is dearer to her than the love of power.

The symbol of orb and cross turned upside down is, of course, the astrological sign for Venus. It seems highly appropriate that she holds her

Fig. 23   Vierge Ouvrante (Closed)   Fig. 24   Vierge Ouvrante (Open)

(Painted wood, France XV century)

symbol aslant, leaning (shall we say) in the direction of Venus, for love is the unifying and regenerative force that connects yang and yin, spirit and flesh, heaven and earth, binding together the opposites in creative embrace until something entirely new can be born which includes both.

Whenever we find our lives blocked out into rigid dichotomies, we might seek the Empress's help. One way to do this is to initiate a dialogue with her similar to our previous conversation with the Popess.

Since both the Popess and the Empress embody the feminine principle, they preside jointly over the four feminine mysteries: formation, preservation, nourishment, and transformation. But each emphasizes different aspects, as one can see by contrasting the portraits of these two sisters.

Whereas the Popess holds her arms in a closed position, protecting the secrets of her body, the Empress's arms are open, indicating a more outgoing nature. Her hair is not concealed by a wimple; instead it falls free. She has thrown off the Popess's almost wooden-looking yoke to expose herself as a woman. In place of a nunlike habit, the Empress wears a tunic and skirt with graceful embroidery and sash. In place of the solid, egglike tiara, she wears an open, gold crown, similar to a halo. Its center is blood-crimson, for it is essentially the Empress who fills out the hollow crown with the maternal blood of earthly reality and warm love.

These concepts are further illustrated by the fact that the Empress is not confined between the pillars of a temple; instead she is pictured in an open, natural setting. The creative potential concealed with the Popess is now brought forth into reality. Whereas the Popess is connected with Isis and gestation, the Empress is associated with Ceres and vegetation. Indeed, one way to look at these two sisters is to consider them as if they were the same entity pictured in successive stages of time:

The Popess is High Priestess and Virgin; the Empress is Madonna and Royal Queen.

The Popess serves the spirit; the Empress fulfills the spirit. With the Popess, the spirit (the Holy Ghost) descends into matter to be made flesh; with the Empress, the spirit is born into outer reality as the Son of Man and ultimately rises heavenward again as the Spiritual Son, the Redeemer.

The Popess is patience and passive waiting; the Empress is action and completion.

The Popess is ruled by love; the Empress rules by love.

The Popess guards something old; the Empress reveals something new.

In short, the Popess holds the book of prophecy and the Empress enacts and fulfills this prophecy. The book is no longer needed, for the new King is born. As Madonna, Great Mother, and Queen of Heaven, the Empress is the connecting link between the Magician's fiery yang energy and the Popess's watery yin power. One might say that the Magician's wand has touched the Popess's depths, and out of this union, through the mediation of the Empress, something new has come into being . . . one world which includes both aspects. Numerologically, the Magician's number one plus the Popess's number two added together produce the Empress's number three which unites these opposites and embraces them both.

Generally speaking, this function of the number three is reflected in all sets of trinities: Father, Son, and Holy Ghost; past, present, and future; mother, father, and child; Isis, Osiris, and Horus. In all of these the third member acts as an equilibrating factor, combining the "parent numbers" in such a way as to produce a completely new reality. An interesting side light in this connection is that Pythagoras considered the number three to be the first *real* number. The first two numbers, he said, were merely *essences* for they did not correspond to any geometric figure, hence they had no physical reality. But the number three creates the triangle, a plane surface with a beginning, a middle, and an end: a tangible reality that corresponds to human experience.

The poetic truth of Pythagoras's statement is beautifully illustrated in Blake's *God Creating the Universe* (Fig. 11). As we look at the Creator's compass, we can see that its two arms diverge at such an angle that they grow farther and farther apart. In order to function together they must be set down somewhere. Before He can create the microcosmic world in the image of the macrocosmic one, the Creator must ground the two points of his compass in reality. When he does this, he will have connected the two arms of his compass with a base, thus creating a three-sided figure – the first triangle. Visualizing this triangle dramatizes the truth of Pythagoras's insight. It demonstrates how, with the advent of the triangle, Divine Intention became concretized. and nebulous essence was made manifest in terms of human experience.

I like to picture the Empress as the base of this triangle, for it is through her that the ephemeral is first brought within the realm of human experience. She connects us with external reality in a most dramatic way, and one which is familiar to everyone. For we all have moments when, touched by the Magician's wand, our creative waters are stirred. We are all familiar with the long, dark period of brooding gestation that follows when we are almost submerged in the watery, lunar world of the Popess. Then, with luck, dawns a new day, a golden moment when these dimly felt ideas and images begin to burst forth into reality! Suddenly, that empty white canvas is alive with color; or the lump of clay in our hand, almost by itself, begins to take shape; or the blank piece of paper in our typewriter is covered with words. Or perhaps it happens that the two seemingly irreconcilable horns of a dilemma which has impaled us for weeks are magically connected, offering an entirely new solution to our problem. These are some of the ways in which the Empress works for us in relation to our creative endeavors. Of course, her empire, like nature's vegetation, is apt to be over lush and somewhat helter-skelter. The reality which she produces is not the finished product. For this, as we shall see, we need the Emperor's discrimination and organization. One of the Empress's chief functions is to connect the primary energies of yin and yang and to give them a body in the world of sensory experience.

Until very recently, modern science took a Pythagorean view of the universe, equating external experience with scientific reality and describing as "mere essences" the forms which appear in that mysterious inner world, the human psyche. But with the advent of Heisenberg's uncertainty principle and Einsteinian physics, it has become apparent that external reality cannot be accurately sensed or measured by man because, in the very act of viewing external phenomena, man distorts them. Furthermore, it appears that because of the nature of light and the limitations of man's sensory apparatus, no instruments can ever be devised which can reinstate external reality as the touchstone of ultimate truth. This being irrevocable, we must at last turn to the inner world, to the human psyche itself, in our search for truth. The purely mathematical equation $E = MC^2$, no longer a "mere essence," now shines forth as the one eternal verity, incorruptible as gold.

The Empress connects us with this new dimension of awareness; for it is through her intuitive understanding rather than through masculine logic that the spirit leaps forth into outer space to connect with celestial insights. That the poetry of modern physics was not born in man's sterile laboratory but burst full blown from the Empress's garden of imagination is movingly documented in *The Creative Process,* a book edited by Brewster Ghiselin,[2] in which many scientists, writers, painters, and other creative people relate how their original ideas first reached them via daydreams, images, or other irrational manifestations welling up spontaneously from the unconscious.

It is the Empress, then, who bridges the gap between the Mother World of creative inspiration and the Father World of logic and laboratories – the kingdom of the Emperor, where her ideas and intuitions will be pruned and tested. It is she who carries the seed from which ultimately will spring a new transcendental awareness in which mysticism and science, spirit and flesh, inner and outer, can be experienced as one world.

But the Empress has many facets, all of which are active today. In order to better understand her influence on our present culture, we have included here three more nearly contemporary illustrations of the Empress archetype. The first of these (Fig. 25) shows the Empress as she appears in Waite's twentieth-century deck. Here she is pictured as a golden-haired matron in a flowered robe, seated on a red velvet couch in the midst of a lush garden. Beside her flows a stream which waters the garden. She wears a crown of stars and holds aloft an orb with no cross. Leaning against the couch is a shield displaying the emblem of Venus. Ripe wheat grows in the foreground, its golden color echoed in a dramatic yellow sky.

The startling juxtaposition of this velvet couch with its tasseled border, and the wild, natural garden, combined with the dramatic sky, suggests a stage set. This seems appropriate since the way the Empress appears to us is often very dramatic. Everything in her garden, all new life, manifests itself as a drama. Be it new sprout, butterfly, sudden blossom, or childbirth, she always functions with a dynamic flair.

Both she and her virgin sister were central figures in courtly love, but in different ways. The Virgin type inspired her knights to feats of daring and creative activity. Troubadours sang her praises and artists tried to catch her essence in paint and sculpture. Her quiet influence moved Dante and Petrarch to immortality. The Empress type acted more outspokenly as *femme inspiratrice*. Sometimes she manifested herself literally as queen or

Fig. 25   Waite Deck

empress whose court became a center for the creative arts. Queen Elizabeth the First was an example of such an empress. This kind of woman has always had a genius for bringing people and ideas together in a dynamic way. The ladies of the grand salons were such women. As she appears in our present culture, the Empress type still enjoys dramatizing herself and her ideas. A contemporary example of this type of woman was Peggy Guggenheim who ruled supreme both as a generous patron of the arts and as a truly liberated woman whose independent life style and daring innovation blazed the trail for other women seeking creative self expression. Here we see Empress Guggenheim seated on her throne surrounded by

Fig. 26   Peggy Guggenheim as The Empress

four courtly attendants (Fig. 26). Actress, community leader, art patron, or artist – wife, mother, mistress, or psychologist, she moves others to action and self-realization. The key to her power is active inspiration and love.

As exponents of women's liberation, these two sister types may both be active but in different ways: the Virgin type by setting an example; the Empress type through public activity. In the Virgin category one usually finds nuns, teachers, nurses, and poets, whereas the Empress type more often appears as an activist campaigning for women's rights. Sometimes the force of her personality can sweep us off our feet, driving us into activity beyond our limits.

Another Empress type can swamp us, submerging our individuality in the saccharin sweetness of her unconscious lure. For example, Waite's buxom blond pictured with her couch and shield suggests this kind of Wagnerian magic. One can almost hear the Venusberg music welling up from the pit to submerge and drown us, pulling us back into the womb. This tendency to smother-love is sometimes characteristic of the modern Empress type, especially in her role as Mom. It also appears in other areas, where the charm of such a woman can lure us into her realm in such a subtle way that we don't realize what's happened.

The Empress-woman herself is often as unconscious as others of her powers. It seems to her that everybody else should quite naturally share her enthusiasms. Being touched by Venus, this woman loves beauty in all forms and is often eclectic in her taste, combining things in a new and interesting way. For example, notice the flowered robe which she chose to wear for her portrait in the English deck. Do you recognize it? It is similar to those created by the famous Italian artist Sandro Botticelli. The Empress probably borrowed it from one of the dancing figures in Botticelli's *Spring*.

In this card, Waite chose to emphasize the qualities of Ceres and Venus. He has omitted the golden eagle of spirit and the cross surmounting the orb. Instead he has given his Empress a crown of stars. This connects her with the figure in Revelation, of whom it is written: "And there appeared a great wonder in heaven; a woman clothed with the sun, and with the moon under her feet, and upon her head a crown of twelve stars." The Madonna as Queen of Heaven is often pictured with such a crown and with the crescent moon lying under her feet. At her highest and brightest, the Empress illuminates the heavens, synthesizing all their powers: sun, moon, and the great wheel of the zodiac. In her lower, more earth-bound aspects, the goddess's unbridled fertility can lead to overindulgence and stagnation.

In the contemporary figure by Henry Moore (fig. 27) the Empress appears in a more earthy but equally commanding aspect as the Great Mother. She is leaning back and taking her ease as she surveys her empire, which is all of nature. She is relaxed, yet she is ever alert to the silent, secret workings which are hidden from us: the movement of the sap with-

Fig. 27   Reclining Figure (Henry Moore. Hirschorn Museum and Sculpture Garden, Smithsonian Institute. Reprinted by permission.)

in the plants, the bursting open of the tiny seeds buried in the earth. She hears the music of underground streams.

But the Great Mother is not always the Good Mother. On the grand scale her negative devouring and smothering aspect is called the Terrible Mother. In fairy tales we meet her as the wicked queen or cruel stepmother who jealously tries to keep Cinderella from rising out of the ashes to meet her prince and become queen. In myths she appears as the devouring mother who eats up her own children. We know her as cruel Mother Nature who seeks to repossess all life – all civilization – to pull it back again into her primal womb. As earthquake she literally opens her womb to suck man and his creations back into herself. As volcano she spews forth hot lava to bury whole cities alive. Every day in our gardens we see her ambivalent soul at work. By day she seems to smile on our endeavors, protecting and nourishing our flowers. But at night while we sleep, she busily plants innumerable weeds, which she fosters and tends with equal solicitude. In relation to all culture and human achievement, she is equally paradoxical; for it was she who furnished the creative inspiration that made our spaceships possible, and it is also she whose gravitational pull constantly seeks to draw them back to her bosom. She is indeed a jealous goddess, particularly where man's curiosity is aimed at woman's province, the moon!

Sometimes she is pictured as a dragon, guarding that indispensable treasure, the "pearl of great price." As such, she represents the devouring, regressive aspect of unconscious nature which the Hero (symbolic of humanity striving for consciousness) must slay in order to obtain the pearl of wisdom transcending mere animal existence. Another familiar representation of this Terrible Mother aspect is Kali, the bloodthirsty wife of Shiva. Here she is pictured holding by the hair the human victim who will be her next morsel, her incredible red tongue slavering in anticipation of this delight (Fig. 28). This devouring aspect of the goddess becomes apparent whenever woman neglects her true kingdom, which is relationship, and becomes power hungry; then she becomes truly a man-eater. Her strength, no longer the subtle power of love, turns into the strident love of power.

Sometimes the transition from the first to the second is so gradual that it can only be observed in retrospect, so that a woman falling victim to her own power drive may become estranged from her deepest self without realizing what has happened. Something like this seems to have developed in the women's liberation movement where, fascinated by power, many women seem to have lost touch with the very feminine creativity which they set out to demonstrate. In the depths of their being, most women in and out of this movement truly seek a peaceful equality and a creative relationship with men rather than dominance and power over them. Yet despite the frequent admonition "Make love, not war!" ours is a time of terrible violence, much of it wholly irrational. In the general hubbub, the bloodthristy cry of the man-eating feminist is heard throughout the land. The Empress, it seems, too long denied her rightful realm, rises from the depths with the hellish fury of a woman scorned.

One contemporary cartoon satirizes this situation nicely (Fig. 29). Here the "man eater," instead of developing her own creative femininity to assume its rightful place beside King Logos as co-ruler of our realm, sets out instead to kill him and usurp his throne.

But this witch, Hecate-like, wears many faces. If we treat her with civility she may show us a more civilized aspect. After all, woman, like her psychological counterpart, the anima, is still a primitive creature. It was only yesterday that Eve, emerging from her imprisonment as a function of Adam, stood exposed to the cultural influences and opportunities for differentiation which have long been man's privilege. Understandably, in her search for her true essence, woman will appear in many guises. As with the Empress Cleopatra, one of her earthly incarnations, "Age cannot wither her, nor custom stale her infinite variety."

Fig. 28   Kali, the Terrible

The Empress at her most "various" and whimsical is the nineteenth-century camera study made by Braun, a pioneer in the art of photography

"*The king is dead! Long live the queen!*"

Fig. 29   The King is Dead, Long Live the Queen!

(Fig. 30). Here sits Woman, caught at last in her own real flesh and blood, yet her essence still remains hidden. Paradoxically, the ebony and gold frame that catches our eye (and hers) also serves as her mask. She is the Countess Castiglione, no doubt descendant of the famous Renaissance humanist Baldassare Castiglione, whose book *The Courtier* was a model for the courtly life of its time. Unquestionably, this modern countess had her courtiers too, in the grand tradition set by her famous ancestor. This frivolous and bewitching pose indicates that the countess herself may have become the victim of her own enchantment.

Fig. 30   Countess Castiglione holding frame as mask
(Braun, Adolphe, 1811-1877. The Metropolitan Museum of Art,
New York. Gift of George Davis, 1948.)

Who is The Empress? Is she witch or goddess, devouring mother or Madonna, *femme fatale* or *femme inspiratrice*? The answer is probably all of these – as who among women is not? And what man does not have lurking in his depths a powerful feminine aspect by turns creative and vindictive; moved to compassion one moment and in a jealous rage the next! Perhaps by studying these pictures we may come to a deeper realization of our own powers and potentials – of our own infinite variety.

Fig. 31   L'Empéreur (Marseilles Deck)

7. The Emperor: Father of Civilization

> One becomes two, two becomes three, and out of
> the third comes the one as the fourth.
>
> Maria Prophetissa

Here is The Emperor, Trump number four (Fig. 31). He may be seen as an active, masculine principle come to bring order to the Empress's garden which, if left to grow by itself, can become a jungle. He will carve out room for man to stand erect, will create paths for intercommunication, will oversee the building of homes, villages, and cities. He will protect his empire from the inroads of both hostile nature and barbarians. In short, he will create, inspire, and defend civilization.

Heretofore we have been dealing with the primitive world of unconscious nature; now we step into the civilized world of conscious man. With the advent of the Emperor we leave the nonverbal, matriarchal realm of the Empress with its automatic cycles of birth, growth, and decay. Here begins the patriarchal world of the creative word, which initiates the masculine rule of spirit over nature. This ruler is an embodiment of the Logos, or rational principle, which is an aspect of the Father archetype. He orders our thoughts and energies, connecting them with reality in a practical way.

Although like the Empress, he represents an archetypal power, the Emperor is obviously more human and hence more accessible to consciousness than she, for his is not the rigid pose of a figurehead enthroned above the mass of humankind. Instead, he sits jaunty and relaxed, legs akimbo, fearlessly offering us a profile view of his left, or unconscious side. Only a ruler secure in his authority can afford to expose himself in this way. That his is a realm of peace, fearing neither attack from without nor treason from within, is indicated by the fact that this ruler wears no armor and carries no sword. His shield, embossed with the golden eagle, is no longer needed for protection. It is displayed here as an emblem symbolizing his connection with the heavenly powers, his rulership by divine right. He has nothing to fear from man or beast, nor from the gods above.

The Emperor presents himself informally seated on terra firma in the field of action, indicating that, instead of operating as a god behind the scenes (unconsciously), he is a practical leader, connected openly and intimately with humanity and its activities. In keeping with this idea, he wears his field helmet, a utilitarian headdress more graceful and individual than the severe crown worn by the Empress. The elegant lines of his helmet are repeated in the ornamentation of his royal chair and on his shield, the design of which is more elaborate and less severe than that of the Empress. Obviously, the empire which this ruler has created is one of cultural refinement; and equally obviously, this has not always been the case. Notice the size and strength of the hand with which he holds his sceptre, in contrast to which his left hand seems dwarfed and effeminate. No doubt this old warrior's sword hand has been strengthened in many a battle. His kingdom was hard-won. Man's struggle to consciousness involves almost superhuman feats of strength, for Mother Nature guards her kingdom jealously. In matriarchal cultures, the royal succession was via the female line. Thus the new king was he who conquered and won the princess. It was often he who was responsible for the death of the old king.

Historically, and in our own personal biographies, this transition from the matriarchal phase to the patriarchal era is always difficult. To leave the loving, protected, and nourishing world of childhood, to face the exposure and responsibilities of adulthood, is a tremendous task. Community life is the necessary intermediary step between the unconscious identity with all nature experienced in infancy and the more conscious and individual standpoint of adulthood. During this transition phase, ideally, one needs to experience oneself as a member of an ever widening group (family, clan, state, nation) at whose head stands a powerful and just authority figure.

The Emperor pictured here seems to be the ideal representation of such a figure, for he transcends the merely personal father, or even the leader of a homogeneous clan or state, since an empire often embraces diverse people and climes. Although secure in his own realm, the Emperor still retains a connection with the matriarchal world of the Empress, for he is pictured looking back toward her. The royal pair are also connected through the two eagles emblazoned on their respective shields. Not only do the two birds face each other, but the way each bird is depicted seems to connect Emperor and Empress in a subtle way. Whereas the Empress's eagle, wings uplifted, seems to be rising heavenwards, thus symbolizing the far-seeing masculine spirit of her spouse, the Emperor's bird is drawn in such a stylized way that its wings repeat the shape of the apparent "angel's wings" formed by the design of the Empress's throne.

Fig. 32   Eskimo Eagle

William Blake has said: "When thou seest an Eagle, thou seest a portion of genius; lift up thy Head!" However much the Emperor's golden
eagle may connect him with the heavenly spirit and inspire him to divine
rulership, he would do well to remember that the eagle is also a bird of
prey. Pictured here is the shadow side of the Emperor's golden eagle (Fig.
32). This Eskimo Indian creation shows the eagle as a rapacious bird,
ruthless and cruel. It is an apt symbol for the power-mad rulership which
often seizes kings and others in positions of authority when the golden
ideal of "divine right," tarnished and corroded, turns into "ego might."

Fortunately, there is evidence that the Tarot Emperor will not fall prey to the eagle's archetypal shadow. His number four suggests that this ruler's perspective, not limited to tunnel vision, includes all four dimensions of life.

The number four is symbolic of wholeness. It marks out our orientation to the human dimension. Its geometric equivalent, the square, represents law and order superimposed on the chaotic disorder of Mother Nature. The four directions of the compass keep us from feeling lost in uncharted areas. The four walls of a room give us a feeling of secure containment which helps us to concentrate our energies and pinpoint our attention in a rational, human way. The rectagonal windows of a house serve to scale down to human size the wide panorama of nature, so that its essence and detail can be more readily encompassed by the human eye and brain. Similarly, the guiding spirit of the Emperor helps us to examine the realities of our human condition and to relate to them in a conscious and creative way, a talent which is specifically human.

The Emperor's number four brings us into reality in many ways. The three dimensions of time (past, present, and future) are mere abstractions until we have located them in space. Similarly, events in three-dimensional space do not become concrete until we pinpoint them in time. To become civilized, man needs to place himself in space and time.The Emperor brings permanence, stability, and perspective. He stands as the figurehead for the state. He represents the principle upon which the fertility and the welfare of the kingdom depends. If he is harmed, the entire community suffers. (Significantly, in the legend of the Wasteland, it was the wounding of its Fisher King that caused the kingdom to become sterile and unproductive.)

At this stage of cultural development, the structure of the earthly kingdom or state mirrored the imagined structure of the cosmos. Calling this phase in the development of civilization "the archaic era of incarnated myth," John Perry discusses it further in *The Far Side of Madness:*

> . . .in that brief epoch the human world and the mythical world were seen as reflections of each other, and the government of society was regarded as fashioned in the image of the ordering of the cosmos. The mythical world was embodied in social forms, and the city kingdom was a model of the cosmos on the human plane. In this the king at the head of his kingdom was the counterpart of the king god in the divine realm; each was now "King of the Universe" or "Lord of the Four Quarters."[1]

As Perry goes on to say, it was at this point in man's history that the first differentiation of the mythical gods took place. He elucidates this as follows:

They came upon the scene as a function of the differentiation of culture itself, which in turn was an expression of the differentiation of the psyche. We can only suppose that culture-making is at the same time psyche-making, that the creative work of structuring the one is equivalent to the same work upon the other.

On both the heavenly and the earthly planes, the number four plays a decisive role as an ordering factor. Here is a partial list of some of the many "fours" that order our thoughts:

The four directions of the compass
The four corners of the earth
The four winds of heaven
The four rivers of Eden
The four qualities of the ancients (warm, dry, moist, cold)
The four humours (sanguine, phlegmatic, choleric, melancholic)
The four Evangelists (Matthew, Mark, Luke, John)
The four prophets (Isaiah, Jeremiah, Ezekiel, Hosea)
The four angels (Michael, Raphael, Gabriel, Phannel)
The four beasts of the Apocalypse
The four elements (earth, air, fire, water)
The four alchemical ingredients (salt, sulphur, mercury, azoth)
The four seasons
The four basic geometric figures (circle, line, square, triangle)
The four phases of the moon
The four Hebrew letters of the Lord's sacred name (Yod, He, Vau, He)
The four basic operations of arithmetic (addition, subtraction, multiplication, division)
The four cardinal virtues (justice, prudence, temperance, fortitude)

The list of "fours" that have helped man throughout the ages to direct his spiritual and physical life is endless. Four is also a number connected with the creation of man. The Syrian "Book of the Cave of Treasures" tells the story this way:

And they saw God take a grain of dust from the whole earth, and a drop of water from the whole sea, and a breath of wind from the upper air, and a little warmth from the nature of fire. And the angels saw how these four weak elements, the dry, the moist, the cold, and the warm, were laid in the hollow of his hand. And then God made Adam.[2]

In summary, then, the number four symbolizes man's orientation to reality as a human being. One pictorial representation of the number four is a square, symbolic of the order superimposed by Logos on random nature. But in the square the elements are still separate and hostile to one another. With the number five, the quintessence, a further development toward unity will take place, as we shall see when we come to examine the next card, which is Trump number five.

In the Tarot card under discussion, the Emperor's legs are crossed so that they create the number four. This suggests that he not only knows with his mind but also understands in a more basic, rooted way, the responsibilities which he embodies as the carrier of human consciousness.

Numerologically, the number four has unusual and magic properties. It not only marks the end of one cycle but it also furnishes the impetus for a new one. The reason it bears this double valence is this: when we add the numbers in sequence from one through four together, we get the number ten, which begins a new cycle. As the Magician (number one) furnished the energy which began the cycle of his creation, so the Emperor now completes this phase and at the same time initiates a new kind of creation – civilization. Like a kernel of corn, he is the result of all that has gone before, yet at the same time he is the seed for an entirely new growth.

Perhaps it was this magic quality inherent in the number four that inspired the wise saying of Maria Prophetissa that "One becomes two, two becomes three, and out of the third comes the one as the fourth." In any case, the truth of her statement is evident at many levels of experience because, psychologically, it is indeed the number three that brings with it the four and offers a new experience of wholeness and unity. This can be demonstrated in the following way. When we develop ego consciousness, we think of ourselves as *one*. But as we grow in awareness, we gradually come to realize that we are *two* – conscious and unconscious, ego and shadow (the one who rises early and the other who prefers to lie abed). If we are to reconcile these opposing aspects of ourselves, we must discover an inner mediator, a number *three* which can correlate these two so that they can work together harmoniously. When this happens, then "out of the three" – through the activity of this third factor – comes "the one as the fourth," an emergent feeling of wholeness, a unified personality that can again function as *one*, but now at a new level of awareness.

In Jung's psychology too, the number three brings up the four, resulting in a new feeling of unity. It was Jung's observation that every human being is born with four characteristic potentials for apprehending raw experience and sorting it out in order to deal with it. He called these four potentials *the four functions* because they represent characteristic ways the psyche functions. The two functions by which we *apprehend* the world he called *sensation* and *intuition*. Because these two operate spontaneously rather than rationally, he characterized them as *irrational functions*. The other two functions, *thinking* and *feeling*, he termed *rational functions* because they describe ways we order and evaluate our experience.

According to Jung, we are all born with the potential to develop each of these four functions to some extent. But early in life it usually becomes apparent that there is one function for which we show a special aptitude. This is called the *superior function*. Then we gradually find that we have some degree of competence in two other areas so that we ultimately have available, in a limited way, a second and third function. Jung called the second and third functions *auxiliary functions* because we can call on them to help our superior function.

But our fourth function always remains relatively unconscious and therefore unused. Jung called this the *inferior function* because it is not directly accessible to conscious training. Consequently its performance remains unreliable compared to that of the other three functions.

Because we tend to choose tasks that are easy, avoiding difficult chores, most of us automatically develop and improve our more accessible functions, leaving our inferior function unrecognized and undeveloped. Usually our families and society further reinforce this tendency by calling on us to serve chiefly in areas where we have demonstrated some competence. As a result, our inferior function drops farther and farther behind. Often it is only when this function intrudes itself in unexpected, inappropriate, and immature ways that we become aware that it exists at all. Meanwhile our superior function may have learned to operate so smoothly and automatically that it has lost its original vitality.

As time goes on, we begin to be "typed" according to our superior function, and we even begin to think of ourselves as if we were psychic cripples, limited by nature to perform adequately in only one—or at best two—areas of awareness. Here are a few of the more obvious characteristics of one who is "typed" according to his superior function.

An *intuitive* in not very observant of the world around him. He lives primarily in a world of future possibilities. He is little concerned with present reality, and he hates coping with details. For example, after attending a committee meeting an intuitive might be relatively unaware of many details of this conference, but he would probably come away from it inspired with a dozen ideas for projects this group might "some day" accomplish. The practical problems involved in this accomplishment he is apt to leave to others.

A *sensation* type would be best at observing the practical realities with which the committee would have to cope if the intuitive's ideas are to be carried out. A sensation person is not given to fanciful notions; his sensory awareness is geared to reality. He will observe in accurate detail the conditions of his outer environment. Like a good news-reporter, he is interested in specifics: who, what, when, where, why, and how. Just *how* can the intuitive's dreams for the future be squared with existing conditions? Is the room large enough to seat the audience? Can a piano be brought through the door? Is there money in the budget for this project?

Each of these two types reacts to life spontaneously. The intuitive smells out future possibilities and gets hunches without knowing how he arrives at this information. In a similar way, the sensation person records sensory experience automatically. For example: while the intuitive is busy "smelling out" a golden future, the sensation person may be observing that the air at this moment smells of leaking gas, and that this, if not dealt with immediately, may obviate any necessity for considering the future. In both cases, these observations are immediate and automatic. They arrive unconsciously and present themselves as proven facts, despite any logic or reasoning to the contrary.

Thinking and feeling, on the other hand, operate more deliberately. The *thinking* type organizes his experience into logical categories and arranges them in a systematic order. On a committee, for instance, he might make a list of the things to be done before the next meeting, and he might work out an agenda for this meeting. If there is to be a speaker on the program, the thinker might express concern that the lecturer be an authority in his field.

The *feeling* type would react differently. He would not care so much that the speaker be an authority, so long as he expresses himself well and presents his material in an interesting way. He would evaluate any program more according to its feeling tone than its content. "Feeling," as Jung uses the terms, does not mean unbridled emotion. Quite the contrary. Jung characterizes feeling as a rational function because it can be exactly as precise and discriminating as thinking. It too is a means of evaluating experience. On a committee, the feeling person might be good as hospitality chairman or toastmaster. He would help everyone to feel at home but, at the same time, he would be quick to discourage behavior that does not "feel" appropriate to the occasion. He would probably accomplish this tactfully, but he could be very firm – even cold-blooded – if circumstances seem to warrant it.

This thumbnail sketch of the four function-types is, of course, greatly oversimplified. But viewing oneself in the light of this summary can be well worthwhile in terms of self-understanding. Even more valuable is the insight a study of the types can offer as to how others function. It can, for instance, help us to understand that a child of the intuitive type does not keep losing things because he is stupid or disobedient; he is simply unconcerned with material objects. In a similar way, realizing that our neighbor is a thinking type can help us to understand that he is not being disagreeable on purpose when he disturbs the feeling tone of a party by interjecting tactless truths which seem to him apropos. Or again: if our spouse operates by intuition, we can avoid practical problems on a motor trip by remembering to slip a map into the glove compartment. As another example: suppose that thinking is your best function, whereas your mate is a feeling type; if both of you understand this, you can approach areas of disagreement more consciously and cooperatively. When your spouse impulsively spends money budgeted for future needs on an antique vase that "feels just right" for the living room, you can understand how, for a feeling type, this object has a value that transcends your logic. Knowing this, you can avoid a head-on collision which would ruin the feeling tone of the moment with futile arguments. But later you and your partner may help solve future problems of this kind by sitting down together to revise the budget to include values important to both feeling and thinking types.

This sketchy discussion of the four functions will offer the uninitiated reader a few clues toward discovering his own function-type. But I present here two hints that I have found helpful. In order to discover your superior function, observe how you behave, or might behave, in an emergency. Imagine yourself in a forest at nightfall far from civilization and separated from your companions. Would you sit down and try to think out a plan of action? Or would you try to intuit where your companions might have gone and set forth in that direction? Or would you take stock of the realities of your situations (warmth, shelter, water etc.) and plan to stay put where these were available? Or what?

Sometimes it is difficult to decide which is your first function because your superior and your first auxiliary function are both so well developed that it is hard to tell which one represents your innate type. In this case it is sometimes easier to locate your inferior function. One way to do this is to observe what sorts of tasks you consistently postpone doing because you have "no time" for them. Often you will find that certain kinds of jobs are ignored day after day, whereas other tasks (which are actually more time-consuming and complicated) do get done. Once you have discovered your inferior function, you can easily locate your superior one, because it will invariably be the *other* function in the same category as the inferior one. For example, if your inferior function is an irrational function (say, intuition) then your superior function will be the other irrational function (sensation) and vice versa. If your inferior function is a rational function (say, feeling) than your superior function is bound to be the remaining rational function (thinking), or vice versa. The reason that this formula is so dependable will be discussed later in another chapter.

For those wishing to delve deeper into this area, *Lectures on Jung's Typology* (Hillman and von Franz)[3] offers a complete description of the four function-types and gives illustrations of how these operate in practical life. But the abbreviated outline presented here is sufficient as a guideline for the following exploration of Jung's type-theory in relation to the wise saying of Maria Prophetissa quoted above.

As we first become aware of these four potentials within us, we tend to label ourselves according to our superior function. In other words, our ego becomes identified with our superior function. We may not describe our feelings in the exact terminology used here, but we do tend to think of ourselves as *one unit* – a person with one special aptitude, excluding other potentials of which we are less aware. We become recognized by ourselves and others as "the one who is clever with his hands," or "the one who is good at mathematics," and so on. But later we usually come to recognize

and develop our secondary functions – at which point "one becomes two."
We are "good with our hands" but we also enjoy reading and writing
poetry, for example. Later comes a beginning awareness of capacities in a
third area, corresponding to our third function. But this function is so
buried in unconsciousness that it is difficult to excavate, so that it is often
many years before one begins to have a sense of himself as having *three*
areas of competence.

During all this time, the fourth function usually remains hidden. It is so
buried in darkness, so unpracticed and therefore so threatening to our ego
status, that we cannot approach it directly. But as we continue to develop
and use our third function, the fourth function also begins to emerge into
consciousness. By employing this third function, it is then, "out of the
third," that we gain access to the fourth. When this happens, there even-
tuates "the one as the fourth." For now there is potential for unity—a
wholeness that includes all four aspects of our psyche and transcends the
ego-unity with which we began our explorations.

Let me illustrate how the types function in this way by citing a brief example from my own experience. I am an intuitive with feeling as my second best function. My third function is thinking, and my fourth (and still
hopelessly undeveloped) function is sensation.

Obviously, writing a book and preparing it for publication is going to
require skills in all four areas. My interest in the Tarot was first sparked
through intuition. I was attracted to the mystery of the cards, and smelled
out the possibility of connecting them with figures in my dreams. For a long
time I did nothing whatever about this except to muse on the cards and
make sporadic attempts to feel into their possible meaning.

Since my thinking is not yet well developed, it took me several years
to organize my intuitions and feelings and find the words to express them. I
didn't want to think about the Tarot cards or read factual books on this subject. I was not interested in learning the history of the Tarot. Being an intuitive with little interest in reality, facts and dates bore me. For a long time
I was content with the vague generalization that the Tarot was "very old"
and made no effort to explore its specific origin. I was concerned with the
cards' imagery rather than their reality.

In giving lectures and seminars on the Tarot, I constantly have problems with the hard facts of reality in many areas—especially those involving space and time. I will, for instance, arrange the chairs for participants in
an inviting circle, which makes everyone feel good, but later discover that
the chairs are so placed that several cannot see the exhibits which will be
the topic of interest. My unawareness of time caused trouble, too, until I
solved this problem by planning to arrive half an hour early and appointing
a timekeeper to signal when the allotted time was up.

Gradually my third function, thinking, is helping me to contact these
realities more directly. By constantly reminding myself to do so, I am beginning to observe street signs and other landmarks when I go somewhere

for the first time. I am even learning to draw crude maps, but I still have trouble making proportions accurate. To improve my sense of time, I play games with myself. "What time is it now?" I will ask myself suddenly. (I must answer, of course, without consulting a timepiece.) Learning to observe the angle of the sun and to hear the "plop" of the evening newspaper on the sidewalk is helping me to guess when it is time to put the cover on my typewriter for the day and repair to the kitchen so that dinner will be ready when my hungry husband returns from his office. In many similar ways, by thinking and planning I am able to make a bridge to my inferior fourth function, sensation. Someday I may be able to contact sensory awareness more directly. When this happens I hope to experience the new unitary feeling described by Maria Prophetissa as "the one as the fourth."

Culturally as well as personally, the Emperor's number four heralds a new beginning, for it is he who initiates the beginning symbolized by the Word. With his advent, we leave the matriarchal world of nonverbal, primitive order which expressed itself largely through music, dance, and imagery. Here we enter into to world of verbal, logos order.

In our biblical accounts, there are two beginnings described. The first tells us that "In the beginning God created heaven and earth." One might see this as the supreme magus creating the primary yang and the primary yin (represented by the Tarot Magician and Popess), these two then being joined together, as we have seen, in the matriarchal world of the Empress. But now, with the Emperor, comes a *second* beginning which we might equate with the second biblical account that reads: "In the beginning was the Word." Originally, the Word (symbolic of idea, breath, spirit) was "with God." Now, with the advent of the Emperor, the power of the Word is conferred on humanity.

The oldest meaning of "Logos" is "that by which the inward thought is expressed." Words are the basis for all organized thought, all self-examination, all science, all recorded history, all civilization. They are the tools whereby we learn to abstract ideas and to separate our ego selves from the primary, unitary world of the unconscious. The moment a child first says "I" marks an important step on the road to self-realization, because it records the initial break between himself and the infantile identity with all creation into which every new babe is born. This magical phase of identification with all nature is sometimes referred to more poetically as *participation mystique*. As the child becomes more proficient in the use of words, he gradually moves away from the realm of primitive magic and feminine Eros into the civilized world of masculine order and Logos, which is the Emperor's domain.

We tend to think of words chiefly as tools for communicating with others; but we need them, first of all, to communicate with ourselves. From earliest childhood on, words are the primary key to self-knowledge and intellectual growth. We need them in order to think—to sort out the chaotic images and events of the world about us and establish our own identity in relation to them. Without the gift of language, we would be like savage beasts, caught forever in a state of *participation mystique* with our surroundings.

This fact was dramatized in the story of Helen Keller, who, being both deaf and blind, had no access to words. As a small child, she experienced herself pretty much as a subhuman animal, and she therefore behaved like one. Then, with the help of a gifted teacher, there came that long-awaited moment when little Helen was able at last to connect the word "water" (telegraphed on her palm in a sort of Morse code) with the cool fluid which she knew by touch and taste. In that magic moment Helen's humanity was born.

Words are indeed a new kind of magic, different from the Magician's powers. They are useful tools, indispensable in helping us to name and classify the objects of our environment. They help us to detach ourselves from things so that we can experience ourselves and the world about us more objectively. They help us to recall nonverbal experiences and to transmit these recollections to others. But words are, of course, not substitutes for experience. The word "water" alone could neither have quenched Helen Keller's physical thirst nor slaked her thirst for knowledge. Without the experience, the word alone has little to offer.

In bygone times man used words more sparingly. The ancient Egyptians spoke only when filled with the spirit; the word was the action of the spirit. Today we speak at random—our words are mere footprints, the substance is gone.

It would seem that in our present ververbalized computer culture, we have so far detached ourselves from the raw stuff of life that we ourselves have become abstractions, lost in a verbal maze. We behave toward words as if they were the experiences to which they refer, do in fact swallow them whole, as if they were nourishing reality. We have spiritual indigestion. As a result, the pendulum is now swinging back toward nonverbal experience. Young people are leaving their books and moving back to nature. Groups abound in sensory awareness, bodily encounter, and meditation. It has even become fashionable to denigrate words as useless, dry, and purely intellectual.

"How," the question is sometimes raised, "would you express a Bach fugue or a Klee painting in mere words?" How indeed? Equally impossible, one may reply, to capture Shakespeare's *Hamlet* in a medium other than words. For that matter, it is even debatable whether this or any other creative work can be adequately translated into words of another language. For words are not signs or counters used solely to designate specific things. Words are symbols whose reverberations, to the educated ear, always include nuances that transcend their overt meaning. We tend to forget that words, like music and other art forms, are not only tools of the intellect. They, too, arose at the gut level of human experience. Historically, words in every language come to us "trailing clouds of glory."

Each reverberates with hidden echoes of the human experience out of which it intially arose and was refined and reshaped by succeeding generations.

Therefore, far from throwing them out the window altogether, we might use words themselves as yet another technique for capturing sensory awareness. Studying the etymology of the words we use can be a useful tool to help us to connect with the exact feeling tone of the experience which they describe. For example, in an earlier chapter a connection was made between our verb "to remember" and the Old English word *mournan*, which meant "to mourn." For me, this knowledge added a new feeling tone not only to the word under discussion but to the experience of remembering. One might say that it added dimension to "the remembrance of things past."

Words have power—many kinds of power. Words produce vibrations in nature. The vibrations of the sacred word AUM are said to correlate with the three forces of nature: creation, preservation, disintegration. A primitive idea, still alive in the most civilized parts of the globe is that words exert a magical influence over the persons or objects with which they are connected. In Jewish tradition, the sacred name of Jaweh must never be pronounced, and one of the Ten Commandments admonishes us not to "take the name of the Lord thy God in vain."

It is worth noting here that even in the first account of the Creation, the word plays a magic role. For it was only at the point where God *said* "Let there be light" that the logos principle itself could be called into being. It is as if even the Creator needed to separate the concept of light from his own inner chaos and pinpoint it with a name before he could make it manifest in outer reality.

Names shape reality and influence its character. In token of this fact, we devote time and thought to the names we give our children. Before selecting a stage name, an actor sometimes consults a numerologist. Manufacturers often have contests to discover a name with alluring "vibes" for a new product. Another superstition connected with names that still flows silently in our blood, is the idea that knowing the name of a person, place, or object gives us a specific power over it. Upon meeting a new person we may feel uneasy until we know the stranger's name, although the name itself may not identify this person in any real way. Conversely, we may feel reluctant to share our name too readily with certain strangers.

Naming things is an important part of the Emperor's task. By no means a purely intellectual matter, finding the correct name for things is a creative act—an art involving not only the thinking faculty but also feeling, intuition, and a good connection with sensory experience. As a demonstration of this, the following ancient legend is apropos. It appears that Satan, jealous of God's attention to Adam, complained to the Lord, asking that he be put in charge of the birds and beasts in Adam's stead. Whereupon the Lord instituted a contest between Satan and Adam to see who could name correctly all the creatures. He ordained that the winner of this contest should rule the kingdom whose creatures he had correctly named.

Satan, of course, flunked the test, for imaginative discrimination and patient dedication to disciplined order are the very last talents in the repertory of one whose genius is pandemonium. So Adam won the naming contest and became the emperor of Eden. And that's how Adam, rather than Satan, became our ancestor. But the Lord didn't banish Satan from the garden altogether. He's still much in residence and extremely active. Perhaps one of his functions here is to remind us what a near thing that contest was.

In recognition of this fact, and fearing confusion above all else, our forebears tended to idolize the logos principle of the Emperor, leaving the Empress out of the picture almost entirely. Now, quite the opposite, we tend to denigrate the Emperor and worship the Empress. Our monstrous one-sidedness made reason, law, and established order seem, and to some extent become, excessively rigid. Many individuals, young and old alike, have revolted against the established order. Some hope to destroy its empire entirely while others have turned their backs on civilization in a futile attempt to recapture the preconscious matriarchal world of vague dreams and feelings.

The obvious truth is, of course, that Emperor and Empress are, as their names indicate, a wedded pair. One cannot function creatively without the other. The sceptre of each displays the orb of Nature surmounted by the cross of Spirit, symbolizing the harmonious union of their energies and their two kingdoms. Each displays the golden eagle, indicating that the powers of each are equally God-given, the rights of each equally divine. With the advent of the Emperor a new cycle is initiated involving new aspirations and new and more sophisticated connections between the mundane realm and the heavens above. Under the influence of the Emperor man will reach up, not only symbolically but actually, to the sun, the moon, and the stars.

Inevitably, if we are to implement our soaring spirit, we cannot always keep one foot in the Empress's garden. There are times, in both our cultural and our personal lives, when one or the other of these great ruling powers must have a stronger influence on our lives than its opposite number. Actually, like all opposites, the two operate best in a sort of alternating current. There are times when it is even necessary to hold one of these in abeyance in order to experience the benefits of the other.

The Emperor rules primarily by Logos and thinking; the Empress is chiefly concerned with Eros and feeling. For the Emperor, objective fact is honest truth; for the Empress, inner fact is primarily important. In her realm, to reveal an objective fact that might hurt a relationship would be dishonest, whereas in the Emperor's world, to conceal such a fact would be reprehensible. Obviously, in a given situation, both cannot rule at once.

But if we give each one in turn a chance to speak, we may find a solution which will be true to the fact of outer reality without doing violence to the equally important fact of inner feeling.

In all kinds of creative work, it is particularly useful to arrange an audience with both these powerful figures – but never, of course, at the same time. For example, during what we might call the Empress's phase of creativity, when images and ideas are bubbling up from our depths in an abundant and spontaneous way, it is usually best to ask the Emperor to wait in the wings while we uncritically capture the bounty of all that presents itself. Later on, we will invite our Logos to sit in as editor, helping us to winnow and choose, to arrange and order our ideas. But if he steps in too soon, he may wither up the fresh new sprouts of our imagination which need, like all tender young things, first of all a mother to nourish and sustain them.

An excellent way to observe in graphic detail how our inner Emperor and Empress work together is to compare successive drafts of, say, a poem by Keats. There one sees how the rich imagination of the poet's feminine, feeling side was later pruned, refined, and shaped by his critical Logos to create the finished product. One is struck not only by the perfection of what remains but equally by the sheer beauty of much that has been sacrificed. For this delicate job of discrimination, the artist's Emperor needs to be sensitive, insightful, and courageous.

One of the specific uses of Tarot number four is to help us to become aware of the kind of Emperor, symbolically speaking, who influences our culture and our own personal lives. Is he relaxed, energetic, imaginative? Or is he rigid, disenchanted, unreceptive? What are some of the unconscious notions which underlie our personal and cultural "empire"? Does our inner Emperor believe in perfectibility? Utopia? The permanent abolition of evil? White supremacy? Black supremacy? What?

One way to examine the Emperor might be to study his picture for a few moments and then jot down without editing or censoring whatever you feel he might answer to the kinds of questions asked above. Do you agree with his answers? If not, where do you differ? If you find it difficult to feel into the character of the Emperor, a useful technique is to contrast him with other pictures of similar kinds of figures. Comparing this card with its counterpart in other Tarot decks is most helpful. For example, the Emperor pictured in the Waite deck appears to be much older and more imposing than the figure we have been discussing. Waite's Emperor has a long, gray beard, and is seated on a large throne, his legs encased in mail. One might imagine that his answers to some of our questions might be different from those of the Marseilles Emperor.

Whatever answers you succeed in getting, please file them away in your Tarot notebook. Later, after studying some of the other cards, it might be interesting to "interview" this character again. He may have come up with some new ideas in the meantime.

Fig. 33   Le Pape (Marseilles Deck)

8. The Pope:
The Visible Face of God

The soul of man is naturally religious.

Origen

So far, each card discussed has pictured only one figure, a personage of magic proclivities or of supra-human proportions. Card number five (Fig. 33) shows something new. In addition to the usual archetypal character (in this case the Pope) we see for the first time figures of human size. They are pictured as two men of the cloth kneeling before the Pope. The one on the left has what appears to be a cardinal's hat, and both display priestly tonsures which, like miniature halos, proclaim their dedication to the spirit.

The Pope sits enthroned as the central figure, framed by the two kneeling men in front and the two upright pillars behind. Thus he reiterates his number, five – a number symbolic of the quintessence, that precious and indestructible quality which is known to man alone and which transcends the four earthly elements common to both men and beasts. We might see the Pope, then, as an externalized embodiment of man's striving for connection with the godhead – of his dedication to the quest for meaning which sets man above the animals.

Whereas Freud saw this religious tendency as a mere sublimation of sexual libido, Jung viewed man's urge toward transcendent meaning as an instinct *sui generis* in the human psyche – as an innate predisposition of mankind – a creative force more compelling even than the urge to physical procreation. Like the sex instinct, the religious drive aims to unite the opposites. As a symbol of such unification the Pope, with his beard and his flowing robes, is androgynous, uniting in his person both the masculine and the feminine elements.

The Pope is a powerful figure both symbolically and in the world of reality. Like the Magician, he connects the inner and outer worlds, but in a more conscious and outspoken way. One might say that it was the Pope's function to make accessible to man the transcendental world heretofore reached only through intuition. He has been called "The visible face of God" because he is endowed with the mana of the Lord Himself.

As is always the case with these archetypal powers which move us on the inside, we must first experience them as existing in our outer environment. All of us have, from time to time, projected onto others the qualities of the Magician, the Popess, the Empress, and the Emperor. By experiencing these qualities as belonging (often erroneously) to persons of our acquaintance, we ultimately come to realize that we ourselves have potentials and characteristics of a similar nature. As we become increasingly aware of our inner powers for weal or woe, the exaggerated projections with which we have clothed our friends and enemies gradually fall away. As we mature, the preachers, teachers, psychologists, and politicians of our acquaintance no longer carry for us those characteristics which properly belong to ourselves. In the end, they (and we) assume more human proportions.

But this is a long, long trail – both historically and in our own personal development. Human consciousness – humanity itself – is young and weak. We need strong, reliable projection holders in order to become aware of the many forces operating within our human psyche. An ideal carrier of our faith and aspirations is the Pope pictured here. In contrast to the two puny figures before him, he appears to be of superhuman size. And rightly, too, for he is God's representative on earth. The word "pope" is cognate with the Latin *pater* and the Italian *papa*. As the Emperor was the supreme father in governing the life of the secular community, the Pope stands as the supreme father figure of the Church, governing his "children" in the religious community.

His appellation "pontiff" is related to the Latin *pontifex*, which means bridge. He is a bridge between man and God. He connects the codified experience of the Church (symbolized by the pillars seen behind him) with the living, human experience of the figures before him. In areas where they have not yet learned to listen to their own inner voice, or have lost connection with it, the Pope offers them the wisdom of a collective value system to sustain and guide them along the way.

In the primitive world of the Magician, the Popess, and the Empress, men and women lived in close connection with their instinctual side. They functioned, not as discrete individuals, but more like atoms revolving around a center, each living out a certain function for the group, somewhat like bees in a hive. Before the advent of the Emperor, with his emphasis on the deeds and words which are the stuff of civilization, people still knew how to listen to the voice of the unconscious as it spoke through dreams and visions.

But with the Emperor, this *participation mystique* between humans and nature began to weaken. Energy was necessarily wrested free to clear away forests and to build an empire. In the inner landscape as well, islands of ego awareness began to rise above the primeval mass of tribal consciousness. Through outer works and words, man gradually began to lose touch with his inner being. The more man lost contact with his own immediate experience of the spirit, the more he came to rely on the dogma distilled from the mystical experience of others. And gradually, through the centuries, as he became involved in the complex personal relationships inherent in a competitive, individualistic society, man came to feel increasingly the need for individual confession and counseling in matters of personal conscience. Out of these needs, the Church arose and grew, with the Pope as its titular head. As God's spokesman, he is the final arbiter of all moral questions. It is also he who must determine the ultimate authenticity of all mystical experience.

The Tarot Pope shows us symbolically the scope of his domain. His right hand, raised in the traditional sign of benediction, reveals two extended fingers. This indicates that moral problems involving the opposites of good and evil are under his domain, to be openly recognized and dealt with. The thumb and two remaining fingers, which he holds concealed, might signify that the Trinity is a holy mystery, not to be examined scientifically, but rather to be experienced emotionally. The Pope holds the key to this holy mystery concealed in the palm of his hand.

As the bridge between dogma and experience, between the code and its practical application, the Pope interprets the spiritual law. He determines knotty problems of sin and sainthood. He protects the Church from splitting apart into individual sects; yet at the same time, he can amend the law when necessary to fit individual circumstances which seem to him exceptional. Unlike the Popess he holds no book; he does not consult the law – he *is* the law. As God's earthly spokesman, he is infallible. His power is supreme, above all humankind. Even the Emperor must kneel before him.

The Pope pictured here holds his staff of office in a gloved hand, indicating perhaps that it is not his individual, human hand which possesses infallibility and supreme power. His is a sacred trust, not susceptible to the temptations of mortal flesh. On his glove is marked the cross *patée*, an ancient form of the cross, indicative of the great age of the Church. This glove may be as old as the institution it serves. It has no doubt been worn by many popes before this one, and will be worn again by many more after he is gone. His three-tiered headdress, similar to that worn by the Popess, is echoed in the triple cross of his staff. The Pope's dominion over the three worlds (spirit, body, soul) is reaffirmed and made more outspoken. But he holds his staff in his left hand; he rules from the heart rather than by force of will.

The two prelates pictured here appear to be almost twins. In our dreams, whenever a new quality or function is about to emerge into consciousness, it often appears as twins – symbol par excellence for the dual aspects inherent in all life. The two priests in this card might symbolize the many sets of twin impulses in man's religious nature of which he is just now becoming aware. Among these, one might imagine, would be conflicts between outer fact and inner meaning, ambiguous impulses toward both good and evil, problems involving public power versus private conscience, and the many subtleties of individual relationship – problems of which the Emperor and his subjects were relatively unaware.

The two kneeling figures have their backs to us, although awareness of the opposites is emerging, it is still unconscious. The prelates do not face the conflicts directly; they turn toward the Pope for guidance. Contrasted with the imposing figure of the pontiff, the priests seem small and weak. They bow to his authority. Almost identical in dress and posture, they have as yet no individual standpoint. Their appellation, "brothers," indicates that they are still functions of a larger family unit, children of Mother Church, yet they are beginning to experience themselves as individuals with personal questions and problems.

The Pope, with his patriarchal beard and flowing robes, plays the role of both mother and father to these brothers. He expresses the concern of Mother Church for the personal development of each of her parishioners, yet he enunciates, preserves, and defends the general law. In contrast to the Popess, who communicates largely through intuition and feeling, the Pope can organize and verbalize his ideas, bringing them together in a formal, rational system. Like the Emperor, he is an embodiment of the masculine Logos, but his concerns are more inclusive than those of the Emperor, who dealt chiefly with the physical well being and social welfare of his subjects; and he is also concerned with the inner world of conscience and responsibility.

The differences between the Emperor and the Pope are clearly indicated in the way each of these archetypal figures is pictured in the Tarot. The Emperor is shown gazing out toward distant horizons; his eye encompasses the totality of his empire. The Pope looks toward the individuals before him; he grants them an audience – he communicates with them. This interaction between the archetypal and the human marks an important step in the historical development of human consciousness. It is at this point that man emerges as a separate entity and begins to experience his own human beingness in relation to the suprapersonal powers. Heretofore in this Tarot series, the archetypal figures have occupied the entire canvas; they held full sway.

In our infancy, and in the infancy of human consciousness, the powers symbolized by The Magician, The Popess, The Empress, and The Emperor controlled our lives without challenge or question. Their magic seemed so powerful that weak ego consciousness could not confront them. In fact, the infantile human ego was still without form. As the first four cards of our Tarot series plainly show, individual ego consciousness had no place in the picture, much less a speaking part. In The Pope card, for the first time, *humanity confronts the archetype.* A dialogue is taking place between consciousness and the instinctual powers of the psyche. To be sure, the kneeling figures have not yet the strength to stand up to the suprapersonal power; but they have sought him out with their questions and problems.

The Pope, although enthroned as befits his godlike stature, is none-theless also human – he exists in earthly reality. Like the Christ, the Pope has a dual origin: he is God's heavenly representative – yet he is also a human being, meaning that although in his person he belongs to time, in his essence he is immortal. The individual Pope pictured here will die, yet as long as the Church endures, the Pope will always have a successor.

In other ways, too, the Pope partakes of the Savior archetype of which the paradigm in our culture is the Christ image. Like Christ, the Pope poses moral problems, sharpening man's awareness in the area of human conscience. Yet as Savior, he absolves man of the guilt inherent in the human striving for knowledge of good and evil – that ancient sin which is "original" with man alone.

Viewed psychologically also, the Tarot Pope is a savior, for accord-ing to Jung, the kind of confrontation he dramatizes is the salvation of human consciousness. Were it not, says Jung, for the continuing dialogue between ego and archetype man would never be able to disentangle his identity from the archetypal womb and free himself from the blind power of his instincts. As Jung has pointed out, without this kind of interaction between the human and the transcendental, neither man's consciousness nor the spirit itself could evolve and mature.

In his "Answer to Job,"[1] Jung uses the biblical encounter between Job and Jehovah as a paradigm for this kind of confrontation between man and archetype. Jung shows how, in the course of this encounter, both figures are changed. Job comes to realize and accept the all-powerful ambivalent nature of his God, and Jehovah himself begins to become aware of his own questionable relationship to Satan. Symbolically speak-ing then, both questioning mankind (Job) and his image of the Omni-potent Spirit (Jehovah) evolve and grow through such an inner dialogue. Although the humble obeisance of the two priests pictured in card five is a far cry from the astute interrogation with which Job confronted Jehovah, nevertheless it is a beginning. The priests have sought out the archetypal figure and he has granted them an audience. The Pope is willing to listen to their questions and to communicate with them.

But such dialogues between the human and the archetypal are not always so serene as they appear in this picture. Here the Pope commun-

icates. But he can also ex-communicate. The hand raised here in benediction, viewed in a certain light, can become the sign of malediction.
Figure 34 shows the image created by the shadow of this hand. It suggests
the head of Baphomet, the devil. There is an old superstition that should
this shadow fall upon one, the Pope's blessing would become a curse.
Even today, those who believe this always take care, when attending papal
ceremonials, to avoid standing where this shadow might fall on them.

Psychologically speaking, all the major archetypal figures we have
been discussing, being large and powerful, naturally cast shadows com-
mensurate with their size. The shadow of religious authority can be devilish
indeed as history has shown, dogmatism and fanaticism being among its
more obvious manifestations.

Whenever the ego is identified with any archetypal figure, it emanates
a force which is both fascinating and compelling but at the same time terrifying and repelling. This kind of power, being supra-human, is difficult to

Fig. 34   The Sign of Excommunication

relate to in a human way. Especially is this true of the archetypal Old Wise Man whose public aspect we see pictured in the Pope, and whose card more individual portrayal we shall discuss as it appears in card nine – The Hermit. Each of these figures is imbued with a special mana, because each seems to speak with the voice of God.

Sometimes people who are seized by the passionate intensity of this archetype espouse causes which are outspokenly religious or philosophical. But, if no adequate container for this energy can be found in an organized religion or philosophy, individuals caught by the archetypal Old Wise Man or Savior will pour their religious passion into other causes, such as vegetarianism, ecology, organic gardening, or group therapy. Imbued with the supra-personal power of these archetypal forces, human beings, otherwise quite ordinary, will accost strangers on street corners, exhorting them to seek God. Even one's next door neighbor, formerly retiring or even shy, when moved by this archetype may take to the soapbox on social occasions to expound the merits of T.M., E.S.T., Freud, Jung or macrobiotics.

The Pope is a logos figure; as such, he also symbolizes the *animus*, Jung's term for the unconscious masculine principle as it appears in the psyche of woman. The animus can take many forms, several of which are pictured in the Tarot. In her study entitled *Animus and Anima*, Emma Jung outlines four stages in the evolution of the Logos as it appears externally in the culture and internally in the unconscious of women generally. The first stage, she says, embodies the idea of *directed power*. This stage is pictured in the Tarot as The Magician. The second stage, *deed*, is personified by the Tarot Knight. (it will also appear later as the young king pictured in card seven, The Chariot.) The third stage of animus development she calls *word*. It is personified in the Tarot as The Emperor. And the fourth stage, *meaning*, is portrayed as The Pope.

In her discussion of animus development in women, Emma Jung says: "Just as there are men of outstanding physical power, men of deeds, men of words, and men of wisdom, so, too, does the animus image differ in accordance with the woman's particular stage of development or her natural gifts."[2] She then points out that coming to terms with *the animus of meaning* is the special problem of woman today. "In the first place," says Emma Jung, "she seldom finds satisfaction in the established religion, especially if she is a Protestant. The church which once to a large extent filled her spiritual and intellectual needs no longer offers her this satisfaction. Formerly, the animus, together with its associated problems, could be transferred to the beyond (for to many women the biblical Father-God meant a metaphysical superhuman aspect of the animus image) and as long as spirituality could be thus convincingly expressed in the generally valid forms of religion, no conflict developed. Only now when this can no longer be achieved, does our problem arise."

In her discussion of women's struggle for equal rights with men, Emma Jung emphasizes the fact that this is "no idiotic aping of man, or a competitive drive betokening megalomania"; that the need to find spiritual and intellectual expression is as instinctive and as necessary for women as it is for men. Coming to terms with her spiritual animus, she says, is the special problem of women today because, through birth control and modern technology, energies formerly needed for childbearing and housekeeping are at last freed for spiritual development. . . "we are not," the author continues, "like Eve of old, lured by the beauty of the fruit of the tree of knowledge, nor does the snake encourage us to enjoy it. No, there has come to us something like a command; we are confronted with the necessity of biting into this apple, whether we think it good to eat or not, confronted with the fact that the paradise of naturalness and un-consciousness, in which many of us would too gladly tarry, is gone forever."

To find meaning, it would seem, is the need of our time – perhaps especially for women, but also for men. We are now culturally in the fourth stage of logos development. We cannot expect magic solutions to our problems – healing ceremonials performed by a tribal medicine man. The chance to escape spiritual confrontation by setting forth to conquer new geographical frontiers – to exhaust our energies in deeds – is long gone. And sterile words no longer assuage our spiritual hunger. For many of us the pope, as a figurehead in the Church, no longer serves our needs. We must somehow discover within ourselves his internal counterpart and find a way to relate to this archetype.

The Pope's number is five. The symbolic meaning of this number fits beautifully with all that has been said about this character. It embodies the four elements common to all creation, synthesizing these through the One of the spirit, which is the special province of man. Five is also the number of humanity, because man has five senses and five fingers or five toes on each hand or foot. The number five makes a bridge between man's physical being and the archetypal mystery of numbers. There are many primitive societies which can only count to five; and in many cultures, in-cluding our own, five is used as a convenient measure for counting. Five has a magic quality; when you square it, it always returns upon itself. For this reason, the ancients called it a spherical number and thought of it as connected with infinity.

Five is three plus two: it combines the Trinity of spirit with the oppo-sites of human experience. As four plus one it also embodies the quintes-sence, that precious substance beyond the four elements, the four func-tions, the four directions, and all the other "fours" that define our earthly reality. It has been said that the first four numbers represent principles of reality, whereas the number five stands for Ultimate Reality. In this way it might also symbolize the psychoid level of man, the enduring sub-stratum of the psyche from which all else evolves.

Like all odd numbers, five is considered a masculine number, carrying a special valence of the spirit. The reason for this is that odd numbers, when divided by two, always leave the number one—the prime number of spirit—standing free. The One can never be destroyed or harmed by this division.

The Chinese sign for man is a pentagram. Man as the quintessence of human beingness is sometimes pictured as a pentagram, with outstretched limbs defining four points of this star, and man's head as the fifth point. The pentagram is the star of revelation that guided the Magi to the manger. It is also the star of universal synthesis. According to the position of its points, this symbol can represent order or confusion. With one point up, it represents the Saviour; with two points up, it represents Satan, the horned goat of the Sabbath. With its head down, it represents intellecutal disorder, subversion, and madness. As such, it is an ill omen, warning of black magic. Upright, the pentagram can guide and protect man. Magicians trace the sign of the pentagram on their doorsteps to contain the positive forces so that they will not dissipate, and it is also used to ward off evil spirits.

As we have already observed, the Pope also embodies powers which are both salutary and destructive. In one aspect, the inner Pope is the function in ourselves that governs our spiritual welfare, the inborn conscience that tells us when we have sinned against the Spirit; and like The Pope, this inner voice can be so dependable as to be virtually infallible. But as we all know this inner Pope can also cast a devilish shadow. Whenever that formerly "still small voice" within us starts screaming hysterically, denouncing the world in general and our friends and neighbors in particular, we may well beware. And if the illumination is adequate, we too can plainly see his horned shadow on the wall.

Fig. 35   L'Amoureux (Marseilles Deck)

9. The Lover:
Victim of Cupid's Golden Error

The lunatic, the lover and the poet
Are of imagination all compact. . . .

Shakespeare

In the previous card we saw two identical human beings, their backs to us, kneeling before a figure of superhuman dimensions. As priests, these two have turned away from the mundane world of the flesh and the practical problems of the Emperor's realm. They seek communion, not primarily with their fellow man, but with the Holy Spirit as personified in the Pope. He holds the center stage of their consciousness; they bow before his superior wisdom and his godlike power to guide their lives and absolve their sins.

What conflicts these priests may have are not clearly shown, indicating, perhaps, that at this point they are not yet fully conscious of them. By entering the priesthood as celibates, they may have successfully postponed any overt confrontations between spirit and flesh, so that their questions for the moment are more general and philosophical than personal and practical. In any case, the dramatic action of card number five is presented as a collective ceremonial rather than as an individual confrontation. In that ceremony, the priests as members of the papal audience play a relatively passive role: they have come to ask and receive, rather than to challenge and debate.

Card number six, The Lover (Fig. 35), marks a departure from this format in almost every way. First of all, it dramatizes a specific (and very human) problem: one young man involved with two women. For the first time in our Tarot series the central figure is not depicted as a magic or godlike personage. He appears to be an ordinary human being, facing the world and its dilemmas with his feet solidly planted in everyday reality. Unlike the twin priests pictured in the last card, he is shown as one individual with specific features and dress, thus symbolizing a step forward in the evolution of consciousness – a step toward individual awareness and away from externally oriented group consciousness. We might see this youth as a personification of the young and vigorous ego, ready to confront life and its problems on his own. There is no authority figure available here to whom he may appeal for help. He must therefore find within himself the strength to meet this confrontation; he alone must assume the responsibility for whatever action he takes in relation to it. Now his problem is out in the open light of consciousness where he (and we) can recognize its familiar triangular shape.

Earlier we learned from Pythagoras that the triangle was the first geometric form, symbolizing a fundamental human reality and connected with the soul. The symbolic truth of this statement is seen by examining the card under discussion. Here we see two human female figures. In the psychology of both men and women, male figures usually symbolize consciousness, intellectual attainments, and spirit; female figures (again in the psychology of both sexes) symbolize aspects of the body, emotions, and soul. It is obvious that the young man in this picture is emotionally involved with these women, body *and* soul. Perhaps one of them appeals more to his sexual passion whereas the other one holds in thrall his secret feelings and spiritual strivings.

In any case, each of them has a definite hold on the poor fellow, both literally and psychologically speaking. For, the more dignified woman on our left (the one wearing a headdress) has one hand possessively on the youth's shoulder, while the blonde on our right seems to touch him nearer the heart. Above these three, and apparently unseen by all, a winged archer also aims at the young man's heart. Perhaps the archer is related to the blonde or is an ally of hers in some way.

Inasmuch as all three actors seem unaware of this heavenly figure, let us leave him for the moment and look at the problem as it appears to the central actor. He is obviously immobilized between these two women who hold him, as in a vise. It would appear that each woman represents something important to him, for with his head he turns toward the figure on his right, or conscious side; whereas the rest of his body swings toward the blonde on his left, which is the side of the heart. He is seemingly torn apart by conflicting urges, divided within himself. If he were to turn his back on either of these two women now, he would leave half of himself behind. He would emerge torn asunder, bereft of this chance to disentangle the attributes and potentials projected on whichever woman he left and reclaim them as parts of his own psyche. These valuable powers within himself would remain in the custody of "the woman he left behind."

Each of these women exerts a hypnotic lunar pull, a magic attraction for him; each seems to belong to him in a compelling and mysterious way. He cannot seem to detach himself from either of them in outer reality because *both* of them belong as part of his inner reality. Ideally, by standing his ground, enduring the tension of his conflicting desires, and coming to know each of these women as an individual human being, this young man will ultimately free himself from their magic spell and "come to himself." Thus he will have taken a decisive step toward individuation. Otherwise his feminine, instinctual side will manipulate his emotions and his life.

No doubt these two women embody, in a more human and accessible way, the powers of the Virgin and the Great Mother. We met these powers earlier in a more archetypal form as the Popess and the Empress. It is interesting to observe that the first human embodiment of the yang principle was likewise presented in a dual aspect as two priests. Now the first human embodiment of the yin principle appears as two women. This is because it seems to be a truism of symbolic reality, as it is also of outer reality, that whatever is far away from our awareness appears blurred and confused.

Newly emerging consciousness, like physical distance, often produces a kind of double vision, so that what appears in dreams or other symbolic material at first as "those" women, priests, or whatever, will later come into focus as *one* individual. We have, in fact, just observed this process in operation, wherein the humanity first seen as the priests is now carried by one person, the Lover.

From his name and his overt situation, we know that this youth is emotionally involved with both these women. Both seem possessive and in his present unconscious state, he is therefore "possessed" by them. But, as to the specific details of the drama being enacted here, we have no clue. Unlike modern Tarot decks, which are usually accompanied by books that purport to decode their meaning, the Marseilles cards present a picture story without scenario. We are therefore quite free to fill in the blanks according to our individual insight and need and from our present cultural bias.

This being the case, I invite you to stop reading at this point and to write a scenario of your own describing what you see taking place in this card. *Who are these women? How does the Lover feel about each? Will he elope with one of them? If so, does he live happily ever after – or is there hell to pay?* Perhaps this card will stimulate you to write more than one scenario. I personally found it one of the most challenging in the Tarot deck. One of my many fantasies about it is as follows:

The woman on our left (the one with "the hat") I first saw as a mother figure, for she seems older and more dignified than the blonde. She may or may not be the young man's literal mother; but in any event she represents a motherly type, someone who offers his still tender young ego support, protection, and nourishment. Since she is pictured as having a hold on him, her ministrations are probably excessively overprotective and somewhat restrictive and demanding. They tend to keep him in an infantile pattern, offering him insufficient room to expand and grow. She has the potential of a glorious queen but also the sinister shadow of an infamous witch.

The young blonde, whose hair is so similar to his own, I saw as the young man's feminine counterpart, his *anima* or soul image. (The anima is Jung's term for the female figure in men's dreams and visions which represents the unconscious feminine side.) The fact that the young man and this figure seem to have similar hair indicates that unconsciously they have a relationship. She can be a princess or a harlot, royal and inspiring or petulant and demanding. In the service of her deepest self he could scale the heights, but in slavery to her vanity he could waste away his life.

Whatever the gifts that a conscious relationship with each of these women might offer, the young man is at present caught in an unconscious involvement with them both. Since they seem to him so powerful, he may have to tackle them one at a time. Probably his fascination for the "anima blonde" (however unconscious) will at least lure him away from the womb-like smothering of the mother type. He and his Eve may not live happily ever after, but through his involvement with her he will have severed the umbilical cord and taken an important step toward becoming a responsive and responsible human being. This might even include – much later – a renewed encounter with the motherly one, but this time not on the mother-son axis, but on a more adult basis.

In outer life, The Lover presents a situation which its central protagonist might be forced to resolve *now* by choosing one of these women; but, psychologically speaking, he must ultimately come to terms with the other woman, too, if he is to gain his full stature as a man. Whichever one he might leave behind him now will follow him to the ends of the earth, not necessarily literally – although this can happen – but certainly psychologically. All of us know from experience how demanding, haunting, even hounding any aspect of ourselves can become when we try to leave it behind us in the unconscious. "Hell hath no fury like a woman scorned." If cast aside, either of these ladies might turn on this hapless youth like Hecate's hounds of Hell. One has only to recall how the Eumenides (whose name, incidentally, means "gracious goddesses") pursued Orestes for his crime of matricide.

Since The Lover lends itself to many interpretations, scholars of various times and disciplines have projected a variety of dramas into it. Most of these tend to view its characters allegorically rather than symbolically. A standard plot (and one which still crops up in the literature) is that the lady on the left, seen as wearing a golden crown, personifies Pure Spirit, whereas the blonde represents Sinful Flesh. Past generations always admonished young men to renounce the latter and to cleave to the former. Unfortunately, many took their advice and suffered from the consequent onesidedness, until Freud came along and (again unfortunately?) spun them around in the opposite direction, where many remain. In any case today's cultural bias seems to favor the blonde.

As a result, if the Tarot Trump under consideration is viewed as a triangle involving wife *versus* mistress, the more matronly figure will get less sympathy today than in former times. Current public opinion makes it easier for a man faced with this dilemma to resolve it by discarding the mother of his children in favor of a more youthful model. Or, if he prefers, he may flaunt with impunity his extramarital affair in the public eye, so that the triangle pictured in The Lover presents fewer problems and conflicts than formerly.

Even the classic ménage à trois, which used to be lived out and borne as a guilty secret, now receives public sanction. This form of the triangle is even being expanded (and this quite openly) to become a *ménage à quatre, cinq, six,* or even *sept!* Thus the marital triangle no longer exists as a rack to try men's souls or as an alchemical retort to confine and transform emotions. No doubt the new social customs also offer positive values, but something very important may have been lost in the transition. For old Pythagoras spoke true: there *is* something fundamental and very human about the triangle. It would seem that by eliminating its stresses and tensions we may be losing an initiatory rite of great importance in the development of human consciousness.

One contemporary commentator[1] connects the Tarot Lover with paintings of the Judgement of Paris, another trial in which Eros played an important role. Whether or not there is an overt connection between the two, their psychological relationship is worth exploring. In the Greek myth, Juno and Pallas Athene each offered Paris cogent reasons, even bribes, to award her the golden apple for beauty. But Venus (the blonde in our picture) simply loosened her garment, revealing her charms, and gave her son Cupid the signal to let fly with his love dart. As a result, Venus won the apple and Paris won Helen. But as is always the case, the results of Eros' dart were mixed. Through this act Paris involved himself and his world in bloodshed and suffering, out of which nevertheless came insight and inspiration. For the Trojan War furnished the impetus for the matchless epics of Homer and the most awesome tragedies the world has ever known.

As we shall presently see, the role of Eros is ambivalent in this drama also. But the interesting thing to observe at this point is that it matters little how we furnish out the overt plot of The Lover. At the symbolic level, the meaning is the same in all cases: in order to be his own man, the Lover must free himself from the regressive pull of whatever womb seeks to contain him and step forth into manhood. As at any birthing, there will be bloodshed but there will also be new life.

Sometimes, the Terrible Mother of unconscious possessiveness is pictured as a dragon whom the hero must slay in order to rescue the princess, or whom St. George must vanquish in order to redeem the kingdom. In human form, the "monstrous one" (the lady on the left in our picture) becomes the cruel stepmother, wicked queen, or terrible witch from whose domination the prince must rescue Cinderella, Snow White, or the Sleeping Beauty, his "own true love," his other half, his soul. Whatever form the Mother archetype takes, the point is that the youthful ego conciousness must disentangle himself from her deadly fascination, rescue his soul, and embroil himself in life. It is through this trial that the Lover (symbolic of the ego) becomes the hero (symbolic of human consciousness in quest of self-realization).

At every level of interpretation, this card presents the ego with a challenge that marks an important step in his initiation. The Tarot Pope, one might say, offers initiation into the life of the spirit. In this card, the challenge is to connect this spiritual life with emotional life and, through passionate involvement in all of life, achieve a new relationship with others and a new harmony within oneself.

It is not by accident that the story of Eden equates carnal experience with the knowledge of good and evil, and in the Old Testament the act of sex is often translated by the verb "to know." *And Abraham knew Sarah and she conceived.* With such knowledge something new can be born. Since this is the case, the Tarot Lover is doubtless scheduled for some big insights . . . and some big conflicts. For, as Jung has repeatedly said, conflict is the essence of life and the necessary prerequisite for all spiritual growth. Life cannot be lived in the abstract. It is only through facing each individual conflict and suffering it through to its resolution or transcendence that we reach into our deepest selves. It is often a seemingly insoluble conflict (or a neurotic symptom caused by the repression of this conflict) that brings a person into analysis and starts him on the road to individuation. As the old alchemists knew, such conflict is the *prima materia,* the necessary first ingredient of all spiritual growth.

Eastern philosophy and Western Christianity would probably write very different denouements for the conflict pictured here, since Eastern and Western ideas about conflict are different. The Eastern idea is to eliminate suffering and arrive at perfect peace. Yoga hopes to attain this inner peace by denying the conflict and rising above it. Western Christianity views conflict as essential to salvation. In fact, its central image, Christ on the cross, epitomizes conflict and suffering as the means to salvation. In line with this central teaching of Christian theology, Jung felt that it is only through becoming conscious of our conflicts, facing them and suffering them, that genuine peace can be found. And this peace, far from being the ultimate goal, is a temporary achievement, a plateau as it were, on the long journey. For, each new awareness experienced along the way first presents itself as a new conflict. Paradoxically then, to go into deep analysis means to be plunged into deeper and deeper conflict but at the same time to experience deeper realms of awareness and peace.

In the case of the Lover in our Tarot picture, emerging from his cocoon of innocence may be the first difficult choice which life has presented to him. Fate, both kind and cruel, has offered this young man the precious *prima materia* for what the alchemists rightly called the Great Work. Seemingly he must make a choice, and he must take responsibility for whatever evolves from this choice; yet, as we can plainly see, a divine factor is at work behind his back and over his head which will influence his decision. Were it not for this winged archer with his magic dart, our hero might stand impaled on the horns of his dilemma until the end of time. Only the fire of e-motion can set him *in* motion.

Who is this winged archer? Is it Cupid with his bow and arrow? When I first started to type this paragraph, the Tarot Fool (a close relative of this fellow in the sky) played a trick on me. As a result, I made what the Freudians call a "Jungian slip." The words I was writing emerged from the typewriter as follows: "Is it Cupid with his bow and *error?*" As is usually the case, these unconscious slips speak true, for Eros' dart often involves us in a kind of confusion which seems disastrous from the viewpoint of logic. Uncontrolled, the fiery emotion it engenders can destroy all life, yet without the passionate intensity of emotional heat, no transformation can take place. Man's golden spirit would remain encased in cold lead.

The winged Eros pictured in this card is a powerful pre-Olympian figure, bearing little relationship to the sentimental boy bedecked in ribbons and lace on today's valentines. Eros was a more ambivalent character, akin to Fate, symbolic of the fatal power of attraction which brings opposites together. As such, according to Hesiod, he drew together the primal forces which created the universe, "bringing harmony to chaos" and making possible all life. He is the spirit – the incarnation of the life impulse.

Eros, be it noted, is a masculine figure. As James Hillman points out, its imagery in various cultures confirms this: "Kama, Eros, Cupid, Frey, Adonis, Tammuz, are all male; and the incarnations of enlightened love, Krishna, Buddha, Jesus – for all their gentleness and forbearance in regard to sexual fertility – are masculine. The eros principle is active and aimed. . . ."[2]

As sexual potency, the god Eros can cause strife, upsetting old patterns of law and order and thus making way for new life to come in. But Eros' fiery potency transcends mere sexual passion. In the alchemical sense, his is the "divine fire" whose maintenance is a necessary condition for the Great Work of ego transcendence and self-discovery. A deep experience of love often initiates the search for individuation. Literature offers many examples, of which Dante's love for Beatrice is perhaps the most familiar. In our personal lives, too, an involvement of the heart usually marks a significant turning point in our development. Such a love appears as an act of fate, an inescapable destiny. We all experience both the life-giving and death-dealing aspects of love's arrow. For, to lose oneself in love is a kind of death, the death of a purely ego-centered existence. It marks a new phase in one's evolution toward a transcendent center.

When we first introduced the Tarot Fool we spoke of his connection with this primal, fiery energy and of his habit of dancing unseen through the deck, furnishing new impetus to each card in turn. As we observed a moment ago, he popped into my personal world causing a "slip" from my conscious wording of a question about him. He plays similar kinds of tricks with the Tarot characters. Like Puck, he enjoys spying and meddling a bit in their affairs. In this Tarot picture, one can imagine him coaching Eros from behind the scenes. Well out of camera range, he dances, screaming with delight as the arrow flies: "Oh, what fools these mortals be!"

This connection between the Fool and Eros is not farfetched. Citing the archetypes Fool, Cupid, and Trickster, as aspects of the Alchemical Mercurius, Alma Paulsen writes:

> In whatever form he takes, Mercurius pricks our ego's self-centered isolation and brings us into confrontation with the wider world in which our fellow men exist, a world in which relatedness is required of us.[3]

Or, to quote Jung:

> . . . this many-hued and wily god did not by any means die with the decline of the classical era, but on the contrary has gone on living in strange guises through the centuries, even into recent times, and has kept the mind of man busy with his deceptive arts and healing gifts.[4]

Jung further describes this mercurial archetype and pinpoints its ambiguous role as follows:

> Eros is a questionable fellow and will always remain so, whatever the legislation of the future will have to say about it. He belongs on one side to man's primordial animal nature which will endure as long as man has an animal body. On the other side he is related to the highest forms of the spirit. But he only thrives when spirit and instinct are in right harmony. If one or the other aspect is lacking to him, the result is injury or at least a lopsidedness that may easily veer towards the pathological. Too much of the animal distorts the civilized man, too much civilization makes sick animals.[5]

Plato rightly called Eros "the desire and pursuit of the whole." But, as with any archetype, to live out this instinctual force on the outside without assimilating its meaning can result in imbalance. For example, the Lover archetype, if experienced solely as an external reality, might result in Don Juanism. In such a case the young lover seeks completion and wholeness exclusively via a never ending series of liasons, none of which brings him closer to the anima within, through whom alone the self-knowledge and stability he seeks can be realized.

Many of the ideas expressed here are implied in The Lover's number six. Six is unique in many ways. Pythagoras called it the first perfect number because its aliquot parts (one, two, and three) add up to itself. Six is also the number of completion. In the Genesis account, the Lord created the world in six days. Symbolically, six is pictured as a six-pointed star. This star is composed of two triangles, one with its apex pointing up toward heaven and the other with its apex pointing downward. The upper one is known as the fire triangle and the lower one as the water triangle. In this way masculine spirit and feminine emotion come together to create a new and shining form – a star to guide the hero on his journey. The upper triangle points to Eros, Fate, that quixotic figure in the heavens over which we have no control. The lower triangle points to earth, the realm of human choice. Here these elements are united to create the star of human destiny, a force which includes and transcends both.

This six-pointed star is the great symbol of Solomon, where macrocosm and microcosm intertwine, symbolizing the Hermetic maxim, "As above, so below." It is the sign of Vishnu. It represents the mystic marriage of Shiva and Shakti. It is also the shield of David and the Egyptian sign of regeneration. These ideas are reflected in the number six, which is the only number that is considered both masculine and feminine.

To return finally to the Tarot Lover as he appears in the picture before us: there he stands, poor guy, at the crossroads earnestly sweating out his decision. From our vantage point we can see that a colorful deus ex machina is already making his decision for him behind his back. Perhaps Puck is right. Maybe this young man *is* a helpless fool. Maybe free will is an illusion. Our power to choose is indeed very small. In times of emotional stress, fate does seem to decide our affairs "over our head."

Seeing the gods in operation, as we are privileged to do in this picture, makes one wonder if it is worthwhile for the Lover to bother trying to make a choice at all. On the other hand, one might equally feel that precisely *because* his power is so limited man is doubly obligated to use it as consciously as possible, and at every crossroads, to reach into the deepest part of himself to find his decision.

The significant point is that whatever the Lover decides and wherever he goes, he must take himself with him. It matters less, therefore, *which* *overt* path he chooses than *wherefrom* in himself he does the choosing. The moment pictured in this card is both a fateful and a fatal one. Let us hope that the young man gives it everything he's got – and that he prays a little!

Fig. 36   Le Chariot (Marseilles Deck)

10. The Chariot: It Carries Us Home

> The self uses the individual psyche as a means
> of conveyance. Man is propelled, as it were,
> along the road to individuation.
>
> Jung

Tarot Trump number seven (Fig. 36) shows a vigorous young king wearing royal insignia and a golden crown, who stands facing us in his chariot. In the Lover our hero was immobilized at the crossroads: this kingly personage seems to know where he is going and to be already on his way. Elevated above pedestrian humanity and framed by four posts, he commands our attention. Yet the title of this card is the The Chariot; by implication we are directed to consider his vehicle first.

The word "chariot" brings many associations to mind. It might be worthwhile to pause here a moment to explore some of your own. Do you think of Ben Hur and victory? Or Alexander and world domination? Or do you picture Apollo, the sun god, whose chariot still commands the heavens? Perhaps you also recall the luckless Phaëton, Apollo's son, who prematurely grabbed the reins of power and was felled by Zeus's thunderbolt. All of these associations belong to this card, for the chariot is a vehicle of power and conquest, one in which the hero can ride out into life to explore his potentials and test his limitations.

Perhaps your first association with this card was wafted up from the unconscious on a familiar musical phrase, "Swing low, sweet chariot, comin' for to carry me home. . . ." This, too, belongs here, for in a psychological sense a chariot *is* designed to "carry us home." The outer journey is not only a symbol of the inner one, it is also the vehicle for our self-discovery. We learn about ourselves through our involvement with others and through meeting the challenges of our environment.

Every journey offers numerous opportunities for new awareness and also exposes us to the risk of disorientation. To be alone in a strange land with no support from family, neighbors, or friends, creates a certain time of truth when the hero may discover who he really is – or be destroyed by the experience.

Whether or not he is conscious of this connection between the inner and the outer journeys, the youth who sets out to seek his fortune yearns also for a value that outshines mere worldly gold. Legends about Alexander's conquest of the known world connect it with the hero's triumph over the mysterious world within. And Odysseus' long voyage home has become a paradigm for the journey of self-discovery which finally leads back, after many trials and confrontations with strange humans, monsters, gods, and giants, to the center where one really belongs.

Symbolically, a chariot has heavenly powers which makes it an ideal carrier for the journey toward individuation. As Sun Chariot it is the Great Vehicle of esoteric Buddhism. In the Cabala it is the conveyance on which the believers mounted up to God and the human soul united with the world soul. Thus it can function to connect man with the godhead, as did Elijah's mystic chariot and Ezekiel's Chariot of Fire. The wheels of the Tarot chariot are put on sideways in a most peculiar manner. Ezekiel's chariot, too, had unusual wheels, which symbolized its numinous powers. Perhaps the Tarot means to show us that this chariot also has magical qualities. In its overall design it resembles illustrations of Ezekiel's chariot. Both are, in effect, movable thrones with four posts supporting an overhead canopy, a design still observable today in the palanquin on which the pope is borne during religious processions. That the central figures of the Chariot and the Pope may be intimately connected is evidenced by the similar layout of the two cards.

In card number five, the central figure, located in a square formed by two priests and two pillars, represents a fifth element, one which transcends the four compass points of ordinary reality. In the card presently under discussion, the king, set in a frame created by the four posts, also stands for a quintessential element. By birth a royal personage with special powers and privileges, a king is set above ordinary humankind. His golden crown, like a halo, connects him with the illumination and energy of the sun. Yet he is not pictured here as a gigantic figure, mounted immobile on some distant throne; he is drawn to human dimensions. He acts as a charioteer, a guiding force, centrally located within the psychic vehicle. Psychologically this could mean that these elements, formerly projected onto external figureheads (such as an emperor or pope), have been brought together and internalized as a guiding principle operating within the psyche itself. Unlike the masculine authority figures encountered so far, this king is a young man, indicating that he brings with him new energy and new ideas.

The throne on which the Pope sits is fixed. The king's chariot allows for greater latitude and flexibility. Its motive power is furnished by two horses. They make an odd-looking team, the one so violently red and the other so insistently blue. No doubt each of these beasts fancies himself as that "horse of another color" which kicks the traces of monotony, adding zest and spirit to our lives. These horses may symbolize the positive and negative poles of animal energy as they exist in all nature, the physical aspect depicted as red and the spiritual aspect as blue.

In card number six, two antagonistic women confront human consciousness and hold it transfixed, impeding the ego's progress until their conflicting elements can be resolved. Apparently the outcome is successful, for here the opposing factors are pictured as a team of horses pulling the chariot. Although by no means a perfect team, they are at least moving forward.

Who is in charge of these spirited beasts? One might expect that the charioteer would hold their reins. But to our amazement, these horses have no reins. Instead, the beasts appear to grow out of the vehicle, as if they and it were part of one entity: one psychophysical body in which the king is contained and borne along. To pilot such a vehicle successfully – and this without reins – would require suprapersonal powers. Perhaps the four posts act as a compass.

These posts and the canopy they support form a relatively secure space which protects the king and contains his energies. One might view them in terms of the four Jungian functions, which are the four essential pillars of the psychic being. Two of them are red and two are blue, echoing the colors of the horses. They indicate that the various aspects of the psyche are beginning to work together toward a common purpose.

Through facing the conflict pictured in the previous card, the Lover has now created a mobile psychic structure within which he can move out into life. At its center stands a young king symbolic of an active ruling principle. If he is a ruler of determination and purpose, he doubtless hopes that the overhead canopy which protects him from the elements will also prove impervious to the slings and arrows of that outrageous little Eros, whose activities we observed earlier. This young ruler will need all the protection and stability he can get, for he is piloting a dubious conveyance. Like all two-wheeled vehicles, it demands perfect equilibrium from its driver. Ideally this king might act as a living gyroscope, which may help to keep the opposites in balance.

If you'd like to have the experience of riding in such a magic conveyance piloted by such a human gyroscope, you can easily do so right now. Just shut your eyes and imagine that you are comfortably seated in this chariot in front of the king. Feel the jouncing, swaying motion of the vehicle and the king's reassuring presence. Hear the brisk, rhythmic staccato of the horses' hooves. Now imagine that you are turning a corner.

Lean with the sway. And now, if you are feeling relaxed and secure, keep your eyes shut and enjoy the inner landscape. For a starter you might imagine that you and your charioteer are driving through a green countryside. It is springtime. The sun is shining. *Did you hear that?* What was it? A meadowlark's song? A child calling?

Take it away! From here on it's your own private trip. *What happens next?* Maybe you stop to investigate the sound you just heard. Or maybe you continue on. Perhaps the scenery and weather change and you meet various people or animals and have interesting adventures. Or maybe you decide that you have had enough for one day and ask the charioteer to turn around and head for home. He will do exactly as you ask. You can stop any time you want. But when you want to take another trip, you now know where to find this charioteer. Just get out Tarot number seven, take a deep breath, shut your eyes, and set forth.

Much has been made in recent times of "tripping out." Books and magazines have expounded various methods for doing so. Marijuana, LSD, and other mechanical aids have been suggested as means to this end. Some of these are dangerous and illegal, and some are injurious to mental or physical health. Imaginative voyagers find these mechanical aids unnecessary. They have discovered that having this kind of experience is actually very simple. They know a secret with which all of us were born, but which some of us have mislaid. The secret is this: *each of us has a "chariot" available for use.* It is always there, ready and waiting whenever we want to embark on another imaginative journey into inner space. The reason it is so easy to imagine we are riding in this magic vehicle is that we are actually doing so all the time. To become aware of this, we need only shut our eyes and tune in.

Whenever we do this, we can sit near the charioteer and experience his essence: he is in tune with destiny. He neither drives nor is driven. He rides the uneven road with easy grace. His crown connects him with the golden understanding of the sun. Since he rules by divine right, he must receive divine guidance in some mysterious way. Perhaps as Papus suggests,[1] the two masks on his shoulders are the insignia of Urim and Thummim, objects used by the high priests of Israel to discover the will of Jehovah, or perhaps they are symbols for the guiding lights of the sun and moon.

A chariot seems an apt symbol for the carrying power of the psyche. The psyche is not an object, a thing; it is a *process*. Motion is its essence. Just as the outer landscape flows by when we travel, so before the inward eye images succeed one another in a constant motion picture. It is these which we tune in on when we shut our eyes to outer things and step into our chariots for a voyage within. These images, half glimpsed, sometimes wholly unrecognized, nonetheless shape our lives and actions. They contain the vital seed of life.

The new vitality inherent in The Chariot is seen in the new green shoots which have popped up in the foreground. As each plant is moved to self-expression by the unique image contained in its seed, so the image of the king in the chariot-body drives it forward to fulfill its unique destiny.

The Chariot's number seven connects it with fate, destiny, and transformation. In a pair of dice, the opposite sides of each die add up to seven. There are listed seven separate acts of creation in Genesis, and in the alchemical process there are seven stages of transformation under the influence of seven metals and seven planets. In Eastern philosophy we have the seven-fold law of divine harmony, and the seven chakras. Not surprisingly, then, The Chariot marks the beginning of a new era, and its energy carries us down to the second horizontal row which appropriately is named the Realm of Equilibrium.

As we shall see, every third card in the Tarot sequence similarly signals a transition of some kind. These are called "seed cards" because they contain the kernel for new growth. The Emperor is one of these cards. Others are: The Wheel of Fortune X; Death XIII; The Tower of Destruction XVI; and The Sun XIX. From their names alone one can easily see how each might initiate a new cycle of development.

The Emperor marks a transition from infancy and early childhood to youth, from containment in the mother and intimate family to containment within a larger social group dominated by powerful male figures symbolic of the masculine principle. The Chariot indicates another initiation. Here the hero sets forth as an adult to find his individual place in a wider social context. In doing so, he will discover his unique potentials and limitations. As Jung says: "Our personality develops in the course of our life from germs that are hard or impossible to discern, and it is only our deeds that reveal who we are."[2]

Through the Lover's action in resolving his conflict, a psychic structure is revealed: a chariot to carry him forward into life. Jung quotes an old alchemical text which may amplify the situation pictured in The Chariot. After the flood, it says, "the chariot should be brought to dry land."[3] It is as if the Lover, formerly submerged in conflicting emotions, has now set his psychophysical chariot onto a more solid reality where it can function in a purposeful way.

In the center of this vehicle stands a king, a guiding principle superior to ego consciousness. A king rules by divine right. His powers are both transcendent and immanent, both divine and human. Thus he can symbolize a mediating function between man and God. In Christian symbology, this figure appears in a more evolved form as Christ the King, God made man and dwelling among us – our most royal part.

The king pictured here does not have this stature; he is very young and inexperienced. But he carries within him the seed for future growth. His appearance indicates that our hero has a potential for self-awareness.

The ego (pictured earlier as the Lover) was manipulated by an archetypal figure in the sky whom he could not see. Now there appears a ruling principle operating from within the psyche. Within the breast of this young ego arise now intimations of a power transcending his limited consciousness. Here he catches his first intuitions, however fleeting, of his human psyche as an instrument through which the deeper self can become manifest. He catches a glimmer of his function as the carrier of consciousness and connects, for the first time, his personal fate with a larger destiny.

In view of the fact that the kingly charioteer plays such a central role in this drama, it seems strange that the card under discussion is called The Chariot rather than (as with all cards heretofore) named after its chief character. Since the Tarot seems to direct us specifically to do so, let us look again at the king's vehicle. At its front is a horizontal bar that cuts across it, dividing it almost in half to form a rigid barrier between "above" and "below." It separates the charioteer (guiding force) from his horses (the instinctual energy which can pull him forward). Below the crossbar is a shield bearing the initials "SM," the king's personal monogram, from which he is also cut off. This young man, so intent upon enacting his kingly role, has set himself above his animal nature and his individual identity as a mortal human being. He pictures himself as superior to his instinctual humanity.

Behind his chariot we can see the two problematic wheels whose symbolism was discussed earlier. However appropriate such wheels may be for chariots of fire that traverse the heavens, they are scarcely standard equipment for travels on terra firma. Of these wheels, and all else below, the king seems unaware. Dreaming of future goals, he ignores the small green plants directly beneath, which may be trampled by his horses' hooves. Even a king – and especially he – cannot successfully rise above the realities of his kingdom.

We have said that this personage represents an archetypal presence transcending the ego. If so, what has become of the ego-Lover? Ideally he might appear as a passenger in this chariot to help the king guide its course by keeping him in touch with the realities of human experience. But he appears nowhere in this picture. Since no other human figure is shown here, we must conclude that the young Lover has crowned himself king; he now pictures his individual human consciousness as the kingly charioteer who will direct his destiny.

Understandably, his victory over the women in the previous card has probably given the Lover an exaggerated notion of his masculine ego power. Unaware that he already bears the wound from Eros' dart, he now imagines that he is above all instinctual nature. Formerly stuck fast in earthly reality, he now pictures himself as wholly above it. Formerly entrapped by two women and exposed to unexpected events from the heavens, he now imagines that he travels free and alone, immune to all further encounters with the irrational. He evidently feels that he can ride roughshod toward whatever goal he may choose. If this new-fledged ego has the notion that he possesses such suprahuman rights and powers, he is destined for unpleasant surprises as our story unfolds.

The Chariot pictures a state of ego inflation which the ancients called hubris. In psychological terms this represents a condition in which the ego, or center of individual consciousness, identifies with (imagines itself to have become) an archetypal figure transcending human limitations.

In most Tarot decks The Chariot is presented as a wholly positive card with no hint that its central character may be suffering from an ego inflation. The one exception with which I am familiar is pictured here (Fig. 37).

Fig. 37 The Chariot (Old Florentine Deck)

In this quaint hand-made Tarot, the charioteer is revealed to be a naked babe, naive, defenceless, and vulnerable. He sits precariously atop his chariot displaying twin banners, one of which reads FAMA and the other VOLA. If fame and will power are indeed his guiding principles, this precocious hero is surely headed for disaster.

The crude wood block design that pictures him thus may be as old as it is wise. It belongs to a hand painted Italian deck of limited edition made in Florence. The original pattern from which this deck was struck has no doubt been handed down from generation to generation. This illustration gives us a good idea of how the first ordinary Tarot cards available to the average person must have looked. The crudity of their workmanship stands in marked contrast to that of old Tarots preserved in museums today, of which the fifteenth century "Sforza Tarot" (Fig 2, page 4) is an excellent example. The elegant design and painstaking craftsmanship of the Sforza cards (and others which have survived as family treasures) was the work of professional artists commissioned by royal or noble families to celebrate a marriage or other festive occasions. It is felt that the reason these commemorative decks have survived in such good condition is that they were rarely, if ever, used as playing cards, but were carefully preserved and enjoyed solely as works of art.

In Greek myths, mortals who overreached their human bounds as the Tarot charioteer is doing, were struck down by the gods. Even the gods and their relatives were subject to hubris on occasion. When Phaëton, son of Apollo, stole his father's chariot for a joy ride across the heavens, he was cast into the sea and drowned. Sometimes the fiery intensity of an overlofty inflation can only be extinguished by completely submerging consciousness in the vast sea of the unconscious (meaning symbolically death or its spiritual equivalent, insanity).

Apollo, too, was not immune to hubris, but he showed more self-awareness than his son. Recognizing his limitations, he sometimes sought additional guidance from heavenly powers. This is neatly depicted in a sculpture on a third-century Roman sarcophagus. It shows Apollo holding the reins of his Sun Chariot, assisted by several winged figures who are helping to guide his powerful steeds across the sky.

Unfortunately our young hero has yet to acquire such humility. Indeed, he seems to have cut himself off from any possibility of assistance from the heavens, since the overhead canopy erected to protect him from Eros' darts may also prove impervious to any help from above. His only hope seems to lie in the wisdom of those two masklike figures on his shoulders. Perhaps, like court jesters, they may whisper wise counsel into the ears of this headstrong young man before it is too late.

As things stand, he is doubtless riding for a fall. But with their help and a bit of luck, he may avoid a fatal accident. To be sure, he will probably land in the mud; but if he survives, the ego-Lover will arise restored to humanity, with that golden crown knocked from his head.

Despite the negative features of our hero's situation, The Chariot marks an important turning point in his development. Although he may be identified with his kingly self, he has nonetheless become aware of its existence. He has begun to experience this young and vigorous guiding principle as an entity *within*, a power with which he feels intimately connected. He no longer wholly projects all wisdom and authority on various bearded figures of suprahuman proportions, sitting immobile on distant thrones. He is beginning to feel that he need not necessarily cross oceans nor climb mountains in search of advice and counsel.

In myths and fairy tales, the central character is often represented as a young king or prince who functions as a guiding principle and savior for the collective group. It is often his task to slay a fierce dragon who had brought drought and famine to the land. Symbolically, such a hero-king represents that impulse to a higher consciousness which conquers the dragon-like inertia of the unconscious, restoring psychic equilibrium to the whole community. As a character of unusual courage, strength, and awareness, this young king enacts the drama of individuation for the relatively weak and unconscious group.

The hero archetype appears differently in various myths depending on the cultural climate of its host. Pictured here are three examples of famous mythical heroes (Fig. 38). Seen in the *upper left* is Superman, who obligingly repeats his miraculous feats "live" daily on television and movie screens, to the amazement of young and old alike. In the *upper right* we see a Japanese hero figure killing the Giant Spider, symbol of the negative mother principle, who tries to impede his journey toward consciousness by ensnaring him in her fatal web. The *lower picture* shows St. George killing the dragon, (another form of the Negative Mother), who jealously guards the treasure of consciousness from mankind.

Von Franz defines such a hero as "an archetypal figure which presents a model of an ego functioning in accord with the Self."[4] But this hero figure is not always in perfect equilibrium. As von Franz also points out, we can observe in such stories a constant interplay between the hero as self and the hero as ego.

To be sure, the hero of our Tarot story is not a mythic savior figure enacting a cultural drama. We see him as an ordinary human being about to set forth on his personal journey toward individuation. Nevertheless, much of what has been said about the fairy tale hero applies also to the central character of our story. If his inner kingdom is not to become a sterile wasteland, he, too, must slay the dragons of inertia; he, too, must strive beyond the limits of the unconscious human mass. His journey also will require personal courage, strength, and awareness.

Fig. 38   Three Heroes

Throughout his travels, as we shall see, there will also be a constant
interplay between self and ego. Since psychological development is an

ever moving process, there will be times (such as the moment pictured in The Chariot) when this young ego, inflated with some recent success, will become identified with his kingly self, losing touch with his personal humanity. At other times, out of contact with his inner king, our hero will become again the helpless mortal of The Lover, at cross purposes with himself, caught in some seemingly insurmountable conflict.

Traditionally, the story-book hero is presented with a series of trials, the first of which is to resist the temptation to be seduced from his quest by a regressive involvement with the feminine (pictured as mother, seductress, beast, or whatever). Small wonder that our hero has emerged from his first successful encounter in a state of ego inflation. But this is only the first of his trials. He will undergo many such testings before his human ego can establish its firm identity and maintain a lasting relationship with his inner guiding principle. In the course of these struggles he will change, and the kingly charioteer himself will assume new forms and wider dimensions.

To set forth on any journey takes courage and equilibrium. Commenting on the alchemical significance of the symbol "chariot," Jung has this to say: "If we take the loading of the chariot as the conscious realization of the four functions . . . the question then arises as to how all these divergent factors, previously kept apart . . . will behave, and what the ego is going to do about it."[5]

Obviously this is only the beginning. There will be many pitfalls along the way. One of these might be to act out the journey on the external level only, and by compulsive traveling, avoid the challenge of the inner quest and the repose necessary for its fulfillment. In times past it was usually the jet set or retired persons who indulged in this particular activity. But today many, chiefly young people, have become perpetual nomads who roam in a variety of vans, caravans, and chariots of their own devising. Some of these charioteers are no doubt embarked on a serious quest for meaning. But others wander endlessly to escape the emptiness of their lives.

It seems worthwhile pausing here to note that to interpret any Tarot card only at the literal level, ignoring its symbolic meaning, is to miss its message. For example, if one were to enact the archetypal situation of the Lover literally, he might try to free himself from the mother by plunging into one love affair after another, only to involve himself in a series of emotional triangles with no time to assimilate each experience. Like Don Juan, he would become stuck in an image of himself as the outer lover rather than moving forward to discover his own chariot and its inner king.

Another dubious detour on the road to individuation is the use of drugs. Some travelers, impatient with the plodding pace of their journey to enlightenment, attempt to hasten their development through depressing ego consciousnes by artificial means in order to more fully expose it to the unconscious. Quite apart from the dangers involved in "tripping out," such a drug-induced journey misses the point. As with any voyage into foreign lands, the essential ingredient is not the number of sights, sounds, personalities, and other stimuli to which one can expose oneself, but rather the degree to which one can interact with them and assimilate these experiences.

In a drug-induced state, ego consciousness is submerged, often completely awash with unconscious contents, with no power to challenge any monsters that appear nor to interact with other aspects of this unfamiliar world. Whereas if we pace our travels into this foreign land according to the natural rhythm presented by dreams, fantasies, visionary daydreams, and other spontaneous manifestations of the unconscious, we are not totally submerged by them, and our ego consciousness can interact and assimilate the material presented. In short, one might say that the difference between the imaginary chariot ride described earlier and a drug-induced "trip" is the difference between a voluntary journey and a kidnapping. While it is true that in neither excursion can we plan our exact route in detail nor foresee our specific destination, yet, with our eyes open and an experienced charioteer as guide, we are much less likely to get lost or suffer a latal mishap.

As Jung has repeatedly said, the psyche is a self-regulating system. As long as conscious and unconscious are both active, our chariot may sway violently from side to side but it is less likely to overturn as it might if only one of its team were operating. If you will look at Tarot number seven again, you will see how this is pictured. Although the horses that draw it forward do not seem to be pulling together, they may, by equalizing each other's tendencies, keep this conveyance on the road, whereas one horse of either color may land it in the ditch.

As these skittish horses suggest, and as the title of our next horizontal row reiterates, the problem uppermost now is equilibrium. All along the way our hero will be confronted with new and puzzling paradoxes which challenge his ability to maintain harmony and balance. One conundrum which is implicit in this card, and which will continue to tantalize his intellect (and ours) as we move forward together, is this: The puny ego is not the kingly charioteer; yet the more he becomes aware of this, the more he will blossom forth as a human being of royal stature. It is as if, when our hero can truly say ". . . not I, but my Father who is in heaven," then he can also say with humility: "I and my Father are one."

So here our hero sets forth at last. Let's not fault him if his journey begins as an ego trip. How else could he have found the courage to plunge into life?

An old adage, with which the reader is doubtless familiar, goes as follows: *the unexamined life is not worth living.* To this, some modern jester has added the following corollary: . . . *and the unlived life is not worth examining!* As we bid our hero godspeed, let's hope that he dares and does to the fullest, so that his adventures will be worth examining in the ensuing chapters.

Fig. 39   La Justice (Marseilles Deck)

11. Justice:
Is There Any?

Equilibrium is the basis of the Great Work.

Alchemical saying.

We have completed the top row of Tarot Trumps, those which comprise the Realm of the Gods, province of the major archetypes. (See Map of Journey, Fig. 3.) Now we are about to consider the middle row, the Realm of Equilibrium, so called because it stands midway between heaven and earth. We might see the top row as representing Spirit; the bottom row Nature; and the middle row Man, who functions as mediator between the gods and the beasts. Of all earthly creatures it is man alone who stands consistently upright, connecting heaven and earth, man who embodies and epitomizes the union of spirit and flesh. It is through man that the energies of yin and yang will be synthesized and expanded.

It is said that in six days the Lord created heaven and earth and on the seventh day he rested. As we have seen, the Realm of the Gods, of the primary archetypes which comprised the top row of our map, is completed. Its seventh card, The Chariot, pictures the hero embarked on his quest for self-realization. Now the Creator can rest, for we enter here the Realm of Equilibrium, where man begins to play a more active role in the on-going process of creative evolution.

The top row shows various magic or superhuman figures, culminating in the charioteer whose vehicle is guided by unseen powers holding unseen reins. Now the time has come for man to put his own hand to those reins, to participate in his own development in a more active way.

The first figure whose help we must enlist is Justice (fig. 39). The Fool says she is an optical illusion because (as any fool knows) there isn't any justice. Facetious as this may sound, it is a healthy approach to the formidable figure enthroned in this picture, for it is true that her scales will not weigh eye against eye nor mete out reward and punishment. The intricacies of human behavior are too various and subtle to be thus mechanically determined.

The golden sword which Justice displays is dedicated to a higher purpose than smiting the wicked, and it is much too splendid a weapon to use for splitting hairs in order to please the smugly virtuous. So we must reconcile ourselves to a world where cheaters seem to prosper and the innocent end up on a pile of dung. Job was not the first nor the last to complain about this, and admittedly the situation is not easy to accept. Despite centuries of human heartbreak to which all of us have added our own tears, we somehow still persist in the notion that in the end justice will triumph. Whether we locate her up in the sky or down in the courthouse, there she grandly sits in our mind's eye, incorruptible and omniscient, ready to spare us the bother of moral conflict by adjudicating questions of innocence or guilt.

"In the last analysis," our ancestors used to say, "virtue is rewarded." Maybe so. But we have by no means arrived at this famous last analysis, and some of the intervening ones are very long winded. Perhaps we had better find another approach to the problem of innocence and guilt, because the fact is that we all are innocent – and all guilty.

One meaning of the word "innocent" is *ignorant*. Only ignorance imagines that it is guiltless. So each of us has a double weight to carry: the burden of our innocent ignorance and the heavy guilt that inevitably comes with each new bite from the apple of knowledge. The two pans of Justice's scales stand empty, ready to accept and receive our human duality. Only to the extent that we also accept our twofold nature will we be able to approach and understand her.

The number of this card is eight, and the Arabic numeral 8 repeats in the verticle dimension the two round pans of the scales. Both the heavenly and the earthly axes are clearly involved in achieving balance.

The symbolism of Justice consistently stresses a harmonious union of opposite forces. Sitting on a throne, this large female figure symbolizes superhuman feminine power. Yet she holds a sword and wears a warrior's helmet, indicating that masculine discrimination and courage are also involved in her work.

Her sword is held neither in a position of defense nor of attack, but upright as one might hold a sceptre or other symbol of dominion. Perhaps Justice holds it thus to remind us of the flaming sword at Eden's gates, and to warn us that we can never again return to the innocence of childhood. We must now assume full responsibility for whatever knowledge of good and evil we have acquired. The weapon is enormous and made of gold, which further emphasizes its enduring value.

"I bring not peace but the sword." At this stage in the Tarot series, the hero has left forever the blissful peace of unconsciousness to assume the challenge and the responsibility which the sword represents. Now he must stop berating the Fates, or his parents, for their sins against him however real these may be, and assume the burden of his own guilt. Only the foolish person is interested in other people's guilt, since this he cannot change. If the hero still sees his parents as devils, responsible for his mistakes and limitations, he is just as bound to them as when he imagined them to be his infallible saviors. To sever the umbilical cord means psychologically to cut oneself free from all childish dependence, negative as well as positive. The ritual meaning of Justice's golden sword is sacrifice. As a sacrificial act, the hero must offer up his infantile reliance on his parents. Ideally, his parents also will use the knife to cut themselves free from their unconscious dependence on him. Only then can there be a balanced adult relationship between generations.

The sword also symbolizes the sacrifice of illusions and pretensions of many kinds. Here the young ego steps out of the Garden of Eden forever. He can no longer live the provisional life of impossible dreams. He must use the sword to separate fantasy from reality and the scales to weigh the myriad possibilities of perfection which his imagination envisions against the imperfect realities of space, time, and human energy.

The sword represents the golden power of discrimination which enables us to pierce through layers of confusion and false images to reveal a central truth. In this connection, one is reminded of King Solomon when he was confronted with two women, each claiming to be the mother of the same infant. He suggested cutting the child in half, whereupon the true mother was instantly revealed by her emotional reaction. Without using his sword, Solomon's keen insight cut through to the heart of the matter.

Justice holds her sword with the tip pointing heavenward. Solid and unwavering, it acts as a plumb line to keep her decisions true to the spirit. In her left hand she holds the scales, the two pans of which are connected by a horizontal rod, emphasizing the earthly axis. Unlike the sword, the scales are mobile, suggesting the relativity of all human experience and the need to weigh each individual event as a unique phenomenon. Its two cups, symbols of feminine receptivity and duality, contrast with the uncompromising single statement of the masculine sword. The respective vertical and horizontal lines of sword and scales together form the cross of spiritual striving versus human limitation, of idealism versus practicality – the cross upon which we are all impaled. Justice sits as mediator between these two realities.

She is looking neither at the scales nor at the sword; instead she stares straight ahead, almost as if in a trance. Plainly her function requires spiritual insight rather than intellectual eyesight. Sometimes she even wears a blindfold so that her judgment will not be confused by details nor her impartiality swayed by personal considerations. She is not concerned with matching up eyes and teeth. Hers is a more subtle weighing and balancing. For this reason Aleister Crowley called this card Adjustment.

Our courts of law are concerned primarily with adjustment. They maintain a working balance between the individual and the state and between one individual and another. The correct solution to a legal problem is not determined by means of a slide rule. The plaintiff who wins a lawsuit can never regain exactly what was lost, be it health, material goods, his precious time, or his honorable name. The court can only award him a compensation. Nature also offers compensations although, here again, exactly what was lost is never regained. For example: When one sense is impaired, the other senses become keener. Whatever is gained is never identical to what is lost, nor can it be said to be its precise opposite; but it compensates for the lost ability in some special way.

The psyche, like the body, is part of nature so, not surprisingly, it also seems to operate according to similar laws of compensation. The unconscious always acts in a manner compensatory to consciousness. A dream does not bring up a figure diametrically opposed to the conscious standpoint. Rather, dream figures *modify* the ego position. They are not enemies of consciousness; they are to be viewed more as opponents in a friendly game or as partners engaged in a mutual task. Jung stresses the fact that our dreams are *complementary* to the ego standpoint and that the word complementary means "to make complete." Completion, he adds, is not perfection. The psyche is a self-regulating system whose aim is not perfection but wholeness and equilibrium.

In *Psychology and Alchemy*, Jung shows how alchemy arose as a compensation to the orthodox Christian viewpoint. Similarly, these Tarot figures which we are contemplating can be seen as a compensatory reaction to the sterile intellectualism of the Church. Certainly their revival today acts as a happy counterbalance to our computer psychology. Their silent mystery helps to leaven the ponderous weight of today's statistical facts. Their pictorial messages help us to regain our equilibrium.

Our dreams also present us with pictures – moving pictures. Their characters dramatize aspects of ourselves of which our conscious mind is unaware. Like the two sides of Justice's scales, conscious and unconscious carry on a constant dialogue. Theirs is a teeter-totter behavior, an ever moving ballet of compensation.

Contemplation of the Tarot Justice suggests numerous ways in which the opposites work together. For example: the two pans of the scales are actually part of one continuum. The connecting bar holds them together *so that they can function*. It also keeps them apart *so that they can function*.

The way the pans oppose each other illustrates the original meaning of the word "opposite," which referred solely to location in space. Originally the word had no implication of hostility or conflict. On the contrary, it implied relationship, as in "the north wall of a room is *opposite* the south wall." Yet both these opposing walls act together to hold up the roof. The twin dishes of these scales exist in a similar friendly opposition to each other.

"In the beginning," both historically and in our own personal development, the opposites were originally undifferentiated. Everything was fluid and confused. Even consciousness itself was totally immersed in the watery unconscious. It took aeons and aeons for shining Excalibur to emerge from the waters and to find its way into the hand of Justice. The original identity of the opposites, as Alan Watts reminds us,[1] is exemplified by words still current in several languages. He cites the Latin word *altus*, which means both "high" and "deep"; the German word *Boden*, which means both "attic" and "ground floor"; and our English verb "to cleave," which means both "to hold" and "to divide." We have seen how Justice's sword can be used both as a principle to hold onto and an instrument to divide.

In times of stress, when we lose touch with the sword, we regress to our unconscious beginnings where the opposites are so close together as to be virtually identical. There, possessed by the watery Moon Goddess, our moods fluctuate as suddenly as her own. We laugh and cry in the same breath, or we turn a lover angrily from the door, dissolving immediately in tears of passsionate longing. If the pressures are intense, moral evaluations may become submerged in emotion. Then, in a rage, we may snatch the sword to maim and destroy our friends, psychologically speaking, or we may flail it about literally, committing senseless crimes or acts of passion.

Whenever we feel emotional tensions building up inside, meditating on Justice's golden scales can help us to regain our equilibrium. They are a beautiful pictorial statement of the way in which all opposites can function together creatively. Their golden bar separates them so that such forces as good and evil or love and hate remain differentiated, yet it holds them together so that they cannot split apart and become autonomous. Like Shakti and Shiva, the two are forever bound in a kind of dance. Perpetual, gentle motion is their essence. Fixed immobility would be stagnation. In contrast to the rather heavy-set figure of Justice, the scales pictured here are of a delicate and graceful design. I like to imagine Justice rising to hold them aloft (as she is sometimes depicted). When she does so, the scales' two pans constantly move and sway like a graceful mobile.

One Swiss Tarot deck pictures Justice herself in motion. She is dressed as a duelist, with her sword at the ready to engage in the sport of dueling, which is a ritual drama of opposing forces. This Swiss card dramatizes the fact that the kind of weighing and balancing that Justice symbolizes need not be only a post mortem to be performed in solitude after the fact. With practice, we can have it available in moments of stress, ready to meet the parry and thrust of our daily confrontations as they occur.

Each separation from the womb of unconsciousness brings with it a feeling of guilt, for it appears as a wounding of the whole. Conscience is an activity of the self; as such it is essentially a private and individual matter. Whether we project it into external laws or creeds, or whether we decide moral problems individually, the point at which one feels guilt is relative to his personal insight. I have friends who, in good conscience, can eat neither eggs nor meat. I know others who have no dietary restrictions but who feel guilty if they do not meditate regularly. Several young men of my acquaintance refused to fight the war in Vietnam, each for different reasons and each in a different way. Some of them cooperated with the war effort itself but refused to carry arms. Others faced imprisonment because they refused to cooperate in any way. Each of these young men made a different decision, and each decision was appropriate and, in that sense, right for him.

Jung says it this way: "It should never be forgotten – and of this the Freudian school must be reminded – that morality was not brought down on tables of stone from Sinai and imposed on the people, but is a function of the human soul, as old as humanity itself. . . . It is the instinctive regulator of action which also governs the collective life of the herd."[2] But, unavoidably, there is always a cultural lag between the expression of individual conscience and its codification into public law. And it is the task of the courts to bridge this gap by weighing and measuring individual pleadings against the written law. Surprisingly enough our courts are able to perform this difficult task more often than one might imagine. Perhaps this is because Justice, as she appears in the Tarot and in our tradition, is a woman, and such matters of conscience fall within woman's traditional province, which is feeling.

In his discussion of the feeling function in *Lectures on Jung's Typology*, James Hillman explores in detail the close relationship between justice and feeling. Calling the Bill of Rights "a document of the feeling function at its abstract best," Hillman says:

> Sometimes we forget that the application of law by a judge is an operation of feeling, and that laws were invented not merely to protect property or assure the priesthood and ruling-class of their power, but also to evaluate difficult human problems and to do justice in human affairs. Judging is a matter of feeling, just as in the temples of Saturn a balance was displayed, or as Saturn in a horoscope is said to be well-placed when in the sign of Libra. A Solomonic decision is not one brilliant stroke through the Gordian knot of complexities, but rather a judgment made by feeling.[3]

In the Marseilles deck, Justice looks a bit severe and uncompromising, but she did not always appear so. Shown here are two other portraits of this figure which reveal her more gentle, feminine side. The first pictures Maat, the Egyptian goddess of justice, truth, and law (Fig. 40). Her sym-

Fig. 40   Maat, the Egyptian Goddess

bol, the feather, connects her with the realm of air, and the spirit of birds. It was Maat's task to weigh the souls of the dead in order to determine their fate in the nether world. For this she placed her feather in one pan and the heart of the deceased in the other. Those whose hearts were burdened with more than a feather's weight of guilt were found wanting. To accomplish this task must have required discrimination as subtle and delicate as the balance of her scales. The second portrait shown here (Fig. 41) is from a fifteenth century Tarot, one of the earliest extant. It shows Justice as a young and beautiful woman in a flowered robe. Her appearance is extremely feminine, almost Venusian. This Tarot portrait clearly connects Justice and her scales with Libra, who is also ruled by Venus.

Actually, Justice is related to Libra through her ancestor, Astrea. The latter, a daughter of Zeus and Themis, walked the earth during the golden age and had a benign influence on mankind. However, man's subsequent impiety and strife drove the goddess to heaven, for disharmony went against her nature. She was given a fixed place in the heavens as Virgo. The constellation Virgo was divided later to create the astrological signs Virgo and Libra.

Essentially, Justice is not concerned with mathematical exactness but, like Astrea, with harmony, functional beauty, and a kind of truth which transcends rote measurement. "Beauty is truth, truth beauty. . . ." The reality of Keats' famous poetic equation, inspired by the Elgin Marbles, is again immortalized in the columns of the Parthenon, which appear to be exact but are actually concave at the top. If their proportions had been measured by the rules of logic rather than in the scales of harmony, these columns would have seemed grossly top-heavy. Their dimensions were created to correspond to the limitations and perspective of the human eye. Through their imperfect truth, they have achieved immortal beauty.

This kind of poetic justice is one which, apparently, operates in the courts of both heaven and earth. It is not concerned with grim moralizing nor with questions of crime and punishment. It is, rather, dedicated to the restoration of universal laws of harmony and creative balance. Greek philosophy and poetry echo this idea. According to Heraclitus, "The sun will not overstep his measure; if he does, the Erinyes, the handmaids of Justice, will find him out."

And here is Ovid's account of the downfall of Phaëton:

> Phaëton, son of Apollo, begged to be allowed to drive his father's sun-chariot across the sky for one day. Apollo tried to dissuade him from such a perilous undertaking, but the youth persisted and was given the reins.

> No sooner had the morning course begun than the celestial horses realized that they were being driven by an inexperienced

Fig. 41   Justice (15th century deck)

hand. They ran wild, left the familiar track, and coursed so high
that the heavens smoked; then plunged so close to earth that
the snowy crowns of the mountains melted, the forests blazed,
the rivers dried up, and even the sea shrank.

> Finally, *to save the universe from destruction*, the king of gods
> was forced to hurl a thunderbolt at the runaway chariot, and
> Phaëton plunged flaming to earth. Apollo, sick with grief, hid
> his face, and for a day the heavens were without a sun.[4]

According to Ovid, Phaëton was cast down, not in a spirit of vengeful
punishment, but rather as an act of mercy – to restore the equilibrium of
nature – "to save the universe from destruction." Ideally it is in this spirit,
too, that our courts of law administer justice – in order to preserve the unity of the whole rather than to punish the individual.

Certainly the Justice pictured in our Tarot seems unmoved by wrath
or vengeance. She is not a goddess to be worshiped but a mediator to be
used. As such, she sets her scales to fit the human equation, for it is man's
nature, as it is her own, to create a harmony between opposing forces. To
move forward spiritually one must be constantly alert to the power of these
hidden forces. To forget this would be to tip the inner scales toward author-
itarianism or toward slavery. In either instance, man would forfeit his
humanity.

Identification with any archetypal force is a primary danger. To imagine that we are the beauteous and beneficent Astrea is to inflate ourselves
to a heavenly position above our fellow man. And as with the other Tarot
Trumps, there is also the subtle danger of enacting the card's archetypal
meaning on the outside thus ignoring its inner significance. When this happens in relation to Justice, one might spend his energies on taking his
problems to court rather than using them to examine and correct his own
inner disharmony. Undoubtedly we all can recall individuals who appear
to be "justice prone," those benighted souls, by turns imposing and imposed upon, who are constantly embroiled in legal battles or hopeless cru-
sades of one sort or another.

As noted earlier, courts of law are useful tools for achieving certain
kinds of compensation and social equilibrium. But sometimes it seems that
what is sought in the courts is actually not on trial there. At times, perhaps,
we mistakenly turn to a human court in search of answers which can only
be found in a heavenly one.

We all need to contact a principle of universal harmony and
equilibrium in order to be reassured that, behind all the seeming injustices
of life, there is a Higher Court of appeal, one Supreme Judge with whom
we can plead our case. In his *Answer to Job*, Jung stresses Job's loyalty
and faith in this One Power and his insistence on a confrontation with its
embodiment, Jehovah. One of the major revelations in Jung's treatment
of this subject is that each of these protagonists is revealed as needing the
other. God needs man; man needs God. This idea is also beautifully ex-
presed in a well-known poem by Gerard Manley Hopkins. Its title, "Thou

Art Indeed Just, Lord," is based on the twelfth chapter of Jeremiah. One of the most moving poems in the English language, it begins:

> Thou art indeed just, Lord, if I contend
> With thee; but, sir, so what I plead is just.[5]

Although the scriptural source is translated in a variety of ways, Hopkins' choice of the word "if" in the above offers us the insight that the Almighty can fulfill our image of a Higher Justice only *if* we contend with Him. Hopkins seems to say that justice is in fact *created* only by this kind of dialogue between God and man.

Perhaps at the deepest level of human experience, God and man are the two pans of a set of scales which, acting together, create the One Equilibrium – the lasting harmony whose beauty and truth alone endure.

Fig. 42   L'Hermite (Marseilles Deck)

12. The Hermit:
Is There Anybody There?

Who looks outside dreams; who looks inside wakes.

Jung

In Jungian terminology, The Hermit (Fig. 42) pictures the archetypal Old Wise Man. Like Lao-tzu, whose name means "old man," the friar pictured here embodies a wisdom not to be found in books. His gift is as elemental and ageless as the fire in his lamp. A man of few words, he lives in the silence of solitude – the silence before creation – from which alone a new word can take form. He brings us no sermons; he offers us himself. By his simple presence he illumines fearful recesses of the human soul and warms hearts empty of hope and meaning.

According to Jung, such a figure personifies "the archetype of the spirit . . the pre-existent meaning hidden in the chaos of life."[1] Unlike the Pope, this little monk is not enthroned as spokesman and arbiter of general laws; unlike Justice he holds no scales with which to weigh out the imponderables. This figure appears to be very human, walking common ground and carrying only his own small lamp to light his path.

Like the Fool, he is a wanderer; and his monk's cowl, prototype for the Fool's cap, connects these two as brothers of the spirit. But the pace of this old traveler is more measured than that of the young Fool, and he is not looking over his shoulder. Apparently he no longer needs to consider what lies behind; he has assimilated the experiences of the past. Neither does he need to scan distant horizons, seeking out future potentials. He seems content with the immediate present. His eyes are wide open to receive it – whatever it is. He will apprehend and deal with it according to his own illumination.

His lamp seems an apt symbol for the individual insight of the mystic. Whereas the Pope's chief emphasis lies in religious experience under conditions prescribed by the Church, the Hermit offers us the possibility of individual illumination as a universal human potential, an experience not confined to canonized saints but available, in some degree, to all humankind.

The flame which the Hermit holds could represent the quintessential spirit inherent in all life – that central core of meaning which is the elusive fifth element transcending the four elements of mundane reality. He offers us that inward light whose golden flame alone dispels spiritual chaos and darkness.

This flame is partly hidden behind shutters to protect it from the elements, and perhaps also in order that its brightness will not blind the Hermit or dazzle those whom he meets along the way. He knows that his fire must be carefully controlled in order to be useful. Contained, it can warm him and protect him from the beasts; uncontained, the fire itself might become a rapacious beast devouring the Hermit and destroying his world.

One of the shutters of the Hermit's lamp is blood red, so that the light filtering through it is touched with the color of flesh-and-blood humanity – tinged with the passion and compassion distilled from the experiences of a lifetime. The other colors of this card also bespeak a natural approach rather than an abstract, philosophical one. The friar's robe is sky blue, color of the Heavenly Spirit as it expresses itself in nature. The robe's lining is yellow, suggesting a connection with the "philosopher's gold," that nugget of meaning buried deep within earthly nature and human nature – that precious substance which it was the alchemist's goal to uncover and release. As the Hermit's living flame attests, he himself has achieved this goal.

Although they may use different words to express their aims, many today seek this treasure, both literally and symbolically speaking. On the literal level, energy depletion and overpopulation have spurred scientists to discover new ways to liberate the giant forces locked up in atomic structure. And a parallel impoverishment of the human spirit, with its consequent deprivation of psychic energy, has forced increasing numbers of human beings in all fields to look within in order to tap what Jung has called "the undiscovered self" with its reserves of primal energy and ancient wisdom. It is a time of universal seeking at many levels.

In myths and fairy tales, whenever the hero in search of the treasure has lost his way or reached an impasse, the Old Wise Man usually appears bearing new light and hope. In a similar way, such a figure can materialize in our own dreams. This is especially true whenever our personal dilemma echoes a similar impasse in our culture generally, since the Hermit has found within himself what has been ignored or lost by society. It is no accident, then, that in the cultural midnight of our times, the Tarot Hermit should have reappeared, sudden as a star, to shed his ancient light upon our contemporary problems.

Although his reappearance may seem abrupt, it is actually long overdue. Since the turn of the century, our poets have seen the darkness coming. Over fifty years ago, William Butler Yeats warned:

> Turning and turning in the widening gyre
> The falcon cannot hear the falconer;
> Things fall apart; the centre cannot hold;
> Mere anarchy is loosed upon the world,
> The blood-dimmed tide is loosed, and everywhere
> The ceremony of innocence is drowned;
> The best lack all conviction, while the worst
> Are full of passionate intensity.[2]

What better description of our present dilemma? The infamous "Watergate horrors" of our outer history were but tiny ripples in a sea of confusion and corruption in which the inner spirit of men everywhere has become engulfed. The ceremony of innocence is indeed drowned, and anarchy is loosed upon the world. As Yeats foresaw, the debacle is no longer merely a matter of greed and lust for power – these are peripheral concerns. It is "the centre" that will not hold. Something is dead wrong at the core of life. We are empty of meaning.

According to Jung, the urge for meaning is the prime mover through whose impetus all other aspects of the psyche, including ego consciousness itself, are brought to birth. Unlike Freud, who contended that the urge to selfhood is a derivative of sexual libido, Jung believed that the impulse toward meaning exists at birth as an instinct in the human psyche. He felt that man is by nature a religious animal. If we accept this premise, it becomes increasingly clear that the present devitalization of conventional religious symbolism, coupled with the breakdown of the family structure, has left us all with an insatiable void at the very center of our being. Small wonder that we are prey to false gods and that our "passionate intensity," unused, stands at the devil's service. Viewed in this light, Watergate – and even fascism – become alarmingly understandable.

Man's overpowering need is to feel passionately about something – to find meaning and purpose as part of a grand design transcending mere ego concerns – to dedicate one's life and energies to the service of a higher authority. As we know, we necessarily begin our journey toward consciousness by projecting this authority onto external figures in our environment (father, president, king, emperor, pope, priest, judge, guru, etc.). In our Tarot series thus far, we have followed the hero as he experienced some of these archetypal figures in sequence. Now he confronts the Hermit. If he is open to this friar's message, he will follow his example by beginning to discover and nurture his own inner spark as the Hermit has done. If the hero is ready to observe and listen, the Old Wise Man can help him to find a lamp of his own. But if the hero is not yet ripe for the Hermit's message, he may misinterpret it in a variety of strange ways.

As we have observed in connection with other Tarot figures, one way to misunderstand the meaning of such an archetypal personage is to view the figure literally rather than symbolically. In the case of the Hermit, for example, our hero might grow a beard, don monk's garb and sandals, and set forth – perhaps to some distant land – in search of a guru on whom to project perfect wisdom and enlightenment. Or he may find a ready-made guru close at hand already equipped with a group of similarly attired followers whose ranks he joins.

Failing to find someone on whom he can project the Old Wise Man, the hero may, in desperation, cast his young and inexperienced human self in the role of this archetypal Ancient One. If this happens, the seeker may himself start a cult, attracting his own followers. Or, crushed by the burden of an archetypal role which he finds himself ill equipped to carry, he may retreat from life altogether. We can then discover him sitting cross-legged in the public square, remote and vacant-eyed as any statue, "stoned" out of humanity and normal human responsibility.

To identify oneself with any archetype at any age can have disastrous consequences. One can become inflated, out of scale with human dimensions; or, crushed by the weight of the impossible, one can be reduced to a vegetable-like depression. In either case, one's human beingness is distorted. The plain fact is that an archetypal character is *supra*human. One can never become an archetypal figure. Any such attempt is hopeless – and has elements of tragedy. But when a young person replaces the cap of a happy-go-lucky fool with a hermit's cowl and scowl, the result seems doubly sad: for it would seem that he has not only aimed at the impossible but has, in the process, neglected the golden potentials properly belonging to youth. It is as if his inner calendar had somehow become badly scrambled.

But of course it is our outer calendar and culture which is askew, our time which is "out of joint." In the current muddle, our search for the Old Wise Man who could help us right things has made Hamlets of us all – one minute flailing our swords about irresponsibly and the next minute buried in conflicting soliloquies. Each of us is vaguely tempted to feel that (O cursed spite) he alone was "born to set it right."

Human beings of all ages, awash in the cultural morass and cut off from the god within, will seek the spirit everywhere – often in unholy places. As Hitler's Germany revealed, when faced with confusion, many people will snatch at the first proffered uniform and set forth in goose step to save the world. That all wars are, in a sense, "holy wars" is axiomatic. It is equally true that even the robes of a peaceful monk or guru have the potential to become a uniform as deadly as any government issue.

We seek out the Old Wise Man because it belongs to our instinctual nature to do so, and we are driven toward him by the fears and anxieties of modern civilization. One of the most compelling of these, as W. H. Auden observed, is the terror of anonymity. In his poem "The Age of Anxiety," Auden characterized our age and spoke for us all when he said:

> The fears we know
> Are of not knowing. Will nightfall bring us
> Some awful order – Keep a hardware store
> In a small town . . . . Teach science for life to
> Progressive girls – ? It is getting late.
> Shall we ever be asked for? Are we simply
> Not wanted at all?[3]

But of course we have been asked for – on many occasions. *Is there anybody there?* Walter de la Mare's famous Traveller asked this question half a century ago. We have all been confronted with it at various times in our lives but no one, I think, has caught the drama and mystery of this confrontation more poignantly than de la Mare:

> 'Is there anybody there?' said the Traveller,
>   Knocking on the moonlit door;
> And his horse in the silence champed the grasses
>   Of the forest's ferny floor:
> And a bird flew up out of the turret,
>   Above the Traveller's head:
> And he smote upon the door a second time;
>   'Is there anybody there?' he said.[4]

But no one answered the Traveller. Unlike T. S. Eliot, who pictured us as "hollow men," incapable of response, de la Mare envisioned our inner house as filled with "a host of phantom listeners" who hear the Traveller's knock but do not respond to his call. One can see these listeners clearly as they cower, silent in the shadows, frozen in fear, not unlike many city dwellers today who refuse to answer the cry of a stranger in the streets lest they become "involved." *"Is there anybody there?"* Perhaps the bearded Hermit pictured above has returned to offer us another chance at this question as he holds his lantern aloft and peers into our darkness.

If confronted in reality, with such a figure on a dark night, we might pause in the shadows to observe him before stepping forward to identify ourselves. One look into the kind eyes of this old monk tells us that he has not trudged painfully down the centuries to preach to us or to berate us for wrongdoing. One feels that he really wants to know who, if anybody, is "there," and that he will accept any answer we are ready to give – even our silence if that is all we have to offer. His eyes look fearless and calm, full of wonder – wide open. We might imagine that his mind and heart are equally open. His expression seems to combine the wide-eyed wonder of childhood with the patience of experience.

In many other ways, too, this stranger seems to embody aspects of the two opposite poles of being. His beard and lamp suggest masculine learning and spirit, the fiery yang, the positive pole of energy. Yet his flowing robes and gentle demeanor indicate a close kinship with the dark yin, the earthly feminine nature. Like St. Francis, he must feel an intimate, tender relationship with Brother Sun and Sister Moon and all the birds and beasts; yet at the same time this Hermit must have the stamina of a St. Anthony to withstand the myriad devils, the monstrous aberrations of the human spirit, which beset man in his loneliness. Perhaps the Old Wise Man has come back to teach us the forgotten art of solitude.

Today, the notion that we are a lonely crowd has become a cliché. Psychologists have told us how we mask our stony isolation in a spurious compulsive togetherness which has little connection with human relationship. They have shown us how we defend our tender insecurities with the armor of social conformity. Sometimes we can see these terrifying insights dramatized in a way that shudders the bone. Caught in a subway or in traffic during what is euphemistically called "rush hour," one suddenly finds oneself part of a horde of faceless zombies, each immobilized in public solitary confinement, each encased in his own status symbol, each armed against all human contact, yet each protected against being truly alone.

Being a nation of extraverts, we have naturally turned to group therapy as an antidote for this isolation. Filled with hope and courage, timorous souls dutifully program themselves around the group dynamics circuit from weekend encounters to body awareness, from lessons in joy to group meditation and back again. At each station of this sterile pilgrimage, the lost ones pause sadly to inquire of one another: "Who am I? Touch me. . . feel me. . . react to me. . . tell me who I am!" Have we so strayed from our inner core of being that we exist solely in relation to others?

It seems increasingly difficult for us to accept the lonely path to self-realization. The art of individuation, of becoming one's unique self, is (as the name implies) an intensely personal experience and, at times, a lonely one. It is not a group phenomenon. It involves the difficult task of disentangling one's own identity from the mass of mankind. To discover who we are, we must ultimately withdraw those parts of ourselves which we have unwittingly projected onto others, learning to find deep within our own psyches the potentials and shortcomings which we had formerly seen only in others. Such recognition is facilitated if we can withdraw from society for brief periods and learn to welcome solitude.

As if in compensation, such periods of introversion are usually accompanied by a lively imaginative life. Since we lack outer companionship, the characters of our inner world take over the stage. These personalities often appear as vivid entities. They engage us in spirited dialogue; they clamor to have us paint their portraits or tell their stories in words. Sometimes they sing to us, bringing fresh and enchanting songs. Here the Hermit can be of help. If, inflated with such a flow of creative inspiration, we try to rise above our human selves, he can bring us down to the ground again and help us choose from this golden fire the one small flame that fits our own unique human lamp.

Today, increasing numbers, disenchanted by the spiritual barrenness of our outer landscape and the impersonal collectivity of our present society, are consciously searching for the hidden light within; and there is evidence that human beings generally are ready to welcome more opportunities for introversion than our culture encourages or provides. For example, recent studies show that most commuters resist attempts to organize car pools or to provide rapid transit service because, they say, the time spent driving to and from work is their "only chance" to be alone. Perhaps, with the Hermit's help, we might dare to allow ourselves and others opportunities for creative introversion under more favorable circumstances. Such periods of solitude are not morbid or antisocial. They can return us to the world with renewed energy for action and a keener sense of our own identity and our special role in relation to the world.

In *Ego and Archetype,* Edward Edinger discusses the meaning of the word "solitary" as it is used in one of the Gnostic Gospels. He points out that in the original Greek the idea of "single" or "solitary" can also be translated as "unified." As an illustration, he quotes the following passage from *The Gospel of Thomas:* ". . . .I (Jesus) say this: 'When (a person) finds himself solitary, he will be full of light: but when he finds himself divided, he will be full of darkness.'"[5] But, unavoidably, anyone who achieves this kind of inner unity must pay the Promethean price of loneliness, guilt, and suffering. In "The Relations between the Ego and the Unconscious," Jung amplifies this idea as follows:

> The Book of Genesis represents the act of becoming conscious as the breaking of a taboo, as though the gaining of knowledge meant that a sacred barrier had been impiously overstepped. Genesis is surely right, inasmuch as each step to a greater consciousness is a kind of Promethean guilt. Through the realization, the gods are in a certain sense robbed of their fire. That is to say, something belonging to the unconscious powers has been torn out of its natural connections and has been subordinated to conscious choice. The man who has usurped the new knowledge suffers, however, a transformation or enlargement

of consciousness, which no longer resembles that of his fellow men. He has certainly raised himself above the human level of his time ("ye will become like God"), but in doing so, he has also alienated himself from humanity. The pain of this loneliness is the gods' revenge. . . .[6]

As Jung makes clear elsewhere, the alienation experienced by the solitary does not imply an estrangement from his human beingness. It means simply that he no longer remains contained in the *participation mystique* – the primitive unconsciousness shared by the mass of mankind. Such a person need not remain aloof physically from the world and its problems; on the contrary, having attained a secure inner unity, he may feel better able to expose himself to the chaos of current events, with less fear of becoming confused by them or submerged in the prevalent mass unconsciousness. Ideally, such a person will continue to be involved in life – but in a new way. That this renewed involvement in life need not necessarily manifest itself in world-shaking words or deeds is charmingly depicted in this illustration (Fig. 43). Its subtitle is: *Zen Hermits Jocularly Performing Household Tasks*. It seems to me that these little monks have something important to tell us about what true individuation might mean. Although new insights may bring with them new ideas and fresh opportunities for creative action, yet essentially at the core of self awareness lies the ability to accept one's own life – however simple and unpretentious – and to perform its necessary tasks in a matter-of-fact way. I personally find it much easier to make sententious pronouncements than to sweep the floors and do the dishes in a "jocular" way.

In the sense described earlier, one who has attained any degree of self-realization is a "solitary" in relation to the general run of mankind, and he is destined to remain so until the others – each in his own time and his own way – reach a similar stage of enlightenment. Even more of a hermit, says Jung, is mankind itself, for the human race – by virtue of its unique capacity for consciousness – stands alone on this planet, cut off from all other living creatures by its psychic differences from them. Jung describes man's predicament in this way:

> He is on this planet a unique phenomenon which he cannot compare with anything else. The possibility of comparison and hence self-knowledge would arise only if he could establish relations with quasi-human mammals inhabiting other stars . . . . The differing degrees of self-knowledge within his own species are of little significance compared with the possibilities which would be opened out by an encounter with a creature of similar structure but different origin. . . . Until then man must continue to resemble a hermit. . . .[7]

Fig. 43   Zen Hermits Jocularly Performing Household Tasks

As to whether or not our explorations into outer space will ultimately bring us face to face with humanoid creatures whose insight may further enlarge our present limited aperture of awareness remains to be seen. Jung's comments indicate that such a confrontation might be a welcome aid to greater consciousness.

Traditionally, mankind, confronted with an impasse in his conscious evolution, has looked to the heavens for salvation. In former times this help was experienced as the divine intervention of a god or godlike savior figure who would miraculously descend from the skies. Today, the Savior archetype may be projected into the Saucer Folk, humanoid creatures of presumably superior consciousness who some imagine to be hovering over us like guardian angels, awaiting a propitious moment to descend and illuminate our darkness. But if indeed such creatures do exist, obviously their advent alone cannot save us. As history has shown, a "savior" can, at best, only help us find ways to help ourselves. So, while some leap into the skies to investigate the reality of magic circular objects bearing Old Wise Men embodied in new, strange forms, the rest of us might turn our attention to inner space in search of the archetypal counterparts of these images; for it is they who are the moving forces behind our outer search — who are, in fact, its raison d'être.

In his essay "Flying Saucers: A Modern Myth," Jung discusses at length the psychological significance of our current interest in Ufo's. He emphasizes the idea that (quite apart from whether or not these circular objects will be proven to exist in reality) it is already a fact of considerable psychological significance that human beings all over the world report seeing such objects in the skies and experiencing their presence in dreams and visions. Likening the Ufo to the mandala, the sun wheel, and "God's eye," Jung goes on to say this:

> On the antique level, therefore, the Ufos could easily be conceived as "gods." They are impressive manifestations of totality whose simple, round form portrays the archetype of the self, which as we know from experience plays the chief role in uniting apparently irreconcilable opposites and is therefore best suited to compensate the split-mindedness of our age. It has a particularly important role to play among the other archetypes in that it is primarily the regulator and orderer of chaotic states, giving the personality the greatest possible unity and wholeness.[8]

Viewing the Ufo phenomenon as a compensation to our group-oriented culture, Jung says: "The signs appear in the heavens so that everyone shall see them. They bid each of us remember his own soul and his own wholeness, because this is the answer the West should give to the danger of mass-mindedness."⁹

The Tarot Hermit, then, might symbolize mankind, that lonely wanderer on this earth, carrying only the small lamp of present-day consciousness to illumine the increasing mass-mindedness which threatens to overwhelm his world. Man stands at the brink of a potential revolution in human consciousness. Perhaps the needed help will in fact descend from the skies; perhaps it can only be found in the heavenly constellations of his own inner being.

The Hermit's number nine reflects many of the ideas expressed here. Standing alone, supreme among the single digits, nine represents the height of power attainable by a single number. In the context of Jung's comments, we might view the number nine as symbolic of the peak of consciousness attainable by the hermit, man, until he can confront another creature with similar capacities for awareness – or until he can uncover, within his own psyche, dimensions of consciousness hitherto unknown.

In Arabic numerals, the number nine (written as a circle with a number one as its tail) presages the number ten in which the energy contained in the heavenly circle is brought down to earth to stand beside the number one, thus forming a new configuration initiating a new cycle of expanded dimensions. When this happens psychologically, the present small flame of the Hermit's lamp will undoubtedly be transformed into an illumination of cataclysmic proportions.

On our planet, the number nine is also the number of human gestation, a period of preparation necessary for the creation of a new human self. Ours is a time of preparation and gestation, it would seem. Until each of us has access to his own small lamp, we might well be blinded or destroyed by a too sudden influx of heavenly illumination.

Historically, too, the number nine is connected with the idea of gestation and initiation. Apollonius of Tyana, the Greek Neo-platonist, considered it a sacred number. His disciples wore this number as an amulet and set aside the ninth hour as a time of silence. He forbade his followers to mention the number nine aloud. The Eleusinian mysteries initiated candidates throughout a nine-day period. For the Romans, also, nine played an initiatory role. They celebrated a feast of purification for all male infants on the ninth day after birth. They buried their dead on the ninth day and held a feast called "Novennalia" every ninth year in memory of the dead. This custom is echoed today in the Feast of Novennae, a Catholic service of prayer celebrated for nine successive days to pray the soul out of purgatory.

Mathematically, also, nine has mysterious qualities, for it always returns to itself. For example: $1 + 2 + 3 + 4 + 5 + 6 + 7 + 8 + 9 = 45$, the sum of whose digits is 9. Similarly, $9 + 9 = 18 = 9$. And 9 multiplied by each digit from 1 through 9 produces a result that reduces to 9. It is easy to understand why nine is the number of initiation, because it symbolizes the initiate's own journey into self-realization. In whatever circumstances the initiate begins his journey, and whatever experiences he may encounter along the way, he also must, in the end, return to *himself*.

As in the case with all archetypal figures, if we fail to heed their message voluntarily we may be forced to do so. For example, failure to answer the Hermit's call to introversion may result in the enforced solitude and isolation of a physical or mental illness. But if we can observe and listen, we can learn from this Old Wise Man the art of voluntary withdrawal from society and the ability to effect a smooth transition back into the world again when it is time to return. When the outer world demands our attention, we won't be caught in black introversion like a bear hibernating in some dark cave; nor will we be compelled to forced extraversion, constantly wearing the smiling mask of an innkeeper because our true identity is still hidden away unmined in the cave of our being.

The way the Marseilles Hermit is pictured emphasizes his ability to make a smooth transition between withdrawal and return. He is a solitary, yet he wears the habit of a religious order with which he evidently keeps contact, and he is pictured en route which emphasizes his ability to move easily between his two worlds.

As the rhythm of life's breath is measured in alternate inhalation and exhalation, so our need for introversion and extraversion follows a similar rhythmic pattern. The Hermit is a master at helping us to discover our own particular pulse. The way his curved staff and his garments flow together suggests a rhythm as natural as breathing. The friar's peaceful steps echo the serene tempo of his meditations. Seen in the half-closed light of reverie, this Hermit appears to move steadily; the motion of his withdrawal holds within it the gesture of his return. He seems to be telling us that life is a process, not a problem; that Tao is a journey, not a goal.

Buddha said; "The world is a bridge; walk across but build no house upon it." With his lantern to guide his steps, the Hermit needs no house. He is not burdened with personal possessions. Today, many emulate his freedom from encumbering household goods. Shedding the accumulations of a lifetime, they move into mobile homes, campers, or vans, and head for the woods hoping to recapture the serenity of a lost Walden. Unfortunately, disposing of our psychological burdens is not so easy. The following story may be illustrative. It concerns an eager young man who, having divested himself of all worldly goods, crossed the ocean in order to consult a famous guru.

"Oh, Master," began the earnest seeker breathlessly. "I am ashamed not to have brought you a present. But I now live empty handed."

"I know, I know," the Sage said quietly. "So put it down, Son, put it down."

Our Hermit is doubtless such a sage. It is obvious that his lamp pene-
trates spiritual rather than temporal darkness, for the sky above him is light
and cloudless. His insight pierces through our arbitrary divisions of space
and time to reveal the meaningful pattern of the ever present now. He sees
so deeply into the present that he clarifies all time, past and future and their
interrelationships. That this wise man, like Merlin, possesses the seer's
magic power to master the riddle of time is further evidenced by the fact
that in some of the older decks he holds an hourglass and is called Time.

This Traveler is using his lamp to illuminate his own darkness. His
light shines for others too, of course, but not deliberately so. If lives are
brightened by his passing, it is because he has helped in perhaps the only
way one human being can help another – by being fully himself. For me,
this Old Wise Man illuminates the wisdom of an often misunderstood
prayer attributed to the Friends: "God spare me from being 'helpful.'"

Today, perhaps more than at any previous time in history, we are
walking on wholly new ground. In our world there are no fixed paths – no
central illumination usable by all. Each of us must find some way to strike
his own spark. As history demonstrates, we cannot depend on authority
figures "up there" to supply illuminating answers to life's questions. In recent years, we the people of the civilized world have sat helpless before our
television screens watching, appalled, as real-life sagas of corruption and
defeat, depression and revolution, overflowing all social, political, and na-
tional boundaries, invade our complacent living rooms to touch our conscience and awaken our spirit. During all this time, the Hermit may have
been standing in the wings, awaiting his cue to step forward. Perhaps the
darkness is beginning to lift so that the Hermit's silent message can shine
more clearly for us all: "Each of us must discover his own inward light. The
minute we hand over our insight and responsibility to some imagined Big
Brother – be he political leader, cultist, psychologist, or guru – we have
lost ourselves, our cultural identity, and our very humanity."

If you don't get it from yourself, where will you go for it? This ancient
query rings loud in our ears. Perhaps, more than ever before, we need to
realize that the light we seek is not a ready-made flame which will some
day be borne to us from outer space on a flying saucer. We need to nurture
the understanding that the Holy Spirit is not something outside us,
something which we, with luck, may some day attain. The Spirit is, rather,
a tiny flame, created anew by each human being in each generation. With
every breath we stir the *pneuma;* we recreate the Spirit. The Christus is
"begotten not made," which is to say that He is newly born in us all.

Prometheus stole the original fire from heaven and brought it to
mankind. I like to think that the Hermit is returning some of this holy fire to
its source. That is what each of us does when he recreates the Spirit.

Is there anybody there? The Hermit waits for our answer.

Fig. 44   La Roue de Fortune (Marseilles Deck)

13. The Wheel of Fortune: Help!

Everything goes, everything returns; eternally rolls the
wheel of being. . . . Crooked is the path of eternity
                                                    Nietzsche

The Realm of Equilibrium began with an allegorical figure, Justice, representing a general concept. This was followed by The Hermit, who embodied her wisdom in a more individual way. Now our focus swings from
the intimate contemplation of personal illumination back again to the wider
panorama of universal principles, culminating in the central question of
fate versus free will, as presented by The Wheel of Fortune (Fig. 44).

In this card we see two odd-looking animals revolving helplessly on
Fortune's ever turning Wheel. The animals wear human dress. Is the Tarot
trying to tell us that we, like these animals, are trapped in the endless predestined round of Fortune's Wheel? Or does this card offer us other, more
hopeful messages?

Previous commentators have explored the geneology of the two
beasts on the Wheel in search of clues. The golden creature rising on our
right is usually connected with Anubis, the dog-faced god of Egypt who
weighed the souls of the dead. He is thought of as a positive, integrative
factor. The monkey-like animal on our left is usually associated with
Typhon, the god of destruction and disintegration. Most commentators
see Typhon as a negative character in the pejorative sense, and they are
pleased to note that this rascal is pictured as on his way down, whereas
Anubis (the good guy) is rising to the top.

Although it is true that Typhon is on his way down, he will not thereby
be banished from the scene. Before we know it, the Wheel will have turned so that Typhon will ascend to the position of top dog, whereas Anubis

will be forced to serve time in the nether regions. Both creatures appear to be fixed to this Wheel, condemned to a senseless see-saw. The helpless look on Typhon's face indicates that he is not in the picture by choice. He seems to plead with us to accept him as a necessary passenger on the Wheel.

It looks as though we are dealing once again with our two friends, the opposites, representing two kinds of energy. Previously, we saw these pictured as the Chariot's team of horses and the two pans of Justice's scales. Now they appear as two forms of unconscious animal libido caught in the never ending cycle of nature: the yang urge to dominate and organize, and the yin tendency to receive and contain. As we know, both are instinctual in all of nature, and both operate continuously in all of us. That these animals wear human clothes might mean that the forces which they represent are partially civilized – they have evolved towards consciousness to a point where their energy is now available for human use.

Card eight shows the yin and yang pans of Justice's scales guarded by a goddess with impartial wisdom and upright sword. Here we see them as living animals caught in a system ruled over by a dubious-looking monster of dark countenance who holds its sword in a careless, haphazard fashion. Whatever power commands Fortune's Wheel, it is evidently amoral. Certainly it bears little relationship to justice. One is reminded of the court jester who mocks authority by wearing the king's crown.

This dark creature with its golden crown sits on a platform above the Wheel, set apart from its activity. Although the monster guards the Wheel, it does not furnish its motive power. The helpless creatures in tandem motion seem to provide that energy.

Traditionally, it is the hero's task to befriend the helpless victims of monstrous fate and free those in captivity. Confronted with the situation presented here, he must liberate these beasts, it would seem, without killing or maiming either of them, for both are necessary to keep the Wheel in motion. Or, to put this in more psychological terms, it is the task of all human beings striving for consciousness to liberate animal energies previously caught in the repetitive instinctual round, so that this libido can be used in a more conscious way. The first step in this direction must be to come to terms with the dark creature sitting above the Wheel who holds these beasts in thrall.

Like dragons and similar mythological animals who guard a treasure difficult to attain, this creature is a monstrous conglomeration of bestial parts representing a hideous aberration of the natural order. Perhaps it symbolizes the primal chaos that existed before the first creation. The animal is naked, yet it wears a golden crown which suggests that although its energy is primitive, its power is divine. It has a monkey-like face and the body and tail of a lion. Its red batlike wings mark it as a night prowler related to the Devil, whom we shall meet in card fifteen. To see a sword in the hands of such a monster is alarming. Only its golden crown offers hope that this strange beast may have a redemptive aspect. It is in fact a sphinx.

At first it seems odd to think of the creature as a sphinx. Certainly its dark, almost impish face is very unlike the serene, golden countenance of its familiar Egyptian counterpart. The two sphinxes are actually opposites. The Egyptian figure is a masculine symbol, associated with the sun god Horus, whereas the sphinx pictured here is a female character, closely related to the sphinx of Greek mythology which represents a negative mother principle.

If we take the Empress of Tarot number three as symbolic of a more positive mother principle, then we might see the monster before us as her chthonic counterpart. One might view the creature sitting atop the Wheel as a parody of the Empress. Like her, she wears a golden crown, but it rests absurd and incongruous above her monkey face, and the careless impertinence with which this sphinx holds her sword aslant seems to mock the Empress with her sceptre. Even the sphinx's monstrous red wings suggest the "angel wing" shape of the Empress's throne. That the Wheel of Fortune appears directly below the Empress on our Map of the Journey (see Fig. 3) further underscores the idea that the sphinx may represent her shadow side.

The negative mother sphinx has been immortalized in the Oedipus myth where she waylays its hero, demanding solutions to her riddles before allowing him to proceed. Moreau's painting *Oedipus and the Sphinx* (Fig. 45) pictures this sphinx as a seductive harpy who fastens her claws into Oedipus, impeding his progress, sapping his vitality, and threatening his very life. This predatory harpy still lives on today in those women who pounce upon one at every opportunity with a series of demanding questions.

The meaning of the hero's confrontation with the negative mother perched so smugly atop the Wheel of Fortune may be clarified by exploring the symbolism of the Oedipus story as elucidated by Marie-Louise von Franz in her book *The Problem of the Puer Aeternus.*[1] As von Franz points out, although Oedipus succeeded in solving the riddle propounded by the sphinx, he did not thereby redeem his instinctual nature from her power. On the contrary, he still remained in the grasp of cruel fate, as helpless as any animal revolving on the wheel of instinctually predestined behavior. For, he did indeed eventually kill his father and marry his mother, thus enacting his fate exactly as it had been prophesied. The psychological outcome was equally fatal. By killing his father (symbol of the dominant masculine order) and marrying his mother Queen Jocasta (symbol of the ruling feminine principle), Oedipus identified with the feminine, burying his masculinity in the womb of the Great Mother.

As a matter of mythical fact, it was precisely *because* Oedipus stopped to answer the sphinx's riddle that he thereby won Jocasta as his reward.

Fig. 45   Oedipus and the Sphinx   (Moreau, Gustave, 1826-1898. Oil on canvas. The Metropolitan Museum of Art, New York, Bequest of William Herriman, 1921.)

The irony here, as von Franz makes clear, is that Jocasta herself is a human manifestation of the archetypal Devouring Mother whom Oedipus thought he had vanquished forever when he bested the sphinx at her word games. His superior intellect was punished, for the gods are jealous of such prideful behavior.

For us also, the intellect is to no avail in confronting the sphinx on the Wheel. We cannot free our creative energies with mental gymnastics nor outwit our human fate by clever answers. As von Franz reminds us, it is a familiar plot of the unconscious to distract the hero (human consciousness striving towards wholeness) by proposing philosophical questions at the very moment when he most needs to confront the demands of his instinctual nature. By falling for the sphinx's word games, Oedipus saved his intellect but sacrificed his phallus, his earthly masculinity.

Throughout human history, man has made the heroic attempt to free himself from the automatic control of animal nature in order to discover a pattern behind the meaningless conundrum of endless birth and decay, and to find transcendental significance in the seemingly quixotic ups and downs of Fortune's Wheel. The first step in the hero's quest is universally depicted as an act committed in defiance of the negative mother.

In both Eastern and Western cultures, the female principle is experienced as an implacable and monstrous power presiding over the rotating fortunes of mankind. In his classic work *The Great Mother*, Erich Neumann illustrates and discusses two pictorial examples of this powerful motif.[2] The first of these, originating in the East, is the Tibetan Wheel of Life, which is held in the cruel grip of the dark witch Srinmo, the female demon of death. The second, of Western origin, is called The Wheel of Mother Nature (a figure from the Middle Ages), ruled by three-headed Time, who stands winged and immobile at its top.

One of the earliest known Tarot decks presents The Wheel of Fortune in its most common medieval form (Fig. 46). Four human figures are fixed to this wheel. The one on his way up is saying *Regnabo* (I shall reign), and he is growing a pair of ass ears. The figure atop the wheel has full-grown ass ears. He holds the ruler's sceptre and says *Regno* (I reign). The figure on his way down has lost his ass ears and has grown a tail. He says *Regnavi* (I have reigned). The bearded old man at the bottom, the only fully human figure of the four, is pictured on his hands and knees. He says *Sum sine regno* (I am without reign). Fortune is enthroned in the center of this wheel. She is blindfolded and wears a pair of golden wings, indicating both her indifference to man's plight and her divine power to control his destiny. Plainly, she makes asses of those who, out of hubris, elevate themselves above her. She takes her revenge by flinging them down on all fours like beasts of the field. The old man under the wheel, like Oedipus at Colonus, has fallen from high estate; but, again like Oedipus, through this experience he has at last become truly human.

Fig. 46   The Wheel of Fortune (Sforza Tarot)

The Wheel is often pictured more outspokenly as a corrective for hubris. Medieval art shows it quite frequently as an instrument of torture on which the proud are broken in hell while the devil turns the handle. The Greek story of Ixion deals with a similar theme. According to this myth, Ixion was bound by Zeus to a fiery wheel because he made so bold as to fall in love with Hera, Queen Mother of Olympus. As with Oedipus, the gods inevitably punish those who, forgetting their human limitations, aspire to make cuckold the kingly masculine principle (symbolized in this story by Zeus).

It is worth noting in this connection that Ixion, inflated with pride, ascended so far above the human station that he impregnated a cloud, thus producing the first centaur, a monstrous creature with the head and shoulders of a man and the body of a horse. The physiology of the centaur is such that, although he presumably possesses human intelligence, his head is so placed that he is incapable of observing and modifying his bestiality, for his animal nature and sexual parts are located behind (in the unconscious), where they cannot be confronted and integrated in a human way. As this myth further implies, creations begotten within the clouds of prideful inflation are destined to be monsters. When Ixion, denying his human origins, rose above himself to cohabit with the gods, he did not thereby create a superman of godlike proportions. Instead, he produced a malformity, a psychic split – a bifurcated creature whose brute energy and sexuality had regressed to the animal level.

Since the Tarot sphinx herself is such a monstrosity, her very presence warns us of the fate that awaits all who try to elevate themselves above earthly creatureliness and escape the round of human fate. If we cannot rise above our fate, we must find some other way to deal with the sphinx and her Wheel.

By now it must be apparent that this sphinx, like all females – be they goddesses, witches, humans or monsters – is full of contradictions. On the one hand, she presents us with a heroic task, the challenge of human beingness, daring us to find meaning in a system seemingly propelled by mere animal energy. On the other hand, she deliberately distracts us with her conundrums, deflecting us from our quest and sapping our strength with her insatiable demands.

The Tarot Wheel reflects the paradoxes of its ruler. The beasts held captive on its spokes remind us of the limitations imposed by our animal nature. Yet at the same time they present the challenge of transcending these limitations – pleading, as it were, for our help. We can see the Wheel both as a circular container that holds all nature within certain prescribed boundaries and, conversely, as the very source of energy by which we might consciously transcend these boundaries. The trick seems to be how to liberate some of our captive energy for conscious use without falling prey to this sphinx's wiles.

Meanwhile, there she sits like all of her breed, smiling her smiles and crooning her conundrums: "What is it," she whispers, "that has devil's wings, a cloven hoof, and a tail, but carries a sword and wears a golden crown?" By now we know that it would be fatal to succumb to the creature's alluring invitation to indulge in verbal summersaults. As with the puzzling questions presented by our dreams, the conundrums of The Wheel can best be solved by looking at the images presented and viewing these in a variety of contexts. Each Tarot card, like each dream, poses questions the answers to which it alone holds. Only by letting our imagination spin with the sphinx's Wheel can we avoid getting caught in her web of circular thinking and free our energies, so that we can reach behind the questions she poses to the hidden meanings she guards.

So let us meditate on the Wheel before us. It is, first of all, an energy system whose essence is motion. Thus we may use it (as indeed it has been used throughout human history) as a kind of moving diagram for the inter-relationship of many facets of nature and human nature. Life presents itself here as a process – as a system of constant transformation equally involving integration and disintegration, generation and degeneration. Up and down are not shown here as two fixed forces playing at tug of war. Instead we are presented with the whole spectrum of infinitesimal graduations from upness to downness, all of which blend subtly into one another like the seasons of the year.

As the Wheel's turning reveals, nothing exists per se: everything is becoming and everything is dying – not sequentially in time, but all at once. Even as we read these words, some of our body cells are dying and new ones are being born.

Pondering the Wheel's eternal revolutions can help us to experience the simultaneity of all opposites – even the seemingly irreconcilable forces called birth and death. By meditating on this card we can experience a world not created in time – a system endlessly beginning and endlessly ending. As we quiet our breathing and synchronize our heartbeats to the motion of the Wheel, we can connect with our own birthing and dying – not as two discrete happenings which will mark the beginning and the ending of a linear experience called life, but rather as two ever present aspects of a continuous process whose revolutions stretch forth into infinity. At these moments one can experience the Wheel as moving throughout all time, spinning forth continuous cycles of birth, death, and rebirth. At such times we no longer find its motion a sterile, repetitive gesture, a ceaseless undulation from day to night and back again. We begin to feel how each succeeding sunrise brings up a wholly new day and how each night's darkness envelops us newly in its black womb. At such moments of insight our bones and sinews tingle with new life and our blood sings with the sure knowledge that we arise each day newborn.

There are many pairs of opposites which a wheel dramatizes. For example: motion and stability, transience and transcendence, the temporal and the eternal. If we watch a wheel's turning, we see how these opposites function together – how the wide motion of its outer rim, which is its raison d'être, would be impossible were it not for the stability of its fixed center.

A wheel's small, closed hub offers little room for expansion and differentiation. It is not open to new light, fresh influences, or wide swings of tempo. It is slow and dependable. By contrast, its fast-moving outer rim is exposed to many new sights, presented in rapid-fire sequence. On the wide circumference of this outer rim one might locate a hundred observation points, each with a different view from all the others. The rim is dizzy with new energy and ideas, but it lacks stability and unity.

To put these ideas into another language, one might say that a wheel's hub represents universal laws and its rim the individual applications of these laws; at the center is the archetypal and eternal, at the rim the specific and ephemeral; at the hub the subjective and ideal, on the periphery the objective and real. It is as if the primal creative urge of the godhead, the idea at the center of all manifestation, spins itself out to the periphery where it appears in a thousand different guises. The center expresses the undifferentiated wholeness of pure being whose essence is unchanging, imperishable unity, whereas the rim offers modification, experiment and motion – with, of necessity, less unity.

I find the Tarot Wheel an excellent vehicle to help me visualize and clarify what I think Jung meant by the often misunderstood terms "introvert" and "extravert." The introvert I picture as living close to the Wheel's center. His first concern is with inner space – the primordial images of this inner world, those archetypal figures instinctual to the human psyche whose essential nature remains constant throughout the generations. The extravert I see as living closer to the outer rim where he is attracted first of all by outer space. He likes motion, exploration, adventure, and he is stimulated by people, places, and planets.

For the introvert, all these stimuli appear as a threat. Before he can contemplate the outer world, he must first connect with himself by exploring his inner depths. He discovers life's meaning inside before he can take his place amid the jumble of events which the external world seems to present.

For the extravert, of course, it is exactly the other way around. For him, the excitement of external events is at once attractive and meaningful. It is the chaotic images of the inner world which he dare not approach directly. He reaches immediately toward the outer object, and through his experiences with outer stimuli, he connects with his inner being. To sum up: One might say the introvert learns *to do by being* and the extravert learns *to be by doing.*

Obviously (and fortunately), a "pure" example of neither the extraverted nor the introverted type exists in nature. A wholly introverted person would be planted at the hub, immobile as a vegetable. A wholly extraverted person would live entirely on the outer rim, where his energies would spin off in all directions like the sparks from a pinwheel, leaving only a burned-out empty shell.

The attitude types are not a rigid classification; they merely indicate an inborn tendency, more pronounced in some than in others. As one grows in self-knowledge, his native bent becomes modified. Understood and accepted, one's attitude type can become a source of strength rather than a limitation. Ideally, a mature person develops all facets of his personality so that it is difficult to determine by his external behavior alone which is his native type. For example: that charming woman so at ease on the platform as she addresses thousands may be an introvert, whereas the rather quiet, scholarly looking man sitting next to you in the audience may be an extravert. In other words, the determining factor is not how one behaves overtly but, rather, how one got there. Looking at the introverted public speaker and the extraverted listener as figures on an imaginary wheel, we might say that each has moved a little toward the other so that they now enjoy a common world. Each can speak the other's language and share his environment without losing touch with his own home base.

In his book *The Tarot for Today,* Mayananda uses the center and the circumference of the Tarot Wheel to illustrate some differences between the Eastern and Western philosophies.[3] The Eastern culture, he says, is near the Wheel's center; it is a world af archetypal principles slow to change. Western culture he locates near the Wheel's periphery where these archetypal ideas have been spun out into objective reality. The introverted Easterner is concerned with general principles, eternals, unity, stability, and pure being. The extraverted Westerner is more caught up in worldly objects and experiences. His is a world of motion, freedom, diversification, and specialization. The Easterner begins near the center of the Wheel and works outward; the Westerner begins near the circumference and works inward.

Viewing the Eastern and Western temperaments and cultures in this way can help us to see what Jung meant when he said that Eastern meditation techniques adopted wholesale are inappropriate to Western needs. One cannot live creatively by adopting a style that is not his own. Contrary to what the thinking mind might suppose, it is not by adopting the ways of his opposite number that each type can relate to the other. Rather it is precisely by "doing his own thing," *but more consciously,* that each will come to himself and will ultimately find his way to contact the other's world and speak his language. Then these two can cooperate and share their two worlds harmoniously.

For these two opposites, as for all others, the Wheel makes an ideal projection holder because its function is wholly amoral. Unlike the scales which Justice holds, the Wheel's circular form cannot be used to weigh and measure relative values. Because it is not a linear system, its rim has become a symbol *par excellence* for equality and interrelationship. No position on it is preferable to any other.

I once heard a black woman express this idea in one pithy sentence: "One good thing about a merry-go-round [she said] there's no place on it for a Jim Crow car!" For this reason the rim of a revolving wheel is often used as a device upon which to arrange a series of equal and related concepts, in order to demonstrate their equality and the subtle way that each partakes of the quality of those on either side of it and stands in contrast to its diametric opposite on the wheel's rim. The spectrum of colors, the four elements and their properties, the seasons of the year, and the signs of the zodiac are sometimes arranged in this way on a moving wheel.

In the *I Ching,* an ancient oracular book of Chinese origin, the sixty-four hexagrams that spell out the meaning of any given moment are pictured on the rim of a wheel in conjunction with the seasons of the year. This arrangement, and the fact that the work is called *The Book of Changes,* underscores the idea that the climate of each moment, like that of the seasons, belongs to its time and is equally right and necessary. To the Oriental mind, which is not bound by linear thinking, there is no such thing as a "bad" hexagram – nor for that matter, a "good" one. Each belongs in its season. For example, even such a hexagram as the one called "Stagnation" is not to be considered negative in the pejorative sense, for stagnant waters already swarm with new life. Without such periods of gestation, nothing new can evolve. As a revolving wheel shows, each spot on its circumference already contains the germ of its opposite.

Meditation on the Wheel dramatizes the idea that the moments of our lives are not happenings which suddenly burst forth out of nowhere at a predetermined date on the calendar. Rather, they are part of an ever-changing process in which past merges into present and the present, in turn, leans toward the future. Connecting with the Wheel at any given moment in our lives can help us to accept the paradoxes of that moment. We can visualize the present as fixed at a certain spot on The Wheel of Fortune, and in this sense, unavoidable yet at the same time, we can observe how this instant in time is already moving into another phase of experience as the Wheel turns. It seems that the more we can bring ourselves to look at the present moment unflinchingly and to accept it as what Jung often called a "just-so story," the more we are able to observe the Wheel as a whole and anticipate the motion of its turning.

The Tarot cards, the *I Ching,* and astrology have, of course, no magic powers to insure prediction of specific future events; but these and similar devices can help us to center our awareness so deeply into the present that we move more easily with the Wheel of Fortune. Certainly we cannot free ourselves from it, but with this kind of insight we can perhaps avoid the more obvious pitfalls caused by our own blindness. And by learning to anticipate the Wheel's tempo, we may escape being repeatedly thrown by unexpected jolts.

Another important characteristic of a wheel's circular form is that its center is equidistant from all points on its circumference. King Arthur's famous Round Table was circular. Sitting at a circular table with no head or foot not only underscores the equal status of all those gathered there, but it also focuses everyone's attention at a central point. This dramatizes the idea that all have a common purpose which remains central, no matter how divergent the many individual points of view represented. When attention is so focused, it can sometimes happen that solutions to problems or guiding images can arise spontaneously, bringing new unity and inspiration to the group. This idea is beautifully illustrated in an old print that shows King Arthur and his knights seated at the Round Table, at whose center the Grail suddenly shines forth as a luminous vision.[4]

Significantly, the Tarot Wheel of Fortune does not picture an empty circle. Such emptiness, like the Fool's hollow zero, belongs to an earlier stage of development corresponding to the undifferentiated world before its division into the opposites – the world of the dancing Jester. The Wheel is by no means empty. Its six spokes divide it into a functional pattern which strengthens it by connecting its whirling outer rim with its stable center. Divided thus, it resembles a sun wheel, the ancient symbol for the divine life force. Surely it is no accident that this Wheel's six spokes form the "I" superimposed on the "X", which is the Greek monogram for Jesus Christ.

The wheel itself embodies the central doctrine of all mystery religions which is that heavenly man, the godlike Son, descends to earth and becomes a slave to the wheel of his fleshly nature. It is from this Wheel of Life that he must win his freedom in order to ascend once more to heaven where he regains his original at-one-ness with God. The cards we have considered thus far may be seen as representing the first step in this process: *involution and generation.* In the classic formula, this was expressed as the descent of spirit into matter. In psychological terms: the ego is born, develops strength, begins to free itself from dependence on its parental archetypes, and establishes itself in the world.

Now, after the Wheel's turning, the remaining Trumps will picture the ensuing stages: *evolution and regeneration.* In the classic formula this was stated as the disentanglement of spirit from matter and its ultimate ascent to a new and heavenly unity. In psychological terms, the remaining Trumps represent the second stage of life, where the ego's energies, having conquered the outer world, turn inward toward spiritual development. At this point, "midway in life's journey," we, like Dante, enter into an unexplored and often dark terrain where new monsters must be faced and fresh illumination found.

That man's life is often prolonged far beyond his biological usefulness, Jung took as a sign that human life has a meaning and serves a purpose beyond mere animal nature. As medical knowledge increases, we are offered, it seems, a chance in our middle years for a whole new life – one usually denied our forebears. It is even becoming fairly common today to find hardy souls in their sixties embarking on what one can only call a "third half of life" – a fresh turn of the Wheel sparked by new challenges and interests quite different from those of the middle years.

Conversely, and this is especially true today, one meets many people in their twenties for whom the Wheel has already made one turning. Since the nature of any wheel is motion, we cannot fasten this card's meaning to a fixed moment in chronological time. The Tarot Wheel represents a turning point that can take place at any age – and it will turn for us all many times.

Sometimes it seems to us that our personal wheel is caught in a rut – that the "same" experiences are happening to us over and over again; or sometimes we may find ourselves seemingly stuck with a recurring dream or nightmare. Whenever these things happen, we may be sure that it is not Fortune's Wheel but we ourselves who are stuck. As the adage puts it: "He who forgets history is condemned to repeat it." Whenever it seems to us that history is repeating itself, we might ask ourselves: What have we forgotten? What specifics of our lives might we view in a wider historical context? Then, by feeling into the symbolic meaning of the recurring dream or happening, we may unlock its broader meaning so that our lives will come unstuck and our energies can move forward again.

To use another metaphor, a recurring dream or happening is like the incessant ringing of the telephone. When we finally pick up the receiver, the ringing stops and we can hear the message. Whenever we are able to turn to the unconscious and hear *its* message, the repetitive motion of life's wheel seems to open out into an ever widening spiral. We have probably all experienced the various stages by which we come to apprehend its spiral motion. Here is the way Jung describes them:

> The way to the goal seems chaotic and interminable at first, and only gradually do the signs increase that it is leading anywhere. The way is not straight but appears to go round in circles. More accurate knowledge has proved it to go in spirals: the dream-motifs always return after certain intervals to definite forms, whose characteristic it is to define a centre.[5]

One might imagine the Tarot Wheel as moving through space-time in such a way that whenever we find ourselves returning to "the same place" we can see we are nonetheless at a different elevation and angle in relation to our former position – that we are still revolving around a central point. However we view it, the rotating wheel has been a symbol in many cultures for the inner journey toward consciousness. The alchemists often referred to the opus as *circulare* or *rota*, "the wheel." One seventeenth-century manuscript pictures the process as an eight-spoked wheel with Mercurius turning its handle.

In Eastern philosophy, the mandala (a circular geometric diagram) has been used for thousands of years as an aid to meditation. Since Jung first introduced it to modern psychology, the word "mandala," a Hindu term for "circle," has appeared with increasing frequency in our Western language. As Jung discovered, mandala designs show up spontaneously in our dreams in times of stress when a compensation is needed for a life situation which is full of conflicts. Indeed, all mandalas no doubt originally came into being as spontaneous attempts on the part of the unconscious to create order.

The Tarot Wheel with its six-spoked pattern is such a mandala. As we contemplate its order, we may perhaps find answers to some of the questions raised at the beginning of this chapter and resolve some of our conflicting feelings about fate versus free will. We may see ourselves as inevitably caught on this Wheel, subject to the cyclic nature of all life, to our seasons of external circumstances and inner development. We may recognize that we are born with definite limitations of heredity and environment – that we are certainly not in control of our destinies. But we are by no means flies enmeshed in Fate's spinning web. Within the Wheel's confines, there is great latitude for movement.

The extravert, born near the Wheel's outer rim, can learn to move a little toward its hub. The introvert, born near the Wheel's center, can learn to move toward its periphery. But since extravert and introvert experience the motion of Fortune's Wheel differently, the techniques for moving about within its confines may be different for each.

An extravert is often whirled about so fast from one activity to another that he experiences life as a disconnected series of ups and downs, and himself as a conglomeration of discrete personalities. The exciting events of his life flash by in such rapid succession that he finds little time to consider his actions and observe the pattern of his fate. He accommodates so readily to outer stimuli, reaching so instinctively for a suitable hat to fit each occasion, that it is easy for him to become estranged from his basic identity.

An extravert can play the roles of parent, son, adolescent, church deacon, sober citizen, and revolutionary so easily that he is often unaware of any underlying conflict in the feelings and ideas expressed in these various roles. When momentary conflicts surface, he is apt to dismiss them as unimportant, plunging immediately into the next exciting adventure. It is only when Fortune's Wheel gives him a sudden, nasty jolt that he is forced to stop and examine his own role in whatever fate has befallen him.

Then he confronts the sphinx with a question: *Who am I that this should have happened to me?*

But the sphinx is a wily creature, more given to propounding questions than answering them. She, and the motions of her Wheel, are not accessible to logic. Only through creative imagination can one unlock her secrets. There are various techniques for approaching the sphinx that sometimes prove rewarding. A few of these are sketched out here, in case the reader might like to try them the next time he feels tricked by her machinations.

Find a quiet spot where you are sure not to be disturbed. Then try to detach yourself from the conflict or problem in which you are currently involved. Shut your eyes and allow the whole scene to move across your inner screen as if it were happening to someone else. Visualize the personalities involved in this current problem and watch them interact as if you were watching a play unfold on your television screen. Turn up your inner sound track so that you can catch the dialogue – recapturing the words, gestures, and inflection, exactly as they happened in reality. Then, let your imagination roam in just the way you would if you were in fact watching a play or movie. What's the plot? What sort of person is the hero or heroine? And the villain? How might this conflict be resolved? Capture any "butterflies" of feelings or thoughts stirring inside you. Can you recall feeling this way on other occasions? Do you see any similarities between the plots and characters of past conflicts in your life and this current one? Does the present situation remind you of any similar one in novels, drama, fairy tales, or myths? Do any of its characters call to mind famous personages in fiction or reality? (Hercules? Hamlet? Napolean? Cinderella? Scarlett O'Hara? Joan of Arc?) If none of these techniques ring a bell, you might try spreading out the Tarot Trumps and using them as springboards for reflection. Which card might represent yourself in the present situation? Which ones might represent other characters? Is there a Tarot personality who might be helpful to you now? If so, how do you imagine this character might behave in the situation?

Put this character on stage and observe what he or she does and says. If the character refuses to talk, then try writing the dialogue yourself. Literally write out a script for the denouement of this drama, complete with setting, characterization, and dialogue. Don't worry about details and don't censor any ideas however foolish seeming, that pop into your head. The sphinx has strange ways of answering our questions, and usually her replies are written between the lines in invisible ink. So don't be surprised if nothing happens immediately. But don't be surprised either if, a day or so later, a new idea should suddenly appear in bold, clear script where only blankness existed before.

For the average extravert who may not have easy access to his inner world, these and similar techniques can sometimes make a convenient bridge to the unconscious. By working imaginatively with external events, an extravert can connect with the inner pattern of which these events are a reflection. He can begin to discover which qualities and tendencies in himself may have constellated the present crisis, and at the same time, he may also find within his own psyche the wisdom, imagination, and strength to help resolve his problems. Uncovering the villainous characters lurking within may give him some empathy for the "bad guys" of his outer drama; discovering his own inner heroes and saviors will give him the courage and insight to tackle these fellows on all fronts.

By viewing his life in this way, the extravert can move a bit toward the center of the Wheel. As he does this, he will find that the rhythm of his life will seem less dizzy and chaotic. His myriad interests and activites may now be connected to a central hub, giving them a more solid form and stability.

The techniques described above are, of course, also useful for introverts. But the introvert usually experiences his problems differently, so the questions he might ask the sphinx are not the same as those asked by the extravert. Generally speaking, an introvert, unless he has been forced into spurious extraversion by cultural influences, is apt to have a pretty good contact with the design of his inner being. Since he is born nearer the Wheel's center, the rhythm of his life is usually slower paced and more considered than the extravert's. He rarely rushes into activities and relationships heedlessly, and whenever he does venture forth, he is less apt to leave part of himself behind.

But, although an introvert usually keeps in touch with his inner feelings, he often has difficulty communicating these to others. As a result, an introvert who lives in an extraverted culture often feels – and in fact *is* misunderstood. From an extravert's point of view, the introvert's slower pace and long silences may seem rude, hostile, secretive, or even sly. The introvert's shy gestures of friendliness (unembellished by the usual social amenities) may appear abrupt and inappropriate. When the extravert, puzzled and mistrustful, turns away, the introvert feels rejected. Hurt, baffled, confused, and generally miserable, he then retreats further into his shell to lick his wounds, reinforcing the extravert's original impression that he was "secretive" and "difficult."

When such things happen, the introvert's question to the sphinx is not *Who am I?* (this he knows more or less). What the introvert wants to know is *Who are they?* He needs the sphinx's help in decoding the inexplicable monsters and quixotic happenings he finds "out there." A sensitive, introverted person usually finds misunderstandings between himself and others too threatening to approach directly, and he cannot bear to replay these dramas on his inner screen as the extravert might do. Because outer reality swamps him, he cannot see it objectively. But he may have contact with his dreams. If so, he might try catching some of these on paper and musing on them imaginatively, using the same techniques on his dreams as those suggested above for approaching a real-life drama.

For a dream is, in fact, a drama. Dreams frequently follow the identical thematic structure used by dramatists from Aeschylus to the present day: introduction, statement of conflict, crisis, and resolution. With a dream, as with a play, the time sequence of events is important. For this reason, in approaching a dream, it's a good idea to begin at the beginning with the first sentence – to read this sentence carefully, visualizing whatever is presented there – and then proceed through the dream, sentence by sentence, pausing to consider each one carefully before moving on to the next.

The dream's opening sentence, like the opening scene in a play, usually sets the stage and establishes the mood of whatever is to follow. As the curtain goes up, the dreamer is "discovered" – where? (In a dark forest? At a party? On a train? At a funeral? Climbing a mountain? etc.) What is the mood of this opening scene? (Terror? Gaiety? Grief? Frustration? Boredom? Confusion? etc.) Soon other characters are introduced. These may be persons, giants, animals, fairies, reptiles, insects, birds, or whatever. If the human beings in the cast are persons with whom the dreamer is currently involved, the dream may speak directly to this overt situation. If the characters are unknown persons, fictional or historical personages, or persons from the dreamer's distant past, they are more likely to symbolize inner attitudes or unconscious archetypal patterns that are operative in the present situation.

It is important to remember that in a dream inanimate objects often play a vital role in the drama and should be included in its cast of characters. Sometimes these objects even play major roles in the conflict. For instance: a car that won't start, or brakes that don't work, or an airplane that comes magically to the rescue just in the nick of time, etc.

After the dream's setting has been described and its characters introduced, a conflict or a problem is stated. The tension between the opposing forces then rises to a peak or crisis. At the end of the dream, as in a play, the final scene depicts a denouement where the conflict is usually (but not always) resolved.

Sometimes the dream's action is so vague, confused, and rambling that it is difficult to determine its plot. If so, it is helpful to ask these two questions: *What problem did the dream raise?* and *How was this problem resolved?* Consider the events of the dream quite literally, as if they were happening in real life. What specifically is the problem presented? (Getting your car started? Stopping it? Catching a train? Escaping from a wild beast? Being exposed naked in a public place? etc.) How was this problem resolved in the dream? (Did you finally start your car? Catch the train? Escape the beast? Find clothing? etc.) Did you achieve whatever resolution took place by your own efforts, or did your have help? If so, who or what helped you?

Often answering these questions at the literal level will offer immediate connections with their symbolic meaning in your life. (Is your "self-starter" stuck? Or do you feel as if you were careening downhill with no brakes? Are you running away from something "beastly?" Does the present situation in your life make you feel "naked?" etc.) Observing how the dreamer got into his predicament can have helpful implications in outer life, and observing how dream conflicts were resolved can give important clues for solving outer problems.

Some dreams, though, are cliff-hangers. They end abruptly at the moment of climax with no indication of a possible denouement. With such dreams, a useful technique is to write out the final act oneself. Maybe several possible resolutions to the dream will come to mind. If so, write them all down. Which one do you prefer? Which offers the best possible resolution to your present reality problem?

Try sketching or painting the characters of your dream. Do these remind you of any persons you know or have known? Any characters in fiction or history? Does this dream recall similar dreams you've had on previous occasions? If you record dreams and also keep a journal of daily events, it is useful to turn back to find dreams with similar plots and to observe what was happening in your outer life at the time these dreams appeared. How was the plot (inner and outer) resolved on these former occasions? Perhaps doing this will offer some hints for a resolution of your current problem. Or you might spread out the Tarot Trumps and look for possible connections between them and the characters in your dreams.

By using these and any other techniques that come to mind, the introvert can perhaps begin to find a recurring pattern in mysterious outer events and can connect with the role he plays in their design. By connecting first with the structure of the familiar dream world and applying these insights to the less familiar outer one, the introvert can make the world and its inhabitants more understandable and less threatening. Finding resolutions to his inner dreams can give him the energy and confidence to take a more active role in the resolution of external problems.

Playing around imaginatively with the facts of his inner world creates a bridge to the outer one so that the introvert's feelings, ideas, and inner essence can come across to others intact and be received more nearly as he intended them. As he creates a successful bridge to the outer world, the introvert will find himself inching away from the Wheel's hub and gradually moving out toward its rim. There the wider view will open up new vistas, and the exhilarating motion will wake his blood to new action.

Since none of us is wholly introverted nor entirely extraverted, the ideas suggested here for the introverted person may prove useful also for the extravert and vice versa. The fact is, of course, that all of us have a stake in both the inner and outer worlds. We all need to connect these two worlds within ourselves, and in doing so, to connect with one another. Introvert and extravert need to move within speaking distance of each other so that they can communicate and work in harmony. Yet it is important that each maintain his own identity so that they can work together in a compensatory way toward wholeness.

Unlike the two beasts on the Wheel of Fortune, we humans have the gift of consciousness and creative imagination. Although our lives also are bound to a wheel of circumstances over which we have no control, we are not pinioned to one spot on its surface. Within the borders of our wheel there are more opportunities for free movement than we might imagine. *Imagine* is the key word. As long as we let our imaginations have free play, we can find ways to move about. But when we approach the sphinx with our ego-intellect, we can remain stuck in circular thinking or interminable rounds of philosophizing and psychologizing.

One way to keep the imagination free, I have discovered, is to avoid asking the sphinx questions that begin with "Why." (*Why* did this happen to me? *Why* did I [they] behave like that? *Why* am I so stupid, inept, misunderstood, or whatever.) I find that, for me at least, "Why" questions result only in recriminations or accusations, burying my creative energies under tons of "shoulds" and "oughts" which leave me paralyzed with guilt or self-righteousness. Whereas before I perhaps took too little reponsibility for my fate, I now begin to imagine that the weight of the whole world rests on my shoulders. Either I am "the guilty party" – wholly responsible for whatever has happened – a creature unfit to mingle with human kind; or "they" are the guilty ones, and it is my job to chastise them, setting their feet once more on the path of righteousness. Either way, one's creativity is paralyzed.

"Why" questions, like Harpies, suck out the blood of life. Learning to address the sphinx in a way that evokes her help is an art. If the questions we ask her are too psychological and philosophical, she will pose counter-questions that set one turning verbal summersaults, like a trained seal. If our approach is too literal and specific, her answers may send us forth into reality in ways that are inappropriate, if not disastrous.

According to the Zohar, in every house of the horoscope there is a door through which man can escape. As we have found with all the other Tarot Trumps, the key to this door is symbolic understanding rather than literal interpretation; inner meaning rather than outer environment. We cannot escape our fate by running away from it. But we can perhaps modify it by becoming aware of attitudes that might attract such a fate, and by changing our viewpoint.

Once more, the story of Oedipus is instructive here. When it was prophesied that he would kill his father and marry his mother, he tried to avoid this fate by changing his outer geography rather than by altering his inner landscape. In order to avoid any possibility of killing Polybus, King of Corinth (whom he believed to be his father), and marrying the Queen of Corinth (whom he took to be his mother), Oedipus fled to Thebes. On the road there, he met a stranger whom he killed in dispute over the right of way. Later, he married the stranger's widow only to learn that the man he had killed was King Laius of Thebes, his real father, and the woman he had married was Jocasta, his own mother.

If Oedipus had considered the soothsayer's prophecy symbolically rather than literally, and if he had examined his inner terrain rather than setting forth to change his outer geography, he might have avoided the fate which was prophesied at both the literal and the symbolic levels. For example, he might have taken "killing his father" as a warning to control his impulsive, hot-headed actions, his quick murderous temper, and the over-weening pride of youth, which demanded the right of way in any encounter and turned against all established values. He might have explored his tendency to "marry his mother" as symbolizing an infantile need for overprotective mothering. A modern Oedipus, faced with such dire premonitions, might have sought professional help of some kind, thus perhaps avoiding murder and incest both symbolically and literally.

As a symbol for meditative contemplation, the Wheel of Fortune can spin out endless meanings. At moments when we feel confused, tossed about too fast by the ups and downs of life, meditating on the Wheel's center can calm us by putting us in touch with its eternal stability. Or when we feel dead and lifeless, contemplating the motion of the Wheel's outer rim can bring revitalization by helping us to contact life's boundless energy.

Sometimes we feel that life has tricked us with her nonsense riddles, making monkeys of us all, and flinging us down in an irresponsible fashion. By meditating on the Wheel, we may discover that it is not the sphinx who has tricked us but our own linear thinking that has fooled us into envisioning life as a hierarchy of achievement reaching up and up to an ultimately heavenly perfection. Only those whose image of life is a journey toward perfection can be wholly thrown by its cyclic movement.

Man has stood on the moon and has seen the earth floating high in the heavens. Surely such an experience should free him forever from hierarchial thinking in which *up* is heaven and desirable, whereas *down* is nothing but a humiliating incarceration in the flesh, a condition to be endured or transcended. If an astronaut stands on the moon and looks up to the heavens for divine guidance, he looks up to – us! It is the miracle of this age that our human selves, body and soul, have been elevated to heavenly status, and that we have been reconnected symbolically with the Divine Spirit in a new way.

When our space travelers disengaged themselves from the earth's gravitational pull and leaped heavenward, they brought back astounding photographs of our round planet silently floating in space, which presented us with a breathtaking view of ourselves and our relation to the cosmos and offered us an expanded awareness of the human condition more cataclysmic than any Copernican revolution. Looking at these photographs, each of us, too, is able to transcend the gravity of petty terrestrial concerns – to extricate himself from his daily round of personal problems – and view his individual fate as part of a wider constellation spread out against the eternal patterning of heaven.

Many of these ideas are echoed in the symbolism of the Wheel of Fortune's number ten which – like the Emperor's number four and the Chariot's number seven – is one of those magic numbers that returns to the unitary one, thus heralding a new epoch of awareness and integration. The way the number ten is written is also significant. Here the heavenly zero (which appears in the Hermit's number nine as a kite with a tail extending earthward) has been brought down from the skies (the realm of the archetypal gods) into the reality of human awareness, where it now stands beside the unit *one* (symbolic of man, the upright animal – the uniquely conscious human being). This might presage a new era of consciousness where man, having cut the umbilical cord, as it were, frees himself to stand aside, viewing the cosmos in an objective way never possible before.

With the revolution of the Tarot Wheel and the impact of its number ten, the hero, too, experiences a similar psychic revolution. For the first time, his ego, disengaging itself from the circular prison of endless trivia, stands aside to observe the pattern of his life as a whole – to view the unique mandala of his individual being against the infinitely expanding circle of the cosmos. He begins now to discover in the jumbled chaotic events of his life a thread of meaning – a consistent story line or dramatic pattern. He begins to experience his personal fate as a kind of myth, and to connect his individual myth with those of the archetypal gods and heroes whose stories are immortalized for all time in legend, and whose names are forever emblazoned in the constellations of the sky. Now the hero begins to understand that his life also has an enduring place in the grand tapestry of the universe. The Wheel of Fortune goes round and round, spinning out endless meanings. As the hero contemplates its motion, he comes to feel that life is not a sphinx's riddle to be solved but a cosmic process of mystery and wonder. For the first time, he stands humbly in awe both of the gods and his own humanity – struck dumb by the painful glory of being human.

Fig. 47   La Force (Marseilles Deck)

14. Strength: Whose?

Out of the eater came forth meat, and out of
the strong came forth sweetness.

Judges 14:14

We have followed the hero's fortunes as he established his ego identity as
the Lover, set forth in the Chariot to seek his place in the world of men,
faced the moral problems posed by Justice, and turned to the Hermit in
search of spiritual insight. The Wheel of Fortune marked the end of this cycle and ushered in a new phase of awareness. With its turning, the hero,
too, experienced a revolution. From this point on, his interest will veer increasingly from the outer world to the inner one. Energies formerly caught
up in external adaptation will begin to concern themselves more with inner
growth. Powers previously involved chiefly with competition and survival
now begin to move toward unification and further development. Problems
belonging to the masculine, logos side of life will give way to the basic
questions of instinctual nature, which belong to the realm of Eros, the
feminine principle.

This change is dramatized in card eleven, Strength (Fig. 47). Here,
for the first time, a mortal woman appears as the central actor in the
drama. She is not a goddess, pictured immobile on a throne; she is a
human being, dressed in the fashion of the period. Yet she is obviously no
ordinary woman, for she is taming a lion. The shape of her hat suggests
the lemniscate hat worn by the Magician. Like the Magician, she must
possess magic powers, and like him, she represents an inner figure active
in the hero's unconscious – one more readily accessible to consciousness
than a god or goddess.

We might view this woman as the anima, an archetypal personage
symbolizing the hero's unconscious, feminine side. In card number one,
the Magician initiated our Tarot series. Here now in card ten plus one, we

are ready for a new beginning and a new magic – one in which this lady magician will play the initiatory role. It is she who will act as mediator between the hero's ego and the more primitive powers of his psyche.

As a mediating cultural influence, Strength seems ideally cast. Her clothes and her bearing suggest refinement and breeding. Although she wears a hat similar to the Magician's, she holds no wand. Her power lies in the hands which fearlessly grasp the lion's jaws, indicating that her magic is more human, personal, and direct than that of her masculine counterpart. Her strength is not invested in a baton to be taken up and cast aside at will – or perhaps lost altogether. Her mysterious power resides in her very being as a permanent, intimate part of herself.

Her number eleven, written here in the Roman fashion as X plus I, recalls the Greek monogram for Christ spelled out by the Wheel's spokes in card ten. Here the X precedes the I. Evidently, the new magic pictured in card eleven has the force of the first ten cards behind it. Perhaps, as with Sir Galahad, this lady's strength is "as the strength of ten" because her heart is pure.

With her help the hero, too, will tap instinctual forces within himself. He will learn to sacrifice ego power for another kind of strength. His masculine drive will be modified by a more feminine approach. This new way of functioning, far from being effeminate, is very powerful. The courage and prowess of the woman pictured in Strength is self-evident. This fearless anima figure exists in a deep sector of the young man's psyche relatively unknown to him. She is not under the ego's conscious control, so she roams freely in his dreams and visions. It is she who will put him in touch with the dark forests of his being and with the wild creatures he will encounter there. She will help him tame his animal nature so that he will no longer be wholly under its power.

In the Fool we saw a happy wanderer prancing along with his little dog behind him. The animal was nipping at this master's heels as if he were trying to tell him something. Perhaps the Tarot hero has not paid enough attention to his own friendly instinctual side, for, in Strength, animal nature is now pictured as an enormous lion – a wild beast too threatening for the hero to face directly, yet too dangerous for him to ignore.

Luckily, the lady magician is able to face the lion and give him the attention he needs. Symbolically speaking, this could mean that the hero's human nature is now able to confront his animal nature. But his ego consciousness cannot deal directly with the untamed forces of the unconscious. A relationship between these two aspects of his psyche can only be accomplished through the mediation of the anima.

The role of the feminine as the mediating influence between human consciousness and the primitive psyche is celebrated in countless fairy tales and legends such as "Beauty and the Beast," "The Frog Prince," "Cupid and Psyche," and "Una and the Lion." In these stories, through a woman's loving acceptance of its bestial nature, the animal is not only tamed but is transformed as well. In "The Frog Prince," for example, it is because the little princess overcame her initial repugnance of the slimy frog and accepted him as her constant companion that the repulsive creature was, in the end, freed from a wicked enchantment to stand forth in his true nature as a royal prince. In other stories, it is through a woman's compassion for its bestial nature that a hideous monster ultimately casts off its disguise, revealing itself to be a handsome lover or god.

These tales dramatize the poetic truth that when human consciousness recognizes and accepts its untamed, primitive nature, it not only frees itself from the instinct's autonomous power but liberates and transforms the instinctual side as well. Such a transformation is already taking place in our Tarot series as we can see by comparing Strength with the previous card, the Wheel of Fortune. In the Wheel, the instinctual forces are depicted as two pathetic, rather comical figures, hopelessly entrapped, and dominated by a subhuman sphinx, wearing a man-made crown. Now, under the benign influence of the lady magician, the instinctual side appears as a golden lion, crowned by his own natural dignity as king of his realm. In the preceding card, the little animals ape humans in expression and dress, and by so doing deny their inherent nature. In this card, the lion stands proud in his animal skin, freely exposing his true essence. Whereas in the Wheel of Fortune the civilizing factor is depicted as "monkey suits," absurdly inadequate, here the taming factor is presented as a dignified human figure with magic powers.

Jung has said that the first half of life is devoted to nature and the second half to culture. The woman in this picture appears to be a person of culture and refinement. For although this lion is king of his jungle, he must be tamed before he can join her courtly circle. This taming process requires an intimate connection between lady and lion. Unlike her masculine counterpart, this magician is not performing at the crossroads in order to demonstrate something; whatever is happening here seems to be a more private drama, her personal encounter with the lion. Her number eleven, commonly written in Arabic notations as two ones side by side, echoes the Magician's number one, at the same time suggesting the reflective duality of the Popess's sacred number two. As one might expect, the magic of this anima figure is more subtle and less dramatic than that of the Magician. She does not manipulate objects and forms on a table; hers is the magic of human relationship, the daring of personal involvement, of direct physical contact. With her bare hands she explores the beast's dimensions and needs; at the same time she communicates to him her own atmosphere, her faith and expectations. If the lion is hungry, perhaps the lady will feed him, for she knows that if she does not give the beast appropriate food, he will swallow her up, body and soul. Psychologically this could mean that the hero's eros side, his capacity for relatedness, would be obliterated. He would then become possessed with an archetypal lust for power, pride, primitive rage, or other lion-like attributes.

Doubtless, everyone has had the experience of being "swallowed up" by an affect. We know how sudden emotions can literally seize us – how the animal side of our nature can spring upon us from behind to claim its own. At these times, ego consciousness is thrust aside and our bodies fall prey to a force which is beyond control. We quiver with fear, tremble with rage, blush with shame, or laugh hysterically, at the same time feeling sudden tears wet our cheeks. When these things happen, our ego self, helpless and humiliated, tries to run away, symbolically if not literally. We want to put the incident behind us.

Whenever we try to turn our backs on this "beastly" part of ourselves, it becomes even more ravenous and demanding. If we ignore these demands, we may be visited by a psychosomatic illness. Instinctual energies persistently ignored can burst their bonds in a destructive way, resulting in crimes of passion. In other extreme cases, dissociation from the animal side can produce schizophrenic episodes, where the ego's connection with the body becomes so fragmented that various parts of the body are personified, each seeming to speak and act independently. To be seized, however briefly, by one's instinctual side can be a shattering experience. Anyone who has been "beside himself" with rage, "consumed" by jealousy, or "possessed" by lust can never again imagine that he is wholly above the beasts. Such confrontations rudely remind us that we humans are, at best, animals who have developed in a special way.

If we are to avoid being shaken by the inner beast against our will, we cannot put him behind us. Sooner or later we shall have to pay attention to him, as Lady Strength is doing. We, too, must put our hands on his gaping muzzle and become intimately acquainted with this creature who, like Blake's famous Tyger, burns bright in the forests of our night. We, too, must dare to behold his "fearful symmetry." But experiencing the beast's power does not mean that we must act out our rages and aggressions at the top of our lungs, indulging our hysterics in the name of therapy. On the contrary, whenever we throw our affects at others, we throw away something that belongs to ourselves: the experience of the beast *as our beast* – and we lose contact with his strength.

As the lady magician clearly shows us by her actions, we need to hold onto our raging affects and come to grips with them. The more each of us individually can become conscious of his animal nature, the less will he be compelled to live out this side in personal rages or mass wars. But we fear the untamed beast within and try to avoid encountering this terrifying aspect of ourselves. "It is this fear of the unconscious psyche," says Jung, "which not only impedes self-knowledge but is the gravest obstacle to a wider understanding and knowledge of psychology."[1]

The Tarot Strength is not afraid. Perhaps by observing her we can get some idea of how best to approach and tame our inner lion. *What exactly is the lady doing with her hands?* This question has puzzled generations of Tarot commentators. Some say she is closing the lion's mouth. Others see her as opening it. Perhaps the picture is left intentionally ambiguous, for doubtless the woman must perform each action at various times, depending on circumstances. There are times when the instinctual lion needs to yawn and stretch, or rant and rave, or give forth a joyful roar; and there are other occasions when even kings – and especially kings – need to learn patience and restraint.

Some say that when the lady's hands are opening the lion's mouth it is in order to teach him the magic of human speech. If so, the beast is also sharing with her the wordless secrets of nature since the two figures appear to be involved in a harmonious dialogue. They seem to be united in a state of perfect harmony, for the design and coloring of this old card emphasize an equilibrium between the two figures.

Does the card's title, Strength, refer to the lady or the lion? Perhaps to both, for each is a powerful figure. Actually, their strength seems to come from their mutual involvement. Even though the lady appears to dominate the lion, she also partakes of his essence. Notice how the golden energy of his fiery strength seems to flow up her arms, illuminating her breast, then leaps to her head where it rests like a golden crown in the center of her lemniscate hat. Appropriately enough, the motif of this little crown resembles the teeth of an animal.

Woman's way of relating to the beast is very different from the masculine approach, as evidenced by contrasting *Samson and the Lion* (Fig. 48) with Strength. Samson opposes his beast directly, face to face, in an aggressive, masculine way; the woman in our Tarot approaches her lion gently and calmly, indirectly, from the lion's hidden, unconscious side. Notice how Samson's feet are braced. He cannot afford to give an inch. He must withstand the onslaught of bestial rage or he will be devoured. In contrast, the lion appears to lean against the Tarot lady. Her foot and flowing robes suggest motion, the possibility of a give-and-take adjustment to whatever situation arises. Interestingly enough, Samson's hands and the hands of the lady are similarly placed at the lion's jaws, but his hands seem to challenge the beast, hers to soothe it.

"The Wrath of the Lion is the Wisdom of God," said Blake. Samson's lion, too, was "of the Lord." This hero extracted from the beast's carcass a swarm of bees and rich honey, symbolic of instinctual enrichment and sweet spiritual nourishment. Whenever we successfully confront our inner lion, we feel nourished and revivified by the experience. Contact with our affects shakes us "out of our minds" and takes us into our guts, bursting the bonds of ego limitation. It pumps new blood into our veins. As we have

Fig. 48   Samson and the Lion
(Nicholas of Verdun, 1181, enamel. The Chorherrenstift Museum,
Klosterneuburg, Austria. Reprinted by permission.)

already seen, the lion's golden substance seems to flow up the woman's arms and become a part of her. Tamed by woman's magic, the beast offers his honey freely. She need not kill him to obtain his gifts.

After a successful encounter with such a beast, a male hero usually emerges wearing a permanent token, such as the animal's teeth, skin, or hair, in order to symbolize the fact that he is now imbued with his adversary's strength and cunning. Like Hercules, who wore the skin of his Nemean lion, a victorious bullfighter today proudly bears from the arena the bull's ears or tail. Perhaps the Tarot lady also seeks a permanent token of her protagonist's power. Maybe she is looking in the lion's mouth for another wisdom tooth to add to those which already appear in her crown.

King Solomon's lion was said to hold the key to wisdom in his teeth, and lions generally are associated with wisdom. Leo, with his sunburst mane, often symbolizes the heavenly sun and the illumination of the godhead. The Hindus place the lion higher than man in the hierarchy of being, for the lion is a symbol of reincarnation. An old fable tells that lion cubs are born dead and are revived only by the roar (or breath) of their father. Seen in these contexts, this lion might embody, among other things, the religious instinct, that inborn yearning toward reunion with the godhead which Jung felt was a primitive tendency in the human psyche, as basic and natural as sex.

Wild animals generally symbolize self-fulfillment because they are true to their instinctive nature, which is pure and uncorrupted by pretense, ambition, and other negative aspects of so-called civilized man. The lion, with his golden crown and beard, is an especially apt symbol for the energizing power of the psyche's central sun, the self.

Although as king of the beasts our Tarot lion is set above all other animals, he is nonetheless a *natural* animal. Unlike the sphinx, he actually exists in nature. This means, symbolically, that Lady Strength is dealing with a natural force which can be tamed and integrated to some extent. This idea is further illustrated by the fact that the lion shares common ground with the lady and interacts with her, whereas the sphinx in card ten is enthroned above the Wheel and does not participate in the action taking place below.

In our Map of the Journey, the Emperor stands directly above Strength. Both depict powerful influences in the development of human consciousness. The Emperor represents external authority, the *thou shalt* of civilization, whereas the lion personifies instinctual authority, the *I will* of the self. Without the inner lion's golden blood in our veins, we would be pasteboard puppets, mindlessly obeying the commandments of others; without the authority and leadership of our inner Emperor, we would still be living in caves. Between these two extremes, the lady magician acts as mediator.

The Emperor's realm, civilization, stresses the welfare of the community. Strength's province, culture, nourishes the needs of the individual. A veneer of civilization can be superimposed from without, but true culture cannot be achieved by externals. It is an inner happening, cultivated anew in the heart of each human being. It involves accepting and integrating the lion as he appears within oneself. As Jung reiterates, a change in human consciousness cannot be mass produced; the individual human psyche is the sole host and carrier of consciousness.

Many of us have little access to the amoral layer of the psyche symbolized by the lion. Some, still imprisoned in the shalls and shall-nots of a strict religious upbringing, dare not even imagine what we might be capable of if these superimposed restrictions were removed. Others, not raised within a strict creed or dogma, rush to tie themselves down to some religious or philosophical code in order to create a prison for the fearsome, unknown lion within.

Leo's strength is ambivalent; it can be both life-giving and destructive. His overweening pride and lust for power are legendary. A less obvious instinctual drive which this lion can also symbolize is the lust for redemption. This too can devour our humanity, leaving only the glittering eye and the rasping voice of the religious fanatic.

Long ago Freud put us in touch with our instinctual side as sexual drive. But the instinct for enlightenment can also be a powerful – even dangerous – force. This is especially true because its overt expression usually meets with social approbation. As with all archetypal forces, the problem is how to relate to them and use their creative power consciously without allowing them to swallow up our humanity. Jung saw this as a specific danger in relation to the instinctual forces symbolized by lions generally. He writes:

> Lions, like all wild animals, indicate latent affects. The lion plays an important part in alchemy and has much the same meaning. It is a "fiery" animal, an emblem of the devil, and stands for the danger of being swallowed by the unconscious.[2]

In myth and fable, both the heavenly and the devilish aspects of wild animals are abundantly illustrated. Zeus, disguised as a bird or an animal, often descended to earth and had love affairs with mortals. There seems to be no instance on record in which Zeus assumed the aspect of a lion for his nocturnal prowls, perhaps because such a kingly role would have been a poor disguise for the ruler of Olympus. The gods do not stoop to typecasting. But whenever Zeus, in the guise of any bird or animal, did have intercourse with a mortal woman, the results were always dynamic, with outcomes for both good and evil. Usually this union of heaven and earth sparked a social conflagration and brought forth a new era, cultural and psychological.

Several of Zeus's love affairs have been celebrated in famous paintings, two of which are reproduced here because they offer illuminating amplification of this theme. In both instances, the outcome of intercourse between the beast-god and the mortal woman produced shattering results. In the first painting, entitled *Leda and the Swan*, Zeus, in the form of a beautiful swan, has just raped the innocent Leda (Fig. 49). As pictured here, Leda seems to have enjoyed the inevitable, for she and the swan are linked in tender embrace. At Leda's feet, newly hatched, lie the fearful issue of this union – two sets of famous twins, Castor and Pollux, Helen and Clytemnestra, symbolic both of the grandeur that was Greece and of the fall of Troy.

Yeats said it better in his poem "Leda and the Swan":

> A shudder in the loins engenders there
> The broken wall, the burning roof and tower
> And Agamemnon dead.

At the end of the poem Yeats asks,

> Did she put on his knowledge with his power
> Before the indifferent beak could let her drop?[3]

It would seem that Leda did not. Unlike Strength, Leda wears no crown of wisdom teeth. On the contrary, stripped naked even of the garments of civilization, she has almost assumed the sinuous form of her swan lover. She has been raped of her humanity through possession by the god.

On another famous occasion, Zeus, assuming the form of a bull, carried away the innocent maid Europa. Giorgio's painting commemorating this event is called *The Rape of Europa* (Fig. 50). It seems obvious that the painter uses the word "rape" figuratively, and purely out of courtesy to the poor girl's parents, for Europa is evidently enjoying the ride. She sheds not one tear as she looks back toward the mute hand waving a final goodbye from the home shore. Notice how beautifully the artist has caught the feeling of unconscious identity between Europa and the bull. The two seem to flow together as one being. She is indeed "carried away" by the godly beast. And out of this union comes again a mixed blessed event – King Minos of Crete and the bestial (and magical) Minotaur.

As these myths illustrate, strength and experience are required in dealing with instinctual drives if one is not to be overwhelmed or carried away. The lady pictured in Strength appears to possess the insight and fortitude needed to conquer the lion. She is in no sense carried away by her

Fig. 49   Leda and the Swan
(Flemish artist c. 1540. The John G. Johnson Collection,
Philadelphia Museum of Art. Reprinted by permission.)

Fig. 50   The Rape of Europa (Francesco di Giorgio)

bestial friend. Instead the two move together in harmony. But even with the aid of such a lady magician, the lion can never be wholly domesticated, for he belongs to the realm of Artemis (Diana), goddess of the animals, who is herself a wild creature, untamed and unpredictable.

Artemis is, on the one hand, the virgin huntress, sister of Apollo, sharing his light. But when crossed she can become as vengeful as the witch Hecate and just as artful in black magic. When the mood is upon her, this goddess can change man's best friend into the slavering hounds of Hecate, so that the animals attack and devour even their own master. This idea was dramatized in the myth of the Greek youth Actaëon, who was torn apart by his own hunting dogs at the command of Artemis because he spied on her at her bath. Actaeon's fate illustrates a psychological truth: If we allow our instincts freedom to act without restraint, they can turn on us and tear us apart.

A stunning photograph of Artemis walking her dog in the Tuileries Gardens (Fig. 51) presents the goddess in a chaste and innocent mood. Only the telltale glint in her hound's eye warns us that we are dealing here with a witch and her familiar. Appropriately the photographer who shot this picture took it on a stormy night, a flash of lightning his sole illumination.

As the old myths have indicated, primitive man had great difficulty in controlling his instincts for they were close to the surface and he could not easily deny them. Today we have ignored our instinctual side so long that we are likely to forget that it exists until it bursts from its cage with the fury of an angry lion. Yet, like it or not, our animal nature is our lifelong companion. We must find a way, as our Tarot Strength suggests, to walk beside it in peaceful companionship. Commenting on the problem of relating to our instinctual side, Aniela Jaffé has this to say:

Fig. 51   Artemis, Lady of the Beasts, Walking her Dog in the Tuileries (Photo by M. Brassai)

Suppressed and wounded instincts are the dangers threatening civilized man; uninhibited drives are the dangers threatening primitive man. In both cases the "animal" is alienated from its true nature; and for both, the acceptance of the animal soul is the condition for wholeness and a fully lived life. Primitive man must tame the animal in himself and make it his helpful companion; civilized man must heal the animal in himself and make it his friend.[4]

One way that we can contact the animal in ourselves is through our dreams. Maybe our lost and wounded animal souls come to us in our dreams seeking human help. In Rousseau's painting *The Sleeping Gypsy* (Fig. 52), a lion pauses beneath a desert moon at the edge of a sleeping gypsy's dream. Under the spell of the moonlight, lion and gypsy are each bewitched by the mystery of the other. The gypsy's sleep is haunted by dreams of his lost animal soul; the restless beast sniffs out the mystery of humanity, yearning for its touch.

Fortunately, the hero in our story remembers his dreams and is aware of the lion that prowls around in the night. Apparently he has also made contact with the anima who walks beside this animal. With this powerful lady as guide, the hero may safely explore the inner forests of his psyche. With her help, he may come to know the lion and all the other primitive beasts who inhabit the darkest recesses of his being.

Fig. 52   The Sleeping Gypsy
(Rousseau, Henri, 1897, oil on canvas, 51" × 6'7". Collection, The Museum of Modern Art, New York. Gift of Mrs. Simon Guggenheim.)

Fig. 53   Le Pendu (Marseilles Deck)

15. The Hanged Man: Suspense

> . . . it is not the blood-letting that calls down
> power. It is the consenting.
>
> Mary Renault

In the twelfth Trump a young man hangs upside down, tied by one foot to
a gibbet, the twin poles of which are truncated trees, each with six bleeding
stumps where their branches have been lopped off (Fig. 53). The trees are
growing on either side of a fissure in the earth – a crevice or possibly a
deep abyss. Thus the youth's head is actually lower than the earth's surface, buried, as it were, underground like the roots of the two trees. The
knob of the young man's head, with its hanging hair, suggests a third
underground ball, perhaps a turnip, with the hairy roots characteristic of
that vegetable.

   With his hands tied behind his back the Hanged Man is as helpless as
a turnip. He is in the grasp of Fate. He has no power to shape his life or
control his destiny. Like a vegetable, he can only wait for a force outside
himself to pluck him free from the regressive pull of Mother Earth.

   After experiencing the exhilarating influx of energy indicated in the
previous card, the hero must have been shocked and dazed by this sudden
reversal. With his one free foot he must have struggled wildly at first to extricate himself, kicking against his fate. He must have felt deeply wronged,
impatient to be righted – to be able once more to hold his head high and
set his two feet firmly on the path of his quest. He must have suffered long
before attaining the degree of acceptance, of almost graceful repose pictured here.

   It is easy for us to empathize with this young man's initial fury and
resentment. We find his predicament unbearably humiliating. It makes us
uneasy to see his head, seat of rational thinking, thus debased, and we
long to free his pinioned limbs so that he can stride forth to new accom-

plishments. Western man finds it difficult to tolerate enforced inactivity. We tend to think of meaningful action as taking place on a horizontal, extraverted plane of behavior, to picture spiritual yearning as directed upward toward heaven, and to ignore entirely the growth that may be taking place below our conscious awareness. We have, to quote Paul Tillich, "lost the dimension of depth."

Almost instinctively, it seems, we itch to turn The Hanged Man right side up. If you hand this card to someone who is unfamiliar with the Tarot, he will almost invariably turn it around so that the figure's head is up "where it belongs." After this he will emit a relieved sigh – and then he will smile. If you don't know why he would smile, you can turn this book upside down so that the Hanged Man appears to be standing upright. Now, delicately posed on one foot and with arms akimbo, he is "really" dancing a jig! Viewed from the perspective of the unconscious, he who appeared to be immobilized and stagnant – held captive – is now freed; he who seemingly had lost his balance has now achieved a splendid new equilibrium. What our upright consciousness experienced at first as a time of stagnation and frustration is newly revealed as a moment of liberating action. Even the Hanged Man's facial expression seems to have changed. He now meets our gaze calmly and confidently with a new look of authority; he appears to smile as if he knew a secret.

In order to discover his secret, we must view him again as he first presented himself, dangling helplessly in space. To be thus hanged upside down is traditionally the punishment of traitors. In some old Italian decks, this card is called Il Traditore (The Traitor). Sometimes this Tarot Traitor is pictured with a bag of money in each hand, suggesting Judas with his thirty pieces of silver. In medieval times, cowardly or disloyal knights were thus strung up by the heels and beaten, a humiliating punishment. In relatively recent times, the bodies of Mussolini and his mistress were hung upside down on public display. In all such cases the hanging itself is not an instrument of physical death. Rather it is a mark of ignominy, of censure and public ridicule, a ghastly reversal of everything that the personage in question formerly stood for.

The custom of inverse hanging was formerly called "baffling." Nowadays "to baffle" means to "thwart, frustrate, or confuse." Certainly the young man pictured here looks baffled in every sense of the word. He is enduring a kind of crucifixion. We are reminded of Peter, who asked to be crucified upside down as a mark of humility. There is no evidence that the hero of our Tarot literally requested that he be thus pilloried, but, speaking psychologically, he must have asked for his fate unconsciously. Perhaps contact with the prideful lion of the preceding card led to an inflation, an overweening confidence in his own human strength. As we know, the gods despise hubris. Any notion that human nature is stronger than

Mother Nature, or that man's intellect is the ruling function of all life, upsets the Great Mother and ultimately the human culprit as well. In retaliation, the goddess may grasp her impudent son by his heels and dunk his proud brains once more in the womb of her moist earth.

The tree, and especially the truncated tree, is a universal mother symbol. Osiris's body, for example, was enclosed in such a tree, the lopped branches of which symbolized both the castration of the son (masculine ego consciousness) and also the possibility of new growth – or rebirth – into a larger sphere of awareness. The Hanged Man, enclosed on either side by the twin trees and by the gibbet above, can be seen as encased in a kind of coffin. At the same time his contact with the maternal underground waters suggests baptism and new life. Perhaps nature holds him thus confined in her grip so that he can newly emerge from her womb as one reborn. One might imagine that, like a newborn infant, he is being held by the heels in order to be spanked into new life.

How aptly the hero is pictured here, suspended between the twin poles of all existence: birth and death. We have all felt the loneliness and helplessness of our suspension over this eternal abyss. Such a terrible isolation or trial by endurance plays an important part in all initiation rites. Sometimes, for example, the initiate is forced to spend the night alone in a dark cave or forest. Here he must face and withstand possible physical death with no help but his own inner strength and resourcefulness. By facing this ordeal, the youth being tested is driven to find a new center, hitherto hidden within himself. If he survives this experience, he emerges indeed as one reborn, in token of which he is given a new name and accepted as an adult by the community. According to Mircea Eliade, through this experience the initiate makes a transition from man's ordinary world of time into the sacred, timeless world of the gods. In his *Thresholds of Initiation,* Joseph Henderson discusses this transitional phase and quotes Eliade as follows:

> Between the two (worlds) there is a break, a rupture of continuity. . . . (For) passing from the profane to the sacred world in some sort implies the experience of death; he who makes the passage dies to one life in order to gain access to another . . . the life where participation in the sacred becomes possible.[1]

In our modern culture we have almost no such specific initiation rites so that young men have difficulty in making this transition. Sometimes they seek out almost superhuman tasks by which to test themselves. For past generations, Lindbergh's lonely transatlantic flight and Hillary's conquest of Everest stand out as paradigms for this kind of self-imposed initiation. In more recent times the voyages into outer space have served this function. For some, enduring the rigors of army life, being threatened with physical death and meeting their own murderous instincts in war, can be such an initiation. For others, facing imprisonment by refusing to bear arms and being subjected to the hostility and derision of their contemporaries can serve the same purpose, forcing a young man to tap new reserves of strength.

As history has repeatedly shown, any person whose individual conscience is in opposition to the collective viewpoint can appear as a traitor to the Establishment. Such an individual is subjected to many trials, the least of which is that held in a court of law. Often upside down in relation to his friends, his family, and his government, such a nonconformer can even be branded criminal. His life as a useful citizen is thus suspended – he becomes a dangling man. In a novel aptly called *The Dangling Man*, Saul Bellow explores this theme.

An initiation of this sort can occur at various times in life, usually whenever we have reached the end of a certain phase or stage of existence and life demands a transition to new ways. It is an awesome moment, for we must give up the old and tried ways of functioning and must entrust ourselves to the unseen and untried new life. It demands sacrifice and courage. All of us, perhaps in less overt and dramatic ways than the one pictured here, have undergone periods in our lives when we were similarly hung up by circumstances, times when old behavior patterns could no longer keep us upright, when life pulled out the rug from under us so that we felt suspended between worlds and could only wait and pray. At these times we felt betrayed by life, debased and humiliated, stripped of all pride and of our persona (the public guise or mask we wear as a buffer between our secret selves and the world.)

Whenever, like King Lear, we hold our heads too high above ordinary life, avoiding the "odor of mortality" with its conflicts and suffering, Fate seizes us, it seems, and rubs our noses in all that we have formerly despised. Whenever we crown our superior function king, we are forced down to the level of our wormy underside. Like Lear, we must immerse ourselves in the slime of our humble reality.

In the card Strength, the hero came to terms with aspects of his psychosomatic nature symbolized by the lion, a mammal high on the evolutionary scale. Now he must confront the lower aspects of his psychic being symbolized by worms, insects and plants. With his ear to the ground, he hears the tender grasses grow and feels in the slow undulation of the worm and the eerie song of the insects his kinship with all life. He who may have approached this chasm like the carefree Fool, with his head lost in cloudy dreams of his strength and prowess, has come a-cropper. The focus of his awareness has shifted perforce to the roots of life – the fundamentals from which all growth arises. According to Eliade:

> The Taoist, imitating animals and vegetables, hangs himself upside down, causing the essence of his sperm to flow up to his brain. The *tan-t'ien*, the famous fields of cinnabar, are to be found in the most secret recesses of the brain and belly; there it is that the embryo of immortality is alchemically prepared.[2]

If the hero survives the initiation life has presented in this card, he can declare with William Blake:

> I have said to the Worm: Thou art my Mother & my sister.[3]

It is worthwhile to contrast the situation of the Hanged Man with that of the Lover, which also dramatizes a trial. The Lover is pictured standing upright, boxed in and immobilized by two women who are planted, solid as trees, on either side of him. The resolution of his problem, and the motive force for action, comes from the winged Eros figure in the sky above. But the Hanged Man, immobilized between two powerful maternal symbols, can find inspiration only from the depths.

The supposed physical location of human consciousness varies from culture to culture: in the Old Testament the kidneys are often spoken of as the center of consciousness; for the African, this kind of awareness is located in the heart or abdomen; modern man places consciousness in the head. The African and the Old Testament Hebrew, for whom consciousness resided deep within the body, usually spoke of supraconscious inspiration as descending from above. But for modern man, who lives too much in the head, "The Other" is more frequently encountered in the depths below. We, like the Hanged Man, have been disconnected from our roots. Our need is to descend – to reconnect with our origins in history and in nature. The motif of sacrifice and dismemberment, hinted at in the blood-red stumps of the truncated trees, is repeated in the red legs and upper arms of the hanging figure, suggesting that he too must give blood, must sacrifice his former ways of understanding and acting. Many of his old gods have now fallen from the tree, among them no doubt the image of life as the ever good and beneficent mother whose function he imagined was to protect him from mishap and nourish his every whim. As Jung has pointed out, the word "sacrifice" means "to make sacred." To sacrifice our ego-centered images is to make our life both whole and holy; then there is no longer a split between our image of how things ought to be and the realities of our human existence. Only we human beings are prone to – and capable of – this kind of sacrifice and spiritual suffering. The burden (and the potential) inherent in the legacy of crucifixion sets us apart from the rest of the animal kingdom.

Like the animals held captive on Fortune's Wheel, the Hanged Man is a victim of Fate, at the mercy of the gods. He is as helpless as the animals but with this difference: he has a chance to accept his fate consciously and puzzle out its meaning, whereas the animals can, at best, merely endure their plight.

Whenever we find ourselves in the position of the Hanged Man it is useful not only to explore the conscious attitudes which life may be trying to dislodge and upset, but also to feel into the flavor of the new experience. A good way to enlarge our feeling for what life is offering the Hanged Man is to shut our eyes and to try to enter into his body. If we are students of Yoga, we might be moved to do a headstand at this point. Then we would feel how the blood rushes to our head, bringing oxygen to the brain and reviving our spirit. Our jaded retinas would be revived, suffusing our view of the world with fresh color. If, like the Hanged Man, we were suspended in this posture, alone and without food or companionship, our "doors of perception" would be so cleansed that we might experience heavenly visions and the illumination of satori.

The experience of enforced suspension has robbed the hero of his independence, but it can also offer him something new and precious if, like Parsifal, he can find the right question to ask. Experience shows that the why-did-Fate-pick-on-me approach is a dead end. But if he asks: "Who am I that this should happen to me?" he may unlock hidden treasures that put him in touch with the meaning of his life in a new way. Hanging in limbo he finds his position full of ambiguities: on the one hand he dangles precariously over an abyss, but viewed another way he has been spared the fate of falling into a chasm. Externally he is immobilized, but deep inside there stirs a dance of liberation.

As noted earlier, many adults, especially those reared in the Occident, feel threatened merely by contemplating hanging in this position. But children of all cultures and climes seem to enjoy turning cartwheels and hanging by their heels, heedless of the pennies and other treasures that may fall to the ground. In some versions of the Tarot Hanged Man, several coins, symbolic of worldly values, are pictured falling from the youth's pockets. We all know from experience how, faced with ultimate realities, all the petty burdens and nonessential encumbrances of life drop away. No wonder that in the depths of himself the Hanged Man can be seen to smile and dance with a new kind of joy.

But this joyful denouement, if it is to come, still lies hidden in the future where it will ultimately become visible as the dancer of Trump twenty-one. By turning the Hanged Man's picture upside down we were privileged to catch a magic glimpse of events from the aspect of eternity, where all time is one. But the young man himself is not consciously aware of the dancing figure buried in his depths. For the present he remains immobile, suspended helpless on the fateful tree.

Osiris, too, the legend tells us, hung from a tree like butcher's meat for three days until he was ripe for dismemberment. So also, it seems, must this youth ripen on the sacrificial tree until the old Adam begins to rot and fall away. At the center of this experience (call it initiation or crucifixion) is the terrible necessity to feel betrayed and to face the awful loneliness of being wholly forsaken. Referring to this psychological state, Jung writes: "The patient must be alone if he is to find out what it is that supports him when he can no longer support himself. Only this experience can give him an indestructible foundation."[4]

What supports the Hanged Man is the solid wood of Nature's tree which connects him with the sturdiness of his own inner nature. That this experience results in an indestructible foundation is indicated by the way his legs (seen upside down) create the numeral four, showing that completeness, orientation, and solidity are taking form in the unconscious. The inner experience he is undergoing is no misty dream; it has the full dimensions of reality. The feet upon which he normally stands now point heavenward. He is acquiring a new understanding. The understanding symbolized by the Emperor and his number four is a different kind. The four points of that figure's compass were oriented to external realities on the human plane: civilization, stability, law and order. With the Hanged Man this kind of fourfold ordering has been turned upside down, but it has not been destroyed. It simply lies open now to the light of heaven, exposed to the intervention of the gods in a new way.

The Hanged Man's number twelve encompasses much of what has been said. It marks the time limits of human reality with its alternating twelve hours of day and night and its yearly count of twelve months. It points also to the heavenly zodiac, symbolizing suprahuman dimensions of time and the intervention of destiny beyond man's control. As four times three, the number twelve connects the trinity of spirit with the foursquare reality of earth. Transfixed now at the mercy of the wheeling stars above, the hero experiences himself in this expanded dimension of twelve.

He begins to discover that the journey toward self-realization does not proceed in an orderly fashion from A to B and thence to C. Its rhythm is quixotic. Like the motions of Fortune's Wheel, his spiritual fortunes, too, will suffer many revolutions. There will be periods of depression where insights previously gained and believed to be held secure will disappear again into the unconscious, seemingly lost forever. Then – and this often at the nadir of his fortunes – the sun will shine again, and he will emerge as one reborn to set forth into a new world of fresher colors and grander dimensions than any hitherto dreamed. Or to use another image: it is as if the pattern of spiritual growth were like that of a tree's unfolding. Before fresh branches can blossom forth at the top, the roots must sink deeper and spread wider to support this new growth.

The Hanged Man initiates a long period of enforced assimilation and consolidation at the roots. It will be some time before the truncated trees pictured here will bear new foliage or the hero himself can step out newly into the world. For the moment, and for some time to come, energies and insights dramatized in the previous cards will be sucked down into the unconscious to be deepened and expanded. For example, in The Wheel of Fortune the hero began to view his personal fate against a wider canvas and make meaningful connections between his life and the universal pattern. Now his faith in this pattern is put to the test. In Justice he confronted problems of equilibrium on the horizontal dimension. Now his awareness is stretched vertically in two directions – upward to the planets of heavenly Nature and downward to the subterranean world of vegetative Nature. He must somehow establish an equilibrium between these opposing forces. His hands are tied. He can do nothing to free himself from the rack experienced as a crucifixion.

Fate can bring about this kind of crucifixion at any time in life and in a variety of ways. A sudden business reversal may rob a person overnight of all his worldly goods and of the career to which he had devoted his life, upsetting his present reality and destroying his hopes for the future. Or perhaps a loved one around whom his life revolved will betray him, destroying his confidence in himself and the world, leaving him dangling and forlorn. Or it can happen that a political or religious cause in which he was wholly absorbed fails him (fails, that is, to enact the savior image he had projected there), turning his universe upside down and leaving his life meaningless. Or he may be immobilized by illness.

It can happen also that a spiritual illness may leave him helpless. Then he who formerly set forth confidently each day to master life now discovers that unaccountably he can no longer summon the will or energy to do so. His entire personality is submerged in a depression. In this case his ego intellect is pressed down and debased, exactly as pictured in this Tarot card. Like the Hanged Man, he feels as impotent as a vegetable. In extreme cases a person undergoing such an experience may become almost literally a vegetable. Lost in the world of the unconscious, no longer able to participate in the outer world or to recognize and care for his own physical needs, he may require hospitalization.

Jung saw the neuroses or psychoses which expressed themselves in these various kinds of stalemates, not as diseases inhibiting life, but rather as corrective measures whose purpose it was to further life by establishing psychic equilibrium at a new level. He thought of them as nature's way of healing the psychic organism. He observed that whenever the intellect and will became inflexible and power-oriented, nature resorted to extreme measures to knock out man's "head trip" so that he would be forced to explore other aspects of his psyche. Jung looked upon the situation pictured in the Hanged Man as an invitation to plumb new depths of being – a challenge rather than a punishment. He says:

> For the unconscious always tries to produce an impossible situation in order to force the individual to bring out his very

best. Otherwise one stops short of one's best, one is not complete, one does not realize oneself. What is needed is an impossible situation where one has to renounce one's own will and one's own wit and do nothing but trust to the impersonal power of growth and development.[5]

Until recent years few psychiatrists agreed with Jung's viewpoint. Faced with a patient in the Hanged Man's position, many reacted to him as almost everyone reacts to his Tarot picture: they wanted to turn him right side up, set him immediately on his feet, and get him started once more in the world of outer achievement so that he could resume his life at the point where it was interrupted.

It is hard not to feel this way, for we are all predisposed to value the obvious ever present realities of the external world above those of the inner world whose manifestations we experience less frequently and less vividly. In fact, many lay persons who have never been possessed by a spiritual sickness are apt to deny the reality of such a condition. Confronted with a friend in a depressed state of mind, they often dismiss his symptoms as imaginary and label him a self-centered hypochondriac. "Buck up," they counsel him. "Don't be so introspective. Get out of yourself. Get interested in a hobby." They may even behave rudely to someone who seems chronically depressed, thinking to shock him loose from his state of possession. For similar reasons hospitals sometimes use electric-shock treatments on individuals suffering from severe depression, hoping to jolt them back to "normalcy."

Today a few psychiatrists are beginning to concur with Jung's view that so-called mental illness is itself an instrument for healing an unhealthy condition and re-establishing the equilibrium of an imbalanced psychic system. Instead of interrupting Nature's healing processes by mechanical devices, psychiatrists are now exploring new ways to help Nature and implement her work. Instead of attempting to force the patient back into his previous ego-oriented mold, psychologists are offering him support in his enforced withdrawal from life, encouraging him to accept it as an opportunity to explore the hidden life within. Through analogy with mythological material, a trained analytical psychologist can help give order and meaning to the chaotic images encountered in the unconscious. Then the patient's life can become more ordered and meaningful. When this kind of work is brought to successful completion the results are rewarding, for the patient emerges from this enforced initiation, not merely reassembled within the framework of his former personality, but truly reborn – a new person newly connected to his center. John Weir Perry, one of the pioneers in this kind of treatment, described a schizophrenic episode in this way:

> Because of an activation of the unconscious and a collapse of the ego, consciousness is overwhelmed by the deepest levels of

> the psyche, and the individual finds himself living in a psychic
> modality quite different from his surroundings. He is immersed
> in a myth world. He feels suddenly isolated because he finds no
> understanding of it on the part of those around him. The fear of
> this overwhelmingness and of this isolation causes a wave of
> panic, which sends him into an acute withdrawal. His emotions
> no longer connect with ordinary things, but drop into concerns
> and titanic involvements with an entire inner world of myth and
> image . . . In it there is a clustering of symbolic contents into a
> number of major themes strangely alike from one case to
> another. It is just like myth and ritual text, save only that it is
> broken up in scattered fragments, much as dream contents
> are.[6]

Likening these fragments to a dismantled stained glass window whose
pieces revolve like patterns in a kaleidoscope hovering around a center,
Perry goes on to show how these fragments ultimately stabilize in a balanced harmonious way in relation to this center.

By accompanying the patient through such a chaotic experience, the
psychiatrist who is familiar with this technique can help him to reassemble
these kaleidoscopic fragments in a meaningful way, so that the center
becomes a clear and active force in life. Even with such psychological support and understanding, confronting the monstrous chaos of the unconscious in this way takes patience, acceptance, and great courage.
Regardless of how the situation pictured in The Hanged Man dramatizes
itself in outer reality, such a confrontation always requires sacrifice – a conscious relinquishing of ego-consciousness as the guiding force and an acceptance of one's fate and a submission to it.

As Mary Renault says in the quotation that heads this chapter, "It is
not the blood-letting that calls down power. It is the consenting."[7]

Only through consenting with his heart and soul to this experience
can the Hanged Man summon a helpful heavenly power and reconnect
with the gods and with his transpersonal self. Through his acceptance of
crucifixion, man cooperates with his fate – and in a sense, *chooses* it. And
when he chooses his fate he is released from it, because in that moment he
transcends it.

The meaning of crucifixion is eloquently stated in the biblical accounts
of Jesus' last moments on the cross. After first crying out "My God, my
God, why hast Thou forsaken me?" he accepts his fate with the words:
"Father, into thy hands I commend my spirit." And having said thus, he
gave up the ghost.

If the Hanged Man can accept his fate and "commend his spirit" to a
power superior to ego-consciousness, he can then "give up the ghost" of

his former personality and step into life with a new spirit. If he can endure and understand his crucifixion, he will emerge from this dark encounter on the other side of the chasm – in another world, so to speak. Having reached the other side, he will set forth once more on his journey but this time in a more conscious and dedicated way.

Up to now the hero's chief task has been to live his outer life fully. But now (as pictured in this card) there is a break between the old and the new. He can never again return to his former ego-centered personal life. From now on he will begin to look deeper and deeper into the grim face of impersonal Death, that monstrous figure pictured in the next card.

Fig. 54 La Morte (Marseilles Deck)

16. Death: The Enemy

So long as you do not die and rise again,
You are a stranger to the dark earth.

Goethe

Trump number thirteen pictures a skeleton wielding a blood-red scythe (Fig. 54). At his feet lie the dismembered bodies of two human beings. In the previous card we left the hero hanging upside down and helpless over an abyss to endure spiritual death and the ultimate dismemberment of his former life and personality. Here we see pictured this dismemberment: his former ideas (symbolized by the heads), standpoints (depicted as feet), and activities (shown as hands) lie useless, strewn about the ground. Every aspect of the hero's former life seems to have been chopped down – even his central guiding principle, for one of the heads in this picture wears a crown, indicating that the kingly charioteer pictured in card seven will no longer rule his destiny in the old way.

But the hero has not lost the royal charioteer who helped guide his course when he set forth to conquer the world in the Chariot, for the crowned head at the skeleton's feet already radiates new life. Whatever parts of the old order that are still vital and useful will be incorporated into the new. Nothing in nature is lost. *The king is dead: long live the king.*

In many primitive societies, each year the old king is symbolically killed, dismembered, and ritually "eaten" to ensure the fertility of the new crops and the revitalization of the kingdom. Christian churches today preserve a similar idea in the Holy Communion, wherein the parishioners partake of bread and wine, symbolic of the body and blood of Christ, to dramatize the incorporation of the Christ Spirit newly within themselves.

In this Tarot card, the idea of revitalization and renewal is more than hinted at by the profusion of new sprouts everywhere and by the way the hands and feet seem to be planted in the earth and already springing to new life. This may be taken as symbolizing an inner psychic manifestation rather than an external one, as indicated by the fact that these new sprouts are colored yellow and blue, symbolic of intuition and spirit, attributes of man's psychic inner nature, rather than green, which is the color of sensation – of outer physical nature.

In card twenty, Judgement, which is the card just beneath Death on our Map of the Journey, the seeds of Death's harvest will have reached maturity. In Judgement we shall see rise a new human being, reborn from the dark earth. But this is getting ahead of our story. For the moment, all we know is that the hero, having "ripened" as Hanged Man, now feels as though he is being dismembered. Death pictures that moment when one feels "all in pieces" – scattered – the old personality and ways so mutilated as to be almost unrecognizable. In the face of time's whirlwind dance, we all stand dismayed, shattered and scattered. As we know from such experiences, it will take some doing before the hero can re-collect and re-member himself. It will be a long time before he can be resurrected as a new and whole person into a new and complete life.

"Dismemberment," says Edward Edinger, "can be understood psychologically as a transformative process which divides up an original unconscious content for purposes of conscious assimilation."[1] In Edinger's book *Ego and Archetype,* a woodcut depicts the crucifixion and dismemberment of Jesus, symbolizing the self fragmented for this purpose. In a similar way the crowned head in card thirteen can be seen to represent the hero's guiding principle as it first appeared to him, being prepared for assimilation and integration in order to be resurrected ultimately in a new form.

Even viewed symbolically, as an instrument of change within the context of our earthly life, the skeleton of card thirteen is hard to accept. We are creatures of habit. At the most superficial level we resist changes in our everyday lives – even changes we ourselves have consciously planned. When, after years of saving and anticipation, we finally move to that long-awaited new home of our dreams, we nevertheless feel sad at leaving the old homestead. Or when at last we achieve a desired transformation in our personal lives and conduct, we still mourn the old ways. We miss bad habits as well – those habits which (to paraphrase Rilke) came and felt at home with us and stayed. Parting is such sweet sorrow because we become attached to everything: people, animals, things. We don't want to lose anything that we feel "belongs to us" – even decaying teeth or falling hair. We are especially attached to the instinctual ways of our natural bodies.

Outworn parts of our psyche are also difficult to part with. The alchemists recognized this predicament, and for them, too, the skeleton symbolized the necessity to loosen one's identification with the body. They also recognized the need to make conscious the conflict between the spiritual and the natual man. "In so doing," Jung tells us, "they rediscovered the old truth that every operation of this kind is a figurative death – which explains the violent aversion everybody feels when he has to see through his projections and recognize the nature of his anima."[2]

But between the pruning away of the old and the maturation of the new lies a period of black mourning. In referring to this stage of the journey to self-knowledge, the alchemists used the term *mortificatio. Blessed are they that mourn.* Whoever mourns the amputation of an unconscious reaction which has been a part of him since childhood, or whoever bemoans the loss of some rigid projection which has long served as support for a tottering ego, these may consider themselves blessed. They will ultimately be comforted with more valid insights and more enduring support.

The skeleton is an apt symbol for this kind of revelation. It suggests both movement and stability. It represents the bare bones of reality; the scaffolding for our flesh and muscles, the jointed framework upon which everything else hangs together, moves, and functions as a unit. And yet, paradoxically, this instrument of change also represents our most enduring part. It is the bony self that we leave to future historians – the sole testimony of our existence as individuals. It is all that remains of our ancestors – of our roots buried deep in time. The skeleton is the archetypal homo sapiens. As such, it represents an eternal basic truth revealed to the hero for the first time.

Some Tarot decks (among these one designed by Aleister Crowley) picture this skeleton whirling about like a dervish, brandishing its scythe in the frantic Dance of Death. This concept brings together the idea that death is both change and stability; that though its essence is whirlwind transformation, its choreography is eternal.

The skeleton of card thirteen embraces many pairs of opposites. On the one hand, he is nothing but a bag of bones, a monstrous dead thing that betrays our faith in the warmth and vitality of life, the great leveler which reduces the unique essence of genius and fool alike to a common denominator. On the other hand, he can be seen as a universal diagram through which Pure Being shines; a revelation of the inner workings of things, like the insides of a watch. *What a piece of work is man!* Viewing the skeleton thus, we marvel at the wonder of our creation, and of all creation. In this way it becomes the model of how we work – how everything works. In this diagrammatic figure, macrocosm and microcosm are united.

The skeleton is impersonal and universal; yet he is our most personal secret, hidden thing, a treasure buried deep within ourselves, underneath our flesh. We can touch our skin, our nails, our hair, our teeth, but we cannot touch our bones. Normally we never see our bones; yet, like the deep unconscious, they are our truest self. X-rays of one's bony structure are often used as a means of identification. Awesome thing, an X-ray, like a dream or vision. *Can that be us?* We shudder at the thought; and yet there's a feeling of kinship, too. We feel a connection, both literally and figuratively, "in our bones." The skeleton stands naked before us. How fiendish and unappetizing it looks. Hard to believe, isn't it, that all it asks of us is just what we ask of one another: *to be accepted*. Let us take a good look at it.

As we study this card more closely, we observe that it includes many opposites. Its scythe connects it with Saturn, god of time, of harvest, dissolution and decay; yet the scythe echoes the shape of the crescent moon, symbol of Artemis, offering promise of renewal and regeneration and suggesting unseen phases yet to come in endless recurring cycles. The scythe's blade is red with the carnage and destruction it leaves in its wake; yet the skeleton's warm tint and active pose are charged with creative energy.

All the Tarot characters discussed so far, being archetypes, have of course shown a similar tendency to encompass many opposites, including those of gender. But heretofore each central character has been pictured as outspokenly either male or female. In two cases the masculine and feminine elements were even pictured separately (Pope-Popess; Emperor-Empress); but in card thirteen the sexual characteristics of its central figure are not clearly defined. We are moving toward a more androgynous presentation than has hitherto appeared. Death is so fundamental to life that it can probably best be presented in a somewhat sexless, diagrammatic way which includes all possibilities.

Sometimes the skeleton is shown quite outspokenly as a diagram of the self. In his book *Hara*, Karlfried Dürkheim presents an illustration of this (Fig. 55), picturing the metal figure of an emaciated Buddha seated in meditation. The body is literally reduced to skin and bones, clearly revealing the skeletal structure. The empty eye sockets of this skeleton's taut face, blankly hollow, stare darkly into infinity.

In dealing with Tarot thirteen, commentators usually stress the skeleton as a symbol for change and transformation *in this life*. The ultimate transformation, physical death, is often avoided entirely. Yet to take this card at the level of psychological and spiritual change only is a cop-out – an instance of how we tiptoe around the subject of physical death. Whoever designed this card must have had a similar reluctance to call the skeleton by name. In the original French edition there is no name whatsoever. In the modern English edition of this deck, the title does appear but it is not written in bold letters under the picture as with all the other Trumps. Instead, the caption "Death" is written very gingerly – whispered as it were – in the upper right-hand margin. Whoever put that fatal word there evidently dropped it hastily and ran just in time, one imagines, to escape the next swing of that bloody scythe.

All of us hesitate to speak this monster name. When we do call someone's name, he usually turns and looks in our direction. That's the last thing we want this threatening figure to do. Like truant children cowering

Fig. 55 The Repentant Buddha

in a corner, we seem to have the notion that if we don't attract his attention, death may forget to knock on our door. Do we seriously believe that never speaking his name, taking care always to strew our friends' graves with bland euphemisms, will cause this nameless creature simply to "pass on?" Not this fellow, you may be sure. He has one huge eye cocked in our direction, and for all that he is a skeleton, he moves quickly.

It is not by accident that the number of this Tarot card is thirteen, a number considered unlucky in our culture. Thirteen intrudes itself into the twelve hours of our day and the twelve months of our year, breaking up the tidy rhythm of our daily round. There is no room on our calendar, no spot on our clock for number thirteen. There is no place set at our table for this awesome guest. We experience the intrusion of this skeleton as a betrayal – the twelve and Judas.

Intellectually we search out roundabout ways toward a theoretical acceptance of this creature and his scythe. We tell ourselves that such a housecleanng is necessary in order to make room for new life; we say we understand that the twelve hours on our clocks must expand to include new dimensions of time. Philosophically we accept the logic that death is not the antithesis of life – that birth and death are rather the twin poles upon which life rests. We know all these words, and we can (and do) recite them frequently. But how to come to terms with our personal mortality? Ay, there's the rub.

Pallida mors aequo pulsat pede pauperum tabernas / Regium turres. "Pale death with impartial tread knocks at the cottages of the poor and the palaces of kings." It sounds more awesome in Horace's Latin; but what it means is: "Ready or not, here I come!"

How *can* we "get ready" for death? The simplest way to prepare for that inevitable knock on the door would be, of course, to follow Balzac's advice: "Death is certain. Let us forget it." And indeed if we could encompass the fact that our physical mortality is certain, then maybe we could, in one sense, "forget it." At least this fellow with the scythe wouldn't haunt us as he does.

Balzac's aphorism neatly encapsulates the wisdom of the old fable "Appointment in Samarra," which holds truth at many levels. A servant meeting the black-robed crone Death in the market place, sees her make what seems to him a threatening gesture. The servant, terrified, borrows his master's horse and flees to Samarra. That afternoon, the master confronts the crone in the market place and asks: "Why did you make a threatening gesture to my servant this morning?" Death replies: "That was not a threatening gesture; it was merely a start of surprise. I was astonished to see your servant in Bagdad, for I had an appointment with him tonight in Samarra."

Perhaps if each of us could truly accept his "appointment in Samarra," the activity of that skeleton in card thirteen would not seem so threatening.

In the fable cited above, Death appeared, not as a hostile or vengeful character, but as a servant of life with a job to do and a time schedule to keep. The implications of this story go deeper than Balzac's aphorism. They seem to say that by squandering precious time and energy trying to avoid Death, the servant failed to live his life; so that in the end it was he and not the mysterious figure in black who betrayed life.

Until we can entrust ourselves to death, we never really entrust ourselves to life. We remain slaves, attached to the body, trapped in deadly egocentricity. Shakespeare dramatized this idea in *King Lear*. There the central character, facing death on the heath, finally accepts that his hand "smells of mortality," and in so doing he becomes at last "every inch a king." "To accept the fact that you perish in time," says Jung, "is a sort of victory over time."[3] Through accepting his physical mortality, Lear transcended the limitations of earthly time. Bursting out of his ego self, he stepped into the timeless world of the immortals.

We often use the term "death's door" to convey the idea that at our physical death we step through a door into a radiant world of new life in the hereafter. Many who have literally stood on the threshold of death and returned testify that this glimpse of "the beyond" opened up new dimensions of spiritual awareness. And those whom fate has never called to the threshold of death have found that facing the fact of death through the loss of someone close has liberated the spirit and opened the door to new vistas.

To accept death like birth, as a part of life, is to become truly alive. "Not wanting to live," said Jung, "is synonymous with not wanting to die. Becoming and passing away are the same curve."[4] And again: "Whoever does not accompany this curve remains suspended in the air and grows numb. From middle age on, only he remains alive who is willing to die with life."[5]

If the Hanged Man is not to remain suspended in the air, growing spiritually numb with the years, he must take the next step, which leads through the valley of the shadow to acceptance of death. In recognition of this intimate connection between death and spiritual transformation, primitive religious ceremonies often required the initiate to face death. Sometimes, like the Hanged Man, he was abandoned, helpless and alone – perhaps in a dark forest. Or, like Sir Lancelot, he was forced to spend the night in his own tomb. Traditional in the initiation of a knight was the final confrontation with the mysterious Black Knight, an unknown warrior armed with a primitve axe, who demanded that the initiate lay his neck on the block. If the young man had the courage to obey this fateful command, the mysterious stranger threw down his axe and lifted his visor, revealing himself as a savior of shining countenance.

In our Tarot, the skeleton's face resembles a mask – for Death wears many masks. The myriad facets of this stranger have preoccupied artists of all ages. By recalling some of these, we may get an idea of the true face of Death – and may learn at last to speak his name. If, like Jacob with his Angel, we can come to grips with this personage, he may even speak for us our true name.

Death is frequently depicted as a grinning skull mocking us with a fiendish leer or, as the fourth horseman of the Apocalypse, riding furiously across the canvas brandishing a sword. Before medical science taught us how to prevent wholesale slaughter by epidemic disease and made the causes of fatal illness more understandable, Death was seen as a ruthless stranger who appeared unaccountably from nowhere killing off multitudes and laying waste the civilized world.

The Triumph of Death, a central theme in Petrarch's sonnets to Laura, and a popular one in endless frescoes and paintings of the same period, no doubt influenced the pictorial form of Tarot thirteen. Death's triumph was depicted in a variety of ways, some of which reiterate the motifs pictured in the Marseilles Tarot. In many of these paintings, a pallid skeleton astride a skeletal horse rides roughshod over a group of human figures from all walks of life. The fallen figures are so jumbled together that one gets the same sense of chaotic dismemberment as that pictured in the Tarot Death. Now here, now there, we glimpse an isolated head or foot and an occasional upright "sprouted" hand. Sometimes, as in our Tarot, one of the severed heads wears a crown.

In such pictorial representations, Death is shown as an impersonal force, striking against all mankind, rather than as a personal adversary whom one meets alone. In part, this may be because plagues and other catastrophes frequently attacked and destroyed entire communities. It may also be that in past times death was not experienced as such a lonely business as it is today. Ritual ways of facing death were provided in the sacraments of the Church and in the customs of family and community life. Death usually took place at home and was an experience shared by all who knew the deceased. The services attending the burial brought the entire community together in ritual worship and mourning. With the breakdown of organized religion, these ritual ways of facing death have largely been lost and, since the idea of death is too monstrous to face alone, we have, until recently, simply swept it under the rug. In the last decade, as will be discussed later, we have begun to explore new ways to accept and deal with the universal problem of physical mortality.

Yet the actual experience of death itself is essentially an individual experience. Each of us must face his moment of truth alone. Böcklin's painting *Island of the Dead,* (Fig. 56) catches both the loneliness and wonder of this moment. It shows a small figure in a white shroud standing alone at the prow of Charon's boat which silently approaches a desolate island whose ruddy cliffs and black cypress are framed in utter darkness. There is no sign of life. A single marble doorway cut into the mountain welcomes the

Fig. 56 Island of the Dead (Bocklin, Arnold, 1827-1901. The Metropolitan Museum of Art, New York, Beisinger Fund, 1926)

traveler – to what? It is strange that the habitation of the dead should be envisioned as uninhabited. However overpopulated our planet is now, its numbers are far exceeded by the legions of the dead. But the approach to death, as Böcklin shows, is always a lonely voyage. It is a personal experience.

The uniqueness of each individual's confrontation with death is sometimes dramatized pictorially as a skeleton pointing a bony finger directly at its next victim. Despite the fact that dying is an experience common to all living things, each of us experiences death's summons as a finger pointing uniquely at oneself. Psychologically, death points at each of us in turn, demanding that each, in his own way, find the meaning behind that gesture. Death challenges every living human being in a special way. For, unlike the beasts, man alone has the ability to anticipate death, to philosophize about it, and to experience its happening consciously. "Alas, poor Yorick," means much more than "Alas, poor us." It leads us through the experience of mourning, to soliloquize, Hamlet-like, on the meaning of death and to make a place for it within the spectrum of life.

In his poem "Spring and Fall: To a Young Child," Manley Hopkins speaks to this theme. He begins his poem by asking the young child: "Márgarét, are you grieving / Over Goldengrove unleaving?" and he ends with this couplet:

> It is the blight man was born for
> It is Margaret you mourn for.[6]

Nature does not care a fig about the individual; her efforts are wholly bent on preserving the species. It is up to man, the poet seems to say, to celebrate the falling leaves and to mourn the transience of life. It is man's fateful task to cherish life and honor the individual, for it is through the individual alone that consciousness is born.

The kind of caring that Hopkins describes is very different from a miserly clutching at the things of this world or an ego-oriented fear of death. Margaret's tears, he tells us, come from a deeper level. Her childlike concern for the transience of life even though it may seem a "blight," is a natural and necessary attribute of mankind – one all too easily outgrown. "As the heart grows older," he tells the child, "it will come to such sights colder."

We have all experienced how, as we move into our grown-up world of medical science and statistics, we lose touch with the kind of mourning that Hopkins describes. We offer our children scientific explanations for the falling leaves rather than sharing their tears, and we sterilize the mystery and wonder out of the death experience in the impersonal efficiency of hospital routine. Our adult fear of death often prevents our allowing ourselves to contemplate it at all.

"Only fools and children," said Erasmus, "do not fear death." I still recall vividly an illustration in my childhood edition of Barrie's *Peter and Wendy* which showed Peter Pan standing jauntily, arms akimbo, legs outspread, gazing out over the misty lagoon. The caption read, "To die must be an awfully big adventure." With children, stepping into each new moment of existence represents a big adventure – a voyage into unknown lands. Having few preconceived notions, young people can entrust themselves to the unknown future. They are more able than we to accept the idea of death with both the tears and the awe which properly belong to this "big adventure."

Many adults find it difficult to contemplate the unknown in any context. We prefer being furnished beforehand with a program of events to follow, a synopsis of the plot, an agenda. Krishnamurti, when he was asked, "What happens after death?" replied: "I'll know when I get there. I don't need to know now." *Do we need to know now?* Doesn't a preoccupation with what may happen in the next chapter spoil our enjoyment of this one? Can't we, like Peter Pan, content ourselves by standing on the shore and looking out to sea with a feeling of awe and wonder?

Indian and Mexican art, welling up from the primitive unconscious, often catches the awesome numinosity of the death experience; but here, too, behind the fascination lurks a fear. Two examples are pictured. The first is a human skull adorned with jet and turquoise (Fig. 57). This object of beauty and terror was originally a gift presented to Cortez by Montezuma. Was it intended as a sinister warning that the conqueror's world would also one day undergo dismemberment? If so, the dark prophecy reflected in the blind stare of those empty eyes has come true. Montezuma's dubious gift now rests in the British Museum. *Who will dare accept this stranger next?*

The second plate pictures a Mexican god of Death (Fig. 58). This regal figure, wrought in gold and dressed in full regalia, welcomes us to his kingdom. His smile, open and hearty, seems that of a jolly innkeeper. "You have nothing to fear," it seems to say. Yet we hesitate at the threshold. Already we feel the heavy door closing and hear its bolt slide into place behind us. We feel our soft flesh crushed within King Death's metallic embrace.

The thought of physical death paralyzes us with horror. Yet each day our physical bodies make giant strides toward death's door. The problem is, of course, how to help our souls to move along in rhythm with our bodies. Whenever the spirit lags behind, it clogs the natural flow of life from birth to death, choking off the vital stream with "dead" habits and outworn concepts.

Krishnamurti was asked how he went about preparing himself for death. To this he replied: "Each day I die a little." From the context of his answer, it was obvious that what he had in mind was not a morbid con-

Fig. 57   Human Skull Adorned   (British Museum)

templation of the fact of physical death. The idea was, rather, to meet
change daily, hourly, by freeing oneself piecemeal from unconscious at-
tachments. Instead of anticipating with dread or even with eager acceptance some Grand Transformation presumably awaiting us from behind

Fig. 58   Mexican God of Death

some final door, Krishnamurti's idea seemed to be that each day offers us many doors to new life, if we would but open them.

Jung also stressed the idea that to live life fully is the natural way to approach death. As a psychologist, he saw the dreams of hundreds of elderly persons. He discovered that the unconscious of those approaching death does not speak in terms of some impending grand finale of life. On the contrary, the dreams of the elderly seem to continue on, as if life itself went on. Asked, then, how one should prepare for death, Jung's answer was that one should continue to live as if life went on forever.

The best way to prepare for a long journey of endless duration to an unknown land would probably be to divest oneself of all unnecessary baggage. One way to do this might be to examine one's belongings, selecting only articles essential to one's spiritual and physical well-being, leaving the rest behind. The trick, of course, is to recognize the essential.

Each day presents many opportunities to make this kind of spiritual choice, and in doing so, we may avoid the many tempting detours which can seduce our energies into promising bypaths or lull us back into the indolent womb of childish ways. To refuse to cooperate in the dismemberment of our outworn selves creates a log-jam in the flow of life. It results in spiritual death. According to Jung, such behavior can even end in physical death. He says:

> If the demand for self-knowledge is willed by fate and is refused, this negative attitude may end in real death. The demand would not have come to this person had he still been able to strike out on some promising by-path. But he is caught in a blind alley from which only self-knowledge can extricate him.[7]

To be seduced, lulled, or tempted away from a conscious participation in life and lured into cooperating with death, is a theme often dramatized in the arts. Death as seducer is a favorite subject in painting. Manuel-Deutsch's *Death the Soldier Embracing Girl* for example (Fig. 59), shows a woman locked in obscene embrace with a skeleton lover, seduced by him into a repulsive, sterile union. Sometimes Death is depicted as a seemingly beneficent mother who smothers us with a gentle lullaby into the Great Sleep. No doubt it was this aspect of Death that Dylan Thomas had in mind when he admonished his father:

> Do not go gentle into that good night
> Old age should burn and rave at close of day;
> Rage, rage against the dying of the light.[8]

And so must we all rage against the subtle blandishments of Death, that satanic tempter who can lull us into absent-minded carelessness so that we become accident prone, or who can lure us into more outspoken suicide. "To die: to sleep; . . ." If the temptation to murder our shadow side – to kill off once and for all this problematic, rejected aspect of ourselves – becomes too overwhelming, it can result in self-destruction.

Fig. 59   Death the Soldier Embracing Girl
(Nikolaus Manuel-Deutsch. Offentliche Kunstammlung, Basel,
Switzerland)

There are many even more subtle ways to commit suicide, both physically and spiritually. If we cannot bear the tensions of change, cannot accept that at certain times in our lives we must remain inactive like the

Hanged Man, upside down in relation to our former activities; if we try to force our energies into outworn patterns, then death may appear in the guise of a heart attack, stroke, or other sudden illness. Or it may happen that a person caught in a vicious round of deadly self-preoccupation can simply fade away, both spiritually and bodily. As Jung has indicated, nature finds innumerable ways to snuff out a meaningless existence.

Although death is a concept of fleshly limitation belonging to the yin side of life, it is usually referred to as masculine. In the fable "Appointment in Samarra," it appears as an old woman. Examples of death as a female figure in art are relatively rare. An engraving by Posada depicts a hideously ironic parody of feminine allure with no hint of the genuine seduction offered by death or the powerful call of the Great Mother gently beckoning us back into her soft embrace. This picture is titled *Calavera of the Female Dandy* (Fig. 60). In it, an obscenely flirtatious skull, bedecked in ribbons and bows, poses for a portrait wearing an enormous lacy hat piled high with flowers and fine feathers. The monstrous mouth with its huge teeth is half open in a voracious smile. The subject of this portrait is got up like some ridiculous old whore, parodying the seductive aspect of Death. The fact that the creature is called a "Female Dandy" suggests that she/he may be a transvestite, representing the androgyny of the self in a distorted form.

Fig. 60   Calavera of the Female Dandy (Posada)

The word *calavera* means literally "skull," but metaphorically it also
carries the connotation "madcap – a wild, hot-brained fellow." This further
underscores the transvestite theme and also suggests the idea of Death as
an irrational, uncontrolled entity whose behavior seems to us outlandish,
outside the accepted patterns of society. Satire such as Posada's is one
technique man uses to confront his fear of death. Another way we try to
put death in a hidden pocket is by reminding ourselves that it is nothing but
a mortal concept – a creation of the human intellect. William Butler Yeats,
who always raged at the top of his lungs against the dying light of old age,
tells us how a great man "casts derision upon supersession of breath." In a
poem called "Death," he says:

> Nor dread nor hope attend
> A dying animal;
> A man awaits his end
> Dreading and hoping all;
> Many times he died,
> Many times rose again.
> A great man in his pride
> Confronting murderous men
> Casts derision upon
> Supersession of breath;
> He knows death to the bone –
> Man has created death.[9]

Although Yeats may have been whistling in the dark a bit, it is certainly
true that man has created the concept of death as *a single event which
takes place irrevocably at a certain instance of time.* As we know, death is a
continuous ongoing process in nature. The concept of life and death as a
distinct dichotomy is simply contrary to observable fact.

This simple truth, long recognized philosophically, has now become a
matter of practical concern as well. In connection with heart transplants
and the recycling, as it were, of human organs, it is essential to determine
the exact moment of death so that the necessary organs can be removed
and transplanted while they are still viable, without doing violence to living
donors. (It would appear, incidentally, that the dismemberment and reassimilation of the perfect man formerly re-enacted in church and temple is
now taking place in the operation room. It is encouraging to observe in
passing that we hesitate to dismember a "living" human being – a delicacy,
be it noted, not shared by many primitive societies, including that of
Hitler's Germany.) The question medical science is asking today is a problematic one: *When is the exact moment of death?* Is it when the patient
stops breathing, when his heart stops beating, or when the EEG shows no
brain waves? Since nature knows no specific moment of death, man must

arbitrarily create one to answer these practical questions. In this sense man does literally "create death." The spurious nature of the presumed dichotomy "life versus death" has now been called to our attention in such a dramatic way that we can no longer ignore it.

Our tidy world of opposites is also being challenged at the other end of the birth-death continuum. With increased legalization of abortion, the question *When exactly does human life begin?* has also become of vital concern. As we are coming to realize, questions both of life's beginning in the flesh and ending in the flesh cannot be settled in the laboratory nor in the courtroom – they can only be settled by common agreement selecting one arbitrary spot on the space-time continuum at which we agree to say that the life of an individual human being begins, and another at which we will pronounce that this human life ends. We have set ourselves up as gods to judge the quick and the dead. Throughout all our discussions, deliberations, and decisions on these questions, Nature herself remains, as always, silent.

Yeats is profoundly right. We might well confront supersession of breath with the contempt it properly deserves. It is, in a sense, no more significant than the many transformations of the flesh which happen daily, hourly, and moment by moment. If we "create death," why does its ghost haunt us? Why can't we go cheerfully about the business of living, trusting to our animal instinct for self-preservation to protect us at those rare moments of physical crisis when defensive action is necessary?

But we cannot seem to do this. In all cultures and ages, this self-created phantom has been ever present in the wings, interrupting life's drama with irrational fears and distracting our attention from the business at hand. Many treatises have been written about the art of dying. One such, *Artes Moriendi,* probably originated at about the same time as the oldest known Tarot. One of the illustrations in this treatise is a painting by Bosch called *Death and the Miser.* In this, the miser is pictured on his deathbed. The shrouded figure of Death is seen entering the bedroom, while little black-winged goblins are everywhere, busily despoiling the miser of moneybags and other treasures. Behind him stands a white angel pointing to a crucifix from which streams a luminous beam. Blessed by this light, the miser turns to face Death, seemingly welcoming him. It is made obvious that the light which the miser now sees transcends the truism: "You can't take it with you." As Bosch and his contemporaries knew, the deadly fear of death inherent in our psychic bones cannot be vanquished by logic and aphorisms. The things of this world, he seems to be saying, can only be relinquished and death truly welcomed through the illumination of an experience which transcends all other things.

In Bosch's time, the Church and its living symbology acted as a mediator for this kind of experience. But for many of us in the twentieth century, this mediation is no longer readily available. The symbols of our Judeo-Christian heritage have lost their meaning for us. Death has increasingly become a purely physical phenomenon that takes place in a hospital and is handled antiseptically by strangers in starched uniforms. Even the intimate spiritual and emotional aspects of the death experience are now taken over by strangers – solemn personages in black who mysteriously appear at the graveside, directing proceedings in an obsequious manner. When the burial ceremonials are completed, these same black birds are often the first to swoop down upon the family (whom they barely know) to say how sorry they are that someone (whom they have known only as a corpse) has "passed on." If encouraged (and suitably recompensed), these professional mourners will select and read poetry or biblical quotations deemed appropriate to the occasion and will even concoct a flowery eulogy suitable for "the deceased" – that is to say, *any* deceased.

The ridiculous attempts of our culture to embalm life have been ably satirized in Evelyn Waugh's classic *The Loved One*. It would seem that this kind of idiocy has now reached its last extremity. It looks as though the pendulum has begun to swing back toward an emotional acceptance of death and a more personal involvement of both the dying and the bereaved in dealing with it practically and spiritually. Terminally ill patients are now being told the facts. Families are encouraged and helped to care for such patients at home. Seminars and discussion groups offer opportunities for families facing this experience to meet others confronting similar situations and to share their problems and insights.

Now that Death's name is being spoken aloud at last, we discover that the face he turns in our direction is less frightening than we had imagined. Perhaps some day the skeleton in card thirteen will shine for us with the luminous glow of transcendent light which he shed on former generations.

In his book *Psyche and Death*, Edgar Herzog explores in detail the origins of the two basic approaches to death: the scientific and the religious. It is his thesis that man's confrontation with the fact of physical death may have furnished the first impetus for all science and all religion. According to Herzog, the capacity to feel horror at the death of another is one of the major characteristics that distinguishes man from the animals. This horror, he says, is quite different from the specific fear of one's own death, which operates as an instinct of self-preservation in both men and animals alike. Research indicates that the first reaction of primitive man, and of the primitive in ourselves, is to flee from the sight of a corpse – a reaction not characteristic of animals. Characterizing this reaction as "horror of the incomprehensible," in contrast to "fear of the specific," Herzog offers the hypothesis that this feeling of horror is probably the first human experience of the "utterly unapproachable" – the unique experience which Rudolf Otto has termed a "tremendum."

Herzog goes on to demonstrate how coming to terms with this tremendum is the springboard for the development of a world picture, expanding man's consciousness in two directions: toward religion, which helps man to accept death and fate by enlarging his awareness to include these; and toward science, which meets the facts of death and fate by trying to control them. Herzog concludes his discussions of this point as follows:

> It should not need saying that both these tendencies operate simultaneously in the psyche, and influence human behaviour: yet human development always seems to lead to a point when one becomes more clearly differentiated and gains predominance over the other. The second trend (towards defence against death) suggests an assertion of the ego in *its adaptation to outer reality;* the first (the acceptance of fate) suggests a self-subordination to inner reality. One leads through magic to the domination of the physical order by means of natural science, the other leads to religion and the perception of being.[10]

Throughout our recent "dark age" with its sterile, scientific approach to death and its insane worship of both youth and longevity, the poets among us have kept faith with the religious values. They have caught in words the numinous connection between death and spiritual rebirth, holding it in trust for us all. One poem that communicates effectively for me the relationship between birth and death is T.S. Eliot's "Journey of the Magi." In this poem, one of the three Wise Men speaks as follows:

> All this was a long time ago, I remember,
> And I would do it again, but set down
> This set down
> This: were we led all that way for
> Birth or Death? There was a Birth, certainly,
> We had evidence and no doubt. I had seen birth and death,
> But had thought they were different; this Birth was
> Hard and bitter agony for us, like Death, our death.
> We returned to our places, these Kingdoms,
> But no longer at ease here, in the old dispensation,
> With an alien people clutching their gods.
> I should be glad of another death.[11]

After his confrontation with Tarot thirteen, the hero of our saga also will have taken an irrevocable step into that bourne from which no traveler returns to the same life he formerly led. Like the Wise Man, he will find himself no longer at ease in the old dispensation. He will have become a stranger to his own family and his former friends, an exile in his own land. But there is no turning back. Like the Fool – and the Wise Man – he must take to the road again, in search of "another death." Let us follow him.

Fig. 61   Temperance (Marseilles Deck)

17. Temperance: Heavenly Alchemist

Every blade of grass has its Angel that bends
over it and whispers, "Grow, grow"!

Talmud

In Trump fourteen, an angel with blue hair, wearing a red flower on her forehead, pours liquid from a blue vase into a red one (Fig. 61). The theme of this card connects Temperance with Aquarius, the water carrier, the eleventh sign of the zodiac. Aquarius rules the circulation of the blood and has been correlated with the circulation of ideas. It traditionally symbolizes the dissolution of old forms and the loosening of rigid bonds, heralding a liberation from the world of phenomena.

Aquarius usually is pictured holding only one urn. As for the two containers pictured here, Paul Huson, in his *The Devil's Picture Book*, makes some interesting comments. He reminds us that in the Egyptian zodiac of Denderah, Aquarius was identified with Hapi, the god of the Nile, whose waters were the source of life, both agricultural and spiritual. Like her Egyptian counterpart, then, the Angel Temperance blends two opposite aspects or essences, producing life-giving energy. Huson also points out that a similar idea was dramatized by the second-century Gnostic, Marcos, who celebrated the Eucharist by using two chalices instead of one. "By pouring the contents of one into the other," Huson says, "he mixes water with wine, the water being equated in his scheme with Sophia, 'divine wisdom,' which had fallen to earth and been whirled about in the dark empty spaces, and the wine with the fiery spirit of the Savior Christ."[1]

The Angel Temperance is a crucial figure in the Tarot sequence, inspiring much of the action that follows. Whether we think of the red and blue opposites she intermingles as symbolizing spirit and flesh, masculine and feminine, yang and yin, conscious and unconscious, or whether their interaction is thought of as "the marriage of Christ and Sophia" or "the union of fire and water," makes little difference, for all of these are implied. The liquid which flows between the two jars is neither red nor blue but is pure white, suggesting that it represents a pure essence, perhaps energy.

Of course two elemental opposites such as fire and water cannot at first confront each other directly. Such a confrontation at this point would no doubt be catastrophic. It might end either in violent take-over by uncontrolled fiery elements or in equally disastrous quenching of the flaming spirit by a tidal wave from the unconscious. Before the red and blue elements can safely meet in daylight awareness, a preparation must take place in the dark recesses of the psyche. It is this ceremonial over which the Angel presides.

As in any conflict situation, a creative first step toward resolution is to find an arbiter – someone whose wisdom and understanding can encompass both sides. The winged Temperance, who holds with equal concern both the red and the blue, is such a figure. Her wings tell us that she is superhuman – able to rise above petty, mundane matters. She inhabits a realm beyond mortal reach. No human figure is pictured in this card, indicating that whatever is happening here is taking place in the hero's unconscious, without the awareness or participation of the ego.

Angels have long been seen as winged messengers from heaven, meaning psychologically that they represent inner experiences of a numinous nature which connect man with the archetypal world of the unconscious. These winged visions appear in our mundane lives at crucial moments, suddenly bringing new insights and revealing new dimensions of experience.

In biblical accounts, angels traditionally appeared in order to make an annunciation or a revelation of transcendental import. Usually an angel's message is one of concern not only to the individual who sees the vision, but to the collective group as well. Such visionary experiences mark dramatic turning points, personally and culturally. Sometimes they presage a miraculous birth (as in the Annunciation to Mary) or trumpet a call to rebirth (as in the Last Judgement), a theme which will appear later on in the Tarot series.

The Angel Temperance does not announce herself with blinding light or clash of cymbals. Rather she stands before us quietly as an enduring presence. Unlike the Angel of Judgement pictured in card twenty, who will burst through the barrier which separates the celestial from the terrestrial to appear in a blaze of glory in the skies, the Angel Temperance, as befits her name, stages no dramatic entrance. In fact, she makes no entrance at all. She is simply there, absorbed in the business of pouring. One feels that this winged being is not newly descended from heaven, but has been standing there a long time waiting for the hero to become aware of her.

According to ancient belief, each living person, animal, and plant had its guardian angel. Perhaps this is the hero's good angel. If she bears a message for him, it is conveyed by her actions which seem to say: "Pa-

tience – Faith. There are powers operating in the universe and in yourself
which are beyond your everyday experience. Trust these deeper currents
of life; let yourself flow with them."

For Meister Eckhart, angels represented "ideas of God." According to
Jung, an angel personifies the coming into consciousness of something
new arising from the deep unconscious. He once defined angels more specifically as "personified transmitters of unconscious contents which announce that they want to speak."[2] The Angel Temperance, as we see, has
not yet made a pronouncement. But if the hero wishes to hear the Angel's
message, he could probably initiate a dialogue with her. Such a dialogue
establishes a living relationship to the answering "other" within.

This method of dramatizing one's connection with an inner figure
(which Jung calls "active imagination") was apparently used by the alchemists too. They called it *meditatio*. Ruland the Lexicographer defines
meditatio as "an inner dialogue with someone who is invisible, as also with
God, or with oneself, or with one's good angel."

After quoting Ruland thus, Alan McGlashan adds these words, "and
with one's dark angel."[3] This is a pertinent addition, for (as Jung has
pointed out) angels, like all archetypes, are creatures of questionable
morality. In the Tarot card which follows this one, The Devil, we shall in
fact come face to face with the most questionable and darkest of these,
Prince Lucifer, the fallen angel.

But the Angel Temperance may be safely trusted, for she wears a
flower on her forehead whose five-petaled circular shape suggests a mandala, symbolic of the quintessence. This living mandala is placed at the
spot of the third eye, traditionally the area of supreme consciousness, and
in Jungian terms the spot of individuation. Statues of Buddha always bear
some sign on the forehead. It is the sign of awakened consciousness, the
symbol of the twice-born.

Although the hero's awareness of his Angel is still buried too deep for
his conscious mind to penetrate, nevertheless he begins to understand intuitively that he, too, is marked. He has emerged from his confrontation
with death as one twice born; he feels his own awareness flowering into
new life. Having glimpsed this angelic being, he now feels chosen –
singled out from the multitude.

To be visited by such an angel is a remarkable experience. The poet
Rilke put his experience with such archetypal beings into these words:

> Who can have lived his life in solitude
> and not have marvelled how the angels there
> will visit him at times and let him share
> what can't be given to the multitude,
>
> the all out-scattered and disintegrated,
> who into cries have let their voices loose?[4]

Such a compensatory message of healing and unity as Rilke describes usually comes to us at times when we are most alone – when our lives, inner and outer, seem the most fragmented. It is at these moments, when the ego feels insecure, that figures from the deep unconscious can move into our range of awareness.

The hero now finds himself in such a condition. That this moment marks a psychological turning point is also evidenced by the fact that Temperance is the final card in its horizontal row on our map, indicating that a dynamic change in the flow of libido is about to take place.

The terrors and insights he experienced in confronting the skeleton of the previous card have left the hero feeling shaken and lonely, disoriented and set apart. He cannot return to his old ways and habits; his life as he formerly lived it lies in ruins. His conscious personality is temporarily shattered. Although the shell of his old security is now irreparably damaged, through its very cracks a new light can be seen, a dim vision of potential wholeness.

Amidst the clamorous cries of the many conflicting ideas, feelings, and opinions whirling about inside him, a center of hidden silence begins to become manifest. Sometimes when he looks with the inward eye, he can catch the faint outlines of his guardian angel as pictured in the Tarot. Sometimes when he listens intently he can hear the soothing sound of his subterranean waters as they begin to flow again, and he can feel his energies quicken and spring to new life. The domain of death is finished; fresh libido is available.

Now it is time for this libido to be poured into a new container. But the change cannot be consciously willed or directed. "Psychic energy," says Jung, "is a very fastidious thing which insists on fulfilment of its own conditions. However much energy may be present, we cannot make it serviceable until we have succeeded in finding the right gradient."[5] Life's creative energies cannot be directed by sheer will power into whatever channels the conscious ego might select, however reasonable, logical, and appropriate these channels might seem to the thinking mind. "Life can flow forward," as Jung says, "only along the path of the gradient." To balance the flow of opposites so that energy finds its proper gradient requires the patience and skill of an angel. Since this kind of transformation is beyond our conscious control, it is appropriate that the hero step out of the picture, trusting his Angel to perform this part of the Great Work alone.

At any level of meaning, reconciliation of the opposites is not a matter of logic and reason. Generations of men have struggled to reconcile the search for meaning, exemplified in religion, and the search for fact, embodied in science, to no avail. The supposed dichotomy between these two basic urges in men cannot be reconciled through the intellect. Like all opposites, they cannot be resolved by logic; they can only come together at the point of *experience*. This truth is illustrated most eloquently in a filmed interview with Jung in which he was asked: "Do you believe in God?" to which he replied, "I don't *believe* . . . I know."

The Angel Temperance might personify this kind of inner knowing which will increasingly supplant "belief" and "opinion" in the hero's response to life. We might see in this card the beginning of the Aquarian Age in the psyche, leading to the rediscovery of man and his world as a whole. Originally, the word "whole" was synonymous with "holy," and the verb "to heal" meant "to make whole." It was Jung's conclusion that neuroses represent a lost capacity for the wholeness and holiness of religious experience. In Temperance, contact with the numinous is re-established. Her two urns, like the Holy Grail and the communion chalice, have magic powers to gather together, contain, preserve, and heal. And this winged personage herself will remain as a kind of archangelic guide for the hero on his journey. She will stay with him as a constant reminder that his thoughts, his energies, and his plans are never wholly under conscious control.

The liquid in the Angel's urns seems to spring by its own vitality from some inexhaustible source, like the mythical waters of the miraculous pitcher. The pattern of the liquid's trajectory can be seen as a lemniscate opened out. The closed lemniscate, which appears as the Magician's hat in the first Trump, suggests the unitary system of primal creative energy before the separation of the opposites, the motion of the tail-biting uroboros. In Temperance the lemniscate has unfolded so that the opposites are now separated and clearly defined as two vases, with the precious liquid being transferred from the higher to the lower container, generating a new kind of energy.

The libido, thus revivified, begins to flow in another direction. After the enforced inactivity of the Hanged Man and the cruel dismemberment of Death, the hero's energy now leaps, like an electric current, from the higher to the lower potential. A fresh connection is being made between the sky-blue clarity of spirit and the bloody red of human reality. Aquarius, the sign of ideal relationship, is concerned with the interplay between perfect principle and perfect form. Since the Angel both pours and receives in one gesture, she creates a new rapport between the directive thrust of the positive yang and the quiet containment of the receptive yin. In this way, she unites the magic of the Magician with that of his female counterpart, Strength.

In The Magician and in Strength, the lemniscate is pictured as a hat. Such a hat is a kind of trademark or insignia of office. It indicates that its wearer is but the custodian of the magic powers or divine talents which it symbolizes. The Angel Temperance wears no hat. Her divine powers are invested in herself.

A good way to understand the drama of this card is to contrast it with the theme of interaction of the opposites as it is pictured in other Trumps.

For example, in The Chariot, which is the card directly above Temperance in our map, the red and blue opposites appeared as two headstrong horses yoked together. Although these two seemed an ill-matched team, their mysteriously invisible reins hinted at divine guidance. In Temperance, this divine guidance comes directly from the winged Angel, its central, and sole, figure.

The symbolism of Temperance is more impersonal and abstract than that of The Chariot. It offers us a view of the situation from the aspect of eternity, putting us in touch with the Aquarian realm of pure, unitary knowledge which exists behind our world of appearances. Here energy, formerly experienced as two separate beasts, is now revealed to be one vital current. In The Chariot the task of the libido was to move the hero forward on his journey. In Temperance the libido itself undergoes transformation. The opposites, which were pictured at the beginning of the Realm of Equilibrium as the two pans of Justice's scales held apart by a fixed bar, are now shown as red and blue containers for the one unique fluid of Being. They have now become alternate forms which shape and hold this *élan vital*.

In the previous chapter, Death, brandishing time's weapon, threatened to cut short the hero's mortal existence. The grinning skeleton represented time in its most threatening aspect. By facing this monstrous reality, the hero began to be lifted into a realm beyond time, to step out of the prison of earthly limitation into the world of eternals. The Angel makes a connection between the everyday world of historical time and "sacred time," to use Mircea Eliade's term. Eliade describes this realm as "a sort of eternal mythical present that is periodically reintegrated by means of rites."[6]

In Temperance, the ritual of the pouring reconnects the hero with the sacred world he had glimpsed before as Hanged Man but has since lost. In the future there will no doubt be times when he will again find himself out of touch with his Angel and her world of immortal verities. But never again will he feel wholly bereft, for he has now experienced the sound of her waters deep in himself and baptized his petty cares in the mainstream of her creative energy.

This ritual is by no means a purely philosophical concept. The help which the Angel offers is a practical one, vital to both outer reality and to the inner journey. If we take the two vases to represent outer and inner, conscious and unconscious, the Angel, by her ritual pouring, helps the hero to reconcile these two aspects of life. As Jung emphasizes, the necessity arises daily to reconcile the world of our dreams with that of our daily lives. Otherwise these two worlds are apt to intrude on each other in a most confusing way. When the unconscious steps into our outer world to borrow as its dream symbols the events, persons, and objects of our daily experience, it threatens the accustomed order of everyday life. In a similarly confusing way, the rational ego mind can intrude into the image world of the unconscious, disturbing and disrupting its healing work.

When these two worlds get mixed up unconsciously, with no guardian angel to preside, our lives become muddled and confused, often with disasterous results. If we try to live on the outer side a drama that more properly belongs to the inner, the plot could end in tragedy. We might, for example, project the Angel Temperance onto some person of our acquaintance, handing over to this person's care and keeping all our conflicts, problems, hopes, and dreams, expecting this seemingly superior being to guard and regulate the flow of our life. If so, it goes without saying that the Angel of card fourteen would one day pop up in our deck as the Devil of card fifteen.

It is equally impractical, of course, to attempt to squeeze into our inner world events which properly belong in outer reality. If, for example, we have a problem with our spouse or neighbor, it is futile to take this drama wholly on the symbolic level, spending long hours concocting imaginary dialogues with this person or theorizing in solitary confinement about possible reasons for the other's behavior. Although some introspection is valuable, there comes a time when one must step into reality and initiate a real-life dialogue with the person in question. Quite often, when we summon the courage to do this, we find the outer reality to be much less threatening than the inner drama we had concocted. It can even happen that what had appeared in our imagination as a tragedy of antagonism turns out in fact to be a comedy of errors.

So, like the Angel, we must find two containers for our two worlds so that they won't accidentally get mixed up, and like her, we must always keep a firm hold on both. When and how to intermingle the contents of these containers is something we can only learn by trial and error.

This fourteenth card has been called The Alchemist. The theory of alchemy was that all matter could be reduced to one substance out of which, by devious processes, the base and corruptible could be distilled away, so that ultimately only the pure and incorruptible, the philosophers' gold, could be bodied forth. Perhaps something similar is beginning to take place in the deepest waters of the hero's psyche. It is as if Death's harvest of partial aspects, of outworn concepts and modes of behavior (symbolized by the assorted heads, feet, and hands of card thirteen) have been reduced to one substance, out of which a new psychic being can begin to form.

The Angel who performs this subtle alchemy is rightly called Temperance. To temper means "to bring to a suitable or desirable state by blending or admixture." We temper steel to make it strong yet resilient. Ideally we temper justice with mercy and for the same reason. Justice appeared as the first card in the Realm of Equilibrium on our map. It is useful to compare that card with Temperance, the final card in this row. In

Justice, the central figure sat enthroned, as rigid and inflexible as the vertical thrust of her sword, the opposite pans of her scales held apart by an equally inflexible crossbar. As we saw, she demonstrated the law of the opposites and how they functioned together in a complementary manner. The instruments which Justice held were man-made devices for discrimination and measurement. Although she presided over moral considerations, she sat above them; she was not personally involved. She appeared as an allegorical figure, neither a human nor one of the gods.

Temperance, although a heavenly being, looks more human than Justice. She is winged, yet she stands solidly in our reality; thus she partakes of both the heavenly and the earthly realms, connecting the two. Unlike Justice, she seems to be very much involved and deeply concerned with the process at hand. In contrast to the rigidity typified by Justice and her scales, everything about Temperance seems as fluid as the magic liquid she pours. The Angel's body sways and flows in a rhythmic dance which matches the ripple of the waters. The red and blue panels of her skirt, their colors significantly placed in opposition to those of the vases, suggest that the transfer of libido pictured here is part of a continuous process, an endlessly alternating current. It is a natural happening, taking place outdoors against an uncultivated background whose twin green plants echo the vitality contained in the twin vases. The play of waters pictured here could not be controlled or measured by even the most refined instruments of civilization. The drama of Temperance happens only by the grace of God and under the ministration of the angels.

Having come now to the end of the Realm of Equilibrium, it might be fruitful to review its overall pattern. Taken as a whole, the middle row of Tarot Trumps emphasizes what one might call moral problems. In medieval philosophy, Temperance was one of the three cardinal virtues, all of which appear in the Tarot Trumps. Although the psychological implications of this Tarot card have taken us far beyond the literal meaning of *temperance,* which is simply *moderation,* this meaning is nonetheless implicit in all that has been said. The second cardinal virtue, Fortitude, pictured as the lady and the lion of card eleven, demonstrates the patient courage, moral strength and endurance usually associated with fortitude. The third cardinal virtue, Prudence, is not specifically illustrated in the Marseilles Tarot, but according to Moakely,[7] a dancing man called Prudence takes the place of the Hanged Man in some decks. Prudence, it appears, was not left out in the Tarot; he was merely (imprudently?) turned upside-down.

Another recurring pattern in the middle row of Tarot Trumps is, of course, that of equilibrium, or the balancing of opposites. Throughout this row we see a continuous interplay of masculine and feminine energy. Justice pictures a woman, but she holds a sword, symbol of masculine

Logos. The Hermit presents an archetypal Old Wise Man, yet he wears the flowing robes of Mother Church. The Wheel of Fortune dramatizes the cyclic interaction of all opposites, to be followed by Strength, in which a lady and her lion intermingle their two kinds of energy in harmonious symbiosis. Following this, the Hanged Man shows us someone achieving balance between heaven and earth. In Death, other opposites, such as king and commoner, male and female, are being chopped up and plowed under, preparatory to reorganization and reassimilation, a process that begins in the final card of this row, Temperance.

It is worth noting that much of the action in this second row is initiated or presided over by feminine figures. Justice, the sphinx on Fortune's Wheel, Strength, and Temperance, all clearly feminine, dominate the action. The Hanged Man is passive, unable to act. Encased and immobilized in a kind of coffin composed of Nature's trees and earth, he is held captive by the feminine. Only the Hermit and Death (both androgynous figures) portray the masculine principle in action. The gentle Hermit, armed solely with a small lamp, initiates no action; he merely sheds his soft, inquiring light on whatever is happening. Death is pictured as very active, but he is not his own master. His scythe, with its crescent shape, belongs to the Moon Goddess Astarte, mistress of time, tides, and change.

Another pattern to be discovered in this Realm of Equilibrium is the way the cards alternate in theme between the general and the specific. First the general problem is presented, then is illustrated and amplified by specific instances of its application in an alternating rhythmic pattern. First, Justice pictures the universal moral dilemma, the problem of determining and measuring guilt and innocence. Next comes the Hermit, whose lamp illuminates a more individual and human approach to the problem. Card number ten, The Wheel of Fortune, brings us back again to the universal. It poses the eternal question of fate versus free will: Are we, like the animals, forever trapped on the not-so-merry-go-round of instinctual behavior? By way of answer, the next two trumps show us two alternatives. First the lady with the lion who demonstrates how bestial nature might be tamed, and second, the Hanged Man, whose body seems as helpless as the animals on Fortune's Wheel, but whose spirit (unlike theirs) is free to find meaning in suffering. Card Thirteen brings us back again to the universal, reminding us that man and beast alike are powerless to avoid the skeleton, Death. And now Temperance cleanses our faulty perceptions, connecting us in a divine yet human way with the immutable world beyond the reach of time's scythe. In doing so, she makes a graceful transition between the world of moral problems and the world of divine illumination, which will be a theme expressed in the last seven cards of the Tarot series. But even for an angel, the process is a slow one. The work which she initiates here will only be consummated at the end of the Tarot journey.

Since Temperance is referred to as "The Alchemist," it might be worthwhile to restate some of the things we have been saying in the language of the old alchemists. In doing so, we may observe how accurately this Tarot Trump and the cards that follow it reflect the symbolic language of those pioneers who blazed the trails toward individuation.

In alchemical language, the "gluten of the eagle" and the "blood of the lion" were mingled in the "philosophical egg," or alembic, then subjected to heat. In Temperance we see pictured the beginning phase of this Great Work, the Angel's compassionate concern furnishing the heat necessary to start the "cooking" process. The next two cards (The Devil and The Tower of Destruction) will show ways in which various other kinds of heat – speaking both alchemically and psychologically – will be applied.

The action of the Angel Temperance as she works with the waters of the hero's psyche is like that of the sun, Nature's alchemist, on our earth's waters. The sun makes of our planet an alchemical retort in which the ocean waters are lifted to heaven and then, their impurities distilled away, are returned to the earth in drops of rain. This continuous circular process epitomizes the natural interrelationship between heaven and earth – between the archetypal figures of the collective unconscious and man's ego reality.

It is Temperance who first introduces this kind of fluid discourse between the heavenly and the earthly realms or, speaking psychologically, between the self and the ego – a dialogue which will be the central theme of all the cards to follow. Significantly, Temperance is the only winged being in the Tarot who descends to earth, confronting man face to face. The winged Eros of card six, it will be recalled, appeared only in the heavens, hovering unseen in the background to shoot his potent arrow and disappear. That the hero's guardian angel stands before him in earthly reality, indicates that he now experiences the reality of the unconscious in a new way. Never again will he dismiss figures of the inner world as creatures of his imagination. Although he may still think of "inner" and "outer" as two worlds, henceforth he will grant the inner world a validity equal to that of the outer world. Perhaps as he gains confidence he will be able to move toward the inner world and interact more freely with its inhabitants.

In this connection, it is interesting to study the development of bodily movement as depicted in the Tarot cards. The top row of cards shows no reciprocal movement between heaven and earth, and even on the horizontal plane movement is restricted. Most of the figures in this row sit or stand in somewhat rigid poses. Only the Magician's hands and his lemniscate hat, and the horses pulling the Chariot depict motion. But in the second row, movement in all directions becomes an important theme, as its central card, The Wheel of Fortune, makes clear. Although this row begins with the rigid figure, Justice, and the somewhat mechanical movement of her scales, the activity becomes humanized in the Hermit and Strength, both of whose movements suggest a sort of dance. Death too is engaged in a dance. Only the Hanged Man is immobile, but (as we know) he is really dancing.

The motif of the dance is an important one in the Tarot. Dancing is an art form in which body and soul interact in an individual and expressive way. A dancer reaches out to objects and other human beings, expressing relationship on the earthly level; and he reaches his arms toward heaven, invoking the gods. There are several dancing figures in the Tarot. The Fool, as usual, begins it all unconsciously as he prances along in his happy way. The Hanged Man, whose dance is equally unconscious, can be seen as the brash Fool, come a-cropper on life's realities. The skeleton's Dance of Death is followed by Temperance's ritual dance with the living waters. We may view these two dances, if we like, as one single event. If you will look for a moment at Death and Temperance, you will see how their bodies lean toward each other in such a way that they form an ellipse.

This ellipse is a symbol for the kind of alchemical interchange between heaven and earth which we have been describing. As we shall see in the following chapters, it is a recurring theme in the bottom row of the Trumps, culminating in The World, which pictures a Dancer. If you will look at card twenty-one, you can see how the fluid movement of this final figure is almost exactly foreshadowed in the body movements of Temperance. Notice also how the ellipse formed by the swaying bodies of Temperance and Death appears in The World as an elliptical wreath surrounding the Dancer.

But the transition from the dance of Temperance to that pictured in the final card is not an orderly one. As we know, life's choreography does not proceed on steppingstones of logic. Rather it follows a spiral course which alternately swings us high and casts us down again.

We have stayed with our Good Angel long enough. It is now time to look the Devil in the eye. He stands waiting to meet us in the next card.

Fig. 62   Le Diable (Marseilles Deck)

18. The Devil: Dark Angel

You have the devil underrated
I cannot yet persuaded be
A fellow who is all behated
Must something be!

Goethe

The time has come to face the Devil. As a major archetypal figure he properly belongs in heaven, the top row of our Tarot chart. But he fell. . .
remember? To hear him tell it, he quit his job and resigned from heaven.
He said he deserved a better break; he felt he should have been given a
raise and more authority.

But that isn't the way others report the story. According to most accounts, Satan was fired. His sin, they say, was arrogance and pride. He
had an overbearing nature, too much ambition, and an inflated sense of
his own worth. Nevertheless, he had lots of charm and considerable influence. His ways were subtle: he organized the angels to rebellion behind
the Boss's back, at the same time currying the Master's favor.

He was jealous of everyone – especially mankind. He likes to think of
himself as the favored son. He hated Adam and resented his rulership of
that tidy Garden of Eden. Complacent security was (and still is) anathema
to him. Perfection made him reach for his firebrand. Innocence made him
squirm. How he did enjoy tempting Eve and busting up Paradise! Temptation was – and continues to be – his specialty. Some even say it was he
who tempted the Lord to harass Job. Since God is good, they tell us, He
could never have played such devilish tricks had He not been conned into
it by Satan. Others argue that, since the Lord is omniscient and all-powerful, He must bear the sole responsibility for putting Job through the third
degree.

The argument as to who was responsible for Job's suffering has been going on for centuries. It hasn't been settled yet and it may never be. The reason is plain: the Devil is confusing because he himself is confused. If you will look at his Tarot portrait (Fig. 62), you will see why. He presents himself as an absurd conglomeration of parts. He wears the antlers of a stag, yet he has the talons of a predatory bird and the wings of a bat. He refers to himself as a man, but he possesses the breasts of a woman – or perhaps more accurately, *wears* them, for they have the appearance of something stuck or painted on him. This odd breastplate can be little protection. It is perhaps worn as an insignia intended to camouflage the wearer's cruelty; but symbolically it might indicate that Satan uses feminine naiveté and innocence as a front in order to charm his way into our garden. And, as the Eden story makes clear, it is through this same innocent naiveté in us (as personified by Eve) that he operates.

That his breastplate is rigid and superimposed might also indicate that the Devil's feminine side is mechanical and uncoordinated, so that it is not always under his control. Significantly, his golden helmet belongs to Wotan, a god who also was subject to womanish temper tantrums and sought vengeance whenever his authority was threatened.

The Devil carries a sword, but he holds his weapon carelessly by the blade, and in his left hand. It is obvious that his relationship to his weapon is so unconscious that he would be unable to use it in a purposeful manner, meaning symbolically that his relationship to the masculine Logos is similarly ineffectual. In this version of the Tarot, Satan's sword seems only to wound himself. But its blade is all the more dangerous because it is not under his control. Organized crime operates by logic. It can be ferreted out and dealt with in a systematic way. Even crimes of passion have a certain emotional logic that makes them humanly understandable and sometimes even preventable. But indiscriminate destruction, wanton murder in the streets, the berserker who takes random potshots on the freeways – against these we have no defense. Such forces, we feel, operate in a darkness beyond human comprehension.

The Devil is an archetypal figure whose lineage, direct and indirect, reaches back into antiquity. There he usually appeared as a beastly demon more powerful and less human than the figure pictured in the Tarot. As Set, Egyptian god of evil, he often took the form of a snake or crocodile. In ancient Mesopotamia, Pazazu (a malaria-bearing demon of the southwest wind, king of the evil spirits of the air) embodied some of the qualities now attributed to Satan. Our Devil may also have inherited certain attributes from Tiamat, Babylonian goddess of chaos, who took the form of a horned and clawed fowl. It was not until Satan appeared in our Judeo-Christian culture that he began to assume more human characteristics and conduct his nefarious activities in ways we humans could more readily understand.

In Blake's *Satan Exulting Over Eve* (Fig. 63), for example, Satan has lost his horns and talons. He even rises grandly above the huge snake coiled around Eve, with which he seems to disavow any connection. In contrast to the Devil pictured in our Tarot, Blake's Satan is an experienced warrior, equipped with a shield and lance which he bears with obvious authority. Evidently centuries of practice have improved his aim and purposefulness. But he still holds his lance in the left or "sinister" hand, for his energies continue to be directed at conflict rather than peace, and at power rather than love.

That the Devil's image has become more humanized in the course of centuries means, symbolically, that we are more ready now to view him as a shadow aspect of ourselves rather than as a supernatural god or an infernal demon. Perhaps it may mean that we are ready at last to wrestle with our own satanic underside. But human – and even handsome – as he appears in Blake's portrait, he has not shed his enormous bat wings. If anything, they have grown darker and larger than those worn by the Marseilles Devil. This indicates that Satan's relationship to the bat is particularly important and requires our special attention.

Fig. 63   Satan Exulting Over Eve (William Blake)

The bat is a night flyer. Avoiding daylight, he retreats each morning to a dark cave where he hangs upside down, gathering energy for his nighttime escapades. He is a blood sucker whose bite spreads pestilence and whose droppings defile the environment. He swoops around in the dark and according to folk belief, has a penchant for entangling himself in one's hair, causing hysteric confusion.

The Devil, too flies at night – a time when the lights of civilization are extinguished and the rational mind is asleep. It is at this time that human beings lie unconscious, unprotected, and open to suggestion. In the daylight hours, when human consciousness is awake and man's ability to differentiate is keen, the Devil retreats to the dark recesses of the psyche where he too hangs upside down, hiding his contrariness, recharging his energies, and biding his time. The Devil metaphorically sucks our blood, sapping our substance. The effects of his bite are contagious, infecting whole communities or even states. Just as a bat could cause unreasoned panic in a crowded auditorium were he to swoop down among the spectators, so the Devil can fly blind into a crowd, literally threatening to entangle himself in everyone's hair, messing up logical thought and producing mass hysteria.

Our loathing of the bat goes beyond all logic. So, too, our fear of the Devil – and for similar reasons. The bat seems to us a monstrous aberration of nature – a squeaking mouse with wings. As with the Devil, his disparate parts defy natural laws. We tend to view all such malformations – the dwarf, the hunchback, the calf with two heads – as the work of some sinister, irrational power, and the creature itself as an instrument of this power. One uncanny talent shared by bat and Devil is the ability to navigate blind in the dark. We intuitively fear such black magic.

Scientists have found ways to protect themselves against the bat's dangerous, filthy habits so that they can re-enter the beasts' cave and examine the inhabitant in a more rational way. As a result, the bat's peculiar form and repulsive behaviour seem less frightening than formerly. Even his mysterious radar system is now discovered to operate according to understandable laws. Modern technology has decoded its black magic to create a similar device whereby man, too, can fly blind.

Perhaps, by a similar kind of objective examination of the Devil, we can learn to protect ourselves against him; and, by discovering within ourselves a proclivity toward satanic black magic, we may learn to conquer those irrational fears that paralyze the will and make it impossible to face and deal with the Devil. Perhaps in the ghastly illumination of Hiroshima, with its aftermath of twisted and warped humanity, we can at long last see the monstrous shape of our own devilish shadow.

With each succeeding war, it becomes increasingly apparent that we and the Devil share many characteristics in common. Some say that it is precisely the function of war to reveal to mankind his enormous capacity for evil in such an unforgettable way that each of us will ultimately acknowledge his own dark shadow and come to grips with the unconscious forces of his inner nature. Alan McGlashan views war specifically as "the punishment of man's disbelief in those forces within himself."[1]

Paradoxically, as man's conscious life becomes more "civilized" his pagan, animal nature, as revealed in war, becomes increasingly ruthless. Commenting on this, Jung says:

> The dammed-up instinct-forces in civilized man are immensely more destructive, and hence more dangerous, than the instincts of the primitive, who in a modest degree is constantly living negative instincts. Consequently no war of the historical past can rival a war between civilized nations in its colossal scale of horror.[2]

Jung goes on to say that the classic picture of the Devil as half man, half beast "exactly describes the grotesque and sinister side of the unconscious, for we have never really come to grips with it and consequently it has remained in its original savage state."[3]

If we examine this "beastly man" as he appears in the Tarot, we can see that no one individual component in itself is overpowering. What makes this figure so obnoxious is the senseless conglomeration of its various parts. Such an irrational assemblage threatens the very order of things, undermining the cosmic scheme upon which all life rests. To face such a shadow would mean facing the fear that not only we humans but Nature herself may have gone berserk.

But this strange beast within, which we project onto the Devil is, after all, Lucifer the Light Bringer. He is an angel – albeit a fallen one – and as such he is a messenger of God. It behooves us to get acquainted with him.

His face is not unattractive. Its quizzical cast reminds one of Pan, a character connected with panic and pandemonium. Actually, the word "pandemonium" was coined by Milton especially to describe the activities of Lucifer and his cohorts. It has remained in our language, and it still best defines the kind of insane and destructive confusion that the Devil can cause in our world and in ourselves.

Despite the fact that this Tarot figure is equipped to pounce and seize in the dark, he has one redeeming feature: a pair of golden antlers. Horns are an ancient symbol for new life and spiritual regeneration, and golden antlers are specifically symbolic of divine fire. The ones pictured here almost look like tongues of flame shooting out on either side of the creature's head.

As noted earlier these magic horns do not belong to the Devil's person; they are part of a golden helmet reminiscent of Wotan. The golden fire, then, is not the property of Satan but belongs to his godlike office as messenger. When he remembers this, his fire can illuminate and purify. But when he steals heaven's fire for his own aggrandizement, his activities can call forth heaven's thunderbolt.

As Adam and Eve discovered, the Devil's role is so ambiguous that it is often impossible to know just what he is up to. On the one hand, he tempts us to disobediance, urging us to taste the forbidden fruit and swallow the bittersweet morsel of good and evil. On the other hand, were it not for his inducement to action and knowledge, we would still be like small children, caught in the idyllic round of a secure but limited paradise. Without this devilish involvement in the crucial problems of good and evil, we would have no ego consciousness, no civilization, and no opportunity to transcend the ego through self-realization. Like animals, we would be forever imprisoned within the rigid formulae of automatic behavior.

Through the activities of Satan, it seems, we human beings were cast out of the Eden of instinctual obedience and animal nature in order that we might fulfill the destiny of our specifically *human* nature. And now, having tasted of the knowledge of good and evil, we are faced forevermore with the responsibility of moral choice. We are no longer able, like obedient children, to remain safely within the limits of a superimposed code of ethics. We are, in the apt phrase of Jean Paul Sartre, "condemned to be free."

Without freedom to choose, there can be no true morality. The fact is that most of us today have more free choice than we realize; but many, still unconsciously imprisoned within cultural mores, refuse to accept the responsibility for moral choice. Most of us simply have no idea what we might be capable of if we were freed of all superimposed restraints, both real and imagined. As long as our obedience to a moral code is automatic, we are not free. As long as we refuse to turn and confront our own inner devils – whatever form these may take – we are not human.

That is exactly the situtation of the odd-looking couple pictured in Tarot fifteen. They are neither wholly human nor entirely free. The faces these two turn toward the world seem human enough, but their bodies are equipped with animals' ears, horns, hoofs, and tails. The two figures are tied by ropes to the platform on which the Devil stands; but they seem to be wholly unaware of this. They appear to be equally unconscious of their cloven hoofs and tails. These imps of Satan dramatize a familiar aspect of the human condition which Jung amplifies as follows:

> . . . we always forget that our consciousness is only a surface; our consciousness is the avant-garde of our psychological existence. Our head is only one end, but behind our consciousness is a long historical "tail" of hesitations and weaknesses and complexes and prejudices and inheritances, and we always make our reckoning without them.[4]

The two Tarot slaves are reminiscent of the assistants at a magic show who pose smirking on either side of the magician while he does his tricks. They never turn around to see what he is up to. They hand him the necessary implements as if performing a ritual dance wholly unconnected with the proceedings. Afterward they turn away and resume their innocent pose at the footlights.

As long as these lackeys remain unaware of their role in the Devil's machinations, they can continue to perform their little ritual with no conflicts, no problems – and no growth. Notice how diminutive their figures appear in this picture. They are ludicrously small in stature because the energies bound up in their animal parts have not been consciously recognized, assimilated, and made usuable for growth. These imps wear the smug look so often seen on the faces of those who presume that they are in complete control of their behavior. Whenever sudden emotional outbursts, unexplained forgetfulness, or other lapses of consciousness threaten to destroy the complacent self-image of such persons, they never look behind to observe the long tails that connect them with their animal ancestors. They are usually too busy pointing the finger of blame at someone else. They remind one of the small boy who, when scolded for getting into a fist fight, cried: "But, Mommy, he hit me back first!" The philosophy of such finger-pointers is embodied in more sophisticated language by André Gide. "Evil," he solemnly assures us, "is a thing one does in return." It will probably be some time before the two Tarot slaves can assume reponsibility for their actions. It may even take a thunderbolt like the one pictured in the next card to disrupt their complacency, and a flash of lightning to make them aware of their long tails.

What specific quality does the Devil represent? He is such an admixture of parts that it is difficult to pin him down. But this is as it should be, for according to Jung, any kind of psychic function that is split off from the whole and operates autonomously is devilish. To be slavishly and unconsciously bound to even the most altruistic code as surely marks one a creature of the Devil as to be victimized by one's animal appetites. It is the unconsciousness and autonomy that are crucial here. With Jung's guideline in mind, let us look at card fifteen to explore some of the kinds of unconscious autonomy that might be represented here.

The design of this card (a central elevated figure with two small assistants at his feet) is not unlike that of The Pope, with certain important differences. The Devil operates behind his assistants' backs, whereas the Pope faces his two priests. The Pope holds up his right hand in the sign of benediction, with two fingers upraised to remind his children that moral conflict must be dealt with; the three remaining fingers are concealed to symbolize the unknowable mystery of the Holy Trinity. By contrast, in card fifteen, the Devil's clawlike hand with its four upraised fingers indicates that his sole concern is with the limited dimensions of earthly power. His hand appears to be flipped up in an arrogant salute, not unlike that which was used to trigger the automatic response *Heil Hitler*.

The Pope is seated on a throne as befits his office. The Devil stands on what appears to be an anvil whose ashes have gone dead. He will have us think that it is he who is the heavenly fire. Not content with his role as Light Bringer, he likes to present himself also as The Light. The Pope holds his staff in a ritual manner in a gloved hand bearing the cross patée to indicate that he holds his power in trust for the Church. But the Devil holds his sword haphazardly in a bare clawlike hand, indicating an unconscious, egocentric use of power.

The sword is an instrument bespeaking a high degree of civilization. This weapon, often of supernatural origin, is a symbol of chivalric honor and of action in the service of an ideal. In card eight, immediately above this one, we see how Justice holds her sword ritually as a sort of plumb line connecting above and below. One might see her sword as a lightning rod to bring down the divine fire to illuminate our blind confusion. In The Devil the central figure makes a mockery of all that Justice's sword symbolizes. Like a small boy showing off, he boasts a personal invulnerability and unconcern for any power other than himself. We, sitting out front where we can look him in the eye, are able to see through his pretentions. But the two slaves remain unaware of his existence.

According to Baudelaire, who had considerable experience with this fellow, "The Devil's cleverest wile is to convince us that he doesn't exist." To outwit the Devil, the Navajos placed him up among the gods where they could keep an eye on him. Eastern religions have always considered the daemonic aspect as part of the godhead. In the Hindu-Buddhist iconography, even the most malevolent figures have one hand uplifted in the mudra meaning "Fear Not" in order to convey the idea that such an apparition is another form of *maya*, one of the million masks of God.

In the Old Testament, evil also was seen as an aspect of God. To quote Jehovah himself: "I am the Lord and there is none else. I form the light and create darkness: I make peace and create evil: I the Lord do all these things."[5] Early Christianity also placed the capacity for both good and evil in the hands of God. Clement, Bishop of Rome in the first century, taught that God rules the world with a right hand and a left hand – the right hand being Christ and the left hand Satan. But in later times Christianity amputated God's left hand, relegating Satan to the nether regions, thus leaving a wholly beneficent God to reign supreme in heaven. Today we have become so enamored of the light, bright aspect of creative power that we have lost sight of the Devil altogether, apparently thinking that when he fell from heaven he was no longer active anywhere, least of all in ourselves.

Many psychologists agree that such neglect of our own devilish side is the major cause of much of the pandemonium loose in the world today.

Our own individual emotionalism, bigotry, vindictiveness, violence, and confusion (not recognized and dealt with in our personal lives) now burst forth on a massive scale as world wars, riots, conflagration, and general destruction. For it is a truism of life that when negative aspects of ourselves are not recognized as belonging to us on the inside, they appear to act against us on the outside.

In the face of contemporary world events, it becomes increasingly imperative that we come to terms with this satanic force. The Hebrew word for devil means "adversary," "turned against," "hostile." In Webster's International Dictionary (1914 edition), the Devil is described as being "the adversary of God. . .although subordinate to Him and able to act only by His sufferance." In other words, the Devil is a very shady, ambivalent character. On the one hand he is hostile to God; but on the other hand, he is subject to God's authority, acting only with the Deity's tacit permission. This seems to be the essence of the conflict with which generations have struggled. Either the Lord is not omnipotent, or the Devil belongs within his creation. We can't have it both ways. If we embrace the concept of monotheism, then obviously God must have created the Devil as part of his divine scheme.

We may find this concept hard to accept consciously, but unconsciously most of us have lived with it all our lives. It has seeped into our blood stream as part of our cultural heritage. "Lead us not into temptation," we pray. To whom do we offer this prayer? To the Devil? That we address this plea to God can only mean that, unconsciously, we experience the temptation to disobedience as part of the godhead.

The ambivalence of the Deity is clearly implicit in the Genesis story of Eden. In this account, the Lord created the tree of the knowledge of good and evil, put it in the garden, and then deliberately called his children's attention to it by forbidding them to eat its fruit. This psychology is reminiscent of the familiar tale about Epimonandas, whose mother baked some savory mince pies and put them out on the floor to cool. As she left the house she said to her small son, "Now, Epimonandas, you be careful how you step on those mince pies." And Epimonandas *was* careful. He stepped with great care right smack in the center of every single pie!

In the story of Job, the Lord *himself* is tempted by Satan to torment Job. In this drama, as Jung points out in his *Answer to Job,* even the godhead is portrayed as having a dark unconscious side – a devilish alter ego or shadow. It is difficult enough to accept the personal shadow in ourselves and our friends, but to encompass the idea that God himself might also have a shadow aspect seems at first counter to the basic teachings of our Christian culture. Many of us have been unconsciously steeped in church-calendar Christianity, where a benevolent Father-God, draped in pink cotton, smiles down protectively on His children, putting the wicked Black Devil to rout. The idea that the godhead might embrace all opposites, including an area of dark unconsciousness, and that the Devil, for his part, might possess some bright, redeeming qualities, seems shocking.

Most Tarot decks make a sharp distinction between the Good Magician of Trump number one who is painted as light, bright, and positive, and the Bad Magician of card fifteen who carries all the unappetizing, negative qualities. But this is not true of the Marseilles deck whose characters seem always to present both light and dark elements. We have already observed how the Marseilles Magician with his lemniscate hat and motley dress, standing casually at the crossroads, appears as an ambivalent character in contrast to Waite's priestly Magician in his bower of lilies and roses. As one might expect, the Devils pictured in the two decks reflect similar differences. In the Waite deck he is a loathsome, fearful fellow with hairy legs, cloven hoofs, and a stern expression (Fig. 64). His symbol is the inverted pentagram, hex sign of black magic. If the Devil were as completely repulsive as this fellow, sin would be no problem. By contrast, his

Fig. 64   Waite Deck

counterpart in the Marseilles pack (like its Magician) embodies both attractive and unattractive qualities. One can easily imagine becoming involved in a love-hate relationship with either of these Marseilles characters.

In Christian art, this archetypal figure is sometimes pictured as Jesus' shadow. In Duccio's famous painting, *The Temptation of Christ on the Mountain,* this shadow appears to be very large and black indeed (Fig. 65). Psychologically as well as physically speaking, it is true that the brighter the light, the darker the shadow. Translated into practical experience this means that the more conscious we become of our creative potential, the more alert we must be to the tricks of our shadow side and the more responsible we must be in relation to it. As consciousness expands, conscience becomes more refined so that one becomes increasingly aware of the potential harmfulness of even the most casual word or deed. Since every human drive is essentially amoral, what makes an instinctual action immoral is simply its unconsciousness. Any drive that manifests itself un-

Fig. 65   The Temptation of Christ on the Mountain
(Duccio di Buoninsegna, copyright The Frick Collection, 1937. Reprinted by permission.)

consciously is primitive, uncontrolled, compulsive, and therefore potentially harmful.

As we can verify by our own experience, increased awareness, far
from turning us into placid vegetables, plunges us deeper and deeper into
moral conflict, demanding ever keener penetration into the mysteries of
good and evil. Christ said, "I bring not peace but the sword." To take up
the sword of moral discrimination disturbs our peaceful innocence and inevitably entails feelings of transgression and guilt. Like Eve, whose first bite
of the apple marred forever the symmetry of unconscious nature, so too
our sharpened consciousness disturbs our infantile identity with all life and
is experienced as a violation of nature. On a grander scale, the cultural
heroes (men and women of superior consciousness, foresight, and energy)
further wound the sacred order when, Prometheus-like, they steal the fire
from heaven for the benefit of mankind.

According to myth and legend, such acts of disobedience and daring
are always punished by the gods. Adam and Eve having taken that fatal
first bite, were then able to observe their nakedness (meaning symbolically
that they had lost their blind innocence and were forced to new self-awareness). As a result, they were cast out to seek further self-realization. No
longer could adequate nourishment for their expanding self-awareness be
supplied effortlessly by nature; human consciousness must now seek sustenance by its own efforts.

Prometheus, too, was punished for invading the hitherto heavenly
territory of consciousness and creativity; chained to Mt. Caucasus, he was
forced to suffer untold pain as each day a vulture ate out his liver – which
then grew back again each night. Symbolically, this might indicate that persons of genius must necessarily suffer the fate of isolation, living in realms
of the spirit above the grasp of their contemporaries. Chained to their
unique task as bringers of light, such heroic figures are forced, day and
night, to sacrifice their life's blood to the demands of their genius.

Feelings of transgression, guilt, and punishment are inherent in the
quest for consciousness. Whenever we break with the parental image of
how things "should" or "ought" to be done, we feel guilty. So deeply are
such feelings embedded in the unconscious that acts of no moral consequence whatever frequently evoke guilt feelings, if these actions offend the
propriety of that unconscious "inner parent" – a creature whose vestigial
remains can endure intact throughout a lifetime. In a similar way any
break, however inconsequential, with the prevailing customs of the outer
social milieu can be experienced as an offence against the whole and is
often accompanied by feelings of guilt. But if "everybody's doing it," one
can wear, say, or do the most bizarre things – or perform illegal or even
criminal acts without experiencing guilt.

To put some of these ideas into broader psychological terms: any
break away from the original unconscious identity with the self involves
feelings of guilt. Yet, if we are to move on toward a conscious relationship

with the self, we must make this break and absorb the guilt. Paradoxically, one is driven by the self to move away from this original identification in order to establish a reunion with the self on a different level of awareness.

The weight of guilt is not only personal, for each of us bears some unconscious guilt for the general criminality and inhumanity of mankind which one reads about daily in the newspapers. "Even if, juristically speaking, we were not accessories to the crime," says Jung, "we are always, thanks to our human nature, potential criminals. In reality we merely lacked a suitable opportunity to be drawn into the infernal melée. None of us stands outside humanity's black collective shadow."[6]

For this reason, Jung says, we human beings "do not feel quite right when we are behaving perfectly; we feel much better when we are doing a bit of wrong. That is because we are not perfect. The Hindus when they build a temple, leave one corner unfinished; only the gods make something perfect, man never can. It is much better to know that one is not perfect, then one feels much better."[7] Nevertheless, the image of perfection is so ingrained in our culture that we feel guilty when we can't achieve it. We sometimes need a scapegoat to help us bear the weight of our all-too-human imperfections. Otherwise we project these onto our friends and relatives, or are crushed by their weight. "The Devil made me do it," we say, half in earnest when we have done something less than perfect, or "I don't know what the devil got into me!" The Devil is a useful scapegoat.

In commenting on the psychological function of the scapegoat, Jung makes this profound statement: "This is the deeper meaning of the fact that Christ as the redeemer was crucified between two thieves. These thieves in their way were also redeemers of mankind, they were the scapegoats."[8]

From all that has been said about him here, one can see that the Devil is a very complex and ambivalent character. According to Goethe's classic description of Mephistopheles, he is "that power that would only work evil, but engenders good." He is the fellow who betrays us into unconscious criminality but who also lures us into consciousness. As Lucifer, he can offer us heaven's fire for our salvation, or he can plunge us into the fires of hell to our destruction. And all the while he outwits us by appearing in so many forms that we can't keep track of him.

The Christian Devil, whose epithet was "The Great Beast," was a caricature of Pan and Dionysus, both of whom, significantly, were worshiped in mass rites of an orgiastic nature. Today, as Jung points out, this Great Beast is aroused again to mass hysteria by the increasing collectivity of our contemporary culture:

> A large company composed of wholly admirable persons has the morality and intelligence of an unwieldy, stupid, and violent animal. The bigger the organization, the more unavoidable is its immorality and blind stupidity. (*Senatus bestia, senatores boni viri.*) Society, by automatically stressing all the collective

qualities in its individual representatives, puts a premium on mediocrity, on everything that settles down to vegetate in an easy, irresponsible way. Individuality will inevitably be driven to the wall.[9]

The Devil's name is legion, and when we are "possessed of the Devil," our name, too, is legion. Filled with conflicting ideas, aims, interests, and emotions, we lose touch with our central self. To be out of harmony with the self is to be in sin. Cast out of Eden, like Adam and Eve, we must then pay for our transgression by wandering the wide world in search of a new connection with the center. The Devil does his best to impede this search by tempting us to procrastinate. He uses procrastination deliberately as one of his most effective weapons, as witness the following account:

Once upon a time, the Devil, unhappy with the way his work on earth was progressing, held a council of his cohorts, asking for volunteers for a mission to earth, and requesting suggestions as to what mankind might be told that would further the Devil's work. One evil spirit suggested telling men that there was no God. Another suggested spreading a rumor that there was no soul. The Devil was not pleased.

Finally one imp slithered forward and asked that the mission be assigned to him. The Devil asked him what he would tell man. The imp replied: "I would tell him that there is no hurry." He was promptly awarded the job, and the corridors of hell rang with shouts of glee.

Sometimes the Devil is pictured as a skeleton, connecting him with the seven deadly sins of medieval theology which were: pride, lechery, envy, anger, covetousness, gluttony, and sloth. One thing that makes these sins so deadly is that they are not always recognizable on the basis of overt action. Often these sins can even appear to be virtues. To identify and combat them in oneself is difficult. As is often the case in moral questions, the determining factor is not so much what one does as wherefrom he does it.

For example, when Satan appeared to Jesus on the mountain and tempted him to turn stones into bread, the overt act suggested would have been harmless enough. Viewed from a purely material standpoint it might have been beneficial. But for Jesus to have performed this miraculous feat merely to demonstrate his power would have been a misuse of his God-given creativity. The question he faced and dealt with in that encounter with the Tempter was the eternal problem of ends and means whose resolution makes the difference between a true miracle and a shoddy trick.

Fortunately, for most of us the temptation to perform miracles is not a problem, but the temptation to imagine that we can is always present. Whenever any archetypal force breaks through into consciousness, we feel an influx of energy and illumination of such superhuman dimensions that we are apt to become so inflated with our own power that we lose touch with our limitations as an ordinary human being.

The masks worn by the Devil and the temptations he is seen to offer vary with the culture. To our forebears, the Devil was pictured as an embodiment of the flesh, epitomized as sexual passion. Today, sex and the body are no longer looked upon as sinful. In fact, sexual freedom has now become de rigeur so that it is prudish restriction that wears horns.

Any function of the human psyche that operates unconsciously is devilish. Goethe's Mephistopheles is the classic personification of this kind of autonomous activity. "Mephistopheles," says Jung, "is the diabolical aspect of every psychic function that has broken loose from the hierarchy of the total psyche and enjoys independence and absolute power. But this aspect can only be perceived when the function becomes a separate entity and is objectivated or personified . . . ."[10]

The Delacroix portrait of Mephistopheles is such an objectification of the Devil (Fig. 66). Here he appears as "aerial spirit and ungodly intellect." See how grandly he sails across the night sky far above sleeping humanity and safely beyond the reach of even the tallest church spires. He is not a bad-looking fellow; sometimes he can look very distinguished. After all, he must be attractive or he wouldn't attract us, compelling our energies to his use. One of the most handsome, and surely the most arrogant, of devils is one we have already encountered as the central figure of Blake's *Satan Exulting Over Eve* (Fig. 63). No wonder "poor motherless Eve" (to quote Ralph Hodgson's classic phrase) fell for his line.

How would we picture the Devil today? In our present mechanized culture, one devilish aspect is surely the dehumanizing effect of our computer psychology. Pictorially we might visualize today's Devil as a monstrous robot computer moving with relentless, mechanical stride across the earth, crushing beneath its metallic weight all humanity and all nature.

Having examined the archetypal Devil in detail, let us compare his portrait briefly with that of the Magician, who appears above him at the top of the first vertical row on our map. The Magician stands on terra firma. The Devil sets himself above us. The Magician confines his attention to certain specifics on the table before him — the action of his two hands coordinated toward a single purpose. This is not the case with the Devil, one of whose hands is raised in a rigid, mocking gesture, while the other holds a sword in a dangerous way. Obviously his right hand has no awareness of what his left hand is up to. He is as irresponsible as a small child. His childishness betrays itself in his sheepish grin and his boastful bravado, a pose intended no doubt to mask his obvious ineptitude with the sword. Because he has been ignored in our Judeo-Christian culture, he has not matured with the years so that he has remained immature, and like all children (and like us, too) he craves recognition. If we continue to ignore him, he will deliberately commit outlandish acts in order to attract our attention.

One Italian Tarot pictures the Devil and his attendant imps sticking out

Fig. 66   Mephistopheles   (Delacroix)

their tongues like naughty children (Fig. 67). In Medieval paintings of hell, the Devil's tongue is sometimes shown protruding phallus-like from his genital area, underscoring his well-known proclivity to sexual license, and implying that the unbridled use of the spoken word can be just as devilish as sexual promiscuity. Since the phallus can symbolize the creative urge at every level of expression, this representation of the Devil may also mock the notion that genius, love, and other so-called spiritual attributes, descend solely from the white clouds above. Apparently we still need to be reminded of this. Not so long ago Yeats' Crazy Jane shocked the Bishop (and many readers) with her outspoken testimony that ". . . Love has pitched his mansion in / The place of excrement; . . ."

Between the Magician and the Devil sits Justice, the two pans of whose scales are empty, ready to weigh and assess the potentials of both light and dark magic. She is concerned with harmony and balance. If we overload one pan of her scales with sweetness and light, the power of positive thinking, and other such images of perfection, leaving the second pan empty, we know what must happen: the Devil will load the empty pan with the penalties of our neglect: street crimes and riots, arson and mayhem. Nature abhors a vacuum.

We have been discussing his Satanic Majesty on the grand scale. Before we leave him, let us try to connect him more directly with our own

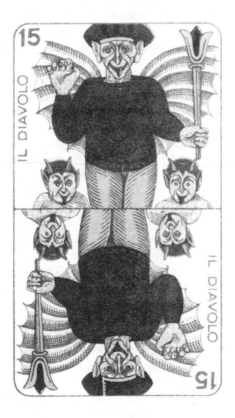

Fig. 67   The Devil (Italian Tarot)

personal experience. It is there, after all, that we confront him daily. Unless one has been "possessed of the Devil," the idea of such a possession sounds too fantastic for credibility. To the uninitiated, the word "possession" is merely a metaphor describing the psychological state of certain disturbed personalities. We like to think this can't happen to us – that modern science with its knowledge of preventive psychology, endocrinology, and balanced vitamins precludes such a possibility. But it can happen to anyone given conditions of sufficient stress; and it does in fact occur, in small ways, more frequently than we realize.

In Paul Klee's disturbing portrait, *A Girl Possessed* (Fig. 68), we can see what such an invasion of the psyche looks like from the outside. Perhaps the look on this girl's face reminds us of friends who harangue us about politics. Or perhaps studying this portrait can put us in touch with the way we ourselves have briefly felt when all our energies were caught up in one project to the exclusion of all else. The subtle thing about this kind of possession is that whatever has swallowed us up may, in itself, be a thoroughly laudable, worthwhile concern such as ecology, world peace (or even the P.T.A.!). It is the unconscious take-over that is so devilish. Jung's comment on such unholy virtue is pertinent: "We quite forget that we can be as deplorably overcome by a virtue as by a vice. There is a frenzied, orgiastic virtuousness which is just as infamous as vice and leads to just as much injustice and violence."[1]

No doubt everyone has had the experience of being confronted on the street or at one's door by a stranger who, like the Ancient Mariner, fixed us with his glittering eye and exhorted us to clean living and brotherly love. Our first instinct is to recoil, not because we are for sin and against love, but because instinctively we fear possession. It smells of the Devil. Conversely, a good clue that we ourselves may be possessed by an archetypal force is the look of panic in the eyes of others when we become involved with our "thing" to the exclusion of the other important values.

The Devil is repulsive, but as we have seen, he is also attractive. Swayed by his alternate powers of attraction and repulsion, we weave our spiral way toward self-awareness. Even as children, we feel these twin forces working within ourselves. One beautiful and revealing account of such an experience is told in Hermann Hesse's novel *Demian*. This sensitive story connects the reader personally and emotionally with the Devil's dubious role throughout our lives.

Literature abounds with personifications of the Devil as varied as they are illuminating. Of these, Shakespeare's Iago is perhaps the most familiar. In Stephen Vincent Benét's popular story "The Devil and Daniel Webster," the Devil appears as a contemporary citizen of considerable persuasion and charm. Since the story is laid in New England, virtue triumphs in the end. But in Thomas Mann's chilling "Mario and the Magician," the Devil is portrayed as a professional magician who uses sinister hypnotic powers in a ruthless and destructive way. In religious polemics Satan was viewed as

Fig. 68   A Girl Possessed   (Paul Klee)

the author of all vice. Playing cards were even called "the Devil's picture book." No doubt Satan had a hand in creating the Tarot Trumps and is watching with amusement as we puzzle our way through their mysteries.

No discussion of His Satanic Majesty would be complete without considering the role played by the two subhuman victims pictured in Tarot number fifteen. It is easy enough to see how the Devil contributes to their delinquency, hampering their growth and development; but it is not so easy to imagine how these two relatively helpless creatures might be contributing to the Devil's delinquency and impeding his maturation toward consciousness. In our personal lives also, we usually think of "devilishness" in terms of overt action, often overlooking the less obvious truth that passive acquiescence and blind naiveté can be equally devilish.

For example, it is easy for us to recognize that manipulation in oneself or others is the Devil's work. Pictured here is Richter's *Devil With Claws* (Fig. 69). As we look at it, we can feel the monstrous qualities of this manipulator constructing a web to catch some unwary victim. In moments of soul searching, we earnestly try to ferret out such monstrous qualities in ourselves and put to rout the temptation to ensnare others to our purposes. But when we find ourselves enmeshed in this kind of web, caught and bound by the machinations of others, the soul searching often stops and the finger pointing begins. We usually imagine ourselves to be wholly victimized and entirely guiltless. We loudly protest our innocence, flaunting it proudly like a banner, not stopping to question whether such innocent naiveté is necessarily a virtue.

Gerald Heard, the late British philosopher, used to say that every murder (psychologically speaking) usually requires two co-conspirators – equally guilty – a murderer and a murderee. It is hard to belive that allowing oneself to be victimized is just as devilish as playing the role of aggressor. But another look at Richter's classic manipulator demonstrates the truth of Heard's thesis. This Devil is not chasing us; he appears to be wholly absorbed in constructing his trap. In order to become caught in its strings, we must, of necessity, take at least one innocent step forward!

The Devil, whose forms are indeed legion, presents many serious problems. We must not take him lightly. Nevertheless in dealing with him, we might learn to laugh a little; for humor can act as a bridge to connect his world with ours in a way that humanizes them both. In their use of humor as an approach to the Devil, the Orientals have a master touch. Their demons, however scary, always leave room for a mocking humor. Even their most grotesque masks possess a Halloween absurdity that makes them seem approachable.

Let us therefore conclude this chapter with a bit of Chinese wisdom, taken not from Confucius, but copied from a contemporary road sign which reads: "Go soothingly on the slippery road, for therein lurks the skid demon."

Fig. 69 The Devil with Claws
(Richier, Germaine, 1952, bronze, 34½ x 37¼". Collection, The Museum of Modern Art, New York, Wildenstein Foundation Fund.)

Fig. 70   La Maison Dieu (Marseilles Deck)

19. The Tower of Destruction: The Stroke of Liberation

I am the Lord and there is none else.
I form the light and create the darkness;
I make peace and create evil. I, the Lord,
do all these things.

Isaiah

Trump sixteen pictures two human figures being ejected violently from a lightning-struck tower (Fig. 70). They look dazed but seem otherwise unhurt. The tower itself is not demolished, but a flamelike tongue of lightning has knocked off the gold crown that served as its roof.

Perhaps your first association to this picture was to the Tower of Babel, an edifice built by Nimrod to storm heaven. According to the biblical account, Nimrod's impious act evoked God's wrath and vengeance, resulting in disharmony and confusion of tongues on earth. The connection between this Tarot and the Tower of Babel is an apt one, for it looks as if the two humans pictured here have incurred heavenly wrath and are being thrown from a position of lofty security into one of exposure and confusion.

What made Nimrod's act seem doubly impious was that the towers of ancient Mesopotamia, far from being built as fortresses to defy heaven, were usually created as temples of worship. It was their function to elevate the mind and heart of man and to provide ways for the gods to descend to earth, thus insuring intercommunication between the heavenly and the earthly realms. According to ancient myth, a rupture between the World Parents (heaven and earth) had occurred in former times, and it was hoped that by building such towers this break might be healed and a fruitful interaction between the two primal powers might be restored.

Symbolically, then, a tower was originally conceived as a vehicle for connecting spirit and matter. It provided a staircase whereby the gods could descend and man ascend, thus dramatizing the concept that there is a correspondence between the earthly and the heavenly orders. The ancient Sumerian idea of cosmic order is amplified by Alfred Jeremias as follows:

> The whole cosmos is regarded as pervaded by a single life, in such a way that there is a harmony recognized between the upper and lower modes of Being and Becoming. The informing thought of the Sumerian world feeling is: "What is above is below"; and from this two directions of spiritual movement are projected: the Above comes downward, the Below mounts aloft. . . .
>
> Moreover, the entirety of the Above and Below is thought of as filled with spiritual godly presences,which pass as "heavenly energies" upward and downward.[1]

Obviously the Tarot tower was not built as a stairway for such "heavenly energies." It appears to be a small, private tower inhabited by two persons. Sealed off at the top, it invited no visitations from heaven and permitted neither warmth nor illumination to enter from above. The two who built this edifice crowned it king, indicating that they recognized no authority above their own creation. There are no doors pictured in this structure whereby its inhabitants might come and go at will or receive guests, and its windows are very small.

One can imagine how dark and isolated the life of these two tower dwellers must have been, elevated above nature's earth, cut off from their fellowman, and barricaded against the gods. They must have lived like prisoners. No doubt their minds and hearts, too, were as cold and dark as their surroundings and as firmly closed to the possibility of miraculous intervention. In such cases, the gods must find a way to enter – by force if necessary. For, as the ancient saying states, "*Vocatus atque non vocatus, deus aderit.*" (Called and not called, God will be there.)

The French title for this card is, in fact, La Maison Dieu (The House of God). Some commentators say that this title came about accidentally, through a faulty transcription of the card's original name La Maison De Feu (The House of Fire). If so, it was a happy accident, for, as is often the case with slips of tongue or pen, this one brings with it hidden meaning, reminding us of the tower's true function as a place of worship and an earthly habitation for the gods. All "God's houses" (temples, churches, monasteries, nunneries) traditionally offer a safe refuge for any who are sick in body or soul. Even criminals who seek shelter in the house of God are granted asylum there. For this reason, La Maison Dieu carries the meaning of "hospice," "hospital," and "asylum." Viewed in this context, one can see that the two sick souls in this picture are being liberated from an enforced incarceration rather than cast forth from their own true home. In retrospect, the effect of this thunderbolt on their lives will seem almost magical. That the lightning pictured here has magic powers is underscored by the shower of multicolored balls like those used by a magician or juggler. They would indicate that whatever is happening here is a miraculous event, arranged by the grand magus. The rainbow colors of these balls suggest the rainbow covenant between God and man in the Old Testament. They would seem to indicate that, despite appearances, the Deity is concerned with the welfare of those two unfortunates in the picture.

Lightning has always been experienced as a symbol of divine energy, a numinous force emanating from God. It represents naked power and illumination in its most primitive and immediate form. It comes from heaven to touch the lives of these two Tarot mortals directly, without the mediating influence of the Magician and his wand, the Emperor and his sceptre, or the Pope with his crosier.

Greek heroes and the lesser gods stood in awe of the thunderbolt, for it emanated from Zeus; and old diagrams of the Cabalistic Tree of Life depict lightning as the divine force that connects the Sephiroth. In Christian art, the Holy Ghost is sometimes shown as a flame from heaven. To be struck by lightning means, symbolically, to be touched by the hand of God; it marks one forever as someone deserving special attention. Asklepios, slain by Zeus's thunderbolt, later became known as the god of medicine. Speaking of his fate, Artemidorus says, "No one who is slain by a thunderbolt remains without fame. Thus he is also honored as a god."[2]

The two mortals in our Tarot may not be destined to become gods but it is true that they have not remained unknown, for generations have studied this old card and puzzled over its meaning. Due to a stroke of lightning, it seems, the personalities of these two will become known to us – and possibly also to themselves – in an illuminating way.

According to Plutarch, lightning was the originator of all life. He saw it as a heavenly phallus, fertilizing the primal waters with its primitive energy. His intuitions have been confirmed by some scientists today who tell us that the first life to emerge from the waters may indeed have been fired by a lightning stroke. The idea of lightning as a life-giving power is echoed in this Tarot picture, where the concrete tower, like the hard outer shell of a nut, is being cracked open to release the two living inner "kernels," seen falling toward the soil. There they will presumably take root and begin a new life.

In most Tarot decks, the lightning is depicted by jagged, zig-zag strokes that slash across the sky like angry teeth, spelling destruction for all below. The Marseilles deck pictures lightning in its more benign, creative aspect. Here it seems to have a feathery, spiritual quality not unlike that expressed by lightning itself as seen in this photograph (Fig. 71). A feather is soft to the touch, yet it is surprisingly strong and enduring. "You could have knocked me over with a feather!" we exclaim on those occasions when our image of reality proves to be quite different from its actuality. Whenever we use this metaphor, we reveal to the world (albeit not necessarily to ourselves) that we were already in a precarious state of psychical imbalance before the feather's touch – that we were ripe for a fall.

This is true also of our Tarot tower dwellers whose recent incarceration obviously indicates a state of psychic imbalance. It seems evident that, had this feathery spirit not touched their lives, they were destined for a fall more drastic than the one pictured here. It is easy for us to recognize this enforced evacuation from their stronghold as a saving grace, rather than a dire punishment. We can understand that, like Phaëton, they have been struck down in order to prevent the destruction of their universe. These falling figures would say that their universe is being destroyed; but deep in the unconscious, there is a wisdom beyond their knowing. Their body language tells us this: *They are turning summersaults!* We are reminded of the Hanged Man pictured in Tarot number twelve, who, when viewed from the aspect of eternity, was "really" dancing a jig.

If we were to ask the tower dwellers why they are turning summersaults, they would probably deny that they are doing so. Such people live too high up in the head to be aware of the body and understand its language. But we, sitting in the audience, as it were, viewing this picture-ballet, can observe the choreography of these summersaults. They express the freedom and youthful joy of summertime; their circular motion suggests the Fool's energy and potential for wholeness, and more importantly, they indicate an *about face* of some sort. The acrobat who performs such stunts emerges right side up, impelled forward *in a new direction*.

Some of the ideas expressed here are again underscored in The Tower of Destruction's number sixteen which (like four, seven, ten, and thirteen) is one of those magic numbers that reduces to one, marking the end of one phase of development and the advent of a new one. The psychological phase that is being so abruptly terminated here is symbolized by the tower.

A tower is a man-made structure; it is tall, rigid, enduring, and impervious to the elements. It is useful for defense, protection, observation, and retreat. Such a tower could also be used as a lighthouse to warn of danger, a platform to call the faithful to worship, or a pedestal from which to harangue the multitude. Today political rantings and other propaganda are broadcast from towers that constantly send forth networks of sound and sight to ensnare our minds.

Towers have also been used as prisons, sometimes quite consciously so, and other times in more subtle ways. Today, for example, in our cities

Fig. 71 Photo of Lightning (Photo by M. Brassai)

millions of human beings are almost literally imprisoned in concrete. It is
shocking to consider the many office workers whose feet never touch the
green grass and who have no contact with the warm, moist earth. These
people descend each morning from their tower-like apartments to a subter-

ranean garage from which they drive to other basement garages, ascending by elevator to towering offices where they spend their days. At
night the pattern is reversed and, like rats imprisoned in a concrete maze,
each finds his way in darkness back to his own cubicle.

Imagine the effect of this daily routine on a living organism. For, whoever lives exclusively high above the earth loses contact with it, with his
fellow men, and inevitably with the instinctual, earthy aspect of himself.
He becomes isolated. The panoramic view, statistical and intellectual,
tends to obliterate the warm personal contacts of everyday life. No wonder
such lonely tower dwellers enroll by the hundreds in sensitivity classes, encounter groups, and be-ins, where, for a fee, they are permitted to walk
barefoot on the grass and are instructed in the lost art of touching and communicating with one another.

Psychologically speaking, many of us live "up in the air," imprisoned
in ideological towers of our own making; for the tower can symbolize any
mental construct be it political, philosophical, theological, or psychological, which we human beings build, brick by brick, out of words and
ideas. Like their physical counterparts, such towers are useful for protection against chaos, for occasional retreat, and as a vantage point for taking our bearings in relation to the wider view. They are useful as long as we
allow room for a little remodeling from time to time and keep the doors
open so that we can come and go at will. But when we build a rigid system
of any kind and crown it king, then we become its prisoners. We are no
longer free to move and change with the moment, to touch the vital earth
and to be touched by its seasons.

Something like this must have happened to the two tower dwellers in
this picture, for their edifice has no door whatever. They have walled
themselves in. In such cases, only an act of God can liberate them. This
liberation can take the form of a severe physical or spiritual illness, a violent
change of fortune, or another cataclysmic event which brings them suddenly "down to earth."

All important psychic changes are experienced as acts of violence. We
resist change. If we maintain a rigid position, then a breakdown may occur. The two humans pictured here are still in a state of shock. They don't
yet know what has happened; but notice how, like sick animals, they instinctively reach out toward the two little green plants at the base of the
tower. Notice also that the tower itself is not destroyed, only its crown is
knocked asunder. Like Nimrod, those two apparently envisioned their
tower as reaching up to heaven. Now they know its limitations. Nimrod's
tower was reduced to insane and meaningless "babel." Their tower is not
demolished, but it is no longer king. Now it is open to superior illumination
from above.

To the humans in this picture, what is happening seems like a catastrophe. They experience only the shock and cannot yet see the illumina-

tion; it is still behind them (in the unconscious). Like Phaëton, Apollo's son, who was struck down by Zeus for running amok with the sun chariot, these two experience this catastrophic happening as retaliation and punishment inflicted on them by an angry god. But this may not be the case. According to Ovid, Phaëton was struck down neither in wrath nor punishment, but in order to save the universe from destruction.

Looking at this card from our detached vantage point, we can see that these two mortals are similarly saved from psychological destruction and liberated from the prison of their prideful egocentricity. Symbolically speaking, they had built for themselves a towering edifice of rational thought by which they hoped to rise above the mundane world. Fearing the chaotic complexities and individual responsibility involved in moral choice, they had retreated into a rigid system of philosophy by whose concrete general laws all decisions were automatically made.

In the previous card we saw two subhuman creatures held in unconscious bondage to the Devil. There the threat was seen as devilish animal instinct (symbolized by bat's wings, talons, horns, and tails). Although the two subhuman creatures were unaware of their animal parts or of the Devil's machinations, these were clearly present in the picture, meaning symbolically that they were close to consciousness. The two had but to turn around or look into a mirror to see them. But apparently they were not ready to do this. Instead they built for themselves – or perhaps borrowed ready-made – a towering philosophy, a construct of ideas, rigid as bricks and fitted together in a permanent, unchanging pattern. They encased themselves in this system, preferring to live within its restricted confines rather than expose themselves to the moral problems and choices they would otherwise encounter. Within this edifice, these two lost even the contact they previously had (however unconscious) with their animal characteristics, for these no longer appear in the picture.

In the previous card, the two figures were naked meaning psychologically that their primitive nature was exposed. In The Tower of Destruction they have covered their true identity with the uniform of civilization. Whereas formerly they were slaves to their devilish instinct, in the tower they became prisoners of their equally devilish intellect. Like Satan himself, their intellectual pride had driven them too high, and like him they must inevitably fall. Perhaps, like him also, they will bring with them new illumination.

Of course these fallen ones are too involved in their immediate predicament to face the lightning. Their backs are turned to it. When they reach the ground, they will probably spend a lot of time licking their wounds and bemoaning their fate. Like Job, they will no doubt devote many hours to complaining about God's injustice and calling Him to task. It may even be years before they can see the light in the lightning. When this happens, their experience of the Divine, like Job's, will transcend all human logic and moralizing. But deep in the unconscious, the seed is already there. According to Jung, lightning signifies "a sudden, unexpected, and overpowering change of psychic condition."[3] We may expect to see the fruits of this experience in future cards, the next three of which (The Star, The Moon, and The Sun) all depict forms of heavenly illumination.

One of the possible outcomes of our own meditation on the Tower of Destruction might be to help increase our awareness of areas in our own life where we are in danger of psychic imprisonment; of attitudes or ideas we have crowned king. Where do they constrict our freedom? In what ways do we use religious, psychological, or philosophical systems to elevate ourselves above the mass of human kind?

Towers, both external and psychological, sometimes come together in an interesting way. For example, William Butler Yeats literally retreated to a tower in later life. Here, in absolute seclusion, he examined his soul and wrote beautiful poetry. But he also spent much of his time resenting old age. One might say that psychologically he was imprisoned in worship of youth. In his poem called "The Tower," Yeats writes:

> What shall I do with this absurdity –
> O heart, O troubled heart – this caricature,
> Decrepit age that has been tied to me
> As to a dog's tail?. . . .
> . . . .
> I pace upon the battlements and stare. . . .[4]

Many in our Western culture are similarly imprisoned in the adulation of youth. One hears elderly persons remark. "Well, I've lived a good life." Past tense. They speak as if their lives were already finished, which indeed is true if they feel that way. With any luck, a stroke of illumination may some day free them from "pacing the battlements" to stare forever at their lost youth.

Often, in small ways, one can be imprisoned momentarily in a rigid mental construct that prevents the free enjoyment of life. For example, when you are waiting for a train or a bus, are you trapped into the notion that you are nothing but "a person who is waiting"? Do you stand rigid as a tower, peering into the distance, impervious to everything else that is happening around you? Or are you relaxed, open to the sights and sounds of your environment and interested in observing the passersby?

Sometimes when we are enveloped in a dense cloud that temporarily hinders communication, we are jolted out of our preoccupation – not by a stroke of lightning, but by a small jolt almost like an electric shock, small but still of sufficient force to crack open our shell and put us in touch with reality once more. Some years ago this happened to me in a way that opened up new dimensions of meaning for this Tarot Trump and showed me a practical application for its use.

This incident occurred at a week-end conference which I had attended chiefly because one of its panel of speakers happened to be Dr. X, a woman whom I knew slightly and very much admired. On the second morning of the conference, a small group of us, including Dr. X, became involved in a lively discussion about new techniques in cancer therapy. I was particularly interested in this topic, and so obviously was Dr. X, who had much to tell us about new research in this field. To everyone's regret her remarks were cut short by the luncheon bell.

Later, finding myself seated next to her at the luncheon table, I re-opened the subject of our previous conversation, knowing it to be one of mutual concern. To my profound amazement, Dr. X turned to me somewhat abruptly and said, "Please, I'd rather not talk about that just now. My mind feels like freewheeling." As Dr. X told me later that day, she had intended to add a word of explanation for her sudden change of mood but she did not have the opportunity to do so because, immediately after she had spoken, someone called her name at the other end of the table and she turned away, becoming involved with others in lively reminiscences about travels in Italy. Since the person on my other side was also involved in a discussion, I sat alone with plenty of time to explore my hurt feelings. I felt stunned and shocked, exactly as if I had been hit by a bolt of electricity. I felt as if I'd been knocked for a loop and sent spinning through the air like the Tarot tower dwellers. And like them I imagined myself to be a victim – I experienced myself as an "innocent" person unreasonably singled out for punishment and humiliation. I prayed that the meal would soon be over so that I could crawl off into a corner alone and lick my wounds.

But, as it turned out, there was a lecture scheduled immediately after lunch, so I decided to postpone my orgy of self-pity and go along with the others to the auditorium. Luckily so, for when I took my seat and saw Dr. X on the platform waiting to be introduced as our next speaker, I understood instantly what had happened at lunch. Of course, just before giving a lecture her mind would have felt like "freewheeling" through sunny Italy rather than plowing through a serious and depressing subject! As she stood before us speaking for an hour extempore and later fielding difficult questions from the floor, I felt grateful for all our sakes that she had had the good sense to protect her wits from my stupidity and to maintain her equilibrium in the face of my one-sidedness. By the time Dr. X and I spoke together later, I felt that it was I who owed her an apology for being inconsiderate rather than the other way around.

You may think that this is the end of my story. And too often this kind of tale does end at the point of its resolution in overt reality. After all, what more is there to say? When a momentary misunderstanding occurs, is immediately cleared up, and rapport established, it is all too easy to forget the incident entirely – to sweep it under the rug as if it had never happened. But something *did* happen that day at lunch, and I wanted to feel into this small event while it was still fresh in my memory. So my story continues.

When I got to my room, I took out the Tarot Tower of Destruction and studied it. I deliberately forced myself to relive the feeling I'd had at lunch of being struck by a bolt from the blue. I experienced again the sensation I'd had immediately afterward of being disoriented as if I were falling. I recalled how I had felt personally singled out as a target. But as I studied the Tarot picture, I realized that the lightning wasn't aimed at the human beings in the picture, it was directed at the tower.

Towers attract lightning. Had I, perhaps, been encased in a tower at lunch? Symbolically we use the word "towering" and similar words to denote something out of proportion – beyond human scale. We speak of a "towering rage," a "towering ambition," a "monumental ego," etc. As I thought about this, I began to see how my "towering preoccupation" with the topic had momentarily imprisoned my human beingness. Inside the formidable fortress of my immediate concern I had sat peering out through tiny slits – or, more aptly, manipulating through them a searching beam of inquiry. Exactly like a searchlight, my inquiring mind pinpointed only certain factors in the environment, leaving everything else in obscurity. Had my aperture of awareness been more open I might have taken a few minutes to enjoy the sunny patio where we were sitting, to sense the mood of my companion, and to recall the program of events in my pocket which clearly listed her as the next speaker!

Having relived the drama from my standpoint, I then tried to imagine how the situation must have felt from Dr. X's point of view. How could she communicate with someone encased in a "tower"? Wouldn't she necessarily have to speak forcefully to be heard?

In using the cards to feel into the meaning of any happening, I've found it useful to study the card in question as it relates to the others in its vertical row. In the case of The Tower of Destruction, these are The Hermit and The Popess. I found this technique to be particularly helpful in meditating on my small but significant contretemps with Dr. X. In studying the Hermit, I was impressed by the friar's flowing mobility and his look of open inquiry. How alive he seemed to every sight and sound in his environment. I noticed that his light was not a spotlight with a piercing beam but rather a small lantern that cast its diffuse illumination in several directions at once. I observed that this lantern had shutters to protect others from its glare when need arose.

Then I looked at the Popess, at the top of this second vertical row. The Lady Pope is a symbol of patience, receptivity, and obedience to the true spirit. She sits quietly, absorbing the atmosphere about her. She would rarely initiate a conversation, and then only after first sensing the other's mood.

Since *l'affaire* X occurred, I've had several conversations with the Popess similar to the one recorded in the fifth chapter of this book. She is more introverted than I, so she is helping me to contact my own introversion. From her I'm learning how to sit quietly in the sun with someone – even a new acquaintance – without necessarily feeling compelled to converse. She has also taught me that, even at a committee meeting or business conference, where time is valuable (perhaps especially there) it is important to share a few moments of gentle "freewheeling" together before plunging into the matter at hand.

Sometimes I have conversations with the Hermit, too. From him I have learned to distinguish true creative introversion which provides its own special glow, from the sterile blackness of a cold and stony tower. Before I learned to emulate the Hermit, the unconscious forced me to compensate my one-sided extraversion by repeatedly sending me colds or other minor illnesses which provided the introversion necessary to inner harmony and health. But in recent years, through conversations with the Hermit, I have learned to maintain a more conscious and voluntary balance between my extraverted and my introverted sides.

With the two tower dwellers, I have not yet had a conversation. For one thing, they are obviously still too caught in their own misfortune to be available for such dialogue. Perhaps later, after they have digested the rainbow-colored manna we see falling from the heavens, they will be able to talk about this experience. Lest we be tempted to offer them the towering theology of Job's comforters, let us look at these poor souls once more and try to empathize with their situation. We have all been there in one form or another. And each time it is again a shock to be brought low and knocked out of our imagined security. Sometimes we are too dazed to react at all; other times we react in surprisingly inappropriate and often humorous ways.

Illustrative of the latter is the following one-liner which was told to me as a true story. A woman, knocked flat by a California earthquake, was heard to cry out: "Please rescue me first; I am from New York and not used to this sort of thing!"

Fig. 72   L'Etoile (Marseilles Deck)

20. The Star: Ray of Hope

Heaven above
Heaven below
Stars above
Stars below
All that is above
Also is below.
Grasp this
And rejoice!

Alchemical Text

In the previous card, we saw two human figures being forcibly ejected from a tower. Although they had lost their former viewpoint and their protective walls, they still had each other and they still wore the clothes which represented their social identity. In The Star we see for the first time a naked human (Fig. 72). Stripped of all identification and robbed of every pretention, her essential self is exposed to the elements. Wearing no social persona or mask, she reveals her basic nature.

The woman is kneeling beside a stream, pouring water in a ritual way from two red urns so that one jet of water flows back into the stream and the other falls onto the earth. She appears at the point where the living water of the collective unconscious touches the earth of individual human reality. She is concerned with both, and through her ministrations the two interact creatively. The water that falls on the earth nourishes whatever seeds lie dormant there. The water from the other jug, now aerated and purified, flows back into the common stream to revivify and replenish it.

Psychologically speaking, the kneeling figure might be dividing and sorting out insights newly available to consciousness, separating out the personal from the transpersonal. Perhaps she ruminates on the catastrophic event pictured in The Tower of Destruction. Meditating on its meaning, both humanly and symbolically, she relates the external happening to the internal psychic situation with which it corresponds.

From this point in our Tarot series, as we shall see, we enter a new dimension of understanding within which life's vicissitudes will be viewed under the aspect of eternity. No longer seen through the narrow apertures of the Tower, the world will spread forth new vistas under a wide and starry sky. Aspects of the psyche, formerly imprisoned within stone walls and now freed, will come down to earth where they can begin to operate in a more realistic way. In The Star, a nature priestess initiates the task of discovering in the events of terrestrial existence a pattern corresponding to that of the heavenly design. One feels that the rhythm of her pouring is attuned to that of the cosmic dance above.

Her two urns bespeak a kinship with the Angel Temperance, connecting her with the archetypal powers. Yet she is a human figure without wings, and the urns are blood red, symbolic of physical nature and human feeling. She kneels on the ground beside the stream, playing with its waters with the earnest concentration of a child. Being naked, her contact with nature is immediate and direct. She can help to ground the lightning of the previous card, bringing it down into reality and connecting it with the primal waters and basic earth of existence.

Her posture and general demeanor suggest humility, a state of being quite different from the humiliation experienced by the two figures falling from the lightning-struck tower – the humiliation we all experience when a cherished self-image is blasted from its stronghold. As we all know, the laborious transformation of such painful humiliation into a feeling approaching humble self-acceptance is a heavy task – one requiring suprahuman help.

Behind and above the kneeling figure, seven varicolored stars revolve around a central double star. No two of these seven stars are alike; each seems to have a unique personality. They are drawn in a vigorous, freehand way, suggesting the twinkling of stars as they actually appear in the heavens. The alternating pattern of their colors gives one the feeling that they are whirling around the larger double star. By contrast, the central star is drawn with geometric exactitude. This double star is created by superimposing a yellow eight-pointed star upon a red one in such a way that the two appear to emit alternating sparks of light. Black lines connect the yellow star's eight points to a center where they converge like the spokes of a wheel. The black dot at the hub suggests that the double star is pinned to the heavens where it remains fixed, but the alternating colors of its sixteen points indicate that this giant wheel revolves on its own axis. In essence, this star system represents a sun wheel or mandala.

Such a stabilizing center or image of wholeness often appears in dreams and visions during the periods of chaos and confusion that typically follow catastrophic events such as the one pictured in the preceding card. The great star's sudden appearance in the sky suggests that a new vision of wholeness has risen from the depths and will soon be available to consciousness. It pictures a fixed center, uniting the yellow spirit, intuition, and light with the red of body, emotion, and flesh. Around this focal point, the lesser lights, the diverse fragments of the personality, can begin to revolve.

Alchemical texts often picture similar configurations showing a giant fixed star (depicting the process of enlightenment) around which revolve the seven planets (representing the seven stages of the alchemical process). The alchemists called this process the Great Work for they believed that the priceless "philosopher's gold" could only be achieved by man's own labor, in contrast to the Christian idea of salvation by the grace of God. It was the alchemist's central idea that not only humanity but all of nature was imbued with the divine spirit, and that it was man's chief task to free the spirit thus imprisoned in matter. Only by engaging in this Great Work could man's own spirit be freed. The alchemists saw man's redemption as a by-product of this lifelong labor rather than as its goal. Theirs was a lonely task to be practiced in solitude or with one devout partner of the opposite sex. They felt that reunion with the godhead could never be achieved *en masse* but could take place only within each individual as a result of his own dedicated effort.

Jung's concept of individuation, as its name suggests, is similar to the alchemical viewpoint. Jung contends that man's salvation lies within the depths of his psyche, and that each of us must labor in his own individual way to discover and free the golden essence which lies buried within our psycho-physical nature. The alchemists, for whom the inner world was still a mystery, projected the elements of their psyche onto the elements of outer nature with which they constantly worked. It remained for Jung and psychologists who followed him to devise ways of withdrawing projections from external objects and persons and confronting these as archetypal psychic elements.

Viewed in this context, The Star pictures an important step toward a more conscious and active participation in the process of individuation. In The Tower, enlightenment came in a blinding flash which was too dazzling and cataclysmic to be faced directly, much less assimilated. In other cards the action has been carried by winged figures or other heavenly personages. In The Star the central figure is pictured as a naked human being, humbly kneeling. In her calm, natural setting there is room for contemplation and space for silent growth.

In the background are two green trees on one of which is perched a black bird. Unlike the eagles emblazoned on the royal shields of the Empress and the Emperor, this bird is a living creature, indicating that the connection between heaven and earth has become a living reality. The trees, too, are alive and flourishing. The dormant, truncated trees which formerly imprisoned the Hanged Man have put forth new growth, liberating him for new development and offering him wider vistas.

Symbolically, trees express both the transpersonal and the individual in a beautiful way. Rooted deep in the earth and towering up into the sky, they connect heaven and earth. The structure of a tree, from the ends of its elaborate root system up through trunk and branch to twig and leaf, presents a paradigmatic diagram, as it were, of the interconnection and interdependence inherent in all nature. Trees draw into themselves all four elements, synthesizing and transforming them into vital new growth. Hence trees are symbolic of the transpersonal, universal self. Yet the shape and pattern of each individual tree differs from all others. So trees can represent the unique way the transpersonal self is made manifest in each individual.

The two trees in The Star might also remind one of the twin trees in the Garden of Eden: the Tree of Life and the Tree of the Knowledge of Good and Evil. Perhaps, like Eden's trees, the two in this picture stand for twin impulses rooted in the human psyche which move us to action — the one which impels us to *live* life, and the other which motivates us to *know* life.

When a symbol appears in duplicate in dreams or other unconscious material, it ofter indicates that a new aspect of the psyche, hitherto unconscious, is now moving into consciousness. In the unconscious the opposites are not separated; all qualities and essences are intermingled. But when we first become aware of a new content, it begins to become differentiated, appearing often at first as twins – two of a kind. Later, as this archetypal content beomes more conscious, the two figures which embody its essence may show themselves as two similar but not identical entities.

For example, in the fifth Tarot, The Pope, man's questing spirit was represented by two prelates. These twin figures knelt side by side and wore identical dress, indicating that their characteristics as individual human beings were still concealed from consciousness. In the next card, The Lover, we saw two women. These women were not identical in dress, age, or character. This indicated a differentiation between the various aspects of the feminine principle dramatized there. Roughly speaking, they represented those of "the virgin" (formerly embodied in the Popess) and those of "the mother" (formerly portrayed by the Empress).

In a similar way, The Chariot pictured animal libido as two horses. Although these horses, identical in size and character, were yoked together as one team, their contrasting colors (red and blue) revealed a sharp differentiation between the two kinds of libido they symbolized: the red horse representing the impulse toward physical activity (the instinct to *live* life) and the blue one representing a more spiritual tendency (the equally powerful instinct to *know* life). In The Star, we now see these two impulses pictured as two trees. Unlike the horses. they are not seen as an unruly team pulling against each other. Although the trees are widely separated, both are rooted in the same Mother Earth, and the black bird flies from one to the other, connecting the two.

The "twin" theme is again repeated in the two vases which are similar in size, shape, and color. But although the two vases are almost identical, their functions are different. As we have observed, one empties the water back into the stream and the other pours it onto the earth. The Star Woman's actions here might dramatize Jung's idea that the two kinds of libido – the spiritual and physical – are really one essence, but each is adapted to a different purpose.

Significantly, this card is named The Star, thus directing our attention to the heavens and implying a connection between the heavenly bodies and whatever is taking place below. Stars usually symbolize guiding forces. Mariners use stars to find their way across uncharted seas. Astrologers use stars to predict future trends and to help human beings match the rhythm of their lives to the revolutions of the planets. The star of Bethlehem guided the Magi to the manger. Both practically and symbolically, it seems, the starry map spread out upon the skies corresponds to our inner constellations. This heavenly map is alive, vibrating with energy. Whether we study it consciously or turn our backs to it as the Star Woman is doing, its emanations nevertheless spark forth to influence our lives.

Stars are pinpoints of illumination scaled down to human dimensions. Unlike the lightning in the previous card, starlight cannot blind or destroy man. Unlike sunlight, it cannot wither and burn. Like the Hermit's lamp each star offers us limited and controlled illumination – spiritual insight – dismembered into small pieces suitable for human assimilation. Their ever changing yet predestined pattern sheds light on the unique moment of ordinary time; but the light that reaches us today from the stars began its vogage to earth milleniums ago. In this way, the stars connect each individual moment with transcendental time. They shed the wisdom of old knowledge upon our current dilemmas.

Stars are also connected with immortality. One ancient legend tells that at death each soul is elevated to heaven where it shines eternally as a star. Heroic figures or gods were often immortalized as planets or constellations which to this day bear the names of those so honored. Another popular belief held that, at birth, each human being was given his own personal star representing his transcendental counterpart or guiding star. Such a star was believed to watch over the affairs of its earthly charge, guiding his destiny and protecting him from harm. This idea finds echoes today in the popular superstition that if we wish upon a star our wish will come true, and when it does, we thank our "lucky stars."

Another ancient legend speaks more specifically about the correspondence between the realm above and that below or, to use psychological terms, between the self and the ego. It was believed that at birth the soul descended to earth through the planetary spheres picking up, as it went along, the qualities belonging to the various planets. At death, the downward movement was reversed, so that these qualities were returned to their respective planets to be used again by the next generation of newborn souls. In a continuous circular rhythm, then, not unlike the Star Lady's pouring, we human beings borrow illumination, energy, and talents from the stars to complete our earthly selves, returning these to the heavens (perhaps replenished and enhanced?) when our life on earth is done.

The idea that the stars were intimately connected with human fate preceded astrology. When man first discovered that the motions of the planets could be predicted, he took heart in the idea that man's fate might also be guided by some divine order. He experienced himself no longer as a creature tossed about willy-nilly by the gods. For him, ever afterward, the stars shone forth as beacons proclaiming that each individual life was connected with the divine pattern, offering hope that the seemingly random events of everyday life created a meaningful part in the universal scheme. Through his empathy with the stars, man, no longer a plaything of fate, became inspired with a feeling of destiny. It is as if the twinkling stars were little windows or eyes through which man glimpsed eternity.

Meister Eckhart has said: "The eye by which I see God is the eye by which He sees me." Stars are often seen as the eyes of heaven whereby the gods look down upon our doings. In Jungian terms, they symbolize the archetypes which are the images that influence our lives and through which we experience the myriad aspects of the godhead. As we move along the path of individuation, these many discrete points of splintered light tend to blend together until they are seen as one giant light whose glow is more constant. One might imagine this great light hidden behind a heavenly curtain through which it shines down on us via tiny pinholes until the curtain ultimately drops away so that we can experience the source more directly.

The stars in our Tarot are not pictured in a dark night sky as they would appear in nature, but are silhouetted against a white background. As with the lightning in the preceding card, this suggests that these phenomena are to be viewed symbolically, as manifestations occurring within the psyche rather than as events in outer nature. The Star Woman does not turn her eyes to the heavens; perhaps she sees their reflection in the waters. In any case, hers is a reflective mood; one feels that she is aware of the planets as inner presences and that they influence her actions.

Significantly, the hero himself does not appear in this picture. He is, for the moment, lost to himself and to us. The narrow, rigid tower in which he was formerly encased no longer contains him. The lofty edifice of words, maxims, and concepts that he has constructed brick by brick to defend himself no longer protects him. Formerly, sitting proudly in his tower, he had thought of himself as a superior being, solid and secure – a somebody. Now he discovers that he is nobody. He has lost all contact with his ego intellect. His self-image has now been knocked for a loop. The watch by which he formerly ticked off the events of his life is broken; the compass that guided his journey is lost. Even his chariot, the golden vehicle he counted on to "carry him home," is no longer available. His ego consciousness and his motility lie helpless. Only through the ministrations of the Star Woman can he be saved.

This woman is an archetypal creature of the deeps. She lives and moves in the timeless world of the planets – a world that existed millenniums ago, long before the advent of man and his clocks. Our ego concept of time is so geared to our man-made devices that it is difficult to remember that timepieces are a comparatively recent invention. For centuries, man along with all other creatures, lived and moved solely by sidereal time. Within each of us, buried deep in the unconscious, there still lives a primitive Star Woman whose counterpart is pictured here. She moves beyond time, subject only to nature's rhythm. Like the woman in this picture, our inner woman matches her rhythm to the motions of the stars. This archetypal figure is an important part of the psyche, but when the ego is overactive, we sometimes lose contact with her: when the ego is depotentiated, as happens in The Star, we can find her again.

In the psychology of a man, such a female figure represents his anima, or unconscious feminine side. In a woman's journey this figure, being of the same sex, would symbolize a shadow aspect of the personality. Since the Star Woman is drawn on the grand scale, larger than life, she could personify a quality far beyond the personal shadow and more akin to the self, that all-encompassing archetype which is the central star of our psychic constellation. In either case, the kneeling figure represents a hitherto inaccessible aspect of the psyche which, like a fairytale princess, was formerly imprisoned in a tower and held captive there by cruel King Logos, ruler of our masculine-oriented society.

In the Tarot Strength, we encountered a similar female figure who dominated the canvas. There, dressed in the fashion of the period, she represented a more personal aspect of the archetype – a humanizing influence. By confronting the lion, she helped the lonely voyager to recognize and tame the emotions so that they did not run rampant in a destructive way. Here, as Star Woman, she demonstrates how to put these reclaimed energies to more creative use. Emotions which formerly might have erupted, jagged as lightning, in rages against fate can now be poured forth as nourishing and healing balm.

One portion of this transmuted energy flows back into the stream. It belongs to the unconscious depths which can never be wholly understood or assimilated. The other portion waters the fertile ground of everyday reality. She works with these opposites simultaneously, connecting their two worlds through the activity of her body and the devotion of her spirit.

In the psychology of a typical twentieth-century woman, isolated from contact with nature and from her natural, inborn feeling of religious awe, the appearance of this Nature Priestess might presage a reconnection with the transcendental self. The Priestess is kneeling in a prayerful attitude. The position of her limbs suggests the swastika, a primitive form of the cross. Called the "hammer of creation," the swastika symbolized the continuous motion of the cosmos, connecting once again the pattern of the woman's circular pouring with the circulation of the planets overhead. Her atmosphere is deeply religious.

As Jung has pointed out, the Latin origin of the word "religious" means "to consider carefully." The Star Woman seems lost in careful consideration of the imponderables. As she meditates, she pours out the waters in a ritualistic way as if making a libation to the gods. It will be her task to initiate the ego into the inorganic layers of the psyche. Here consciousness will become aware of inner regions more remote and mysterious than those symbolized by the lion; layers deeper and more elemental than those inhabited by the insects and worms encountered by the Hanged Man.

The psychological importance of the Star Woman can be seen by contrasting this Tarot with Van Gogh's well-known painting *The Starry Night* (Fig. 73). This picture was painted in 1900 at St. Rémy, a mental asylum to which the artist was committed in his later years. Forcibly removed from the world of ordinary life, Van Gogh, like our Tarot hero, found himself cast into a parlous and lonely place. But in Van Gogh's canvas no mediating figure appears to help him deal with the sudden onrush of elemental contents from the deep unconscious. In the heavens, too, no central star shines forth to hold the planets in their orbits. Here the stars appear as masses of fire whirling about in a turbulent sky, each a law unto itself. One wind-swept star, comet-like, seems to have burst its moorings, for it careens madly across the heavens, threatening even to invade the earthly realm below.

In the foreground, a dark cypress writhing in agony shoots flamelike into the sky. It is as if the natural boundaries of heaven and earth had burst asunder and all of creation had gone mad. The sole image of unity and harmony in this chaotic canvas appears in the upper righthand corner where sun and moon are wedded together in a symbolic union of opposites. But this image is not central; it seems distant and unattainable. Without the intervention of human imagination, as symbolized by the Star Woman, the elements of Van Gogh's psychic being seem to have reverted to the primordial chaos of the deep unconscious – to the time before the Creation when "the earth was without form, and void; and darkness was upon the face of the deep."

Fig. 73   The Starry Night
(Van Gogh, Vincent, 1889, oil on canvas, 29″ × 36¼″. Collection, The Musem of Modern Art, New York. Acquired through the Lillie P. Bliss Bequest.)

By contrast, The Star pictures an ordered harmonious world. Here we see represented for the first time all four elements of creation: earth, water, air and fire. Kneeling on the earth, the woman is working with the water, while behind her in the airy sky, the fiery stars hold sway. It is through contact with these elements in outer nature that we experience the elemental nature within. In Jungian terms, the four natural elements could symbolize the four functions of the human psyche. Not all analytical psychologists agree as to which element best symbolizes which function. My own notion is that air and water might represent thinking and feeling; whereas fire and earth might symbolize intuition and sensation. No doubt one's function type influences the way he experiences and classifies the functions. The reader might find it useful to pause here and ponder on which classification feels right to him. Although this activity may not reveal anything new about the four elements of outer nature, it might produce fresh insights about the four functions of inner nature.

In The Chariot, these basic four were pictured as four posts or fixed concepts which supported a canopy to protect the charioteer from the elements. In The Star, the central figure has no such protection. She is exposed to all nature. The four elements of the psyche, no longer experienced as stationary rigid concepts, have come alive. Vibrant with energy, they reveal their true nature as completely as does the Star Woman herself.

Like Aquarius, the Water Bearer, this woman is kneeling on the earth pouring out water from two urns. Like him, she devotes her attention to the unconscious and to nature. Her appearance may signal a new phase in the hero's development, one akin to the Aquarian Age upon which we are now embarked. In this phase the hero, like many seekers today, will move away from fascination with outer nature toward exploration of inner nature, from ego concerns to relationships, ultimately combining and unifying all experience, inner and outer, to create a new world.

Indeed the Star Woman appears to have begun this task. For although she concentrates her activities on the water and earth, the stars and the wide sky are also prominently featured in the picture. One feels that with her help all four functions of the psyche will move toward integration. Despite the fact that the ego is "out of the picture," perhaps even because this is the case, it can now become passively aware of an expanding universe with dimensions hitherto undreamed. Flat on its back, the ego cannot participate in ordinary human activity; it can only lie inert in a deep depression. When the ego is immobilized, intuitions are free to soar. At this point the ego begins to be filled with a new sense of destiny and to experience its individual fate as part of the universal design. Purely ego-centered ambitions are now lost in contemplation of the stars, and life begins to revolve around a new center.

It is only through the inner images of the unconscious that such realizations can shine forth. The night light of fantasy, rather than the searching beam of consciousness, reconnects us with the eternal wisdom of our inner constellations. These inner eyes never sleep; they glow within us all the time. But sometimes we lose contact with them. Only through our natural eros side can we get in touch with our psychic heavens. This way of connecting – fluid rather than static, contemplative rather than rational – is pictured here as pouring.

In Temperance, we saw an angel pouring a white essence from a blue container into a red one in order to determine a new gradient for psychic energy. The Star Woman is doing something quite different. She is pouring blue water from two similar red urns. Temperance's task was to collect and amalgamate the disparate parts of the psyche which Death had dismembered, and to direct this new-found essence into new channels; the Star Woman's task appears to be one of separation and redistribution. Perhaps she is separating out the archetypal elements of the unconscious from the more personal contents, so that ego consciousness will not remain inundated by material with which it is not at present equipped to deal. She pours the archetypal contents back into the collective stream shared by all mankind; the more personal, she pours onto the dry land of everyday reality to encourage new life and growth. As the dry soil at her feet becomes wet, it grows malleable like clay. From this new substance a new world can be shaped – one more surely grounded in natural reality than the towering brick structure built by the intellect, which invited the lightning from on high.

The woman is both active and acted upon. She moves with a trancelike grace. Hers is the godlike absorption of a child creating a new world out of water and mud. Her intense dedication and total participation in this act of creation is not unlike that of the Deity himself as depicted in the illustration already presented from Ovid's *Metamorphoses* (Fig. 14). There we saw God evoking the great round world out of chaos. But the Creator, as Ovid tells us, did not fashion the world directly out of chaos; he had first to separate out the four elements. Only then could he recombine them to fashion the universal whole of absolute reality.

In a similar way, the Star Woman is now separating out the elemental waters in order to create a new reality. The rhythm of the dance of creation, as presented in Golzius's engraving, is active, overt, and masculine; the rhythm of the Star Woman is calm, introspective, and feminine. One feels here the healing serenity of this woman and the tranquility of silent nature. According to an ancient maxim, "Silence is the inner space we need for growth." This moment of inner growth is not one for extraverted doing; its essence is inner vision.

One Tarot student, musing on this card, wrote the following couplet:

> Star-struck woman by the stream
> Pouring water on a dream. . .

Our innermost dreams need to be watered, tended, and planted in outer reality. Whenever we work with the unconscious through active imagination or meditation, we "pour water on our dreams." We nourish them and connect them with consciousness, redeeming potentials that have hitherto remained hidden so that they can be used in our daily lives. By bringing our unconscious fantasies into contact with our conscious intentions, we free the spirit imprisoned in matter, liberating new intuitions and insights formerly locked up in our unconscious depths so that they can blossom forth into reality. We give life in the here and now to ideas and dreams formerly held captive in towering rationalizations. In doing so, we transform not only ourselves but nature as well. In other words, we change both the quality of our personal lives and the character of the collective unconscious. At this holy place where the earth and the waters meet, both the personal and the universal are touched and transformed.

It is evident that the waters with which the woman is working are changed by her activity. Containment in the two urns seems to have touched them with new life so that the streams now pour forth from the urns with fresh energy. In the process of pouring, the waters have become aerated and purified. Now air and water, fire and earth all come together in a new way. Psychologically speaking, the four functional elements of the psyche are revivified and recharged through contact with the eros, or feeling, side. It seems appropriate that the element emphasized here is water, for water, says Jung, "occupies a middle position between the volatile (air, fire) and the solid (earth), since it occurs in both liquid and gaseous form, and also as a solid in the form of ice."[1]

The Star Woman looks sad. Perhaps she adds a few tears to the waters as she pours. Tears cleanse and purify. They wash away the dust that life has thrown on our eyes so that we can look at the world more clearly. We say we are "dissolved in tears," "reduced to tears," or "broken up" by emotion. When we cry, our superficialities are panned out, as it were, so that the essential gold can shine through. Rigid aspects of personality are liquefied, leaving us more receptive and malleable. When we are flooded by emotion, the dam between conscious and unconscious gives way and consciousness is awash with new images, potentials, and ideas. Some are illuminating, some are terrifying, but all bring with them new energy and power.

At first we feel swamped by this sudden inundation. The Star Woman, being herself a creature of the deeps, understands this. That is why she is dividing and pouring the waters with such loving care. But she is, by nature, unconscious. Soon she herself will sink back again into the water which is her element, leaving the hero bereft of her ministrations – totally alone in the silent world of elemental being to confront the monstrous deeps as best he may. Then he will be plunged into further darkness where he must endure a confrontation with darker waters before he can emerge into the light of a new day, baptized and reborn.

Perhaps the black bird in the background brings dire premonitions that this will be his fate. Yet birds are symbolically messengers of the gods. As long as the bird is in the picture, one knows at least that the gods exist and that they are concerned with life on this planet. Like Elijah's raven, the bird may bring nourishment and sustenance to the suffering hero. Like Noah's dove, he may then bring hope of a promised land.

The bird now appears to be spreading his wings to lift himself bodily above the earth. But he will not leave this earth permanently, for he is a creature of the garden, too, sustained by its waters and fed by its fruits. Fly high into the light as he may, he must perforce return to his humble nest; and to whatever regions of air he may soar, he must always carry with him his little black self. The wings which transport him body and soul into unknown realms belong to him. Unlike those of Icarus, these are no artificial appendages affixed by wax, destined to melt in the sun. The bird's feathers are an integral part of his nature, designed especially to withstand the elements. Soon the bird, lifting himself above the earth and leaning effortlessly upon the air, will be borne higher and higher until he seems to soar among the stars. As the hero muses on this, he prays that one day he, too, may learn to entrust himself to the winds of spirit in such a simple, natural way. He hopes that he also may explore unknown regions of air and light without losing contact with his earthly home so that, like the bird, he will move easily between heaven and earth. But for the moment there is still work to be done.

It seems significant that the alchemists referred to their opus as the Great Work. Today we, too, speak of "working with an analyst," or "working on our dreams." Whenever we do such work with the unconscious, we distill out its essence. Such work is a kind of active meditation. It is not guided by written dogma or proscribed formulae. As one can see, the Star Woman consults no book; she simply deals with whatever material nature presents. "Imagination," said the alchemists, "is the star in man, the celestial or supercelestial body." Jung, too, believed that one's own imagination should be the guiding star in working with the unconscious. He did not set forth specific rules for creative meditation nor suggest specific images toward which to direct one's thoughts. He felt that the rhythm of each individual psyche was unique, and that one must work with whatever images the unconscious presented, following the rhythm best suited to one's own nature.

Yet Jung's method of active imagination and dream amplification is by no means "free association." In free association, as the name implies, one uses the original image merely as a springboard for fanciful flights which often lead one far away from the central idea. For example, one might start with the image "star," leaping from there to "movie star," and thence to "Hollywood," "celluloid," and on and on in a never ending trajectory. By contrast, the Jungian method of amplification follows a circular course. Keeping the original image central, it moves around its periphery, amplifying its meaning by analogy and contrast, using associations which proceed from it and remain connected directly to it, like the spokes of a wheel. In Jung's method, the secondary images revolve around the central one as the planets pictured in The Star revolve around their central sun. The circular motion of the Star Woman's repetitive dipping and pouring eloquently dramatizes Jung's way of working with unconscious material.

The Tarot Star emphasizes the autonomous nature of the psyche. Even this nature goddess is powerless to control the free-flowing stream which is a natural phenomenon operating independently, its motion and direction governed by gravity. Significantly, she makes no effort to direct the stream's course. She accepts the waters as they come, dealing only with those she is able to collect in her two small urns. But through her actions she effects a change, however small, in the character and quality of the stream. Jung's technique of active imagination affects the mainstream of the unconscious in a similar way.

As the Star Woman demonstrates, this form of meditation is by no means merely a passive process. Although she makes no attempt to control the direction and flow of the stream, she does not sit idly by, allowing herself to become hypnotized by its music. As Jung's term "active imagination" suggests, she *interacts* in an imaginative way with the waters, relating them to her earthly standpoint.

In a similar way, Jung suggests that we must never passively accept whatever a figure from the unconscious may say or do, as if it were gospel handed down from above. For, as we have already seen, archetypal figures, like human beings, possess both positive and negative characteristics. Sometimes they offer us sound advice; sometimes they talk nonsense; and on occasion they can make diabolic suggestions. It is Jung's contention that we must confront these archetypal characters actively and directly, by raising questions or presenting objections, exactly as we might do with some stranger who appeared suddenly to offer us suggestions or advice. Only by engaging in a spirited dialogue in which the conscious standpoint and the drives of the unconscious both find expression can we hope to resolve our conflicts and problems in a practical, human way. Having achieved such a resolution, it is important that we act upon it, for the function of this kind of meditation is to help us find a creative way into life rather than to use meditation as a soporific escape from life.

Sometimes, though, the problem with which we are confronted seems an insoluble one, unreachable by *overt* action. In such cases, it is often astounding how, by attaining inner harmony, we automatically resolve outer problems as well. Just as the Star Woman, through her actions, effects a change, however small, in the character and quality of the stream, so, too, active imagination can effect miraculous changes in the mainstream of the unconscious. Or, to use another analogy: the collective unconscious is like a vast sea full of archetypal fish. Each fish that is brought up into the light helps by that much to relieve the density of the dark waters beneath. It is not so much the number of individuals who go fishing that counts (and in any case their numbers will be relatively few); but what is of supreme importance is that new denizens of the deep become known and identified, and that increasing areas of the bottomless sea get explored and differentiated. Jung's active imagination is one way to conduct such an exploration.

As the Star Women makes clear, this is not a group technique. It is best performed in solitude. For after all, it is only through the individual that new ideas come into being. Later these ideas may be adopted by the general public and their influence spread throughout the world. But as artists, musicians, writers, and scientists have all testified, the initial "fishing expedition" is best conducted alone. It is a private ceremony whose mystery can only be realized within the secret recesses of the psyche.

Jung's comments on the significance of such a mystery in human development, both cultural and individual, seem pertinent.

> As the importantce of the inner life increased, the meaning of the public mysteries of antiquity decreased in value. To own a mystery gives stature, conveys uniqueness, and assures that one will not be submerged in the mass. . . . Mystery is essential to the experience of oneself as a unique personality, distinct from others, and for growth through repeated conflict.[2]

The mystery enacted in The Star cannot be shared with others or even, for that matter, with one's own critical intellect. Up to this point in the journey, the hero, ruled by intellect, has had little contact with his imaginative side. But now his Star Woman shines forth for him clearly. There is a Cabalistic saying to the effect that "When you have found the beginning of the way, the star of your soul will show its light." At long last, it seems, our hero has found the beginning of the way.

Before leaving The Star, it might be worthwhile to contrast it with the previous card, summarizing some of the salient features of each so that we can observe more clearly the relationship between the two. In The Tower of Destruction we saw two human figures being forceably ejected from their edifice. They were stunned, acted upon, passive. All the action in that card came from the heavens – traditionally the realm of spirit, Logos, and yang energy. The phallic shape of the tower further emphasized the masculine principle, indicating that the two tower dwellers were themselves prisoners of their intellectual aspirations and their strivings for power. They lived far above the sensations of their earthly, animal nature. They had lost contact with the ground of their being and the fluid waters of their inmost nature. The light of intuitive insight was blocked out of their lives by the massive crown which capped their dwelling. They wore fashionable clothes, symbolic of their personae, or stations in society, but these only served to make them look ridiculous by emphasizing the inadequacy of all human pretensions in the face of nature's elemental powers. The clothing of the two figures was almost identical, suggesting that neither of the two had a strong sense of his unique nature; even their sexual identity was unclear.

In The Star, all man-made covering and pretensions have been stripped away revealing one individual woman, naked and exposed to the elements. Although she may be only dimly aware of the fateful stars overhead, she is not passive. As we have observed, she takes action. Hers is the realm of earth and water, symbolic of the feminine eros principle. Unlike the lightning whish thrust forth violently to crack open, inseminate, expose, and destroy, the stars shed a passive, gentle light whose influence is calming and healing.

In The Tower, the human figures were too stunned by the thunderous flash from the skies and too preoccupied with their plight to observe what was happening to them. But in the calm aftermath of the storm, the hero, depotentiated and inactive, is open to new awareness. As he observes the

Star Woman, he marvels at her unself-conscious nakedness. Exposed to herself and to all the world, she makes no effort either to hide her imperfections or to accentuate her positive features. Without shame or pride, she accepts herself and the circumstance in which she finds herself. She makes no attempt to rise above it. She seems absorbed in her task, not as a means to an end, but as something useful and interesting in itself. She offers herself completely to the situation that life has presented.

As he observes her, the hero begins to accept himself and the helplessness of his situation. He begins to realize that such acceptance is necessary for change – and is, in fact, the sole motivation for all change. He understands now how, formerly clothed in a pleasing persona and imprisoned in towering rationalizations and defenses, he not only hid his true nature from others but from himself as well. Encapsulated as a tower dweller, he could not know who he was or where he was in relation to the elemental facts of life. Now the energy formerly dedicated to pretense and defense is free to observe the universe more objectively and to find his true place in it.

As he watches the Star Woman at her cyclic pouring, he begins to understand that the journey toward consciousness is itself a continuous, circular process. As soon as one uncovers, recognizes, and integrates an aspect of the hidden shadow side, another, hitherto unrecognized, comes to light. Each sudden breakthrough of illumination, like the disastrous one pictured in The Tower, brings with it new archetypal contents to be assimilated and integrated. Now the hero begins to view his journey as a series of such breakthroughs followed by periods of relative calm and integration. He no longer imagines the lightning to be an irrational act of the gods, an undeserved bolt from the blue. Neither does he experience it as a vindictive punishment for his many sins. Rather, he accepts his present situation as part of a meaningful design, a necessity, a challenge, and an opportunity. Deep in his heart a sense of life's meaning shines forth to illuminate his suffering and make it bearable.

The suffering is acute; he cannot deny it. But he no longer struggles to do so. He begins to understand that it is only through such anguish, such wounding, that the puny self-satisfied ego will be goaded forward on its journey toward the self. He no longer feels that he is an outcast; he feels, at last, *included* as part of life's pattern. Jung describes this kind of experience as follows: "You no longer see yourself as an isolated point on the periphery, but as the One in the centre. Only subjective consciousness is isolated; when it relates to its centre it is integrated into wholeness and finds in the midst of suffering a quiet place beyond all involvements."[3]

Reviewing now the events of his journey thus far, the hero begins to discover in their seemingly haphazard nature many recurring patterns. He observes how his psychic pendulum swings constantly back and forth between the opposites in an attempt to achieve equilibrium, and how his human helplessness invariably calls forth unexpected help from the unconscious. For example, as the Lover, confronted by his unconscious feminine side, he was inspired by Eros and moved to find the king in his golden Chariot. Faced with the enigma of Justice with her impersonal sword and scales, he was led to a more personal meeting with the gentle Hermit. Discouraged by the endless revolutions of a mechanized Wheel of Fortune, he was able to tap new reserves of energy through Strength. And in a similar way, his stalemate as Hanged Man, and his dismemberment by the dark angel Death, were assuaged by the ministrations of the bright angel, Temperance. Now he feels how the humiliations dramatized in The Devil and The Tower of Destuction are being bathed and soothed in the healing waters of The Star.

If the Fates had kindly furnished the hero with a map of the journey similar to the one we are using, he would be able now to look upward with us and make connections between The Star and the two cards that lie directly above it on the map. The Empress, at the top of this vertical row, pictures the Great Mother in her postive aspects as Mother Nature whose creative imagination brought all life into reality. Just below her, in The Wheel of Fortune, we see the sphinx, representing the Great Mother in her more negative phase, holding all libido captive, chained to her purposes. Now in The Star, we see this libido liberated from the Wheel of predetermined, repetitive circling, free to interact with it in a creative way.

Whereas the animals are chained to the Wheel and clothed in a ludicrous travesty of helpless humanity, the Star Woman is an independent being, able to deal with her fate in a specifically human way. The Star Woman shows how, through our creative imagination, we can be freed from bondage to a cyclic pattern each to live out his individual potential. Like the planets, we are all held within a specific orbit by a power beyond our control, but within our prescribed boundaries, each of us is destined to shine forth in a way uniquely our own.

According to an old maxim, "What the soul imagines. . . happens only in the mind, but what God imagines, happens in reality." By helping the hero to bring his soul's imaginings into harmony with nature, the Star Woman gives him a new reality. By connecting the hero with the world-creating imagination of the godhead, she imbues his life with new meaning and purpose.

Fig. 74   La Lune (Marseilles Deck)

21. The Moon: Maiden or Menace?

A savage place! as holy and enchanted
As e'er beneath a waning moon was haunted
By woman wailing for her demon-lover.

                                          Coleridge

Card eighteen presents a desolate landscape, eerie and terrifying, seen in the dark of the moon (Fig. 74). Directly before us, in the murky waters a fearful crawfish, with claws outstretched, seems to bar our way. On the other side of this water (perhaps a moat) two hounds, furiously barking, guard access to the two golden towers which mark the entrance to the Eternal City, the hero's destination.

As in The Star, the hero himself is out of the picture. His ego intellect, still submerged, has plunged even deeper into depression, for in this picture no human figure appears to help him confront the darkness. Psychologically, this means that he has lost contact with every aspect of his human self. Sunk now to the level of the animal kingdom, he is as wholly submerged in the watery unconsious as the prehistoric crawfish imprisoned in the moat. No helping hand reaches out to pull him up; no guiding star illumines his sky. This is the bleakest moment of his journey.

It seems he is lost in the vast desert whose yellow sands stretch out in all directions, unrelieved by green trees or shrubs. To be sure, two small golden plants are pictured in the distance, but these are not green as they would appear in nature, indicating perhaps that they are to be viewed symbolically rather than literally. Their golden color hints at the golden flower of immortality, that precious blossom traditionally sought by the heroes of ancient mythology. Whether the two plants exist in reality or appear only in mirage, they are inaccessible now. Our hero cannot reach them until he has crossed the waters and passed between the howling beasts.

That these plants are seen in duplicate, as are also the two dogs and the two towers, reiterates the "twin" motif which, as we have observed, marks the advent of new contents emerging for the first time from the unconscious. The territory on the other side of the water is indeed a strange new land, a foreign country hitherto unknown and unexplored. To set forth into this place of abysmal terrors and infinite promise requires great courage. This fateful transition is one the hero must face naked and alone. Leaving behind him the familiar world, he must venture forth blindly with no assurance that he will achieve the golden towers that beckon him on.

The hero cannot turn back. Already cast out of the wordly tower of outworn ideas and conventional patterns, bereft of the Star Woman, he stands between worlds, in a kind of no man's land, with no apparent bridge to make his crossing easier. He is an outcast from civilization and indeed from all humankind. Like a beast, he can only submit to his fate, relying on his animal instinct to see him through.

It takes courage and faith to set forth, like Abraham, "from your country and your kindred and your father's house, to the land that I will show you." (Gen. 12 : 1.) Even greater faith and courage is required of our hero who cannot yet hear the voice of the Lord. His only hope lies in the face within the darkened moon, which is framed in a rainbow collar, symbolic of hope and promise. As the moon, reborn from darkness, will transform herself to shine again so, too, may he emerge reborn from this night of terror. But other portents in the skies are not favorable, for the multicolored droplets appearing there (unlike the manna which fell to earth to nourish the tower dwellers) seem to be rising heavenward. It is as if the Moon Goddess, like a devouring mother, is sucking up into herself all creative energy from the earth, leaving it desolate and barren. The hero himself feels depleted, hypnotized by the crawfish lurking in the depths of the moat.

This is the hero's moment of truth, a time of terror and awe. The experience of the crossing is a familiar one to all who have made the jorney into self-realization. The mystics called it the "Dark Night of the Soul." In myths and legends it appears as the "Night Sea Journey." There, traditionally, the hero, like Jonah in the whale's belly, must overcome the monster which can devour his consciousness and hold it captive. In psychological terms, this symbolizes his victory over the devouring aspects of the unconscious, which would otherwise engulf his ego consciousness, resulting in psychosis.

In the Moon, the regressive pull of Mother Nature is symbolized by the crawfish who lives in the depths and walks backward, the rapacious hounds, and the moon herself, who seems to suck away his energies, deflecting the hero from purposeful action. The Goddess Moon is a witch and bewitching. As Luna, she can drive man to lunacy. Like Circe's, her magic can turn human beings into swine, and like Medusa, her hypnotic gaze can paralyze the will.

It is not to be forgotten that Artemis, the tranquil moon goddess, is cousin and companion to Hecate, that black witch of the crossroads whose slavering hounds could tear the hero limb from limb, or send him, rabid and frothing, into a perpetual night. Such a confrontation can spell spiritual death or it can presage rebirth. Only in the region of greatest terror can the golden treasure be found.

The motif of the watchdog as guardian of the underworld is a familiar one. The entrance to the Vedic underworld, the Realm of Yama, was guarded by two hounds. According to Greek mythology, the entrance to the infernal regions was guarded by Cerberus, the three-headed dog. Traditionally, the hero must not kill the animal; he must find other ways to come to terms with this instinctual side in order to proceed on his quest. Orpheus lulled Cerberus to sleep with his lyre. The Sibyl who conducted Aeneas through the Inferno, put the dog to sleep with a cake seasoned with poppies and honey. Hercules subdued the beast with his bare hands and afterward, according to one version of the legend, brought Cerberus back with him into the upper world. Psychologically, this myth seems to say that the hero – in search of individuation – cannot make the crossing from mundane ego-oriented reality into the land of the immortal self until he has conquered his instinctual side and brought it into consciousness. Ignored or suppressed, the hero's animal nature could turn on him and dismember his growing awareness. Yet he dare not destroy these beasts, for he will need their energy and help if he is to move forward into the Eternal City whose portals they so jealously guard. He knows that he cannot merely appease these beasts; he must make friends with them. Good watchdogs cannot be bribed or tricked. Perhaps if he can find a way to approach them, their night-prowling eyes will help guide his footsteps through the moon-darkness to the golden towers.

As our Tarot hero lends himself to the enchantment of the moonscape, the hideous yelping of the animals seems less threatening. Perhaps they are simply baying at the moon. He begins to feel a creaturely kinship for these two hounds, caught, like himself, under the spell of the Goddess of Night. Now their yowlings, no longer vicious, begin to sound to his ears like pleas for help. It occurs to him that just as he needs their instinctual guidance to achieve his goal, so too may they need the help of his superior consciousness in order to become free.

To descend into the depths means to be deprived of one's usual daytime orientation. In this condition, described in some primitive cultures as "loss of soul," one can be guided and ultimately saved only through instinctual knowledge. One is thrown back on the primitive wisdom of the body. As "man's best friend," the dog symbolizes this instinctual wisdom in a form sympathetic to man.

The idea than man and dog have an unconscious empathy is an ancient one. In *The Odyssey* it is recorded that Odysseus's dog, Argos, was the only earthly being to recognize the hero when he returned home from his long voyage. Although Odysseus appeared disguised and much aged, his dog's keen nose could detect his master's true essence. The dog cannot be fooled by a superimposed persona. By sniffing out everything that doesn't belong to our natures, he keeps us true to ourselves, and we in turn give new meaning to his "dog's life."

As we have seen, the alchemists thought it was man's task to redeem nature. Creation, they felt, had been left incomplete, and man must finish the job that nature had left undone. They felt that not only man's bestial inner nature but also the beasts in outer reality look to him for redemption. For the alchemist, even inanimate objects cry out to man for recognition and salvation. In his *Duino Elegies*, Rilke expressed a similar idea:

> These things that live on departure
> understand when you praise them: fleeting, they look for
> rescue through something in us, the most fleeting of all.
> Want us to change them entirely, within our invisible hearts,
> into – oh, endlessly – into ourselves! Whosoever, we are.
>
> Earth, isn't this what you want: an invisible
> re-arising in us? Is it not your dream
> to be one day invisible? Earth! invisible!
> What is your urgent command, if not transformation?[1]

Now the hero looks more kindly upon the crawfish, viewing it through the new-found eyes of his primitive, nocturnal self. Does this creature bar his way, or does it too seek redemption? Unlike the Mother Crab who once sought to pull Hercules into the waters, this crawfish seems to be reaching toward the opposite shore. The hero sees the creature now as a fellow traveler seeking, like himself, to rise out of the water and slime. He feels that the crawfish, whose armor has protected him from change down through the millenia, may be ready to cast off his cumbersome encasement and move upward along the ladder of evolution as other creatures have done.

But as he watches, the hero realizes that this is impossible. The weight of centuries is too much for the little creature. Time and again its clumsy shell pulls it backward into the waters; its unaccustomed claws can find no toe hold in the sand. Observing the crawfish's struggle, the hero begins to empathize with this poor creature who, like himself, is ambivalent: with outstretched claws it reaches toward the Eternal City, yet its habitual armor resists change.

Unlike man, whose flesh is exposed to the elements and willy-nilly subjected to change, the crawfish protects his tender flesh with an armor so impervious that his form has endured intact from prehistoric times. He even seems to wear his skeleton on the outside proudly, as if in mute testimony to the enduring structure underlying all life. Observing this, the hero feels that it is perhaps the crawfish's unique destiny to remain forever trapped in the waters in order to reassure wayfarers like himself of the basic stability behind all life, without which creative innovation would be impossible.

As if in response to the hero's musings, the little creature begins to emit an incandescent glow. Caught and emblazoned against the blue water, it shines forth as a symbol of transcendence. The crawfish, true to himself throughout the millenia, now seems to the hero a symbol of his own indestructible essence. Through empathy with the crawfish, he feels connected with his own cold-blooded prehistory, and with his future as it will be made manifest in the generations to come. Through this despised creature of the depths, the hero feels akin to the immortals. He takes courage now to move forward on his quest, for he knows that never again will he walk alone. Henceforward, the gods will accompany him.

For primitive peoples, cold-blooded creatures often symbolize immortality and are worshipped as gods. The Egyptian scarab is such a symbol. Another example is the golden lobster amulet from Costa Rica in figure 75. It seems charged with the same numinous intensity evoked by the Tarot crawfish.

The crawfish, far from barring the hero's way, seems now a stable rock to support his faith, a stepping stone to help him make the dangerous crossing. He sees his quest, too, in a new light. No longer concerned chiefly with his own safety, he experiences his journey as a sacred trust, a task assigned by nature. He sees man's evolution to consciousness as an unfinished aspect of creation – one left by nature for him to help her complete. His journey and its terrors shine with new meaning.

As the hero muses, the crawfish surfaces in the water. Rigid and immobile, it clearly offers its back for his step, as if urging him to move forward. Now the hero begins to feel reassured. He feels confident that, with the help of his ancient, new-found friend, he can achieve the other bank, bearing within his heart the "invisible re-arising" for which this creature, and all nature, yearns.

Even the dark moon holds no terror for him now, for he recalls a legend which tells that each night Lady Moon gathers unto herself all the discarded memories and forgotten dreams of mankind. These she stores in her silver cup till dawn. Then, at first light, so the story goes, all these forgotten dreams and neglected memories are returned to earth as moonsap, or dew. Mingled with *lacrimae lunae*, "the tears of the moon," this dew nourishes and refreshes all life on earth. Through the compassionate care of the Goddess Moon, nothing of value is lost to man.

Seen in this light, the multicolored droplets, no longer sucking out his energies, offer instead hope of future nourishment. The rainbow collar

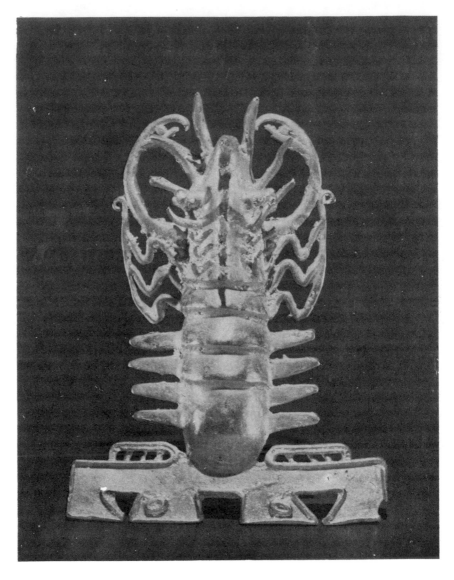

Fig. 75   Golden Lobster (Banco Central de Costa Rica, San Jose, Costa Rica)

which frames the Moon's face now reminds him of the Fool, whose pensive face even seems to be revealed and concealed within the orb's darkness. He feels that perhaps the Jester himself, God's little friend, is watching over him. With the help of the crawfish's proffered back, he is ready to make the leap to the unknown shore.

It has taken the hero a long time to prepare for this transition. Confronted with this card, almost everyone has an equally difficult time finding a way into it. At first, one is terrified, hypnotized, and immobilized. One cannot empathize with any of its figures, and one can see no way to get across the water. Like the hero, one feels depressed and tempted to turn back. Yet the golden towers are enticing; one wants to move forward to discover what lies behind them. No detour is possible. The path clearly lies ahead.

In some Tarot decks, this onward path is more explicitly drawn. In Manley Hall's deck, for example, the pathway is well defined and evidently well trodden, giving one the feeling that others have passed this way before (Fig. 76). Here the crawfish, too, is less threatening. It is not pictured lurking in the waters with possible evil intent; it is obviously reaching out to the opposite shore. This card shows other significant changes. The

Fig. 76   The Moon   (Manley P. Hall Deck)

two beasts, seen in the Marseilles deck as two dogs, appear in Hall's card as a black wolf and a light-colored dog. The latter even wears a collar, indicating that he is thoroughly domesticated. Hall seems to be saying that our path lies between these two instinctual drives, that we must maintain contact with the wild beast in ourselves and also with the domesticated animal without identifying with either one. To regress to the level of the howling wolf would spell insanity; yet, to become wholly domesticated with chain and collar would mean to distort and violate our instinctual side. Only by keeping contact with both of these animal tendencies can we move forward along the path.

The motif of the differentiated opposites is reflected again in Hall's towers, but here the one on the left is light-colored and the one on the right is dark. Perhaps this symbolizes the relativity of all opposites once one has crossed the waters and faced the howling instincts. Far ahead on the path, Hall pictures a tiny figure. Here, it seems, the hero has successfully made his crossing, confronted the dogs, and is on his way. Appropriately, Hall shows the moon-tears falling to earth, for the dark night is over. Dawn approaches. In the upper right corner the moon-cup appears on a shield.

One might say that the Marseilles card and the Hall card complement each other. In the Marseilles card, we stand at the edge of the Dark Night of the Soul, and in the Hall card, the darkness is behind us. We have made the crossing. In Hall's card, the crawfish is colored a realistic lobster-red. For all his antique armor, he looks to be a contemporary fellow whose strange shape holds no terrors for our kitchen knife, and whose innocent flesh frequently graces our table. Hall's Moon, too, no kin to Hecate, seems also quite tame – even benevolent.

By contrast, the crawfish in the Marseilles deck lurks menacingly in the waters, a mythological beast as ancient as time. His home is in their murky depths where he will continue to glow forever under the dark moon in the witching hours of night. Only the Marseilles deck offers us the hopelessness of depression, and at the same time its numinosity.

But like Lady Artemis herself, the Marseilles Moon does not share her secrets readily. In fact, she was so reluctant to have her picture painted that she started to disappear at the top of the card before the Tarot artist could finish her portrait. I, too, found her difficult to deal with. When I first approached this card, I was nonplussed. No amount of research on crayfish, dogs, towers, or moons could put me in touch. Then one day, ignoring the notes I had so painstakingly assembled, I simply let my imagination play with these symbols. The following little prose poem is what emerged.

This is the dark of the moon. A time of mystery, wonder, and terror. The witching hour when Hecate haunts the crossroads and her hounds stand guard, baying. No god or human being is seen. We are lost even to ourselves. Deep in the waters lurks a crawfish with claws outspread. Do we dare go forward? Or will this monstrous creature reach out to pull us back? The moon looks down on all – silent. Whose mask is that she wears? Maybe it's the Fool's, for she wears a band of rainbow colors not unlike those of our Jester, reminding us that the Moon is concerned with man's welfare. At dawn she will cry her moon's tears, with magic powers to nourish and heal. The Moon Goddess of the Terrible Night is also the giver of dreams, the revealer of hidden mysteries.

Is the crawfish really our enemy? Or is it, too, struggling toward the distant towers? How like Death's skeleton it looks! It wears its bones on the outside like armor to protect the mummy flesh within from change. And with what monstrous success! This crawfish, like the Egyptian scarab, is exactly the same creature as its great, great, great ancestor, some ten milleniums ago.

Like the scarab, it is immortal. See, now, how its truth glows darkly under the phosphorescent moon. A revelation. . . Now terror is dissolved in awe. The creature no longer seems menacing. Like a fly immobilized in amber, it stands impaled against the blue water, emblazoned there like the eagle on the royal shield, scorpio rising. Her claws reach up to embrace the moon, the ever-changing, changeless moon. Upright, she salutes the Man in the Moon. *Le Mat, Le Fou, L'Ami de Dieu,* God's little Friend, and ours.

And now at last the hounds are quiet. Their blood-thirst will soon be slaked by the Moon's tears. The crawfish offers his back for our step. Come, friends, take hands, take heart. It is now or never. Forward! Let us dare or die.

The Fool smiles now and fades out of the picturre. His work is done. In the dark of the moon, the sun is preparing himself to rise.

Although I cite this active imagining last, it really came first. It was actually out of this fragment that the entire chapter evolved. As in facing a depression in real life, so too in facing the darkness of this card one's intellect is of no use. Only through intuitive insight one can uncover the illumination of the depths. As Jung has so truly said, "One does not become enlightened by imagining figures of light, but by making the darkness conscious."

Having crossed the waters of The Moon, let us pause for a moment to take our bearings in relation to The Emperor and Strength, the two cards directly above it on our Map of the Journey. The Emperor, we said, represents civilization, the logos order which man attempts to impose on primitive nature. Strength represents culture, a more feminine and individual way of dealing with nature. The Moon represents Nature herself, within whose seeming chaos exists order of a very different kind from the conscious categories imposed by a masculine ruler. Her diffused illumination reveals to us many aspects of reality not visible under his sunlight consciousness.

Unlike the sun. which is bright, dependable, and warm, the moon is pale, inconstant, and cold. Yet by her illumination we can see shadows hitherto unknown. Whereas in sunlight objects stand out clear-cut as separate entities with sharply defined forms, under the moon's pale glow these man-made categories dissolve, offering us a new experience of ourselves and our world. Transformed by moon magic, a bush can become a bear, a tiger, a rock, a house, or a human being. It is frightening at first to find our tidy compartmentalized world thus dissolved into shimmering moon-flux; but as our eyes grow accustomed to the moon's revelations, our fears, too, begin to dissolve in wonder and awe.

Symbolically, and in actual reality, the Moon does not unveil herself to man's intellectual curiosity. She keeps one face always turned away from earth. Generations of men have been intrigued and challenged by her virgin modesty. Figure 77 shows a fifteenth century version of the Moon. Here a monkish figure, perhaps an alchemist, with the help of a female assistant, tries vainly to capture the moon's mystery with calipers and equations. But the moon eludes him. She continues to float serene above the clouds far beyond the grasp of his puny instruments and intellect.

Today modern man has shot through the clouds in his space ships to land impudently on the moon's dark face. But to no avail. The secret of her inner glow still remains hidden. Our spacemen brought back no magic moonbeams to illumine our dreams and astound our children. They established no other-world colony of moonchildren. They departed carrying with them only a sackfull of dullish rocks and leaving behind on the moon's virgin surface the trademark of modern man – a parking lot!

No wonder Lady Moon presents only her pockmarked witch's mask to man's gaze and offers him an inhospitable and barren body. She has every reason to resist his approach. She rightly fears that he will defile and poison her nature as he has long since ravaged and despoiled that of his own Mother Earth.

The Virgin Moon does not give herself to any man. Her essence is reflection. It seems in character, then, that the only gift of value that the spacemen brought back to earth was a breathtaking new image of the earth itself – a stunning photograph of our planet floating like a great balloon in the heavens (Fig. 78). An Italian poet, Guiseppe Ungaretti, recorded this experience succinctly:

Fig. 77 The Moon (15th century deck)

Fig. 78 The Earth (NASA photograph)

What are you doing , Earth, in
heaven?
Tell me, what are you doing, Silent
Earth?[2]

It is as if the moon in her quiet way were both challenging man's temerity in storming heaven, and at the same time directing him to seek heaven on his own planet and within himself. "Look to your own earth for the answer to your restless questing," she seems to say. "Why should man aspire to conquer the upper regions when he has yet to conquer the ecological problems on earth? Why should man yearn to unveil the mysteries of the heavens, when he has still to uncover the secrets of his own inner geography?"

The Tarot cards seem to be posing these questions too, for the mediating card between The Emperor and The Moon is Strength, who moves in harmony with her lion. She suggests that nature's veil cannot be pierced with ships of steel, nor her heart pried open with crowbars. The secrets of nature, she tells us, will only reveal themselves through the intimate contact of gentle hands and an understanding heart.

Strength's message is beautifully stated pictorially in the astronaut's photograph of our earth. By reflecting on it, we may reconnect with the lost values that the Moon Goddess has so long held in trust for us.

In our Map of the Journey, the Fool, striding free at the top, seems to pause over the Moon's vertical row. He and his little dog have already made friends with the baying hounds and learned the Moon's secrets, for the Fool is Luna's own moon child – a vague creature of rainbow possibilities with a penchant for madness. Some even say the Fool is the Moon's lover, that elusive Man in the Moon!

Fig. 79 Le Soleil (Marseilles Deck)

22. The Sun: Shining Center

Nor dim nor red, like God's own head,
The glorious sun uprist. . .

Coleridge

Behold the sun! The black depression of the previous card has lifted. The menacing crawfish and the howling dogs have disappeared. The Sun appears in all his glory, shedding his blessings on two children at play (Fig. 79). He wears a benevolent human face similar to that pictured in alchemical manuscripts where he personifies "golden understanding." The Tarot Sun possesses inherent human characteristics with which man can establish conscious relationship. The motif of human relationship is further emphasized by the two children who play lovingly together.

We have stepped now from the dark complexity of the inhuman, impersonal moonscape into the simple world of sunny childhood, where life is no longer a challenge to be overcome but rather an experience to be enjoyed. It is a world of innocent play, where we can recapture the lost spontaneity of our natural selves. Here we can rediscover the inner harmony we felt as young children before the opposites split us so cruelly asunder, dividing us from ourselves and from one another. This is the world of Blake's *Songs of Innocence,* where lamb and "tyger" move in harmony and one sees the world with new eyes of wonder.

In his book *The Savage and Beautiful Country,* Alan McGlashan calls this area of experience the "climate of delight." In the following passage, he tells us how to enter this sunny garden:

> Delight is a secret. And the secret is this: to grow quiet and
> listen; to stop thinking, stop moving, almost to stop breathing;
> to create an inner stillness in which, like mice in a deserted

> house, capacities and awareness too wayward and fugitive for
> everyday use may delicately emerge. Oh, welcome them
> home! For these are the long-lost children of the human mind.
> Give them close and loving attention, for they are weakened by
> centuries of neglect. In return they will open your eyes to a new
> world within the known world, they will take your hand, as
> children do, and bring you where life is always nascent, day
> always dawning.[1]

McGlashan perfectly describes the inner state dramatized in The Sun, reminding us, as does the Tarot picture itself, that this "climate of delight" is
not a distant land to be found in the skies but is, rather, simply a new way
of experiencing the known world. We come upon this secret garden, not
through sterile intellectualism, but through imaginative play. When this
new sun dawns within us, it makes the entire spectrum of outer reality
shine for us more clearly than ever before. In The Moon, the Tarot hero
began to connect with his inner "child"; here he does so more consciously.

In *The Creative Process* mentioned earlier, many scientists, writers
and artists – among whom Einstein, Jung, Yeats, and Henry Moore – tell
how they happened upon their most profound insights by simply playing
with words, ideas, or images. In recognition of its value as a means to
plumb creative depths, psychologists today use play therapy as an
analytical technique. One such method is described by Dora Kalff, a
Jungian analyst, in her book *Sand Play.*[2] In this method, the analysand is
provided with a large sand box, water, and dozens of toy figures (miniature
people, houses, animals, birds, vehicles,etc.) with which to create a new
world. Significantly, one important element in this treatment is the size of
the sand box itself, which defines a limited yet free area within which the
analysand can dare to let the undeveloped childlike aspects of himself play
freely without fear of harm or censure. The walled garden in The Sun
creates a similar kind of safe enclosure – a sacred *temenos,* or holy place,
where something dark and hidden can safely be brought forth into the
light. Only within such a consecrated spot could the instinctual opposites
(pictured before as howling beasts) emerge transformed as naked children.

Children often represent the inferior function, childlike and
undeveloped – close to nature. It is through this inferior function, which
has remained spontaneous, natural, and close to the unconscious, that
renewal can come. A good way to relate to this inferior side is through
play. In commenting on this, von Franz has this to say:

> You cannot organize the inferior function. It is awfully expen-
> sive and needs a lot of time, and that is one reason why it is
> such a cross in our lives, because it makes us so inefficient if we
> try to act through it. It has to be given whole Sundays and

whole afternoons of our lifetime and nothing may come out – except that the inferior function comes to life. . . I think nobody can really develop the inferior functon before having first created a temenos, namely, a sacred grove, a hidden place where he can play.[3]

Children symbolize something newborn, vital, experimental, primitive, and whole. Children are not self-conscious. When one is self-conscious, he is divided – riddled with doubts. He feels as if his every action were being observed and evaluated by a severe critic. Although one tends to project this critical voice onto others in his environment, the fact is that it resides, at least in part, within oneself. It is one's inner censor who subjects every act and word to scrutiny, killing spontaneous creativity.

The children in this Tarot play together freely and naturally. Because each is in harmony with himself, he moves in harmony with his companion and with all of nature. Each reaches out to the other with no fear of rebuff, and since each gesture arises spontaneously from the heart, it is not rejected or misunderstood. Contrast these two human figures, for instance, with the subhumans pictured as the Devil's disciples in card fifteen. Those two, each wearing a perpetual smirk, stand stiffly apart, assuming rigid poses. They dare not make a spontaneous move lest they disrupt the set performance, exposing those long tails which they choose to ignore. The children in The Sun have nothing to hide; they play together as freely as two puppies.

One feels instinctively drawn to young children because they symbolize the natural self. When one looks into the eyes of a child, one reconnects briefly with the innocence and purity of his own fundamental nature. The child symbolizes the archetypal self, the central guiding force of the human psyche with which we were all in tune as children. As the ego develops, we perforce move away from this identification with unconscious nature and often, in doing so, lose contact with it. The first half of life is usually an ego trip, a necessary stage of development in our Western culture. But when we have made our mark in the world and our sun stands at its zenith, then we can turn inward to rediscover the lost child within and relate to it in a more conscious way, healing the state of inner alienation imposed by civilization. The Sun pictures the hero's reconnection with his neglected self, which brings with it a direct experience of the illuminating godhead and transcendent life.

In his essay "The Psychology of the Child Archetype," Jung speaks of the "Eternal Child" as follows:

It is thus both beginning and end, an initial and a terminal creature. The initial creature existed before man was, and the terminal creature will be when man is not. Psychologically

speaking, this means that the "child" symbolizes the preconscious and the post-conscious essence of man. His preconscious essence is the unconscious state of earliest
childhood; his post-conscious essence is an anticipation by
analogy of life after death. In this idea the all-embracing nature
of psychic wholeness is expressed. . . . The "eternal child" in
man is an indescribable experience, an incongruity, a han-
dicap, and a divine prerogative. . . .[4]

As Jung clearly indicates, the "eternal child," being an archetypal image,
embraces many opposites. His appearance in our Tarot could symbolize a
regression into the "unconscious state of earliest childhood" where the ego
is contained, immature, and dependent; or it could represent "the all-
embracing nature of psychic wholeness" of a mature ego, relating naturally
to the self. In the first instance, we might characterize the hero's
psychological state as "childish," and in the second instance we might see it
as "childlike." But this Tarot picture offers several clues which indicate that
the hero is in no danger of a disastrous regression into childish behavior.
The children play in a walled enclosure, insuring that the insights available
here will not be flooded or swept away by an invasion from the unconscious. At the children's feet lie two golden nuggets reminiscent of the
philosopher's stone, that indestructible essence which was the desideratum
of the alchemist's Great Work. (In the previous card, this precious
substance was pictured as twin golden plants, which might wilt under the
sun's heat.) And finally, the child archetype presents itself as *two* children,
a boy and a girl, symbolic of all opposites in harmonious, creative interaction.

    That the heavy-set child on our left and the more slender figure on
our right are of opposite sexes is underscored by the fact that their sexual
parts are hidden by loin cloths. As with Adam and Eve, whose sex was
similarly concealed by fig leaves, these loin cloths are not worn in shame or
false modesty, but from an emerging awareness of their individual natures
and in recognition of the creative opposites as a holy mystery whose
essence must be protected and preserved. Like Adam and Eve, these
twins, no longer undifferentiated and contained in a womblike Eden, will
together create a new world.

    In our Tarot series, we have seen the opposites pictured in many
ways. We have traced their evolution from twin pillars to twin priests; we
have seen them as two horses, two pans of Justice's scales, the two
animals in The Wheel of Fortune, the twin vases of Temperance and The
Star, and so on. Never before have we seen them pictured as two human
beings of opposite sexes, naked and facing us. Never before have we
observed these twin impulses interacting directly rather than via another
figure (e.g., pope or angel) or via a mechanical device (e.g., chariot,

wheel, or scales). In The Sun, for the first time all opposites (male-female, spirit-flesh, soul-body, etc.) can interact directly and in a human way.

The motif of twin children is a familiar one in legend and myth, and it often appears in our dreams. Usually it symbolizes a creative potential of unusual proportions. For example: Romulus and Remus, twin brothers, founded Rome. In American myths, twin figures (one representing heavenly powers, and the other representing dark underworld forces) are sometimes cast as cocreators of the world. One famous set of twins from Greek mythology, Castor and Pollux, are still to be seen in our night sky where they have been immortalized as stars. One of these brothers is said to represent man, and the other, his heavenly counterpart. Whenever we look up at them, they can remind us that each one of us, too, is "twins." Each has an ego, and each has a companion figure, an immortal part, corresponding to the self in Jungian terminology. Awareness of *the other* always appears with the force of a revelation. In our Tarot, this awareness bursts forth, sudden as a sunburst.

Although this card pictures a moment of tremendous spiritual illumination, it is significant that its meaning is enacted – *embodied* – in actual physical bodies pictured in a down-to-earth setting. According to an old alchemical saying, "The mind should learn compassionate love for the body." Here body and soul are represented as equals, each reaching out to the other in gestures of compassionate love.

The feeling of body and soul as equals interacting harmoniously is not one easily achieved. As we have seen, our hero has arrived at this point only after many detours and regressions. In his Tarot journey he has recapitulated the psychological development of man in our Western culture from infancy to maturity. At birth, the spirit is identified with the body – buried as it were, in the flesh. To a large extent, an infant *is* his body; the demands of the flesh (hunger, etc.) predominate. But as the child matures, spiritual needs (for belonging, for identity, for meaning) begin to arise. Often these are in conflict with the bodily instincts, so that they must be separated out and recognized in order that conscious choices can be made. (The saints, for example, fasted and denied themselves sex in order to "separate out the spirit from the body.") Whenever we work on our dreams, we catch the spirit embedded in the unconscious and distill out its essence. Only when the spirit has been separated, clarified, and purified can it be reunited with the body in a more conscious way. Then the needs of both spirit and flesh, Logos and Eros, conscious and unconscious, can each receive recognition and become related in a way that renders each its due.

The motif of the *hierosgamos,* or mystic marriage of the opposites, is a familiar one in alchemical symbolism. It is often pictured as twin children – the brother-sister pair – embracing in the waters of the unconscious, as in figure 80. In this picture, the sacred *temenos* is not a garden as in our

Fig. 80   Alchemical Twins in a Vessel

Tarot, but a sealed alchemical vessel which contains and protects the ex- perience, preventing it from spilling out into overt life. That the *hierosgamos* is an inner happening rather than an outer sexual alliance is emphasized by its incestuous nature. Psychologically, incest symbolizes one's relationship to himself. It takes place within one's own psychic family, so to speak.

Naturally such an inner experience of unity will transform the hero's relationships in the outside world also. If the *hierosgamos* is experienced and contained, he will emerge with a renewed sense of wholeness able to relate more consciously and creatively to his wife or lover. But if he pro- jects the lost half of himself onto another human being, he remains forever incomplete.

The fiery illumination of the sun can be dangerous to human beings. Whoever created this Tarot deck used every color at his disposal to create the Sun's multicolored rays. The rays themselves are pictured as alternate sharp spears and snaky waves, presenting the Creator as not wholly beneficent but as the embodiment of all opposites. A similar idea is ex- pressed in the Old Testament where the first name for God was "Elohim," a *plural* noun, in recognition of the fact that the godhead must contain both masculine and feminine. In our Tarot, behind the sun's multicolored aura, we see a collar of black lines which give an illusion of energetic mo- tion to the sunburst. (Compare this to the more static collar worn by the Moon in the previous card.) Since black is created by combining all colors, these black lines may symbolize the ultimate union of all opposing forces to create pure energy.

The sun is the source of all life on this planet. We receive energy di- rectly from its rays and also indirectly from coal and natural gas which hold in store sun power absorbed aeons ago. All wind power, too, comes in- directly from the sun since it is caused by the sun's warmth spreading un- evenly over the earth's surface.

Unlike the pinpoints of flickering starlight, the sun's glow is wide and constant; and unlike Lady Moon, the sun fully reveals his face to us. His influence on our earthly lives is ever present. As the self is the center of our inner skies, so the sun is the center around which our planetary system re- volves. Each night we close our eyes secure in the knowledge that while our consciousness sleeps, the sun will hold our world safely in orbit. Even at darkest midnight we do not feel abandoned, taking comfort in the con- viction that at this very instant the sun is starting his upward climb toward our horizon, bringing with him a new day.

Many people — notably the Egyptians, the Aztecs, and the American Indians — have worshipped the sun as the supreme creator. In matriarchal cultures, the sun is seen as feminine, symbolic of the nurturing mother principle. In patriarchal cultures, the sun has masculine attributes. But in all cultures, the sun has carried the valence of a central supernal Being with

which we humans feel intimately connected and toward which we feel
something akin to a divine responsibility. Jung tells how the Pueblo Indians, for example, arise each morning at first light to worship the sun and
help him to rise – not for themselves alone, but for the entire world.

> "He who goes there," (they explained, pointing to the sun)
> "that is our Father. We must help him daily to rise over the
> horizon and to walk over Heaven. And we don't do it for our-
> selves only; we do it for America, we do it for the whole world.
> And if these Americans interfere with our religion through their
> missions, they will see something. In ten years Father Sun
> won't rise any more, because we can't help him any more."⁵

As these Indians realized, Western man has destroyed his intimate
connection with nature, to the detriment of both mankind and nature.
When man's relationship to nature is broken, the world becomes as sterile,
dark, cold, and desolate as if the sun literally did not rise. As Jung put it,
"Only the symbolic life can express the need of the soul – the daily need
of the soul, mind you!"⁶

In our Judeo-Christian culture we are fast losing contact with the symbolic life. Only once a year, on Easter Sunday, do the Christian faithful
gather on a mountain top to greet the dawn and to celebrate the sun's rising as a symbol of Christ's resurrection.

But most of us, regardless of religious or scientific background, pri-
vately and unconsciously experience the moment of sunrise as one of
mystery, wonder, and promise. Each day the sun brings with it a new day
with new warmth, new light, and new opportunities. When, faithful to his
promise, the sun comes back each morning from his dark Night Sea
Journey, he renews our faith in an ordered cosmos. As the sun, rising in
the sky, spreads out his rays like the spokes of a wheel, he becomes a giant
mandala, symbolic of the radial order existing in the unconscious and in all
nature. To observe the great sun wheel moving solemnly through the
heavens is to transcend briefly the linear time of our everyday existence
with its categories of cause and effect and to touch the acausal world of the
archetypes. There events do not appear sequentially "in time," but seem,
rather, to be grouped cluster-like around a center, like the sun's rays. At
moments of intense illumination, one glimpses a principle of order whose
motif is not linear like a railroad track, but is radial like the spokes of a
wheel. At these moments of intense awareness, one senses that it is *meaningful coincidence* rather than cause and effect which attracts these clusters
of events and holds them together.

Although scientific materialism has done its best to kill our spontaneous connection with the sun wheel, and smog and smoke at times
obliterate our view, nevertheless the great round sun riding high in the sky
still remains a powerful symbol through which we reconnect with our inner

sun. His faithful concern for the welfare of our planet evokes in us a reciprocal feeling of dedication and responsibility to the transcendent self, which the sun has symbolized for man from the beginning of time.

Perhaps it may seem strange that such a dazzling and ever present entity as the sun should be one of the last symbols of the self to appear in our Tarot series. In alchemical pictures, too, the *splendor solis* (as the illumination pictured in the Sun was sometimes called) usually appeared late in the pictorial sequence. Perhaps one explanation for this is that in order to experience the full splendor of this kind of illumination one must first have built or found a walled garden or sacred *temenos* within the psyche to receive the light. Otherwise the sun's rays could wither and destroy. But of all the reasons one might give why "the golden understanding" comes to our hero so late in his journey, the most cogent one is embodied in an old saying sometimes attributed to the Buddha, to wit: "All beings are born enlightened, but it takes a lifetime to discover this."

As one might expect, The Sun, whose number nineteen reduces to one, is one of our "seed cards" which signals the end of one phase of development and begins a new one. Like The Emperor, The Chariot, The Wheel of Fortune, Death, and The Tower of Destruction, The Sun heralds a new stage of enlightenment and nourishment. This quality is further indicated by the multicolored droplets falling from the heavens. Now the memories and energies gathered and stored by the Moon are released to revitalize the earth. It is a time of fulfillment. The two previous cards (The Star and The Moon) pictured a period of deep depression. Here now The Sun heralds a re-arising into the light. Traditionally, "the third" signals rebirth into a new awareness. On the third day, Jonah emerged from the whale's belly. So, too, on the third day Jesus arose from the sepulcher.

The motif of the vertical row also seems clear. At its top the Pope, God's earthly spokesman, sits upright on his throne, while at his feet the two kneeling priests bow to him as the external symbol of the self. Below this card the Hanged Man, topsy-turvy in relation to the codified religion, hangs precariously over the abyss of meaninglessness, suspended only by his own limited human understanding – cut off from humankind. But now, having endured the loneliness and trial, he discovers "the other," his inner companion, and emerges as twins to revel in the sun's glory.

Unlike the kneeling priests, these two children do not depend on faith or the testimony of others to believe in the Creator's existence; they experience the illumination of the godhead directly. Indeed all the Trumps of this bottom row illustrate varying degrees of direct illumination. First Lucifer, the fallen star, appeared in the hero's Eden as the Devil, after this, lightning, stars, and moon revealed their unique light. Now in The Sun this illumination reaches a crescendo. The Sun pictures that moment when the hero, leaving forever the world of sterile opinions and formal dogma, steps into the sunny world of direct experience and pure knowledge.

Fig. 81   Le Jugement (Marseilles Deck)

23. Judgement: A Vocation

Lo! I tell you a mystery. We shall not all sleep, but we shall all be changed, in a moment, in the twinkling of an eye, at the last trumpet. For the trumpet will sound, and the dead will be raised imperishable, and we shall be changed. For this perishable nature must put on the imperishable, and this mortal nature must put on immortality.

I Corinthians

In card twenty, a large angel with a golden trumpet appears in the sky, bearing a banner emblazoned with a gold cross. Below him are three naked human figures, one of whom is rising from the tomb (Fig. 81). The title of this card, Judgement, connects it with the biblical account of the Last Judgement when, at the sound of Michael's trumpet, the just will be called to heavenly life, whereas the wicked will be consigned forevermore to hell. The point to this resurrection is not, of course, that the just are to be rewarded with immortality somewhere in the sky, but that they are to re-awaken to a new and "heavenly" life on earth. Psychologically, they will now be called to enter a new dimension of awareness hitherto unknown.

Judgement dramatizes this moment of spiritual resurrection in several ways. Here for the first time a human figure (the one rising from the tomb) faces the source of illumination. This was not the case in The Lover, The Tower of Destruction, The Star, The Moon, or The Sun, where the activity in the archetypal realm took place above and behind the earthly figures. They felt its effects, but only indirectly, via the unconscious. In Judgement the central figure consciously perceives and hears the call. The immediacy of this connection is emphasized by the angel's size, by the long pointed rays of his aureole which seem almost to pierce the earth, and by his enormous trumpet whose blast bids fair to shatter the eardrums of those below.

Sound is a much more direct, arresting, and primitive form of communication than illumination, as we can all testify from our own experience. A lazy sleeper can turn away from the morning sun to continue his dreams undisturbed; but the persistent clamor of an alarm clock or bugle cannot be ignored. Within our dreams also, sound has an electrifying effect. It reaches us in a more startling, visceral way than visual imagery. To hear any sound in a dream – be it music, a whispered word, a gong, or a shout – is an unforgettable experience. *What was that? Who called?* We are instantly mobilized to action. We cannot believe it was a dream. We feel that we have been summoned by a power beyond ourselves.

Music of whatever kind connects the inner and outer worlds in a mysterious way. It can stir us to action, or soothe the savage breast; it can put the disordered spirit into harmony with the universe, or shatter glass; it can encourage plants to grow or cause them to recoil and wither.

It seems significant that in the two biblical accounts of the Creation, sound plays an important role. In Genesis, God *said:* "Let there be light." And John tells us that "In the beginning was the *Word*." In both accounts, the sound of the word precedes the creation. Quite apart from its meaning, the spoken word is sound. It creates vibrations to which all of nature responds. In Judgement, the sound of Michael's trumpet, like the spikes of his aureole, seem to have impinged on the earth beneath, which reacts by rising up in great billowing waves. It is as if Mother Earth, having yielded forth the figure rising from her womb, still roils about in convulsive labor with yet another birth to come.

Standing beside the open grave, a man and a woman greet the newly risen one in attitudes of prayerful thanksgiving. They welcome the one who was dead (buried in the unconscious) back to new life. One feels that he is closely related to them. Now the earthly trinity is reunited. The angelic figure completes the quaternity, joining heaven and earth to form a new reality. This theme is reiterated in the banner with its golden cross, to which the angel seems to point in a significant way.

The motif of the descent into the tomb and the ultimate resurrection of the "twice-born" (psychologically the death of the old Adam and the birth of the new) is a familiar one in our Judeo-Christian tradition and in many other cultures as well. In the Eleusinian mysteries, for example, the entombment and resurrection was enacted symbolically. In the final stages of initiation, the candidate descended into a crypt where he remained in a state of suspended animation watched over by a priest and priestess. At the end of three days, he was awakened from his trance by a herald to rise reborn as a new member of the Order. In our Tarot series, Judgement heralds the beginning of a new order – a new interaction between conscious and unconscious which will become manifest in the final card, The World.

The central figure of this picture is evidently our hero. When last seen, he and a lady companion were pictured falling down to earth, felled from their seemingly impregnable tower by a bolt of lightning. In the next three cards (The Star, The Moon, and The Sun) he disappeared from view. We imagined him lying in the slimy mud of a deep depression. Now he emerges from his long night to join the two figures standing vigil at his tomb.

A reunion of whatever kind always initiates a new beginning; it can never eventuate in the re-establishment of a former status quo. Whether the wanderer has been on an outer journey or an inner one, he returns a person far different from the one who set forth. And so, too, with those who were left behind. All will have changed in the interim. And the lives of those who kept the faith will undergo further changes by contact with the voyager to realms unknown. This is vividly illustrated by the accounts of persons pronounced clinically dead who have been revived, and whose visions of a wider reality have added new dimensions to the lives of all they touched. When someone is reborn, everyone around him awakens to new life.

The vitality of the figure rising from the tomb is apparent. He is pictured as a young man, solid and muscular, whose flesh glows with health. Although from the viewpoint of everyday consciousness, he has seemed "lost" and "dead," he returns renewed in body as well as spirit, revitalized by his contact with the earth and his adventures in the subterranean depths.

Since there are four figures here, it is tempting to explore them in the light of the four functions of the psyche which Jung called sensation, intuition, thinking, and feeling. I should like to hazard the hypothesis that our hero (the man pictured rising from the grave) has become identified with his superior function, and that this function was probably thinking, because his feeling side seems undeveloped. I take this young man to represent both the ego consciousness and the thinking function, and I see them as now rising to new life after their long sleep underground. Before developing this thesis further, it seems a good idea to recapitulate Jung's theory about the four functions.

As noted earlier, they represent the four characteristic ways a human being perceives and deals with reality. Sensation (the testimony of the five senses) and intuition (information derived via the sixth sense) are the two functions by which we apprehend the world of inner and outer experience. Jung called these *irrational functions* because they bring us information which has nothing to do with logic. For example: Despite assurances by an expert that my typewriter is now in perfect condition, my sensation function tells me that one key still sticks. Or, although Mr. X has just arrived bearing gilt-edged letters of recommendation, my intuition tells me that he is untrustworthy. There is no rhyme or reason to either of these conclusions; they simply *are*. I would find it difficult to support them with logic.

By contrast, the information derived through thinking and feeling is rational. These are the two functions by which we deal with the material presented by sensation and intuition. They are classified as *rational functions* because they involve rational discrimination. In the case of thinking, we make valuations based on logical thought, and in the case of feeling, we make choices according to an equally rational hierarchy of feeling values. To use the instance of the malfunctioning typewriter as an illustration: A thinking type presented with this problem might immediately look up the largest and best publicized repair shop in town and take his machine there for repairs since the first mechanic had failed in his task; whereas a feeling type might be inclined to return it to the original mechanic in order to give him a chance to rectify his mistake.

This kind of conscious feeling decision, as Jung conceives it, is not to be confused with unconscious emotion; on the contrary, it is a very precise value judgement based on how one feels about something rather than what he might think about it. Conclusions reached via the rational functions (unlike those derived through sensation and intuition) can be described and supported in a rational way. For example, confronted with a malfunctioning typewriter, a thinking type might tell you: "I considered this, and this, and this, and finally came to the conclusion that the most logical thing to do was to look in the newspaper and pick the best advertisement." Whereas a feeling type might say: "I felt I owed this mechanic another chance. If the shoe were on the other foot, I'd appreciate an opportunity to rectify my mistake. I wouldn't feel right doing it any other way."

Jung made another observation concerning the functions which is of significance here. He discovered that the two rational functions (thinking and feeling) are mutually exclusive, and so also are the two irrational ones (sensation and intuition). When we are busy thinking about something, we cannot at the same instant be feeling about it; and, if we are concentrating on observing something with the senses, we cannot at the same time be receptive to messages via the sixth sense. It follows then, that if one's superior function is one of the rational functions, the inferior one will necessarily be its rational counterpart; or if the superior function is one of the irrational ones, the inferior function must perforce to be the other irrational function.

Since we tend to use our superior function most often, it constantly improves with practice, whereas its incompatible function suffers more and more from neglect. In some cases the superior function – this dependable right arm of the personality – becomes so adept and strong that it seems almost to take over the entire psychic body. As a result its other three limbs (especially the inferior one) become atrophied for conscious use. After years of successful and happy association with the superior function, the ego can become virtually identified with it.

To become identified with one's superior function is not an uncommon experience. In our culture, this is particularly true when the superior function happens to be thinking. Today we overvalue logical thought (often ignoring its antithetical function, feeling). As a consequence, the thinking type is sometimes pushed into relying almost entirely on his thinking, leaving his feeling side and other aspects of himself relatively undeveloped. Early on, such a person is pegged by family and friends as "the one who is good in school." Tasks involving thinking are automatically handed to him. He is encouraged to develop it further by specialized study, perhaps in physics or philosophy. Such a person will probably end up in a business or profession demanding constant use of his reasoning mind, with few opportunities to develop other talents. By the time he reaches middle age, such a person is identified by others (and, more importantly, by himself) as "the thinker." He begins to perceive himself as a person whose sole mission in life is *to think*. We frequently meet the thinker in the classic cliché of the absent-minded professor who can readily recall abstruse equations but cannot contrive to remember his wife's birthday.

If this professor is successful in his work, such an ego identification may continue all his life. With the aid of one auxiliary function he can limp along quite happily, his stoic calm being interrupted only occasionally by sudden outbursts of repressed feelings on his part, or by misunderstandings with those whom his lack of feeling has offended.

But sometimes the ivory tower of logic within which this professor has become incarcerated is hit by a bolt from the blue, and like the figures in the Tarot Tower, he is knocked from his isolated security to lie helpless in the mud. Usually the lightning bolt appears as a wholly unexpected change in his outer life: He is inexplicably fired from a job he has held for many years; or his "happy" marriage is blown sky high by a "Dear John" note pinned to the pillow; or he himself suddenly falls head over heels for a dizzy blonde. However fate strikes, this professor finds himself helpless and exposed, cast out forever from the solid structure of his old life and unable to marshal his thought and will to devise a new one.

If the blow has been severe, he can remain in a confused and depressed state for a long time. Ideally, with a little luck, and perhaps some professional help, his enforced retreat from active life will not be one of listless stagnation but an interlude of creative renewal. If his journey into the depths is a successful one, the deposed thinker will come back into life reborn. Henceforward he will be able to operate not through thinking alone but with other aspects of himself now available for conscious use. Thinking will still remain his superior function, but it, too, will have been transformed – revitalized by its contact with the wellsprings from which all creativity flows. Then his ego personality, and all the functions of the psyche, will experience the kind of reunion pictured in Judgement. When this happens, what formerly was felt as a stab in the back or a destructive bolt from the skies will be seen as an angel of wonder and glory.

Jung's theory of the psychological types is so complex that he devoted an entire book to the subject. Obviously the above resumé cannot do it justice. But it may serve as a useful springboard for viewing Judgement. If we are to connect the young man in this card with one of the four functions, it seems likely that he must represent the hero's superior function – the one with which he has been most closely associated all his life. The way he is pictured in Judgement seems to bear out this hypothesis: The figure rising from the tomb is not a newborn babe but a full-grown man, and he is being *reborn*, indicating that he was formerly alive and active in the outer world. In stature and age he so closely resembles the hero that one could not tell them apart, which would indicate that the two are pretty much identified with each other. In such a situation, it is easy to understand how, when the superior function is knocked out, the ego also suffers a drastic blow.

This is what seems to have happened to the hero. In fact, the tale of the absent-minded professor might well be his own life story, for there is evidence that, like the professor, our hero is a thinking type. We can observe this first in The Lover. There, faced with a choice involving a conscious discrimination in the feeling area, he was completely helpless; his logical thinking was useless. Unable to get at his submerged feelings, he stood transfixed. He seemed woefully unconscious of the winged god whose erotic darts were about to wound him in the back.

Naturally, this isn't to say that only persons of the thinking type get themselves into such a fix. But this young lover did seem singularly unaware of Eros – unconscious, one might say, of his very existence. Most of us, if we're lucky, can at least catch a glimpse of him out of the corner of one eye before he strikes. In any case, the lover's tolerance for such wounds was limited. As we saw, he chose neither of the two ladies who sought his attentions. Instead he set forth alone in his chariot. There we observed him, fenced in by the four posts, protected by his overhead canopy, and riding high above the instincts, the good earth, and all humankind.

This theme is further developed in The Tower of Destruction. There his relatively fragile and mobile chariot has now become a fixed fortification of solid bricks within which he is encapsulated high above all nature and removed from life. To be sure, he has by now acquired a female companion, but she, too, is a prisoner in this man-made construction.

No doubt all of us tend to identify at first with our superior function, but when the prison is not so towering and rigid, the lightning need not be so violent nor the ensuing depression so severe. The psyche is a self-regulating system; it constantly strives to correct any imbalance between its various aspects. If the imbalance is less pronounced, the force necessary to restore equilibrium need not be so cataclysmic. Sometimes, for instance, the needed correction does not come via some external event but from the superior function which, worn out by constant use, simply lies down in its tracks and refuses to budge.

My own experience is a case in point. As mentioned earlier, I am an intuitive type, with feeling my second-best function and sensation my inferior one. After some analysis, I was able to get at my feelings pretty easily and had even achieved a nodding acquaintance with my thinking function. But my sensation – my ability to perceive and relate to reality via the five senses – was still unconscious and undeveloped. I found my way about the world of people and objects largely via the sixth sense, my superior intuition, assisted by feeling.

I had been conducting adult education seminars in literature and the humanities, first under the auspices of a university and later on my own. I enjoyed these seminars very much and so did my students. We had embarked on a study of Shakespearian drama, and I had built up an extensive library on this subject in preparation for what promised to be a career of never ending challenge and inspiration.

On the overt level, everything seemed to be fine. We were just completing our study of *King Lear* and had voted to do *The Tempest* next. All the current members of this group were anxious to continue, and several prospective members had applied for admittance. Then, quite suddenly, I woke up one morning with the feeling: *I can't do this anymore.* Everything had gone dead for me. It wasn't that the material itself had become stale through repetition. I had never taught *The Tempest* before and was eagerly looking forward to this new experience. But somehow I could not summon the libido to continue. It had simply disappeared – gone underground, taking with it a good part of myself, but fortunately not all of my ego consciousness. I could continue to function in the world; but the zest and joy had gone out of life.

I felt like a zombie, going through the motions of living, waiting for Godot. Every once in a while, I would make an effort to dredge up my lost libido and interest it in some valuable enterprise. To no avail. Once I made an abortive attempt to study the works of Marcel Proust, who had briefly caught my imagination; but this, too, faded to nothing. On another occasion, I decided to embark on a graduate degree in literature but soon dropped out of the program because I found the professors pedantic and the material uninspiring.

Then one day, a close friend gave me a deck of Tarot cards and my imagination was piqued by their curious pictures. These Tarot Folk seemed to "belong" to me, but I could not identify them specifically nor approach them intellectually. To do so would have required using my inferior sensation function to study their reality in minute detail and my thinking to organize this material. Being an intuitive, I was not interested in objective reality and details bored me to bits. If my intuition couldn't connect immediately with something, I lost interest. After all, I dealt in images and words. I loved words. The sound of words, the imagery evoked by them, the reverberations of meaning inherent in their origins – all this I loved. But these peculiar nonverbal picture cards? No thank you. Yet I treasured them because my friend had given them to me, and my intuition kept telling me that there was a key into their meaning if I could but find it.

Several years later, I attended a lecture where Jung was quoted as having said that the Tarot presented a pictorial representation of the archetypes. There was the key! And after that my libido woke up and the juices of life began to flow into new channels. My intuition had risen from the grave revitalized in a new and healthy body. I began to study the pictures in detail and to find meaning in them. Later I regained enough self-confidence to begin giving seminars on this subject and to discipline my sensation and thinking to undertake the more exacting study necessary to write this book.

But sensation still remains my inferior function. For example: Although I have examined Judgement many times with many different groups, I only observed today, as I was writing this chapter, that the yellow earth in the background of this picture is not flat, but appears to be moving in convulsive waves.

In the above discussion of the hero's experience and my own, we have made a wide detour from the specifics of the card before us. (This kind of detour is typical of intuitive types, by the way; we tend to use present reality chiefly as a springboard for flights of fancy into other worlds.)

If you are a psychologist, or even if you aren't, you may disagree with my fanciful hypothesis about the hero's identification with his superior function. But probably we could all agree that in Judgement he has undergone a rebirth. Such a moment of liberation is always experienced as a redemption.

When we redeem an article from pawn, we buy back something of value which formerly belonged to us and which has been held hostage. Individuation is *au fond* a redemptive process. Its aim is not to create something entirely new – something beyond and foreign to ourselves – but, rather, simply to redeem and liberate aspects rightfully belonging to ourselves which have been held hostage in the unconscious. In German, the verb "to redeem" is *erlösen*, literally, "to free from fixation." But freedom from fixation does not imply freedom from all cares and problems. Whenever we redeem something, we must pay a price.

Although our hero appears to be redeemed, his life henceforward is not to be envisioned as one of perfect peace and everlasting harmony. He, too, must pay a price. His increased awareness will inevitably entail increased responsibility. His long trial in the dark dungeon is over; but he must now face the challenge of new light.

At the end of a court trial a judgement is handed down. This marks the termination of the defendant's present ordeal. If the judgement is favorable, the prisoner is set free – not free to do as he pleases, but free of guilt. Although he is now able to move about in the world as he chooses, he will find that his choices and values have changed during his confinement. His increased awareness may bring with it wider areas of choice and a more acute sense of responsibility.

This is clearly pictured in Judgement, where the one who is being freed from solitary confinement is no longer alone. He now has two close human companions and a heavenly presence whose needs and wishes he must consider. If he fails to meet these new obligations, he may find himself back in his prison again. To be redeemed is an honor. It means being summoned to a new vocation. "Who has vocation hears the voice of the inner man; he is called," says Jung.[1]

The gravity of this moment is clearly shown in the emotional atmosphere of Judgement. The couple standing by the grave do not welcome their comrade back to life with huzzas and wild jubilation; theirs is a posture of solemnity and prayer. Their faces reflect thanksgiving for his safe return, but also gravity at the prospect of entering into a new life of wider awareness. They look to the young man, who is central to their family for guidance. He, in turn, faces the awesome angel. The hero, who formerly rose above all he surveyed, now stands in a grave looking up to the heavens for guidance. He, who once considered himself superior, now hears the call to serve a power above and beyond himself.

If he is able to respond to the trumpet's call, he will step forward into an expanded life beyond anything he has known or imagined. If he fails to meet the challenge, he will sink back into his dungeon, perhaps never to re-emerge. The gravity of his situation is amplified by Jung in the following passage:

> When the libido leaves the upper world of light, whether by individual decision, or owing to the decline of vital energy, it sinks back into its own depths, into the source from which it once flowed out, and returns to the point of cleavage, the navel, through which it once entered our body. This point of cleavage it called the "mother", for it is from her that the source of the libido came to us. Therefore, when there is any great work to be done, from which the weak human being shrinks, doubting his own strength, his libido streams back to that source – and that is the dangerous moment, the moment of decision between destruction and new life. If the libido remains

caught in the wonderland of the inner world, the human being becomes a mere shadow in the upper world: he is no better than a dead man or a seriously ill one. But if the libido succeeds in tearing itself free and struggling up to the upper world again, then a miracle occurs, for this descent to the underworld has been a rejuvenation for the libido, and from its apparent death a new fruitfulness has awakened.[2]

In Judgement, an angel suddenly bursts forth out of nowhere to deliver a challenging pronouncement. The advent of such a deliverer is one of catastrophic dimensions, which Jung describes in this way:

The birth of the deliverer is equivalent to a great catastrophe, since a new and powerful life issues forth just where no life or force or new development was anticipated. It streams forth out of the unconscious, i.e., from that part of the psyche which, whether we desire it or not, is unknown and therefore treated as nothing by all rationalists. From this discredited and rejected region comes the new tributary of energy, the revivification of life.[3]

From all that has been said about Judgement, it is easy to make connections between it and the two cards which stand directly above it on the vertical axis (The Lover and Death). One might say that the topic dealt with in this vertical row is death and rebirth; death of the old ego and its resurrection in a new form. What is involved primarily is a sacrifice of egowill and its dedication to a power beyond itself.

In The Lover the hero's young ego received its first wound. But Eros' dart was only a pinprick. As we saw, he crowned himself king and set forth alone to conquer the world. In Death a more complete dismemberment of ego and other psychic aspects took place. From this catastrophe, too, he emerged intact. But now he was no longer alone; he had acquired a female partner. These two first appeared in The Devil as naked subhumans unwilling to turn and confront their devilish (and Luciferian) potentials. We saw how they covered their tails and hoofs with the clothing that "everybody is wearing," and escaped the Devil by incarceration in the Tower.

Now, at last, in Judgement, the hero and his two companions stand naked together, exposed to one another and to the influence of heavenly powers. It is as if the dismembered bodies which Death had plowed into the earth have now sprouted forth in a new and more human way. The angelic figure in the sky has also become humanized. Although he has golden hair and two sets of golden wings, his expression shows more intensity and human feeling than one could observe in the faces of the heavenly figures pictured in previous cards. And, significantly, he is communicating directly with the figures below.

That all the figures in Judgement are humanized and are in communication with one another marks an important breakthrough in the hero's psychic awareness. It gives promise that the qualities of each may be brought together and consolidated into one complete being – a *human* being. The earth echoes the promise of new birth. Perhaps the earthly clay in which the hero has been embedded has been sparked to new life by the angelic fire, and a new creation will emerge in the next and final card, The World

Fig. 82   Le Monde (Marseilles Deck)

24. The World: A Window on Eternity

At the still point of the turning world. Neither
flesh nor fleshless;
Neither from nor towards; at the still point, there
the dance is,
But neither arrest nor movement.

T.S. Eliot

We have reached the culmination of our long journey. In this final picture we see a naked dancer framed by a living wreath of interwoven branches. (Fig. 82). At the corners are pictured a lion, an ox, an eagle, and an angelic figure with a halo. The card is called The World.

The dancer has the face, hair, and breasts of a woman but her slender hips and sturdy legs suggest that she is an androgynous being who combines and integrates within her body the masculine and the feminine elements. The opposites whose development we have been tracing are here combined in one entity. Its neuter sex removes it from the world of the personal into the realm of the transcendental, yet its flesh color marks it as human. The dancer moves in an area of awareness often described as "Thou art *that*." And "I am *that* I am." The flowing scarf suggests the presence of the ever moving spirit. The dancer holds two wands, one in each hand, representing the positive and negative poles of energy. As she moves, these two move in relation to each other in a compensatory way, symbolizing the constant and dynamic interplay of all opposites.

The natural wreath framing the dancer indicates a harmonious interweaving of all aspects of nature, conscious and unconscious to form a continuous and integrated whole. The wreath creates a sacred *temenos* within which the dancer is protectively contained. In The Sun, the twins were partially enclosed by a semi-circular wall of golden bricks; here the *temenos* is alive, natural, and complete. It sets the dancer apart from all that is meaningless and unessential – from all that does not belong to her. Yet she has space to move – her own space – within which she is free to express herself effortlessly. In Jungian terms, she might symbolize the self, center of psychic wholeness.

It may seem puzzling that, although this naked dancer exposes herself freely, without prudery or shame, her sexual parts still remain hidden. Symbolically, she tells us that the creative urge at the heart of all life cannot be revealed. This not in the sense (as the queen said about sex) that it is "much too good for peasants," but simply because it is a holy secret, one that cannot be fully unveiled. In this connection, it seems significant to recall that the twins who appeared in The Sun also kept their sexual parts hidden. Such modesty is an instinctual, archetypal feeling arising from the central self, not a false prudery caused by superimposed cultural restraints. One confirmation of this is that, even in today's permissive society, young children often show a reluctance to expose themselves. If, mistaking their innate modesty for prudery, we pressure them into self exposure, we may thereby do violence to their natural connection with the self. The dancer pictured in The World may be telling us that, although to be naked is indeed natural, to expose oneself to the world is not necessarily so. There are times when the self needs to be protected and contained.

The self is the center of our psychic equilibrium. When we lose contact with the dancer within, we lose our equilibrium. Whenever we lose touch with nature – our inner nature – we experience, deep down, a sense of inferiority. To be in contact with the natural self, Jung tells us, is to feel neither inferior nor superior. A similar idea is expressed in the following:

> In the landscape of spring
>   there is neither better nor worse.
>
> The flowering branches grow naturally,
>   some long, some short.

The dancer's wreath creates a safe asylum for the newly emerging self, so that its unity can never be disrupted by invasion from the outside. It also creates a boundary to contain her energies and protect them from dissipating. This protection is pictured as a natural one, indicating that it occurs spontaneously at this stage of psychological development. Symbolically this means that the self is now fully realized as an incorruptible entity. Regression is no longer possible. For this reason, the alchemists called the final stage of their process *fixation*. Here conscious and unconscious are united, and instinct and spirit flow together as one being whose awareness embraces and includes both.

The wreath is not the round uroboros of primal chaos; its shape is elliptical. A closed circle suggests the womb within which the fetus is contained in the amniotic waters; an ellipse is reminiscent of the vulva, or lips of the vagina, through which at birth a new being, now complete, emerges into a new world of light and air. Whereas a circle is one continuous round with one center or focal point, the ellipse has two foci – one at the top and the other at the bottom – suggesting the coming together of two discrete halves to form one whole. In our Tarot this idea is further indicated by the way the two halves of the ellipse appear to be bound together at the focal points. Such an ellipse is called a *mandorla*. It reminds one of a seed, an egg, and the motion of the planets in orbit. Unlike the uroboros and the wheel, both of which endlessly repeat themselves, the mandorla carries with it the suggestion of future development. It symbolizes the creative interpenetration of the two spheres of heaven and earth. It also connects with the World Egg which (according to Mithraic belief) produced the Creator, and with the Philosopher's Egg wherein the gold was incubated and revealed. Its shape follows the path of the circulation of light, the ever renewing creative light described in Chinese philosophy. Within the wreath, circulation is further suggested by the flowing scarf. A new spirit touches the figure; she dances as the spirit moves. She is contained within that sacred space where reality touches eternity.

This state of awareness is pictured as a *dance*. When we dance, we move in space to a rhythm which marks out time, bringing the two together in harmony with music, symbolic of feeling. Dance originated as a sacred art, a form of prayer, by which man put himself in tune with all nature and with the gods. Through rhythmic dance, man bridged the gap between mortal time and transcendental time and experienced himself as part of an everchanging process. Through ritual dance, the shaman put himself in tune with the universe to restore the equilibrium of nature so that he could call forth needed rain or effect healings. Through ecstatic dance, the dervish leaped outside mortal time, matching his rhythm to the whirling stars.

Dance symbolizes the act of creation. In Greek Orthodox doctrine, Sophia (Divine Beauty) dances. Zen philosophy views all life as a gentle dance, the art of which consists in moving through one's ordinary life in a natural, integrated, yet spontaneous way. Physicists tell us that our world, and we ourselves, are but a dance of particles. At the microscopic level, all dichotomies – inner and outer, mine and thine, subjective and objective – become meaningless. The dancer in our Tarot *is* the World. Yeats expressed the same idea this way:

> O chestnut tree, great-rooted blossomer,
> Are you the leaf, the blossom or the bole?
> O body swayed to music, O brightening glance
> How can we know the dancer from the dance?[1]

The dance has been a frequent symbol in these cards. It all began with the Fool dancing on his merry way and sweeping us along with his boundless energy. But his dance was uncontained and unfocused. Heedless of the present, he pranced forward while looking backward, with little awareness of himself in the reality of *now*. The Hanged Man, too, was a dancer of sorts. But although his feet could be seen to perform a jig, they were not grounded in reality; and the rest of his body remained immobile. Confined within the coffin of his truncated trees and suspended from above like a puppet, he could only perform a mechanical jig. The movements of Strength with her lion and Temperance with her two jugs were suggestive of dance, but these characters appeared as allegorical figures; they were not human beings. The movement of each was restricted by the limitations of the specific task to which her energies were dedicated. In card thirteen we saw the dance of Death, another suprahuman allegorical power who, like Shiva, performed the eternal dance of creation and destruction.

The dancer pictured in The World is quite different from all of these. She appears as a naked human being, intent on no specific act or purpose other than *being* – being herself. Focused neither on past nor future, she moves in rhythm to the ever changing present. As her title indicates, she is not confined by restrictions of a limited allegorical classification (as in Strength, Death, and Temperance). She encompasses all of these and much more. Unlike the Hanged Man who enacted the topsy-turvy jig of Fate's puppet, this dancer moves freely with one foot always touching the earth. Although she is in constant motion, she remains connected with the ground of her being – golden and indestructible.

Von Franz describes this beautifully when she says: "The experience of the Self brings a feeling of standing on solid ground inside oneself, on a patch of inner eternity which even physical death cannot touch."[2]

Heretofore, the hero has had brief intimations of the self as the central guiding force of his journey. Now, in The World, the self stands completely revealed in an unforgettable way. When one has such a revelation, it effects a profound and permanent change. The result is not simply a further widening of the former personality – it is as if one were re-created as a wholly new being. From this moment forward, the self becomes a conscious, ever present reality, which Jung describes in this way:

> Experiencing the self means that you are always conscious of your own identity. Then you know that you can never be anything other than yourself, that you can never lose yourself and never be alienated from yourself. This is because you know that the self is indestructible, that it is always one and the same, and cannot be dissolved and exchanged for anything else. The self enables you to remain the same through all conditions of your life.[3]

Yet, as Jung also makes clear, being in contact with the self does not mean being estranged from the world or unaffected by it. One still reacts emotionally but in a more profound way. He describes the dimensions of the self as follows:

> The widened consciousness is no longer that touchy, egotistical bundle of personal wishes, fears, hopes, ambitions which always has to be compensated and corrected by unconscious counter-tendencies; instead, it is a function of relationship to the world of objects, bringing the individual into absolute, binding, and indissoluble communion with the world at large. The complications arising at this stage are no longer egotistic wish-conflicts, but difficulties that concern others as much as oneself. At this stage it is fundamentally a question of collective problems, which have activated the collective unconscious because they require collective rather than personal compensation. We can now see that the unconscious produces contents which are valid not only for the person concerned, but for others as well, in fact, for a great many people and possibly for all.[4]

Many of these ideas are represented in the Tarot World. For the first time we see pictured symbolically *the whole of creation:* **earth, plant,** animal, bird, man, and angel. The figure in its center is none of these; yet being an androgyne, she encompasses much that transcends ordinary humanity. She is not merely the sum of all her many aspects but, rather, the *quintessence,* a state of being beyond the four dimensions of ordinary reality. At the same time, she is represented in *human* terms. She is not pictured as an abstract design – a hollow tube, an instrument through which the Divine flows unchanged; she reveals herself as an individual, with unique physical characteristics. She gives the light a body – *her body* – and she expresses it in her own individual way.

The four figures at the corners, who stand guard in eternal vigil, symbolize the state of development Jung describes above, where one's aperture of awareness is now open to collective problems rather than those of mere ego concern. Like the four points of a compass, they mark out the new dimensions of this wider world. Although securely placed, they are alive and the dancer is in constant motion in relation to them. Bound to no superimposed rules of behavior, puppet of no "isms" or cults, she is free to move in her own individual way within the confines of her individual space as defined by her protective mandorla.

This dancer does not have to worry about being consistent: She has no need to recall what she may have said or done yesterday so that she can square today's behavior with yesterday's. As long as she keeps contact with the four at the corners, she moves spontaneously in the present, secure in the knowledge that her reactions of today are in harmony with those of yesterday because both have come from her deepest center. As the Tarot so beautifully shows, she is in constant motion in relation to her environment, and her environment (the four corner figures and the wreath of branches), too, being alive, can interact as part of an evolving pattern. Her reaction today will no more be the same as it was yesterday than the events which called it forth will be identical to those which will confront her today.

The Tarot picture blends together this idea of spontaneity and stability in a beautiful way. The dancer is not pictured with both feet solidly planted on the earth. Only one foot touches it; the other is poised in mid-air ready to contact it in a new way with each succeeding step. One can see how, as her dance unfolds step by step, she will never lose contact with her golden touchstone nor will she become affixed to it in a rigid, uncompromising way. Her openness to change is also represented by her flowing scarf, indicating that the space within her mandorla is not a vacuum, a dead-air space. Within it, a gentle spirit moves, bringing ever new refreshment, new ideas, and with these, new dimensions of conflict which will challenge the dancer to seek their resolution at a more profound level.

This dancer is not a stone statue, impervious to conflict. As she is free to move, so also is she free *to be moved*. She holds the wands of both positive and negative energy, and her dance encompasses not only creation but the destruction without which no creation would be possible. Because she is released from neurotic conflict, she is even more open to the fundamental experience of opposites. Calling this state of tension "divine conflict," Jung describes it as follows:

> All opposites are of God, therefore man must bend to this burden; and in doing so he finds that God in his "oppositeness" has taken possession of him, incarnated himself in him. He becomes a vessel filled with divine conflict. [5]

As Jung has frequently emphasized, and as our Tarot dramatizes, to be a vessel filled with divine conflict is a privilege and burden specifically human. It offers no escape into "another world" but presents us with the challenge of living in this world in a meaningful way. Content within the framework of her natural boundaries, the Tarot dancer dreams of no treasure to be sought at the end of some visionary rainbow. To borrow the language of the alchemists, she is concerned with translating the base metals of her everyday existence into golden experience of lasting value.

The self can be pictured in many ways: as a flower, a rock, a tree, a child, an abstract design, and as a king or god. In Revelations, the ultimate goal is presented as the Celestial City, the timeless New Jerusalem, to

Fig. 83   The World (Sforza Tarot)

which after the Last Judgment, the faithful will rise to eternal life and light. In the Moon, the golden towers of this heavenly city were seen as a distant goal guarded by two beasts. In this fifteenth century Italian Tarot The World, the city now stands fully revealed (Fig. 83). It is presented and supported by the two alchemical twins of the Sun whose union makes possible its revelation.

It seems significant that the Marseilles version of this card has abandoned the traditional, collective symbolism of the Heavenly Jerusalem in favor of a more individual, human approach. If, as some say, the Albigenses created the Tarot as a veiled protest against the domination of the Church and its collective formulae, it seems probable that they might have chosen to picture revelation as the unique individual experience pictured in the Marseilles version. In protest against today's collective society, Jung also stresses the importance of the individual human being as the sole carrier of consciousness – the one instrument within whom and through whom the self is made manifest. "The individual alone," he says, "makes history." Jung's lifelong concern was for the fate of the human being, "that infinitesimal unit on whom a world depends, and in whom, if we read the meaning of the Christian message aright, even God seeks his goal."[6]

Often the Christ appears in art as a symbol of the self. Significantly, Christ was referred to in the Scriptures as both the Son of God and Son of Man, thus underscoring the idea that the god within can only be brought to birth through human consciousness and made manifest in a human way through the lives of individual human beings.

The Tarot dancer is not pictured against a specific background. Her illumination does not come from lightning, star, sun, moon, or an angelic presence. Symbolically, her background is everywhere and her light is universal. Everything in this card is seen from the aspect of eternity in the ever present now. When she reveals herself, the hero, like the poet, sees not *with* but *through* the eye. Her wreath is in fact shaped like an eye through which man may glimpse the miraculous. To quote Fausset: "There is only one miracle in the world: that of being reborn from division into wholeness." Individuation means to stand wholly revealed as a whole person – not perfect, but *complete*. An ageless being, this dancer existed before man was, and she represents the essence of man, not a goal beckoning from without, but an emanation unfolding from within. In her, spirit is embodied in flesh – flesh spiritualized in such a way that the two interact as one. Her presence is made manifest, not through death of ego, but through a humanization of the archetypal self. The dancer's two wands suggest self-fertilization – a constant dialogue between all opposites, with ego and self interrelating in dynamic equilibrium.

Although the Tarot figure is androgynous, she is pictured as predominately feminine. This represents a psychological truth, for the feminine side in both men and women is connected with the experience of the self. With a man, his initiation comes through the anima; with a woman, the self is personified in dreams and other unconcious material as a female figure. As woman, the World contains within her the seed of new birth, for self-realization is an ever evolving process, both in the individual and in mankind generally. This dancer is destined to continue moving and growing through all time. Just as the image of the self has been incarnated in various guises through history, so this symbol, too, will doubtless undergo many rebirths and metamorphoses in future generations. Since she is an archetypal figure, the forms she takes as she evolves will always be compensatory to the conscious standpoint of the current cultural melieu. Perhaps the renaissance today of this feminine figure is a compensatory reaction to the denigration of the feminine element in our Western culture.

In response to a similar cultural imbalance, the alchemists frequently pictured a female figure in a mandorla. She was called the *anima mundi*, or world soul. They conceived of her as a force embedded in matter which animated all bodies from the stars in heaven to the animals, plants, and elements of earth. It was the alchemist's lifelong task to liberate the *anima mundi* from her imprisonment in the *prima materia* of unconscious nature. That she represented qualities not unlike those of the Tarot World is made evident by Jung's comment about her. "The idea of the *anima mundi*," he says, "coincides with the collective unconscious, whose center is the self." He further characterizes her as "the guide of mankind" who is herself "guided by God."

Despite his emphasis on the individual as the sole carrier of consciousness, Jung repeatedly stresses the effects of such individual awareness on the community. Individuation is not isolation. Self-realization in one individual will invariably change those with whom he lives, and this will affect the community, ultimately resulting in social changes as well. Not that a self-realized person sets forth to create a new society; but his inner illumination will inevitably shine forth in such a way that it draws others into its orbit. A new realization of the self in a unique person will spark its reincarnation in the collective environment.

"The deepening and broadening of his consciousness," says Jung, "produce the kind of effect which the primitives call 'mana.' It is an unintentional influence on the unconscious of others, a sort of unconscious prestige, and its effect lasts only so long as it is not disturbed by conscious intention."[7] Jung stresses here the idea that to be effective the individual's influence must be *unintentional*. But this, of course, does not mean that it is chaotic or disorganized. For, elsewhere he says: "Resistance to the organized mass can be effected only by the man who is as well organized in his individuality as the mass itself."[8]

Both the spontaneity and the solidity of this kind of influence is dramatized in the concept of the *anima mundi*, which is often pictured as a naked woman standing within an ellipse whose rays shoot forth in all directions like a sunburst of energy (Fig. 84). A similar idea is represented in Christian art where the Christ is often framed in a mandorla of golden rays, presenting the self as a numinous revelation for all to behold. In neither case does the central figure *create* its aureole or even seem aware of its existence.

Fig. 84   Anima Mundi

Sometimes the Christus appears within an ellipse formed by the Tree of Life. Perhaps the two halves of The World's mandorla wreath might symbolize the branches of the Tree of Life and the Tree of Knowledge securely interwoven to create a unified pattern. In The Star we saw these two trees directly connected only through their rootednes in common earth, and indirectly through the black bird who might fly from one to the other. In The World the branches of these two seeming opposites now form a living mandorla, symbolic of a vital enduring relationship between body and spirit, between man's natural enjoyment of his physical being and his equally natural desire to reach out toward life's meaning.

The idea that spirit and flesh, heaven and earth, belong together as equal parts of a unified whole is reiterated pictorially in the four corners of The World. In the upper corners appear two winged beings and in the lower corners, two beasts of the earth. Mandorlas of the Christ often picture similar figures at the corners. These are the four "beasts" of the Apocalypse. They can be seen to symbolize many things, among which are: the four directions, the four elements, the four humours, the four Jungian functions, the four fixed, cardinal, and mutable signs of the zodiac, the four Prophets, and the four Evangelists. Here are a few specifics which may enrich the meaning of these figures:

> THE OX represents earth, Taurus, stability, patience, perseverance, and pure substance. It is connected with St. Luke because Luke's gospel emphasized Christ's work on earth.

> THE LION represents fire, Leo, creation, spirit incarnate, and resurrection. It is connected with St. Mark.

> THE ANGEL represents air, Aquarius, ideal relationship, the search for truth, universal brotherhood, and the interplay of perfect knowledge and perfect form. It is connected with St. Matthew, and appears in human form because St. Matthew stressed the geneology of Christ.

> THE EAGLE represents water and Scorpio (since it is Scorpio risen). It stands for emotional power, death and regeneration. It is connected with St. John, since his special concern was the inspiration and divine nature of Christ.

The four stand guard and bear witness to the dance of life. Together they form a square which contains within it the mandorla. The overall design of this card, which is essentially a circle encompassed by a square, brings together earthly and heavenly reality, present development and future potential, in a beautiful way. In the words of Walt Whitman:

> I am an acme of things accomplished
> And I am an enclosure of things to be.[9]

In alchemy, the miracle of self-realization, the harmonious union of earthly and heavenly truth, was called "the squaring of the circle." It stood for the idea that the impossible was, by God's grace, actualized, that the

Fig. 85   Squaring the Circle

mysterious could, in fact, be "squared" with physical reality. Figure 85 shows an alchemical representation of the squaring of the circle. Here a man and a woman appear within the circle, and the idea was that by squaring the circle, the alchemist would unite these two into one whole. A similar motif is pictured in this old French version of The World (Fig. 86). Modern philosophy and science are now moving toward the squaring of the circle, toward a synthesis between the miraculously intuited world of the mystics and the scientific world of overt observation.

Heisenberg's Uncertainty Principle has destroyed many fixed boundaries with which man formerly marked out various aspects of reality, and this uncertainty is reflected in the language of science in an astonishing way. Since it is now accepted that subatomic particles cannot be accurately defined in time and space, physicists today speak of them as having "a tendency to exist." Following this through to its logical conclusion has brought with it the horrifying realization that we, too, have only "a *tenden-*

le Monde

Fig. 86 The World (Old French Tarot)

cy to exist." The minute particles which constitute our bodies are in constant interaction with those which comprise the people and objects of our environment. Just as we interact constantly with our environment through breathing, perspiration, and elimination, so also are our seemingly solid bodies in constant interaction with everything around us. Our existence as individual entities has become, at best, merely a statistical probability.

Furthermore, physicists tell us, this distressing state of affairs is here for keeps. Since, by the very act of observing matter man changes and distorts it, we do not know and *can never know* what, if anything, exists "out there." As a result, even the concept of an external "real" world as a stimulus which "causes" the way we see the world is just as mystical and unscientific as other ways of viewing reality.

Today all our distinctions between inner and outer, mine and thine, past and present, have broken down. Modern physics has become increasingly mystical, whereas dreams, visions, and other so-called mystical experiences have become increasingly accepted as important factors in our reality. All human experience is fusing together, it seems, to become one world.

This one world is now understood as a continuous state of becoming: a constantly evolving process, of which each seemingly discrete entity (rock, plant, animal, or human) is a part. This, not in the sense that the universe is a giant jigsaw puzzle of which each of us represents one small segment, but rather that each discrete entity is, in fact, *the whole world*. Just as through the technique of holography one can recreate an entire picture from one tiny segment, so too, within each of us, is contained the whole universe.

Long before the advent of subatomic physics, mystics, poets, artists, and philosophers of many cultures connected intuitively with the *unus mundus* underlying the "ten thousand things" of our everyday experience. That each individual *is* this world in microcosm has been beautifully expressed in Cabalistic writing. It is interesting to observe how, in attempting to record this numinous experience, writers of whatever cultural background seem to use similar metaphors to catch the indescribable essence at the heart of all life. It is also surprising – yet understandable – that writers of one discipline often reach for the language of another quite foreign to them in order to reconcile the opposites. This is particularly evident in contemporary writings where physicists who have come to their experience via observation of the outer world write of it in mystical language, whereas analytical psychologists (notably Jung) who have arrived at their conclusions via observation of the inner world often use the metaphor of physical science to describe their findings.

On occasion, both physicist and psychologist write like poets, whereas the poets themselves sometimes try to match square to circle in the language of geometry. The common denominator for all of these as our Tarot shows, is the image: One World.

At the deepest level of being, it is indeed one world. Here now are a few examples of its universal language. The first was written by Erwin Schrödinger, physicist, winner of the Nobel prize for his research in this field:

> . . . inconceivable as it seems to ordinary reason, you – and all other conscious beings as such – are all in all. Hence this life of yours which you are living is not merely a piece of the entire existence, but is in a certain sense the *whole*; only this whole is not so constituted that it can be surveyed in one single glance. This, as we know, is what the Brahmins express in that sacred,

mystic formula which is yet really so simple and so clear: *Tat tvam asi*, this is you. Or, again, in such words as 'I am in the east and in the west; I am below and above, *I am this whole world.*'[10]

Abandoning forever the concept of an external physical reality substantiated by objective observation, Schrödinger opts in favor of the psychic world. He says: "If we decide to have only one sphere, it has got to be a psychic one, since that exists as a given for all experience." He amplifies this statement in the following passage:

> . . . if, without involving ourselves in obvious nonsense, we are going to be able to think in a natural way about what goes on in a living, feeling, thinking being. . . . then the condition for our doing so is that we think of *everything* that happens as taking place in our *experience* of the world, without ascribing it to any material substratum as the object *of which* it is an experience; a substratum which would in fact be wholly and entirely superfluous.[11]

Hear now C.G. Jung, who was often called a mystic (and this when mysticism was considered by some a mortal sin):

> The uniqueness of the psyche is of a magnitude that can never be made wholly real, it can only be realized approximately, though it still remains the absolute basis for all consciousness. The deeper "layers" of the psyche lose their individual uniqueness as they retreat farther and farther into darkness. "Lower down" – that is to say, as they approach the autonomous functional systems – they become increasingly collective until they are universalized and extinguished in the body's materiality, i.e., in the chemical bodies. The body's carbon is simply carbon. Hence "at bottom" the psyche is simply "world."[12]

Unlike Schrödinger, though, Jung did not abandon one aspect of the world in favor of the other. Characteristically, he managed to find the *tertium non datur* at the psychoid layer of being where the two worlds could be reconciled. He says:

> Of course there is little or no hope that the unitary Being can ever be conceived, since our powers of thought and language permit only of antinomian statements. But this much we do know beyond all doubt, that empirical reality has a transcendental background – a fact which, as Sir James Jeans has

shown, can be expressed by Plato's parable of the cave. The common background of microphysics and depth-psychology is as much physical as psychic and therefore neither, but rather a third thing, a neutral nature which can at most be grasped in hints since in essence it is transcendental.[13]

Generations of men and women have attempted to reconcile the fixed square of earthly reality with the circular motion of the infinite. Here Dante describes his struggle with the conundrum of the universe. Like most of us, he first tried to approach it through the reasoning mind:

> As the geometer his mind applies
> To square the circle, nor for all his wit
> Finds the right formula, howe'er he tries,
>
> So strove I with that wonder – how to fit
> The image to the sphere; so sought to see
> How it maintained the point of rest in it.

And, like most of us, he reached an impasse. Then, when he had given up hope, illumination came suddenly, by the grace of God. Divine love, he found, was the key to the mystery of life:

> But mine were not the wings for such a flight
>   Yet as I wished, the truth I wished for came
>   Cleaving my mind in a great flash of light.
>
> Here my powers rest from this high fantasy
>   But already I could feel my being turned
>   Instinct and intellect balanced equally.
>
> as in a wheel whose motion nothing jars
> by the Love that moves the Sun and other stars.[14]

To square the circle is the universal problem of all mankind. We have seen how poets, philosophers, scientists, artists, and psychologists have struggled with it, and we know that each of us, too, must find his own key to the geometry of life. We have observed how the Tarot cards have presented the hero's confrontation with this eternal riddle. And we have traced the motif of the opposites as they confronted him at various stages of his journey until they reached a resolution in The World.

If we look at the Map of the Journey (Fig. 3), we can see how the final card in each of the three horizontal rows dramatizes a specific stage in the hero's progress, and how the three cards on this vertical axis connect with one another and with others along the way. At the top of this vertical row is The Chariot. There the central figure was not a naked human figure but a king, dressed in full regalia. He was pictured standing rigidly above the earth, cut off from the opposites of instinctual nature (represented by the ill-matched team of horses) with which he had no direct contact. The four points of his compass were pictured as four rigid posts which confined him within a small square space. His protective canopy cut him off from illumination from above. It seemed obvious that, although our hero was launched on a journey, it was, at this point, an ego trip. If he imagined himself to be the kingly charioteer. he was destined to experience many humiliations along the way.

We saw some of these dramatized by The Hanged Man and Death. But in Temperance, the card directly beneath The Chariot, all that was upside-down, stagnant, and dismembered seemed to flow together once again in the figure of an angel pouring a liquid essence from one container to another. At this point, the hero's energies, formerly dedicated to ego development and conquest of the outer world, now began to turn toward inner development. But the figure presiding over this change was not a human being; it was an angel, an archetypal figure symbolizing a movement taking place in the deep unconscious. Before he can become aware of this divine presence within, the hero must undergo further depression and darkness, even the danger of psychosis, as we saw in The Moon, whose name, Luna, can spell lunacy.

The bottom row of our map pictured various stages of illumination, from Luciferian confusion to the dazzling sunshine of golden understanding. Now the hero emerges into a new world whose gentle glow reflects elements of all that has gone before. Since this card ends the series, it may seem curious that its number, twenty-one, does not mark it as one of those seed cards which numerically reduce to ten, thus terminating a specific phase of development. But to think in these terms would be to reckon without the influence of the Fool, whose number zero gave him special privileges and powers. He started us on our journey, and as we have seen, he has popped into the other cards from time to time, sometimes to mock the hero and sometimes to sustain him along the way. No doubt he is even now waiting unseen in the wings to lead the traveler back again to a new confrontation with the Magician, and a new beginning on the never-ending maze of individuation.

We have observed how the Fool has contrived to be present at important moments in the Tarot journey; so it is easy to imagine him standing nearby, just out of camera range, to witness the birth of the self. In paintings depicting the birth of Jesus, a fool is, in fact, often pictured in various guises pausing in adoration at the manger. Ferrari's *Adoration at the Manger* (Fig. 87) shows the Fool standing in wonderment at the Nativity. Significantly, this moment of spiritual illumination does not take place on

Fig. 87   Adoration at the Manger   (Gaudenzio Ferrari, c. 1545-6.)

some barren mountain top, but comes to birth in a manger. In this connection it is important to observe that the Fool's dog also participates in this experience. At one level of understanding this seems appropriate because, without the protection and guidance of his animal counterpart, the Jester could never have found his way to the manger. But Ferrari's painting also offers another possible insight: had the Fool rejected his "beastly self" at this supreme moment, he himself would have remained incomplete and found wanting. The artist may be telling us that only those who are pure of spirit and whole of heart can enter the Heavenly Kingdom with the Wise Men.

But as we know, the Fool never remains in one place long. Soon our little mascot, *l'ami de Dieu,* God's little friend – and ours – will be impatient to be off, luring us with him on a new journey into new dimensions of awareness. As the Tarot has shown, life is process, life is motion; serenity is not freedom from the storm but equilibrium at its center. So The World cannot be the end-product of the hero's travels. It is rather the image that inspired him to undertake them. Jung summed it up this way:

> Complete redemption from the sufferings of this world is and must remain an illusion. Christ's earthly life likewise ended, not in complacent bliss, but on the cross. The goal is important only as an idea; the essential thing is the *opus* which leads to the goal: *that* is the goal of a lifetime.[15]

25. On Spreading the Cards

In the previous chapters we discussed the symbolism of the Tarot and suggested some techniques for using the cards to help us in our daily lives. Another way to use the Tarot for personal insight and growth is to spread and "read" the cards. When reading the cards, we ask a question, then deal a specific number of cards in a given pattern and study their symbolism and relationship to one another in order to find an answer to our question. Here we shall discuss the philosophical implications of spreading the cards, some techniques for interpreting their answers, and suggest one method of laying out the cards for this purpose.

Is It Fortune Telling?

Your first association to "spreading" or "reading" the cards was probably *fortune telling*. At any rate, it was mine. But I never use the cards to predict specific future events for myself or others. I feel that to do so is generally not helpful and may, in fact, prove harmful. Instead, I view the cards as symbolic pictures of archetypal forces operating in all aspects of life at various times – forces that demand our attention *now* in the present moment. Page 382 shows a diagram of the spread I use. There you will observe positions marked Recent Past, Present, Immediate Future, and The Year To Come. Whichever card falls under Recent Past I take to symbolize an archetypal force dominant during the past several months. The Present I view as a force currently activated, and the card marked Immediate Future as an influence just beginning to appear on the horizon. This future image in its turn will soon wax and wane, giving way to the card marked The Year To Come, which speaks of a more consistent influence that will glow in the background throughout the following year.

Centrally located within these four cards is a position marked The Card of You. This represents the psychical situation of the querant in relation to life generally in the present moment. It stands in the center because it is of special importance, and because its relationship to the other cards is central to the reading as a whole. These five cards speak chiefly to the general situation of the querant in all aspects of his life, including, of course, the question asked; but they do not specifically answer the question.

The four cards marked The Oracle are concerned with the question asked. The card that stands by itself in this group called The Signifier answers the question. The other three cards modify, expand, or otherwise amplify this answer.

When I say that I do not use the cards to predict future events, I don't mean that a symbolic interpretation bears no relationship to outer events that may take place in the future. Naturally, any technique that expands self-awareness in the present will have profound implications for the future. When we emerge from an illuminating encounter with the unconscious, we are literally not the same person we were an hour ago. Sometimes we step forth glowing with a big Aha! – with lights flashing and bells ringing. More often, we experience a delayed reaction, returning to our daily round with a pocketful of small insights – tiny seedlings that ripen slowly in the days and weeks to follow. But whatever ideas and intuitions come, and however they arrive, they will surely effect a change in our inner images and overt behavior, and these new ways of being and behaving will elicit new reactions from the people and situations in our environment. More importantly, as we evolve and change, new avenues of interest, new contacts, and new choices will open out, so that we will not only return to our old life in a new way, but will begin to attract, in many ways, a wholly new life. Viewed in this way, one might say that reading the Tarot symbolically rather than literally doesn't predict a given future; rather, it offers us opportunities to participate in the creation of a new and unpredictable future.

Interpretations: Predictive Versus Symbolic

Of course, there are many instances where one can observe in retrospect how a predictive interpretation of the cards would have been absolutely correct in that the event thus "foreseen" did indeed come to pass. Nevertheless, I feel that a predictive interpretation, however true it may prove to be on the overt level, misses the inner truth we seek from a Tarot reading, and diverts our attention from true self-understanding.

Let me illustrate this with a specific example drawn from my personal experience as a Tarot consultant. This involves the suit of Coins or Money, which all too readily lends itself to a predictive interpretation of "good fortune" on the literal level. I recall one amazing spread in which coins appeared three times: once as The Immediate Future, once as The Year To Come, and a third time as The Signifier. Although the temptation to do so was almost irresistible, neither my client nor I discussed the coins as predictions of future monetary wealth. We viewed these golden coins as symbolic representations of energy formerly embedded in the dark earth of the unconscious, but now mined, minted, polished, and ready for use. My client took the coin's mandala design as a symbol of the deeper self. She observed that the Ace of Coins had two blue "handles," and she felt that these handles might help her to grasp a new "golden understanding" and to use it creatively. She noted that these twin handles were placed on either side of the coin, which suggested to her that this new understanding might be grasped and held in conjunction with another person. She connected this with a specific person with whom she felt currently at odds. Since her relationship with this person involved, among other things, financial problems, we then discussed the coins as representing money; but we still did not view them predictively as heralds of a future windfall. We took it that the Tarot was presenting the coins as a way of calling her attention to a need to become more conscious about money. One card in particular, the Valet of Coins, seemed to my client to be holding up a coin for her inspection as if asking her: *How do you feel about money? Do you long for it, despise it, try to rise above it, or what?* As she searched for answers to these questions, she discovered that she had never before really explored her feelings about money. Although by no means wealthy, she had always been financially comfortable, with no fears of abject poverty and no prospects of future wealth. She had never stopped to contemplate what it would be like to be desperately poor, nor had she examined the opportunities great wealth might offer and the responsibilities that having it might entail.

As she began to spin fantasies about these things, she came to the conclusion that in some ways she might be better able to cope with poverty than with enormous wealth. Although in certain areas of her life she would welcome the opportunity for the increased leisure and wider choices that wealth would offer, she also felt that she would find these wider horizons tremendously threatening and confusing. She felt that to be able to say *yes* to every opportunity that presented itself would split her up, as she put it, "in seventeen directions." She told me, for instance, that she loved to travel and she was sure that, had she the means to do so, she would be tempted to spend her life on endless cruises to the detriment of her inner journey, which was now the major focus of her life. She also felt that she might not enjoy these cruises because she would always feel guilty about spending all that money on herself "while millions starved."

We spent the remaining few minutes of the hour discussing this guilt. Was it (we wondered) that she would feel guilty about "the starving millions" (about whom she could do relatively little)? Wasn't this guilt more related to her neglect of the deeper self (about which she could do a great deal)? Both of us became so absorbed in this discussion that our time together passed without a single glance in the direction of that "unexpected inheritance," which is the all-too-expected darling of every Gypsy fortune teller.

Interestingly enough, in this instance, such a Gypsy prediction would have rung true. A few months after her Tarot reading, my client did in fact receive a substantial amount of money, not by inheritance, but from a wholly unexpected source. When she phoned me to share the news of her good fortune, she also voiced a complaint. *Why didn't you tell me?* she wanted to know. The answer is two-fold and very simple. First of all, I didn't know. As with predictive dreams, only hind-sight offers 20/20 vision. But, more importantly, even had we been absolutely certain of its outcome, *how, specifically, would such a prediction have been helpful?*

As a means of answering this question, we reviewed together the Tarot cards she had drawn in her spread and our previous discussion about them. Had she found it helpful in relation to her new-found wealth? (I asked). Wasn't it possible that a predictive interpretation might have had a negative effect? Mightn't it, for instance, have set her to day-dreaming about that pot of gold at the end of the rainbow, with the result that she might have begun to lead what Jung has called "the provisional life," instead of (as actually happened) simply returning to her usual activities with a few new insights?

Although my friend felt that our previous discussion had indeed been an excellent preparation for her financial windfall, she could not quite go along with the notion that a predictive reading would have been harmful. There was one point, though, on which we were both in perfect accord: had I made predictions of future wealth that failed to come true, she would indeed have had reason to complain!

There are many situations where a literal interpretation might do greater harm than in the instance cited above. One such is a spread in which a card turns up that reminds you so forcibly of someone you know behaving in such a characteristic way that you take it for real. If you interpret this card to mean that the person in question is acting, or will act, as the picture seems to indicate, you are in for trouble. For one thing, this false assumption will alter your own behavior toward him and set up a chain reaction that may prove detrimental to your relationship.

By "false assumption" I don't necessarily mean that the person in question may not behave in some respects in ways you feel the Tarot pictures him doing. That may or may not be the case; but that is not the central question. By "false assumption," I mean the mistaken notion that the card before you bears a direct relationship to an actual person in outer life. Obviously, it is not this human being; it is not even a photograph of him.

What you see mirrored here is *your own* subjective experience – *your* image of this person, based on *your* reaction to past experiences with him.

When we are tempted to view a card too literally, it is important to remember that neither we, nor the Tarot, have the power to predict future behavior. We cannot foresee another's actions; we cannot directly alter their course; we can't specifically prepare ourselves in advance to deal with them. But we can change ourselves. We can alter our images about others, and by doing so, change our behavior in relation to them. In doing this we affect their attitude toward us. The following hypothetical case will illustrate some of the problems involved in confusing a Tarot character with a specific human being, and will explore some techniques for changing inner images that the cards have evoked.

Let us imagine that the Knight of Swords turns up in your spread. You are already familiar with the symbolic meaning of the questing Knight as he appeared in our discussion of the Knight of Diamonds; and in the chapters on the Emperor, Justice, and the Chariot, we touched on the symbolism of swords and horses. Although you have an excellent spring board for viewing the Knight of Swords symbolically, you find it difficult to do so in this instance because (let us suppose) this Tarot figure suddenly seems to you to be a dead ringer for a person with whom you are currently involved. Let us say that the Tarot Knight seems to you a very determined, aggressive man, charging blindly ahead with his lance at the ready, and that his temperament and behavior remind you very much of a specific person who, you feel, has attacked and wounded you on many occasions.

Let us further imagine that the Knight of Swords has fallen in the position marked Immediate Future just to the right of The Card Of You, so that the horseman appears to be charging with upraised lance, directly at – you! In such a situation, the temptation to view such a card literally is almost overwhelming. It appears to be as convincing as if it were an actual photograph of the person in question behaving, or preparing to behave, in exactly the way we see him pictured.

"Oh, oh," you say to yourself, "here we go again!" You jump to the conclusion that the Tarot has predicted another attack against you, and you begin to relive past occasions where this person has punctured your ego, wounded your pride, hurt your feelings, or otherwise "done you in." As you sit there licking old wounds, you feel anger, hostility, vengeance, and other such emotions rise in your gorge. In this spirit you now begin to prepare yourself for his next attack (which you now take to be a foregone conclusion).

The way you go about preparing for this attack will, of course, depend on your general temperament and momentary mood. You might, for instance, leap to horse with fire in your eyes and lance in hand, determined to seek out this "despicable character" and chop him to bits "in self defense." Naturally, if you take this course, you yourself will begin to resemble this "despicable enemy," who (as you've just observed) is pictured as about to inflict harm – not on himself – but on you!

If you are a person of a more retiring termperament, you will probably prepare for the Knight's supposed attack in other ways. For example, instead of mobilizing your energies for attack, you may decide to retire from the fray altogether. With this in mind, you begin to devise elaborate plans to avoid meeting your adversary at all costs. If you follow such a procedure, the cost will indeed be high. You will probably end up foregoing many creative opportunities and twisting your life generally out of shape, and this to no purpose. In the end you are bound to meet up with the "Knight of Swords," or someone very like him. The woods are full of him. He lives in everyone everywhere, even, lo in thee and me! That's exactly why his image is so compelling.

Obviously this Tarot card bears no relation to a specific human being. It pictures an instinctual kind of behavior typical of all human beings everywhere, among whom no doubt your adversary and also yourself. This Knight, then, pictures an archetypal image, one that, in this case, you have projected onto a specific person.

When we discussed the mechanism of projection in a previous chapter, we noted that it was an automatic, unconscious one, and that the qualities projected were usually those in ourselves of which we were relatively unaware. A good first step in dealing with the Knight of Swords is to pause for a moment and become aware of these latent qualities within oneself. Everyone feels aggressive and hostile at times. *Do you feel that way now?* If not, you can no doubt recall instances where you did feel that way. If you can contact some of these feelings in yourself, it is bound to change your feelings about the person whom you associate with this card. By taking back onto your own shoulders some of these negative feelings, you will lighten the load he has been carrying for you, and you will change your image of him. If you can do this, you will see your adversary in a different light. Now you may find that you no longer think of him as "the enemy," but more as "fellow sufferer," "friend," or even "brother."

Another technique for dealing with this situation creatively is to study the Knight of Swords very carefully in every detail. If your association between it and your adversary was instantaneous, the chances are that you may have leapt to conclusions, missing many important details. For example, if you assumed that this Knight was aiming his lance at you, look again. *Is this really the case?* Viewed less emotionally, he may now seem to be holding his weapon quite casually in his left (unconscious) hand. His eyes may now appear not fixed on you as a target, but rather, to be scanning distant horizons. He is, after all, a Knight on a quest. Perhaps he is so intent on some distant goal that he is wholly unaware of The Card Of You in his immediate foreground. Or perhaps he is so dedicated to this goal that, insofar as he is aware of the existence of anything in the foreground, he sees it only dimly as some object standing in the way of his "holy crusade."

One way to explore some of these ideas more fully might be to write a little drama about this picture. What do you imagine his quest might be? Is the central figure pictured in The Card Of You aware that he stands in the Knight's way? Could the "You" step out of the Knight's way? If not, hadn't he better cry out and make the Knight aware of his existence before he gets trampled to death under the horse's hooves? If he did so, would the Knight pay attention? How would the horse behave if someone in his path screamed for help? You might even stop here and write a dramatic dialogue involving the You character, the Knight, and the horse.

Having refreshed your spirit with a bit of fantasy, you might now turn your attention to your problem with the external "Knight of Swords." Is this person also on a quest of some kind? If so, what do you imagine might be his goal? Can you think of a way that you might inadvertently stand in his path? Have you yourself on some past occasion ever "ridden a horse" with such intensity that you had tunnel vision? Can you recall an instance when you might unconsciously have wounded someone who stood in your way?

Naturally being wounded by a sharp lance hurts, even though the offense was unintentional. But, if you take the time to pursue some of the techniques described here, you will probably end up with the feeling that there is a lot of unconsciousness on both sides of this problem. If the relationship is one you value, and chances are it is or this Tarot picture wouldn't have aroused such deep emotion, then the next step might be to see the person in question and share some of the feelings this has aroused in you.

If you follow some of the techniques described here, you will discover for yourself how approaching the cards symbolically rather than literally can result in practical down-to-earth changes in our everyday lives. When we have projected an archetypal quality onto another person and/or reacted ourselves to some situation in an unconscious, archetypal way, the Tarot offers us a technique for separating the archetypal from the personal and helping everyone involved to his own humanity.

As we already know, the Tarot pictures can become targets for all sorts of projections; sometimes they seem to personify devilish qualities; other times they appear to be imbued with godlike attributes. In either case, it's important to disentangle the human from the archetypal. In the above hypothetical case, the Knight of Swords was viewed as epitomizing certain negative qualities (agression, hostility, lack of consideration, and the like). However, for some persons, this same Knight of Swords might appear to be a benign or even helpful figure. For such a person, this horseman would seem to be a savior figure, a brave knight riding toward The Card of You to rescue the querant from a threatening situation.

Maybe you are one who views the Knight of Swords in this positive way. You might imagine that this "means" some 'knight" in your outer environment is about to rescue you from whatever predicament you find yourself in at the moment. To imagine that this is the case would be nonproductive in several ways. First, because your expectation may not be fulfilled, and second, because when you cast someone in the role of your savior, you automatically cast yourself in the role of a "helpless victim of circumstance," someone who looks to others for salvation, rather than seeking his own solution to his problems.

Here, again, a symbolic interpretation would be more helpful than a literal one. Let us suppose you do take this Knight of Swords as a savior figure. Symbolically, then, this would represent an archetypal quality or potential within yourself. That you tend to project it onto others probably indicates that this quality lies dormant and unrecognised within you. The fact that this card comes up at this time might mean that the moment is ripe for you to begin to recognize and develop this innate quality. How do you imagine this inner "savior" might help you in whatever situation you now find yourself? Could you use his courage just now to put behind you some outworn security and plunge boldly forward? Have you become so sunk in the meaningless routine of daily life that you have lost touch with your questing spirit? How, specifically, could your inner Knight of Swords help you just now?

In order to answer these questions, go back to the card and study it carefully in detail as described above. Look at it in connection with The Card Of You. Is the central figure in that card in need of help? If so, what might the Knight do to help? You might imagine a dialogue between these two figures, viewing these two characters as potentials within your psyche. Or you might try drawing a picture of your inner Knight. Is he similar or different to the one pictured in the Tarot? If different, in what respect does he differ?

Sometimes, in trying to dramatize the situation presented by the Tarot we run into difficulty because the central character in a given card is not pictured as a human being. In the Wheel of Fortune, for example, the central character is the Wheel, and the other characters appear to be animals. Never mind. Select one of the animals, or the Wheel itself, and teach it to talk. The Tarot pictures a magic world. When we enter this world, we become magicians, and when we return once more to our daily reality, we remain in touch with the many magic powers available within the human psyche. After such an inner journey, we usually find that we are no longer the victims of circumstance we formerly thought ourselves to be. After we have contacted our inner savior, we no longer experience ourselves as helplessly awaiting salvation from without. Perhaps our inner resourceful Knight has shown us a way out of our predicament, or, if our problem is insurmountable, he has given us the courage to endure our fate.

What About the Death Card?

Whenever the Tarot Death turns up in a spread, we are apt to feel uneasy. It's the one card that we most fear to take literally; yet it's also the one that most tempts us to do so. Lest you find yourself fearful of this card, let me set your mind at rest by citing my experience with it. I have been reading the Tarot professionally for clients of all ages for many years. I keep a record of each spread. In these spreads, Death has turned up frequently but *never has anyone who drew this card met physical death.* The only two who have in fact made this transition did not draw Death in their spreads. Both of these querants were elderly women of unusual insight and wisdom. One woman was ninety years old at the time of her reading. When we looked at the cards she had drawn, she expressed surprise that Death had not come up, since it was so obviously "in the cards" for her. After puzzling about the meaning of this, we came to the conclusion that it was because she was, in fact, so prepared to meet death, and so open to all forms of transition in her life that the Tarot had not presented Mister No-Name for her consideration.

As a result of these experiences (and others where, for example, Death appeared as Recent Past, with no corresponding connections in outer reality) it would seem that the Tarot doesn't intend us to consider this card literally, but presents it, rather, symbolically in the context of transformation in our lives on this planet. Nevertheless, since physical death is a fact of life that all of us must face sooner or later, it also seems appropriate to use this card as a springboard for exploring our feelings about death. But there's a world of difference between preparing for the known fact of death in a general way, and being scared to death by spooky predictions of impending doom that may have no immediate connection with reality.

Predestination or Free Will?

If we were to pursue our discussion of predictive readings to its ultimate conclusion, we would find ourselves enmeshed in the age-old question of fatalism versus free will. The limitations of this book make such a discussion impossible; but I'd like to throw out a few questions here for your consideration and share with you some of my tentative answers to them. These questions arose from a brief encounter with a complete stranger, and came about in the following way.

One night at a dinner party I sat next to an affable, extraverted young man who seemed very much at home with himself and with life in general. I was very surprised therefore when he asked for a Tarot appointment. I found it so difficult to picture him consulting the cards that I asked him point blank how he imagined the Tarot could help him.

"Oh," he replied, "that's very simple. I play the stock market, and I want the Tarot to tell me which stocks to buy!" I replied, and this with some asperity, that *my* Tarot didn't stoop to predictions of this kind, and that if it did, I'd surely not be sitting there beside him. I'd probably be off on one of my yachts somewhere. The rest of the evening passed pleasantly enough with no more talk of a Tarot appointment.

Later on, when I got home, I sat up half the night brooding about this light-hearted conversation. What, exactly, I asked myself, was wrong with my dinner partner's expectation that Tarot could predict the stock market? Of course, there existed the obvious danger that we might read the cards' message incorrectly. But, assuming that we could accurately tune in on the Tarot's advice, what would be wrong with the notion that consulting the Oracle about stocks might make him rich overnight?

As I mulled this over, it seemed to me that the obvious flaw was this: if the future activities of the stock market were indeed preordained and accurate information about tomorrow's market were available today via the Tarot, then our individual actions in relation to the stock market (and everything else) must necessarily be similarly programmed and foreordained. In which case a Tarot preview of the market would be useless, since one would not possess the necessary freedom of choice to act upon the cards' advice.

Let me illustrate with the following hypothetical case: Suppose my erstwhile dinner partner (whom we'll call Jim) had spread the Tarot cards, received the clear message that stock X would quadruple in value next day, and set forth immediately for his broker's office with the firm intention of investing his savings in this stock. According to our present hypothesis, Jim could only carry out this intention *provided that it were predestined that he do so*. If it were not Jim's prescribed fate to buy stock X, then he would *not* have done so despite the Tarot's clear advice and his own avowed intention. Something would have intervened en route "by chance" to prevent his exercising his "free choice" in this matter. Or, conversely, if it *were* his fate to buy stock X, then he would surely have done so whether or not he consulted the Tarot.

Of course, whichever way it happened, Jim would have preserved his illusion of "free will." Let us say he did *not* buy stock X. On being questioned later, he would doubtless tell us that he had "changed his mind" and "chosen another course of action," and that he had done this voluntarily and for excellent reasons. These "excellent reasons" he would then proceed to enumerate in a most convincing manner.

The difficulty, it seems to me, with Jim's rational explanations is this: if we are to allow him his precious "freedom of choice", then we must also allow the stock market a similar privilege to "change its mind" at the eleventh hour, and to favor a different stock from the one it promised the Tarot it would push. Surely we can't expect the market to hold still for Jim meanwhile leaving him perfectly free to gallivant about the country, at liberty to make whatever new choices should happen to appeal to his "logic" and "intellect"! Or (to look for a moment at the other side of the coin), if the future activities of the stock market are presumed to be predetermined – and we can count on whatever they promise the Tarot Oracle – then surely we must imagine our friend's activities in relation to the market to be similary predetermined. I don't see how we can have it both ways.

But enough now of hypothetical cases. I'm sure each of us can recall choices we ourselves have made which (however rational they may have appeared at the time) viewed retrospectively did seem (come to think of it) enmeshed in a web of startling coincidences. Usually, though, we don't "come to think of it" till much later.

The eternal question of fate versus free will has been around for a long time. Obviously it can't be resolved by us here and now – nor perhaps by any human beings ever. Inasmuch as the subject does not lend itself to examination under controlled conditions, it appears that whichever way we turn, we face an unresolved hypothesis. We are therefore destined (or predestined?) to choose whatever feels right for us.

I personally could not live creatively (if at all) with the notion of a predetermined universe in which all actions – macroscopic and microscopic – were fixed *a priori* for all time. I could not thrive unless I felt that there were some area, however limited, within which I was free to change, grow, and move in new and unpredictable ways. And as to events at the macroscopic level, if I am to imagine these as being instigated and held together by a Central Creative Force or Intelligence, then surely I cannot imagine the actions of such a Creator to be irrevocably set and forever closed to further acts of creativity!

However we may choose to visualize and label this Central Creative Energy, it seems evident that we can no longer think of our universe as *having been* created by Whomever, or Whatever – whenever. In the light of modern physics, we must now view all mankind and his environment as part of an ever-changing energy system rather than as a finished product brought into being once and for all, aeons ago. If we are to allow our human selves the latitude necessary to devise new inventions – to discard the old and produce the new by spontaneous combustion – so, too, must we perforce visualize our universe as ever-expanding, ever-destroying and ever-creating. It seems evident that we must allow Creative Energy the same latitude we allow ourselves, if only for the selfish reason that this Central Energy – this Atman – is the sole wellspring of our own creativity.

To say one finds the notion of predestination unacceptable doesn't mean that he necessarily opts in favor of a philosophy that could be accurately described by the words "Free Will." As Jung makes clear everywhere, and as this book has tried to demonstrate, we human beings are by

no means wholly free to chose our destinies nor can creativity be consciously achieved by will power. Quite apart from the obvious fact that the
number of choices offered any given individual in his lifetime is necessarily
limited, it is also becoming increasingly obvious that our reasoning intellect
and will power play a minimal role in governing whatever choices we do
make.

If we are to reject the hypothesis of predestination and also the notion
that our lives can be guided by reason, are we then to assume that we live
at the mercy of chance happenings where (to paraphrase Einstein)"God
plays at dice with the universe"? Or can we, as Jung suggests, accept the
fact that our reasoning mind is not supreme and find ways to interact with
the irrational world of the unconscious which we now realize, plays such
an important role in our lives?

This is not to say that by getting in touch with the unconscious via dream
analysis, I Ching, astrology, Tarot, or other means, we can avoid all sickness, sorrow, conflict, or the other grievous problems flesh is heir to. But it
is evident that we all possess more freedom than we realize to select, attract, and understand the events in our environment, and that, as we begin
to grow in awareness of who we are, we can also begin to choose more
wisely and to accept situations in which we seemingly have no choice.

To return once again, and this finally, to our friend Jim: I'm sorry now
that I discouraged him from consulting the Tarot. To be sure, had he done
so, he might have been disappointed to learn that the cards are simply not
calibrated to those figures on the Big Board, and therefore are not in a position to give him that "hot tip on a sure thing" that he thought he wanted.
But it is conceivable that by consulting the cards, he might have got in
touch with what he wanted at a deeper level of his being. It is not unlikely
that he might have emerged from such a Tarot consultation with more
questions – and these more relevant to his life than the ones he started
with originally. At least it has been my experience that, although a querant
may initially find the cards' answer disappointing or nonexistent in terms of
the question asked, he ultimately discovers (and this usually fairly soon)
that the question he presented to the Tarot is no longer one of central concern.

The dinner table conversation with Jim described earlier took place
many years ago. As a result of it and the ruminations that it evoked, I have
never since discouraged anyone who wished to do so from making an appointment to consult the cards, however frivolous his reasons for consulting them might appear to be. At times there are problems in our lives
that we can only afford to approach at first on tiptoe, as it were, and with a
nervous smile. Also there are some overt decisions that perhaps can only
be viewed flippantly – decisions with so much to be said for both sides that
one might well decide them by literally flipping a coin. On these occasions,
I recall the axiom discussed in relation to the Lover pictured in the sixth

Tarot: *What* you do is usually less important than *wherefrom* you do it. It seems to me that the Tarot offers us its most effective help when we approach it less in search of advice as to outer choices, and more with the idea of deepening our platform for making these choices.

Having outlined our personal philosophy regarding the Tarot's oracular powers, we now present our method for spreading the cards. The Nine Card Oracle is the one I use. I have never tried any other. I came upon it "by chance" in the instruction booklet accompanying a Tarot deck created to advertise a certain brand of art paper. I tried out this spread, liked it instantly, and that was that! Of course, like our friend Jim, I can cite logical "reasons" for this choice, chief of which is that for spreads I eliminate all pip cards (2's through 10's) in the four suits, leaving only 42 cards in the deck. So it seemed to me important to find a spread that uses a proportionately small number of cards. The reason I eliminated the pips is because these cards as they appear in the Marseilles deck are relatively uninteresting. They can offer us only the symbolism of their numbers which is already available in the twenty-two Trumps.

If you have never before spread the cards, you might begin with the Nine Card Oracle. If this one doesn't feel right for you, then I suggest that you look at other Tarot books in the public library until you find a spread you like. There are, it appears, about as many systems for laying out the cards as there are books on the subject. To my way of thinking, choosing which pattern you will use is exactly as important (or unimportant) as deciding which clothes you will wear to consult the cards. The important thing is to find something that fits and feels comfortable.

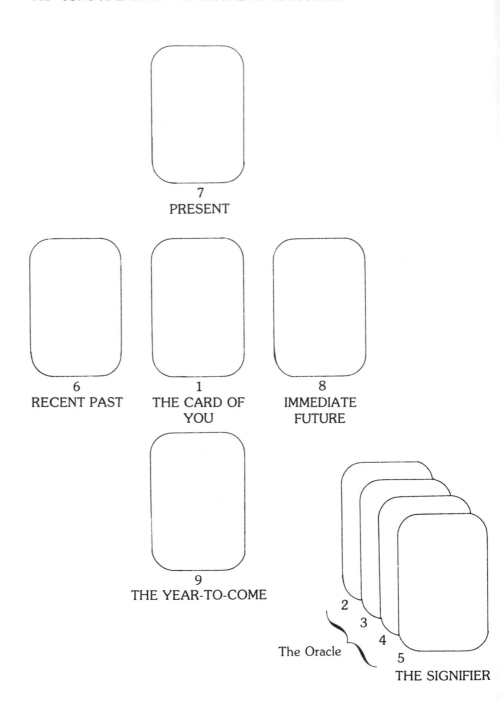

7
PRESENT

6
RECENT PAST

1
THE CARD OF
YOU

8
IMMEDIATE
FUTURE

9
THE YEAR-TO-COME

2
3
4
The Oracle
5
THE SIGNIFIER

THE NINE-CARD TAROT ORACLE

METHOD 1: OPEN FACE SPREAD

(NOTE: This spread is useful only if you are *unfamiliar* with the Tarot. If you are already acquainted with the symbolism of the cards, you will find Method 2 more helpful.)

Place the cards *face up* on a large flat surface. If you can't find a table big enough, use the floor.

Pick out the nine cards that interest you most or catch your imagination. Choose them carefully, but not intellectually. Don't try to decipher a card's title or decode its symbolism. Respond spontaneously and emotionally. Does the picture intrigue you? Does it strike a responsive cord in you?

In choosing these nine cards, it's important to remember that there is no such thing as a "bad" card. As with the sixty-four hexagrams of the I Ching, each belongs to its time and season. Also, as with the I Ching, their meaning is symbolic rather than literal – so that one might choose, say, Death or The Hanged Man with no implication that this "means" literal death, physical torture, suicide, etc.

Having chosen your nine cards, put away the rest, leaving the cards you have selected face up. Now study the cards carefully and choose from their number the one that seems closest to your idea of yourself *at the present moment*. This will be known hereafter as The Card of You (position #1 in diagram). In choosing it, remember that this card represents your self-image at this moment in time. You are not stuck with this selection forever. Next month – or even next week – you might choose another card.

Having selected The Card of You, leave it face up on your table and collect the remaining eight cards. Keeping them face down, shuffle them. While you are shuffling, make a wish or ask the Tarot a question – preferably about a matter that is pending. *The moment you have found your wish or question, stop shuffling.* Cut the cards and complete your cut.

Now deal out four of these eight cards and set them aside in a pile, *face down*. These are the Oracle Cards that speak specifically to your wish or question. They will be discussed later.

Since the exact wording of your wish or question is important, it's a good idea to stop here and write this down exactly as you have worded it to yourself. Remember that the Tarot, unlike the Ouija Board, has no way of responding with an unequivocal "Yes" or "No" answer. For this reason, it's best to word your wish or question so that it doesn't require a definite answer. It is helpful if you can introduce your queries with such phrases as: "What can you tell me about . . . . ?" Or, "What am I overlooking in . . . (this situation)?" Or "Will you please amplify . . . . ?"

At this point you have The Card of You face up in the center of the table, the four Oracle Cards face down in a pile at one side, and the four remaining cards still in one hand. When you have written down your wish or question, it is time to deal out these four cards. Place them face up and clockwise, as shown in the accompanying diagram, starting with Card #6 to the left of The Card of You.

Now you will have a picture-story on the table before you, with The Card of You completely framed by cards #6, #7, #8, and #9, as in the diagram. Study this picture first for a *general impression*. (Favorable? Unfavorable? Pleasing? Displeasing?)

Note any recurring pattern that strikes you as significant (Repetition of symbols? Alternating Yin and Yang rhythms? Emphasis on certain colors, shapes, or bodily movements?)

Next study each card individually in order, beginning with The Card of You. Ask yourself these kinds of questions about each: what first attracted me to this card? In what way might it "belong" to me? Does it remind me of an incident in my life? Of a person or situation? Jot down any findings for future reference.

As you move clockwise from card #6 (Recent Past) to card #7 (Present), and card #8 (Immediate Future), and card #9 (Year to Come), contrast each card with the preceding one. What similarities and/or differences in tone, flavor, color, mood, and action can you find? Which cards face each other? Which seem to reject, or turn away from others? Can you discover any "plot" or progress in the cards as they appear in numerical sequence?

Look especially at card #9 (The Year to Come). Does its action seem to be a gradual culmination of events pictured in the other cards? Or does it seem quite different? If so, in what way different?

The five cards we have just been considering speak to your life situation generally. Of course, they will necessarily also throw light on your wish or question, but less directly so than the four Oracle Cards. These will speak specifically to your hopes and dreams.

Now it is time to consult The Oracle. Turn up the top card (#5) first. This is the Signifier – so-called because it is the most significant card of the four. It deals directly with your wish or problem. What is your first reaction to the Signifier? (Favorable? Unfavorable?) Next, turn up the other three Oracle Cards. These represent influences at work in connection with your wish or question. Pause here to catch first reactions to these Influence Cards.

If you made a wish and the Signifier seems to you strongly positive, then your wish probably has a good chance of being realized – provided that you take into consideration the influences, personalities and/or inner tendencies portrayed in the three Influence Cards. Should the Signifier seem to you strongly negative, then perhaps your wish is not yet ripe for maturation in reality, in which case the Influence Cards may offer a clue as to the forces within and without that need first to be overcome or utilized in this situation.

If you asked a question, the Signifier provides either a direct answer or a veiled clue, and the Influence Cards give additional details or more clues. In deciding the cards' meaning, your own intuition is the best key.

Now study all nine cards together as part of one drama. What connection can you find between the two groups of cards? Pay special attention to The Card of You and the card representing The Year to Come. Are they facing the Oracle Cards, or are they looking in another direction? How might the postures, actions, or atmospheres of these two cards affect whatever answer the Oracle might have given?

METHOD 2: CLOSED FACE SPREAD

In this spread the cards are dealt out in exactly the same order and placed according to the same diagram as above. The only difference between the two spreads is that in this one *you do not choose the cards for your spread.*

After shuffling whatever deck you use, you place the cards in one pile *face down* and write out your wish or question. Now cut the cards. Next turn up the top card of this deck and place it face up in the center of the table in position #1 as before. After dealing out the four Oracle Cards and leaving them in one pile face down, you next deal out cards #6, #7, #8, and #9 and place them face up according to the diagram.

Now proceed to study the cards exactly as described above, jotting down any ideas or associations for future reference.

SUGGESTIONS: Whichever spread you use, be sure to make a chart of it so that (in perhaps a week or two) you can lay out the cards once more in the same pattern. In the meantime keep their pictures and drama in mind and meditate on these from time to time.

Be on the alert for photographs, news clippings, personalities, emotional reactions, or anything else which seems to connect in any way with the cards that turned up in your spread. You may be surprised at the flashes of insight that come to you at odd moments when the Tarot is seemingly farthest from your conscious thoughts.

If you record your dreams, look there also for characters or incidents that might connect with "your" cards. Jot down even the most insignificant-seeming connections; often together they'll create a meaningful pattern. Keep a record of the next spread you create and see if you can find connections between the present spread and the new one. Did you, for example, draw any of the same cards in the second spread? If so, did some of them fall in the same places as before? If so (or if not) what conclusions might you draw from whatever turns up?

As I write these words, the Tarot Oracle whispers that this book which we have been writing together has come to *its* conclusion. We wish the reader Godspeed on his Tarot journey. May the cards bring him good fortune!

References

Chapter 3

1. James Kirsh, *Shakespeare's Royal Self,* New York, C.G. Jung Foundation for Analytical Psychology, Inc., 1966.
2. Charles Williams, *The Greater Trumps,* Grand Rapids, Michigan, William B. Erdman's Publishing Company, 1976.
3. William Willeford, *The Fool and His Scepter,* Evanston, Illinois, Northwestern University Press, 1969, Plate 12, p. 39.
4. E. Tietze-Conrat, *Dwarfs and Jesters in Art,* London, The Phaidon Press, 1957, Plate 65, p. 59.
5. Willeford, *op. cit.,* p. 11.
6. Williams, *op. cit.,* p. 227.
7. Alan McGlashan, *The Savage and Beautiful Country,* Boston, Houghton Mifflin Company, 1967.
8. Joseph L. Henderson, *Thresholds of Initiation,* Middletown, Connecticut, Wesleyan University Press, 1967, p. 36.
9. Marie-Louise von Franz, *An Introduction to the Psychology of Fairy Tales,* New York, Spring Publications, 1970, Ch. 19, p. 10.
10. James Hillman and Marie-Louise von Franz, *Lectures on Jung's Typology,* New York, Spring Publications, 1971, Part I, pp. 6,7.
11. McGlashan, *op. cit.,* p. 39.
12. *C.G. Jung, *Civilization in Transition,* The Collected Works of C.G. Jung, Princeton, New Jersey, Princeton University Press, Vol. 10, par. 723.
13. St. Bonaventure, *Itinerarium,* (trans. by James), Quoted by Jung, *Mysterium Coniunctionis,* C.W. Vol. 14, par. 41.
14. C.G. Jung, *Psychology and Religion: West and East,* C.W. Vol. 11, par. 391.
15. W.B. Yeats, "The Queen and the Fool," *Mythologies,* New York, The Macmillan Company, 1959, pp. 112, 113.

Chapter 4

1. C.G. Jung, Quoted by Ira Progoff in *Jung, Synchronicity, and Human Destiny,* New York, The Julian Press, Inc., 1973, pp. 104, 105.
2. Aniela Jaffé, *The Myth of Meaning,* New York, C.G. Jung Foundation, 1971, p. 32.
3. Aniela Jaffé, "The Influence of Alchemy on the Work of C.G. Jung," *Spring, 1967,* Irving Texas, Spring Publications, University of Dallas, pp. 21, 22.
4. Aniela Jaffé, *The Myth of Meaning,* New York, C.G Jung Foundation, 1971, p. 152.
5. C.G. Jung, *Psychology and Religion: West and East,* C.W. Vol. 11, par. 554.
6. McGlashan, *op. cit.,* p. 147.

*Henceforth Jung's *Collected Works* will be indicated by the initials C.W.

Chapter 5

1. Alan Watts, *The Two Hands of God*, New York, Collier Books, 1969.
2. M. Esther Harding, *Woman's Mysteries*, New York, Longmans, Green and Co., 1935.

Chapter 6

1. Erich Neumann, *The Great Mother*, Princeton, New Jersey, Princeton University Press, 1955, p. 331.
2. Brewster Ghiselin, ed., *The Creative Process*, New York, The New American Library, 1952.

Chapter 7

1. John Weir Perry, *The Far Side of Madness*, Englewood Cliffs, New Jersey, Prentice-Hall, Inc., 1974, p. 43.
2. C.G. Jung, (Quoted by) *Mysterium Coniunctionis*, C.W. Vol. 14, par. 552.
3. James Hillman and Marie-Louise von Franz, *Lectures on Jung's Typology*.

Chapter 8

1. C.G. Jung, *Psychology and Religion: West and East*, C.W. Vol. 11.
2. Emma Jung, *Animus and Anima*, New York, Spring Publications, 1969, pp. 3, 5.

Chapter 9

1. Paul Huson, *The Devil's Picturebook*, New York, G.P. Putnam's Sons, 1971, p. 160.
2. Hillman and von Franz, *Lectures on Jung's Typology*, Ch. II, p. 87.
3. Alma Paulsen, "The Spirit Mercury as Related to the Individuation Process," *Spring*, 1966, p. 119.
4. C.G. Jung, *Alchemical Studies*, C.W. Vol. 13, par. 239.
5. C.G. Jung, *Two Essays on Analytical Psychology*, C.W. Vol. 7, par. 32.

Chapter 10

1. Papus (Gerard Encausse), *The Tarot of the Bohemians*, New York, Samuel Weiser, Inc., 1978, p. 136.
2. C.G. Jung, *The Development of Personality*, C.W. Vol. 17, par. 290.
3. C.G. Jung, *Mysterium Coniunctionis*, C.W. Vol. 14, par. 264.
4. Marie-Louise von Franz, *Interpretation of Fairy Tales*, New York, Spring Publications, 1970, Part IV, p. 13.
5. C.G. Jung, *Mysterium Coniunctionis*, C.W. Vol. 14, par. 265.

Chapter 11

1. Watts, *The Two Hands of God*, p. 28.
2. C.G. Jung, *Two Essays on Analytical Psychology*, C.W. Vol. 7, par. 30.

3. Hillman and von Franz, *Lectures on Jung's Typology,* Ch. III, p. 98.
4. Ovid, *Metamorphoses,* Quoted in Metropolitan Museum of Art Calendar, New York, 1961.
5. Gerard Manley Hopkins, "Thou Art Indeed Just, Lord," *The Pocket Book of Modern Verse,* Revised Edition, Oscar Williams, ed., New York, Washington Square Press, Inc., 1960, p. 144.

Chapter 12

1. C.G. Jung, *The Archetypes and the Collective Unconscious,* C.W. Vol. 9, Part 1, par. 74.
2. W.B. Yeats, "The Second Coming," *The Collected Poems of W.B. Yeats,* Revised Version, New York, The Macmillan Co., 1956, pp. 184,5.
3. W.A. Auden, *The Age of Anxiety,* New York, Random House, 1947, p. 42.
4. Walter de la Mare, "The Listeners," *The Pocket Book of Modern Verse,* p. 220.
5. Edward F. Edinger, *Ego and Archetype,* New York, C.G. Jung Foundation, 1972, p. 172.
6. C.G. Jung, *Psychological Reflections,* Jolande Jacobi, ed., Princeton, New Jersey, Princeton University Press, 1970, p. 28.
7. C.G. Jung, *Civilization in Transition,* C.W. Vol. 10, pars. 525, 526.
8. Ibid., par. 622.
9. Ibid., par. 723.

Chapter 13

1. Marie Louise von Franz, *The Problem of the Puer Aeternus,* New York, Spring Publications, 1970, Part VIII, pp. 12, 13.
2. Erich Neumann, *The Great Mother,* Plates 98, 99.
3. Mayananda, *The Tarot for Today,* London, The Zeus Press, 1963, p. 16.
4. C.G. Jung, *Psychology and Alchemy,* C.W. Vol. 12, Fig. 88.
5. Ibid., par. 34.

Chapter 14

1. C.G. Jung, *Civilization in Transition,* C.W. Vol. 10, par. 530.
2. C.G. Jung, *Psychology and Alchemy,* C.W. Vol. 12, par. 277.
3. W.B. Yeats, "Leda and the Swan," *The Collected Poems of W.B. Yeats,* Revised Edition, New York, The Macmillan Co., 1956, p. 212.
4. Aniela Jaffé, "Symbolism in the Visual Arts," *Man and His Symbols,* C.G. Jung, ed., Garden City, New Jersey, Doubleday and Co., Inc., 1964, p. 239.

Chapter 15

1. Henderson, (Quoting Eliade), *Thresholds of Initiation,* p. 93.
2. Mircea Eliade, *The Forge and the Crucible,* New York, Harper and Row, 1962, p. 117.
3. William Blake, "The Gates of Paradise," *The Portable Blake,* New York, The Viking Press, 1946, p. 276.
4. C.G. Jung, *Psychology and Alchemy,* C.W. Vol. 12, par. 32

5. C.G. Jung, "The Interpretation of Visions," *Spring, 1962*, p. 154.
6. Perry, *The Far Side of Madness*, pp. 8, 9.
7. Mary Renault, *The King Must Die*, New York, Pantheon Books, 1958, p. 17.

Chapter 16

1. Edinger, *Ego and Archetype*, p. 140.
2. C.G. Jung, *Mysterium Coniunctionis*, C.W. Vol. 14, par. 674.
3. C.G. Jung, "Interpretation of Visions," *Spring, 1962*, p. 156.
4. C.G. Jung, *Psychological Reflections*, p. 287.
5. C.G. Jung, Quoted by Kristine Mann in "The Shadow of Death," *Spring, 1962*, p. 95.
6. Gerard Manley Hopkins, "Spring and Fall: To a Young Child," *The Poems of Gerard Manley Hopkins*, Oxford University Press, 1967.
7. C.G. Jung, *Mysterium Coniunctionis*, C.W. Vol. 14, par. 675.
8. Dylan Thomas, "Do Not Go Gentle Into That Good Night," *The Pocket Book of Modern Verse*, p. 574.
9. W.B. Yeats, "Death," *The Collected Poems of W.B. Yeats*, p. 230.
10. Edgar Herzog, *Psyche and Death*, New York, C.G. Jung Foundation, 1967, p. 27.
11. T.S. Eliot, "Journey of the Magi," *Collected Poems 1909-1935*, New York, Harcourt, Brace and Company, Inc., p. 126.

Chapter 17

1. Paul Huson, *The Devil's Picturebook*, pp. 183-184.
2. C.G. Jung, Quoted by Amy I.Allenby, "Angels as Archetype and Symbol," *Spring 1963*, p. 48.
3. McGlashan, *op. cit.*, p. 29.
4. Rainer Maria Rilke, *Poems 1906-26*, Norfolk, Conn., New Directions, 1959, p. 73.
5. C.G. Jung, *Two Essays on Analytical Psychology*, C.W. Vol. 7, par. 76.
6. Mircea Eliade, *The Sacred and the Profane*, New York, Harcourt, Brace, Javonovich, Inc., 1959, p. 20.
7. Gertrude Moakley, *The Tarot Cards Painted by Bonifacio Bembo*, New York, New York Public Library, 1966, p. 95.

Chapter 18

1. McGlashan, *op. cit.*, p. 35.
2. C.G. Jung, *Psychological Reflections*, p. 208.
3. Ibid., p. 208.
4. C.G. Jung, *The Symbolic Life: Miscellaneous Writings*, C.W. Vol. 18, par. 168.
5. Isaiah. *Old Testament*.
6. C.G. Jung, *Civilization in Transition*, C.W. Vol. 10, par. 572.
7. C.G. Jung, *The Symbolic Life: Miscellaneous Writings*, C.W. Vol. 18, par. 209.
8. Ibid., par. 210.
9. C.G. Jung, *Two Essays on Analytical Psychology*, C.W. Vol. 7, par. 240.
10. C.G. Jung, *Psychology and Alchemy*, C.W. Vol. 12, par. 88.
11. C.G. Jung, *Psychological Reflections*, p. 211.

Chapter 19

1. Joseph Campbell, (Quoting Jeremias), *The Mythic Image*, Princeton, New Jersey, Princeton University Press, 1974, Part II, p. 87.
2. C.A. Meier, (Quoting Artemidorus), *Ancient Incubation and Modern Psychotherapy*, Evanston, Illinois, Northwestern University Press, 1967, p. 30.
3. C.G. Jung, *The Archetypes and the Collective Unconscious*, C.W. Vol. 9, Part 1, par. 533.
4. W.B. Yeats, "The Tower," *The Collected Poems of W.B. Yeats*, p. 192.

Chapter 20

1. C.G. Jung, *Mysterium Coniunctionis*, C.W. Vol. 14, par. 717.
2. C.G. Jung, From *Conversations with C.G. Jung*, Margaret Ostrowski-Sachs, Zürich, Juris Druck & Verlag, 1971, p. 30.
3. C.G. Jung, *Psychology and Religion: West and East*, C.W. Vol. 11, pars. 427-428.

Chapter 21

1. Rainer Maria Rilke, *Duino Elegies*, New York, W.W. Norton and Co., Inc., 1939, p. 77, 11. 63-71.
2. Campbell (Quoting Ungaretti), *The Mythic Image*, Part VI, p. 498.

Chapter 22

1. McGlashan, *op. cit.*, p. 156.
2. Dora Kalff, *Sandplay*, San Francisco, The Browser Press, 1971.
3. Marie-Louise von Franz, *The Problem of the Puer Aeternus*, New York, Spring Publications, 1971, Part V, pp. 5, 6.
4. C.G. Jung, *The Archetypes and the Collective Unconscious*, C.W. Vol. 9, Part 1, pars. 299, 300.
5. C.G. Jung, *The Symbolic Life: Miscellaneous Writings*, C.W. Vol. 18, par. 629.
6. Ibid., par. 627.

Chapter 23

1. C.G. Jung, *Psychological Reflections*, p. 283.
2. Ibid., p. 293.
3. Ibid., p. 293.

Chapter 24

1. W.B. Yeats, "Among School Children," *The Collected Poems of W.B. Yeats*, p. 214.
2. Marie-Louise von Franz, *C.G. Jung, His Myth in our Time*, New York, C.G. Jung Foundation, 1975, p. 74.

3. C.G. Jung, "The Interpretation of Visions," *Spring, 1969,* p. 72.
4. C.G. Jung, *Two Essays on Analytical Psychology,* C.W. Vol. 7, par. 5.
5. C.G. Jung, *Psychology and Religion: West and East,* C.W. Vol. 11, par. 659.
6. C.G. Jung, *General Bibliography of Jung's Writings,* C.W. Vol. 19.
7. C.G. Jung, *Civilization in Transition,* C.W. Vol. 10, par. 583.
8. Ibid., par. 540.
9. Walt Whitman, Quoted by Ira Progoff in *Depth Psychology and Modern Man,* New York, The Julian Press, Inc., 1959, p. 90.
10. Erwin Schrödinger, *My View of the World,* Cambridge University Press, 1964, pp. 21, 22.
11. Ibid., pp. 66, 67.
12. C.G. Jung, *Psychological Reflections,* p. 39.
13. C.G. Jung, *Mysterium Coniunctionis,* C.W. Vol. 14, par. 768.
14. Dante, "Paradiso," *The Divine Comedy,* New York, W.W. Norton Co., Inc., 1977, 11s. 139-146.
15. C.G. Jung, *The Practice of Psychotherapy,* C.W. Vol. 16, par. 400.

2. Kalff, Dora, *Sandplay,* The Browser Press, San Francisco, 1971.

3. von Franz, Marie Louise, *The Problem of the Puer Aeternus,* Spring Publications, New York, 1971.

4. Jung, C.G., *The Archetypes and the Collective Unconscious,* C.W. Vol. 9, Part 1, Par. 299 & 300, Princeton University Press, 1969.

5. Jung, C.G. *The Symbolic Life: Miscellaneous Writings,* C.W. Vol. 18, Par. 629, Princeton University Press, 1976.

6. Ibid. Par. 627.

Chapter 23

1. Jung, C.G., *Psychological Reflections,* Jolande Jacobi, ed., Princeton University Press, 1970.

2. Ibid.

3. Ibid.

Chapter 24

1. Yeats, W.B., "Among School Children," *The Collected Poems of W.B. Yeats,* The Macmillan Co., New York, 1967.

2. von Franz, Marie-Louise, *C.G. Jung, His Myth in our Time,* C.G. Jung Foundation, New York, 1975.

3. Jung, C.G., "The Interpretation of Visions," *Spring, 1969,* Spring Publications, University of Dallas, Irving, Texas.

4. Jung, C.G., *Two Essays on Analytical Psychology,* C.W. Vol. 7, Par. 5, Princeton University Press, 1966.

5. Jung, C.G., "Answer to Job," *Psychology and Religion: West and East,* C.W. Vol. 11, Par. 659, Princeton University Press, 1969.

6. Jung, C.G., *General Bibliography of Jung's Writings,* C.W. Vol. 19, Princeton University Press.

7. Jung, C.G., *Civilization in Transition,* C.W. Vol. 10, Par. 583, Princeton University Press, 1970.

8. Ibid. Par. 278.

9. Whitman, Walt, Quoted by Progoff in *Depth Psychology and Modern Man,* The Julian Press, Inc. New York, 1959.

10. Schrodinger, Erwin, *My View of the World,* Cambridge University Press, New York, 1964.

11. Ibid.

12. Jung, C.G., *Psychological Reflections,* Jolande Jacobi, ed., Princeton University Press, 1970.

13. Jung, C.G., *Mysterium Coniunctionis,* C.W. Vol 14, Par. 768, Princeton University Press,

14. Dante, "Paradiso," *The Divine Comedy,* trans. John Ciardi, W.W. Norton & Co., Inc., New York, 1977.

15. Jung, C.G., *The Practice of Psychotherapy,* C.W. Vol, 16, Par. 400, Princeton University Press, 1966.